Long Ago A

JAMES

His Life A

LONG AGO AND FAR AWAY

JAMES TAYLOR

HIS LIFE AND MUSIC

TIMOTHY WHITE

OMNIBUS PRESS
London/New York/Paris/Sydney/Copenhagen/Madrid/Tokyo

Cover designed by Chloë Alexander
Picture research by Timothy White & Nikki Lloyd

ISBN: 0.7119.9193.6
Order No: OP 48785

Exclusive Distributors:
Music Sales Limited,
8/9 Frith Street,
London W1D 3JB, UK.

Music Sales Corporation,
257 Park Avenue South,
New York, NY 10010, USA.

Macmillan Distribution Services,
53 Park West Drive,
Derrimut, Vic 3030,
Australia.

To the Music Trade only:
Music Sales Limited,
8/9 Frith Street,
London W1D 3JB, UK.

Every effort has been made to trace the copyright holders of the photographs in this book but one or two were unreachable. We would be grateful if the photographers concerned would contact us.

Printed in Great Britain by CPD Wales (Ebbw Vale).
Typeset by Galleon Typesetting, Ipswich.

A catalogue record for this book is available from the British Library.

www.omnibuspress.com

To my brother Denis
and his Carolina clan

No writer has interviewed James Taylor and his family in greater depth over the decades than Timothy White, editor-in-chief of *Billboard*, former Senior Editor of *Rolling Stone* and author of the international best seller *Catch A Fire: The Life Of Bob Marley*. White is also the author of the acclaimed Beach Boys biography *The Nearest Faraway Place: Brian Wilson, The Beach Boys & The Southern California Experience*, and three separate volumes that bring together his writings from *Rolling Stone*, *Billboard* and other sources.

Timothy White is married with two sons and lives in Boston and New York.

Contents

A Taylor Family Tree 1601–2001

HERCULES TAILYEOUR

Prominent shipbuilder in port of Montrose on Scotland's Angus coast, and the son of John Tailyeour, treasurer in 1601 of the Montrose town council. Hercules was laird since 1616 of the family lands of Borrowfield, and in 1631 became Master of Montrose's piers. Hercules had two brothers: John, Jr, local magistrate in the late 1650s, and Robert, elected town provost in 1661 and member of the Scottish Parliament until 1678.

ROBERT TAILYEOUR

Son of Hercules, a Montrose provost, and Master of the Hospital in Montrose. He wed Jean Ouchterlony in 1711. She bore him three children (Catherine, 1712), James (1714), and Robert, Jr (1715), who grew up on the family's Borrowfield lands.

ROBERT TAILYOUR, JR

Co-provost of Montrose with brother James, moved away from Borrowfield and purchased the great estates at Kirktonhill and Balmanno. He wed Jean Carnegie, daughter of Pittarrow burgess Sir James Carnegie, in 1750, and they had three children: Mary, James, and John – the last a prominent trader like his father. John was once shipwrecked in Jamaica. Kirktonhill was sold after Robert, Jr's death in 1778.

JAMES TAILYOUR

Robert, Jr's brother and co-provost. He married Christian Card in the Marykirk church at the entrance to Kirktonhill in 1751. A thriving merchant-artisan known for his fine damask-weaving and thread-making firms, James and family resided at Drumnagair Farm and then the Mill of Barns estate adjoining Kirktonhill.

JOHN TAILYOUR

Son of Robert, Jr, a Montrose councilman and merchant active in Caribbean trade. He wed Mary McCall and prospered with shipping associates in Glasgow, London, Bristol, Liverpool and Lancaster. In the 1790s, John regained Kirktonhill and Balmanno.

ISAAC TAYLOR

The sixth of James and Christian Taylor's nine children. Born in 1763 and christened in the Marykirk church, he left Montrose in 1790 at the age of 27, sailing across the Atlantic with his brother John, 24, to New Bern, North Carolina. Isaac became a famed merchant in the American South, and also owned a plantation outside of town called Glenburnie. He and his wife Hannah had six daughters and one son, Alexander. Isaac died on July 4, 1846.

ALEXANDER TAYLOR

Isaac's only son, left out of Isaac's will because his drinking habits were adjudged to be "excessive". He became a successful physician and married Sarah Ann Cole, who bore them two boys, James Cole and Isaac Montrose Taylor I.

MRS ALEXANDER TAYLOR

A spy for the Confederacy during the American Civil War; also known as the "Prison Mother" for her work nursing injured/imprisoned rebel soldiers. She and her husband were friends of North Carolina Governor Zebulon Vance, a former Confederate colonel who served as a character witness in the murder trial of ex-soldier Tom Dula – whose 1868 hanging inspired the North Carolina folk song, 'Tom Dooley'.

ISAAC MONTROSE TAYLOR I

Born in New Bern, NC, in 1857. Attended the University of North Carolina, graduating in 1879, and the College of Physicians and Surgeons at Columbia University in New York. He practised at the Western North Carolina State Hospital in Morganton, NC, and founded Broadoaks Sanatorium in Morganton. Wed Susan Murphy Evans, daughter of a noted NC doctor of Scottish descent, and they had seven children, including son Alexander.

ALEXANDER TAYLOR II

He married Theodosia Haynes of Long Meadow, Mass., his wife dying after complications during childbirth. The attending physician was her father-in-law Isaac Montrose I. Neither Dr Taylor nor his bereaved son ever recovered from the tragedy, so Theodosia and Alexander's child, Isaac Montrose Taylor II, was raised by Alexander's sister, Sarah Cole Taylor, and her husband, Dr James Vernon.

ISAAC MONTROSE TAYLOR II

Orphaned son of Theodosia and Alexander Taylor II, was a graduate of Harvard Medical School, lieutenant commander in the US Navy, chief resident at Massachusetts General Hospital and Dean of the Medical School at the University of North Carolina at Chapel Hill. In 1946 he wed Gertrude "Trudy" Woodard of Newburyport, Mass. The daughter of a successful commercial fisherman, Trudy studied at Boston's Conservatory of Music, and her lineage included numerous New England seamen as well as writer John Greenleaf Whittier. Ike and Trudy had five children, Alex, James, Kate, Livingston and Hugh.

JAMES TAYLOR

Prominent musician, singer, composer, married singer–songwriter Carly Simon in 1972. They had two children, Ben and Sarah "Sally" Maria Taylor; divorced 1983. James remarried in 1985 to actress Kathryn Walker; divorced 1996. James wed Caroline "Kim" Smedvig in 2001; they have two children, Henry and Logan.

1

Lo And Behold

"A reading from the Book of Revelation: 'The New Jerusalem',"
announced the tall, rangy man at the foot of the altar, peer-
ing down at the open book of Scripture through wire-
rimmed glasses as he loomed over the bowed heads of the aggrieved
congregation.

"And I saw a new heaven and a new earth," James Taylor recited,
the gentle nasal sonority of his sombre tone somehow lending him
added authority, "for the first heaven and the first earth were passed
away; and there was no more sea. And I saw the holy city, New Jerusalem, coming down from God out of heaven, prepared as a bride
adorned for her husband . . ."

Several hundred people were assembled in the Church of the New
Covenant on the corner of Newbury and Berkeley Streets in Boston's
Back Bay on the sunny morning of November 30, 1996 for a memorial
service for Taylor's father, Dr Isaac "Ike" Montrose Taylor II, graduate
of Harvard Medical School, ex-lieutenant commander in the United
States Navy, former chief resident at Massachusetts General Hospital,
one-time Dean of the Medical School of the University of North
Carolina, and a past executive administrator at the Boston University
Medical Center, who died November 3 at the age of 75.

The mood of the occasion was sedate, respectful, astringent in its emotional tenor. The proceedings had opened with the strains of J.S. Bach's 'Arioso', as played by a cellist and pianist from the Boston Symphony Orchestra. Another short musical interlude, 'My Father's Eyes', sung by son Livingston Taylor, was framed by concise impressions offered from family friends and lifelong New England colleagues. James' reading was followed by the playing of Rachmaninoff's bittersweet 'Vocalise'.

"I chose to read the 'New Jerusalem' passage at my father's memorial," James Taylor confided afterwards, "because it had a lot of layers of meaning for him. The biblical aspect of a new beginning is there, and settlers coming to this country were looking for the same sort of new start, but also my dad had a sailboat that he dearly loved, and he named it *New Jerusalem*."

Descended from prominent Scottish lairds, traders and shipbuilding seafarers who reached America in the late 1700s, James Taylor is himself an able boatswain, whether toiling as a 12-year-old on the decks of his grandfather Henry's trawlers – "Knee-high in live flounder, tossing the trash fish overboard with a spiked pole" – or passing the summers of his mature adulthood on his own sloop off Vineyard Sound.

Six months after eulogising his parent, Taylor released *Hourglass*, his first Top 10 album in the States since *Dad Loves His Work* 16 years earlier. While the last 10 of Taylor's 17 albums have either gone gold (a half-million units shipped) or platinum (a million units shipped), and he is a leading concert attraction in his native land, the critically acclaimed *Hourglass* would prove the singer-songwriter's biggest popular and artistic success since 1970's three-million-selling *Sweet Baby James* landed him on the cover of *Time* magazine. The *New York Times* called *Hourglass* "His finest album in two decades . . . and possibly his best ever," the record going on to earn two Grammys, including one for Best Pop Album. The 50-year-old Taylor undertook his first full-scale European tour in 20 years, giving 35 sold-out shows in 10 countries, including England, Ireland and Scotland.

"*Hourglass* felt like a good title," said Taylor, "because it reminded me of the hourglass on a ship during the 18th and 19th centuries. A CD disc is also a kind of glass that you can start again and again, most of them lasting about an hour.

"In the old days of British maritime history, the sandglass was used to mark time, to measure how long a sailor has to stand watch while at sea, and to judge how fast the ship was going."

As the tale that ensues will make plain, Taylor's modern *Hourglass* would fulfil many of the same functions, helping to calculate for the first time the distance in both nautical miles and human mettle between the wreckage of his storied family's distant past and the painfully acquired redemption of the present.

It's ironic that, prior to *Hourglass*, Taylor hadn't been a substantial concern for UK album buyers since *Mud Slide Slim And The Blue Horizon* followed *Sweet Baby James* into the Top 10 of the British charts in the summer of 1971 (all chart references are to the US unless otherwise stated), since Taylor's music has always drawn heavily from the music of his English and Scottish ancestry.

It's also well known that Taylor's recording career took shape in London, quite literally in the shadow of The Beatles. Apple Records A&R chief Peter Asher signed James in London and produced his début album (with uncredited assistance from Paul McCartney) at Trident Studios during July–October 1968, the tapings interspersed with the Fab Four's recording and mixing of material-in-progress such as 'Hey Jude' and 'While My Guitar Gently Weeps'.

At that juncture, Taylor, who was living in a flat in Notting Hill, had a music-enveloped sorrow of his own. Before he could promote his self-titled Apple album, he would have to seek treatment at a Stockbridge, Massachusetts hospital called Austen Riggs for a persistent heroin habit he'd acquired two years previously in New York's Greenwich Village.

During the early '70s, the three Taylor singles that would gain the greatest retail and airplay recognition in England were 'Fire And Rain', James' forlorn farewell to a female confrère lost to suicide; a meditative cover of chum Carole King's 'You've Got A Friend', and his remake with then-wife Carly Simon of Inez and Charlie Foxx's frisky 1963 R&B smash, 'Mockingbird'.

That Taylor would ultimately conquer his addiction, survive his initial struggles with fame, and grow in artistic stature in the aftermath of his flamboyant but ill-fated 10-year marriage to Simon are now part of his lengthening legend as a self-effacing kinsman of Jimmie Rodgers, Cliff Edwards, Hoagy Carmichael, Ewan MacColl and other beloved troubadour-stylists of Anglo-American song.

Such hard-won personal triumphs are further accentuated by the out-spoken esteem with which the highly influential singer-songwriter-guitarist is held by such modern country superstars as Garth Brooks (who named his daughter Taylor in tribute to James), as well as latterday bards of Albion songcraft like Sting, who once described Taylor to this writer as the contemporary performer he most admired – "because he's always been both a complete natural and a complete original. His singing and his sound are always contemporary and yet timeless – totally immune to mere fashion – and I find that remarkable." So has the recording industry, with James accorded lifetime achievements honours and assorted hall of fame inductions from 1998–2000 that included receipt of *Billboard*'s Century Award, the trade publication's highest honour for distinguished creative achievement, as well as entry in 2000 into the Songwriters' Hall of Fame beside such diverse colleagues as Carmichael, Paul Simon and Bruce Springsteen.

Equally noteworthy, however, is the degree to which Taylor's immigrant heritage and its thematic underpinnings in much of his music have long been obscured or miscomprehended. Indeed, fans who've spent three decades combing the performer's lyrics for drugs allusions or clues to romantic attachments have allowed a few loose threads to distract them from the larger tapestry.

The bulk of Taylor's songwriting concerns itself with restlessness, the lure of travel and the lives of those (soldiers, troubadours, outlaws, hobos) habitually drawn to wanderlust. And when James hasn't authored such picaresque musical narratives, he has celebrated song-crafting customs of Scottish-Irish derivation, reinterpreting traditional folk laments like 'One Morning In May', 'Wandering' and 'The Water Is Wide'.

Yet of all the subjects and characters woven into the man's music, there are few so prevalent as the topic of the open sea and those who traverse it seeking fortune, glory or forgetfulness in its farther shores. The bounding main and its briny depths are unceasingly evoked – whether to connote beauty and loneliness, signify redemption or renewal, recall a directionless time, represent a new beginning, or simply extend an invitation to sail away for good – in dozens of selections from Taylor's repertoire, from 'Long Ago And Far Away' and

'Soldiers' on *Mud Slide Slim And The Blue Horizon* (1971) to 'Fanfare' –
as well as the album photo of James adrift in a rowboat – on *One Man
Dog* (1972); continuing with 'Hello Old Friend' (*Walking Man*, 1974),
'Lighthouse', 'Sarah Maria' (*Gorilla*, 1975); 'Captain Jim's Drunken
Dream' (*In The Pocket*), 1976); 'There We Are', 'Terra Nova' and 'Bar-
tender's Blues' (*JT*, 1977); on through the *Flag* album (1979), whose
jacket art was the nautical symbol for 'man overboard'; and in 'I Will
Follow', 'Believe It Or Not', 'Summer's Here' and 'Sugar Trade' (*Dad
Loves His Work*, 1981); 'Turn Away' and 'Only A Dream In Rio'
(*That's Why I'm Here*, 1985); 'Never Die Young', 'Valentine's Day',
'Sun On The Moon' (*Never Die Young*, 1988); 'The Frozen Man' (*New
Moon Shine*, 1991); as well as 'Enough To Be On Your Way', 'Gaia',
'Jump Up Behind Me', 'Yellow And Rose' and a pensive rendition of
Livingston Taylor's 'Boatman' on *Hourglass*.

"I've recently been reading the mariner novels by Patrick O'Brian,
such as *Master And Commander* and *The Wine-dark Sea*," explained
Taylor in 1997, "which are ripping yarns of the sea that pretty much
illuminate the evolution of an era that encompassed the migrations of
my ancestors."

What Taylor failed to note is that his forebears merit actual mention in
O'Brian's renowned series of historical fiction regarding the Royal Navy
during the French Revolutionary Wars (1792–1802) and Napoleonic
Wars (1803–15).

Just as the English O'Brian's ultra-detailed epics frequently employ
genuine ships and incidents, they also incorporate real personages from
the late 1700s/early 1800s annals of maritime trade and naval adventure. Thus, chapter five of O'Brian's international bestseller *The
Wine-dark Sea* opens with Captain Jack Aubrey's privateering crew on
the HMS *Surprise* as they sight a bobbing barrel in choppy waters
several miles off South America, surmising that the object signals
another ship is lurking nearby. They examine the wooden cask, seeing
that it's bound with withies (flexible twigs) instead of iron hoops, and
deduce it's a "Bedford hog", i.e. a strong, lightweight hogshead in use
by the whaling ships out of the ports of New Bedford, Martha's Vineyard and Nantucket in Massachusetts.

"Then how come it has Isaac Taylor's mark?" asks a deckhand, referring to an eminent Scottish merchant resettled on the North Carolina

coast. A fellow seaman informs his deckmate that this sort of keg is customarily obtained by New England whalers as they take on stores while plying the coastal waters of America's southern colonies.

That a forefather of the fellow who sang 'Shower The People' should prove grist for what literary critics consider some of the most storm-tossed and impassioned nautical tales ever published may catch some James Taylor fans unawares.

More intriguing still is the fact that even close friends and relations attending the memorial service in 1996 for Isaac Montrose Taylor II – the direct descendant, two centuries later, of the progenitor whose name was pointedly dropped in *The Wine-dark Sea* – remain ignorant or only dimly aware of the grand exploits and aggrieved sorrows that link the destinies of these and other Isaac Taylors and their offspring.

"He was a very principled person always," says James Taylor of his late parent Ike, reflecting on the troubled father who figured prominently in assorted songs James penned over the years, including 'Walking Man', 'Only For Me' and 'Jump Up Behind Me', the last an anthem of rescue from *Hourglass* (1997).

"And he was very liberal-going-toward-socialist in his political leanings," Taylor adds of Ike, "so we shared an adamant outrage at the political system throughout our lives. I'd also describe him as an alcoholic, but in a very controlled way.

"I think he was a very sexy, earthy guy. He was not a dry person at all; he was juicy and powerful. But he was a very lonely fellow, complicated too, and in many ways very driven, and submerged. He was an exceptional kind of being, but there was a very dark thing he came out of."

And there was a very dark thing out of which the entire Taylor pedigree emerged, the great arc of its shadows stretching back 200 years to the Angus coast of Scotland. The stubborn gloom first arose during the social and economic turmoil of Scotland's so-called Age of Transformation (1690–1830), and it spread to New Bern, North Carolina circa 1790 via the ominous voyage of the original Isaac Taylor.

The final respects paid to Isaac "Ike" Montrose Taylor II in Boston occurred 205 years to the month after his 18th-century namesake took a bride in North Carolina. Then, as now, the sun shone on another fateful ceremony observed by one of the most publicly celebrated and secreted bedevilled family trees ever implanted on the Eastern seaboard's edition of the New Jerusalem.

In a world that tends to hide many of its mysteries in plain sight, the tale of the Taylor clan – including musical siblings Alex, Livingston, Kate and Hugh – stands as a startling case in point. This is the saga, across half a millennium, of one of the more accomplished lineages in British-American social history, and yet the many filaments of its remarkable outreach have never before been woven into one comprehensible fabric.

The annals of the Taylors are also the story of the ebb and flow in the fortunes of the British Empire, and its collateral impact on the economic, social and cultural destiny of the United States, from its colonial origins and the Civil War, on through the Civil Rights Movement of the mid-20th century and its unsettled aftermath. Yet it took the most unlikely latterday exponent of the Taylors' elusive legacy to occasion a full examination of its past and present, and the family's unique, ongoing contributions to life along America's eastern shores.

There are other James Taylors in this book besides the renowned singer-songwriter, and each was a role model and even a cultural hero to his contemporaries in the British Isles – much as a young English musician named Gordon Sumner (later famous by his nickname of Sting) drew early career inspiration from a 1970 concert by the contemporary James Taylor. ("I went to see him in my hometown of Newcastle; he played the city hall the year of 'Fire And Rain'; I bought the albums, learnt everything on them, play all the licks.")

By the same token, there are several Isaac Taylors in this chronicle – including a fledgling singer-songwriter now in his twenties named Isaac Cole Taylor – who personally acknowledge the pioneering influence of bygone bards of Albion songcraft. On a chilly November evening in 1997, the modern Isaac took the stage at the new Agricultural Society Hall on the island of Martha's Vineyard, located seven miles off the south-east coast of Massachusetts, to sing a pensive tune called 'Willow', whose lyrics he boasted he'd "stolen" from William Shakespeare.

But we are getting ahead of ourselves in this century-spanning account of Anglo-American borrowings, historical influences, and lineal bestowals. As indicated earlier, the title of this book comes from a ballad written by the modern James Taylor for his semi-autobiographical 1971 album for Warner Bros. Records, *Mud Slide Slim And The Blue Horizon*.

The song's composer laboured at Crystal Recording Studios in Holly-wood between January 3 and February 28, 1971 to capture on tape that album's title piece and the record's other material. Manager Peter Asher supervised the production, boyhood chum Danny Kortchmar playing guitar and congas, close friends Carole King and Joni Mitchell offering piano and vocal accompaniment, and drummer Russ Kunkel and bassist Leland Sklar comprising the rhythm section. Moreover, each of these musician-friends of Taylor's had been fated to exert a pro-found personal as well as professional impact on James.

Among the most wistful of Taylor's vast catalogue of secular hymns, 'Long Ago And Far Away' speaks of "tender dreams", "sailing ships", a "misbegotten guess" and "bits of broken glass".

At the climax of the cheerless chantey, the singer asks, "Why is the song I sing so sad?"

By treading back through the mists of memories since obscured, delving into diaries nearly lost or archives never probed, and picking up the traces of questful journeys that breached unfathomed oceans, un-explored wildernesses, and unprotected human hearts, this book recovers a forgotten world from long ago and far away.

Virtually all of the direct testimony from the principals in the text derives from talks with the author over the course of almost 30 years. Sons, daughters, parents, colleagues and friends each discussed and/or discovered for the first time the personal and historical patterns under-lying the matrix of a family whose modern music was an often-unconscious diary of its ancestral turmoil.

In the process, this story discloses hidden parallels with the present and answers one mournful ballad's truly ancient questions.

2

Boatman

The early 1620s on the Angus coast of Scotland was an era of ill omens and uncertain signs. On a crisp, blustery day in October 1622, Hercules Tailyeour learned of the stern decree that the town council of Montrose, Scotland had issued regarding him and his recent activities. However complaint-like its wording was, the overall tone of awe in the municipal order made Hercules proud: "Cass [cause] fill up that dokk holl [dark hole] quhilk [which] wes cassite [dug] be him and his brother for the bigging [building] of their new schipp [ship], besyt the hinging hill."

The local hummock in question was Constable Hill, a sandy rise that sheltered from westerly winds the muddy lagoon and magnificent adjoining seashore rimming the handsome seaport and market town of Montrose. And the town council's chastising message to Hercules Tailyeour was owed to the mammoth eyesore Hercules and sibling John, Jr had created on the otherwise picturesque community beach, even though their gaping pit was an impromptu shipyard for the largest sea vessel yet constructed in Montrose.

Hercules' audacious act of shipbuilding came at an uneasy time in the superstition-prone Montrose's recent history. It occurred less than a year after a great whale had washed ashore and been pronounced an evil portent. When an armed galleon fleeing an engagement of the

Thirty Years' War between Spain and Holland's United Provinces slipped into Montrose harbour in January 1622, fears of menacing intrusions seemed confirmed.

The gentry of the royal seaport vowed to assemble a volunteer navy to protect Montrose against a dreaded Spanish invasion. Thus, the erection of a truly imposing new commercial vessel by Hercules Tailyeour of Borrowfield signalled the presence among them of a bold modernist willing to confront the shifting uncertainties of the times.

The Tailyeour brothers had designed and constructed their great sailing craft to help facilitate their burgeoning trade in textiles – for the clients of the wealthy Tailyeours could be found in markets as distant as northern Norway, the inner Baltic, Rotterdam, Normandy and Bordeaux.

The Montrose town council's dictum was a diplomatic exercise intended to mollify other council members, since Hercules' father John had served as treasurer of the council since 1601 (two years before the union of the crowns of Scotland and England, whose parliaments nonetheless took another century to unite). The patriarch of the Tailyeours sat in council sessions beside representatives from such eminent families of the burgh as the Ramsays of Balmain and the Erskines of Dun.

For Hercules' part, he had been the laird since 1616 of nearby Borrowfield, a vast landholding described in a royal deed dating back to 1480 as containing "woods, plains, moors, marshes and stagnant waters, pastures, mills and multures, fishings, etc." Known in the region as Tailyeour of Borrowfield, Hercules would rise to the position of premier bailie (a medieval term meaning owner-magistrate) of that burghfield in 1629.

Montrose would become an active centre over the next 150 years for ship and boatyards specialising in both the design and repair of vessels. Along the Angus coast, gentleman skippers and shipwrights were frequently burgesses and the social equals of the foremost neighbouring merchants. But the Tailyeours were all these things and more, being prominent landowners and traders as well as multi-skilled artisans. Hercules of Borrowfield would transcend the censure of the Montrose council. As the leading local master ship-carpenter, he was officially entrusted in 1631 with the contracting and supervision of repairs to the piers of a port with crown-ordained monopolies in wool, hides and other apparel-related products.

Hercules' parent John acted as provost of Montrose from 1640 until his retirement in 1657, formally supported in the role by all three of his sons. John, Jr took over as chief magistrate of the town after his father stepped down, and then son Robert was elected provost on September 24, 1661, sitting in the Scottish Parliament until 1678.

The resourceful Tailyeours were also tailors to the kings of Scotland, hence their surname. Indeed, they had been prominent tradesmen and respected seafarers on the Angus coast of north-east Scotland (also called Forfarshire) since the founding of Montrose in the 13th century, when Montrose (Gaelic for "a sunny promontory on a peninsula") was designated a royal burgh by King David II, son of the famed Scottish king Robert I the Bruce.

The Tailyeours were believed to have come to Montrose from adjoining parishes to the east of Forfar, a fertile vale, once the centre of the aboriginal Picts tribe, in the loch, munro (mountain) and glen-adorned county of Angus. Back in Forfar, the Tailyeour name had known spellings as various as Tailzour and Tayleour. There was no firm rule in the early 17th century regarding the proper spelling of surnames, but with regard to the subscription of Council deeds in the mid-1600s, "Tailyour" became the correct form.

Forfar was known in the 17th century for the chimney stacks of its textile mills, for the mysterious, pre-antiquity allure for wayfarers of its many symbol-encrusted Pictish "standing stones", and for the local persecution of witches. King James VI, son of Mary Queen of Scots, was a sworn enemy of witches. After the "Union of the Crowns" by which James VI inherited the English throne as James I, he revised what he called the "defect" in Elizabethan laws that dared to mark a distinction between good and bad witches.

But the bisexual James was also a devotee of fashion; thus the devout Church of Scotland Tailyours were much in his favour. James' reign (1603–25) was a voguish juncture, during which men and women of the smart set carried umbrellas to protect their waistcoated suits and hoop skirts from the elements. James, who introduced golfing to England, delighted in lace-trimmed satin cloaks, and embroidered livery gowns.

Apparel denoted status. Important citizens wanted to wear what the sovereign wore, and clothes made of linen, damask, and fine wool were sufficiently expensive to spark a thriving enterprise in secondhand outfits – as well as the not-infrequent theft of choice items from bedchambers and washing lines.

Fine garments demanded protection, and were sufficiently valuable to be bequeathed in wills and cited in merchants' inventories of heirlooms. The official Montrose residence of the affluent Tailyours by 1645 was a manor house at Close No. 186 on the west side of the "Hie Way" that lay between the low-roofed cottages dotting the grasslands of St John's Croft (a croft being a small tenant farm) and the walls and gateway of the King's Port.

The Tailyour home in the close was a large mansion facing south, its gables toward the street, with the family's busy address quickly acquiring the centuries-honoured designation of [*sic*] "Tailor's Close". Montrose householders would be known as Gable Endies, due to the unusual manner in which the town's 17th- and 18th-century merchants like the Tailyours, influenced by architectural trends on the Continent, had constructed their handsome domiciles gable end to the main thoroughfares. In the Tailyours' case, an addition was made in 1677 to extend their manse still closer to the carriage traffic of nearby Murray Street.

During the 1670s, Scotland was well into the United Kingdom's Restoration Period under the rule (1660–85) of Charles II after the death of English parliamentary general and self-styled Lord Protector, Oliver Cromwell (whose forces had occupied Montrose in 1651 and installed a military governor). Following years of civil war, the social euphoria of the Restoration was mirrored in the flamboyant frivolity of men's fashions, which included raiment as peculiar as petticoat breeches.

In May 1662, Charles II announced to a disconcerted House of Commons that he "could not but observe that the whole nation seemed to him a little corrupted in their excess of living. All men spend much more time in their clothes, their diet, in all their expenses, than they used to do." Charles neglected to mention that he personally was then deeply in arrears to his own tailors.

The occupants of the Montrose greathouse in Tailor's Close were thriving in their ventures: importing fine fabrics, raw flax and un-finished cloth; exporting finished cloth, bleached and unbleached sail canvas, and building boats to transport textiles. The ports of call for the Tailyours' compact fleet of schooners and barques rapidly expanded to encompass havens in Canada, Virginia, the Carolinas, Jamaica and Antigua.

By 1684, the Tailyeours had relinquished much of their retail inter-ests as they augmented their extensive shipping, and the mansion on Tailor's Close was sold off to be transformed into capacious workrooms for associated firms of royal clothiers (Robert Graham, William Smith, Forbes Dick & Co., James Selby & Co.). The glass entrance door of the Cloth Hall, as it came to be termed, remained engraved with the nation's royal coat of arms.

During the remainder of the 1600s, the Tailyours resided principally on their Borrowfield lands, and strengthened their hold on local politi-cal power, each male head of the family becoming an alderman over the clan's corner of the Angus coast. On May 24, 1711 provost Robert Tailyour wed Jean Ouchterlony, who bore him three children in swift succession: Catherine (1712), James (1714), Robert, Jr (1715). During these happy years, the Tailyours had civic-mindedly embraced the medical profession, with Robert, Sr becoming Master of the Hospital in Montrose.

Privilege was its own reward in rural Scottish society during the 17th and 18th centuries, and the Tailyours depended on this fact as they made plans in the evolutionary decades before the American Revolu-tion. Scotland was still dominated by the royal or gentry-controlled burghs which the crown licensed to oversee internal and external trade. Fiscal and bodily risk were considerable in sea merchantry in the mid-1700s, given the uncertainty of tempestuous seas and fog-engulfed landings where smuggling endured in opposition to unpopular colonial trading laws. Many sovereigns extended official and unofficial letters of marque to captains of private vessels – i.e. privateers or corsairs – allow-ing them to attack and plunder the ships of a hostile government.

With Scotland still independent in its church and legal system but now incorporated (by means of the 1706–07 Act and Treaty of Union) with England in its parliament, its Hanoverian sovereignty and its trading, a new business boom occurred. By 1740, England was importing much more of Scotland's linen cloth, the latter nation's fore-most industry, which also found ready markets in America's planta-tions. Scotland also eased into the American tobacco trade, its cut of Britain's stake in the leafy indulgence rising from 10 per cent in 1738 to 52 per cent in 1769.

The Tailyours were benefiting from every aspect of this interface of old and new. Thirty-six-year-old Robert Tailyour, Jr, currently sharing power as co-provost of Montrose with his brother James, was wed in 1750 to 30-year-old Jean Carnegie, sister of Pittarrow burgess Sir James Carnegie. Five years later Robert, Jr decided to move away from the clan's burgh of Borrowfield, and purchased the huge estates of Kirktonhill and Balmanno in the barony of Rescobie, County of Kincardine. Robert, Jr thereby became the titular laird of the entire picturesque Kincardine village of Marykirk, located six miles from Montrose, since his estates encompassed not only the principal build-ings of the suburb but also the dozen farms that hemmed it.

In the centre of Marykirk stood a stone kirk (church) that had been consecrated to the Virgin Mary in AD1242. The parish of Marykirk supported 1,280 residents in 1755, most of them produce and livestock farmers, fishermen, weavers of linen on hand looms, and mill workers who either spun flax at the sole local flax-spinning concern or sawed fir timber from 1,532 encircling acres of often muirish (boggy, black-soil) woods. Looming in the middle distance nine miles inland were the purple and green Grampian Mountains.

The landscape was splendid, and never more so than on a clear late-September day, when the golden stands of hay that coated the wavelike stretches of hillocks were gathered in neat windrows to dry. More formal efforts to enhance the beauty of the estate included two walled gardens constructed on either side of the ample stables and adjoining dairy, but visitors to Kirktonhill often discovered its greatest vistas by wandering in the high pastures of oats and barley, up above the small grain mill behind the Kirktonhill manor house. One could stroll between the dense copses of elm, birch and larix (larch) trees (some of them concealing romantic gazebos and stone follies) and then follow the cowpaths over the crest of the dell, gazing out at the towering, rain-bow-rimmed curtain of salty mist – known locally as *haar* – that often obscured the nearby ocean. As the day wore on, and prevailing winds parted the twinkling veil of vapour, a shaft of the North Sea would suddenly shine forth like hammered steel: cold, indented and keen. This was Scotland's rural coast at its robust, prismatic best.

As for Robert Tailyour's neighbouring brother James, he was a merchant-artisan, being well regarded locally for his damask-weaving and thread-making businesses. After James' own decision to relocate to lovely Marykirk, he married Christian Card of Logie Pert, Angus, in the tiny medieval Marykirk church on October 17, 1751, the couple settling on Drumnagair Farm beside the Kirktonhill estate. For the next thirty years, these two branches of the Tailyour brood oversaw every aspect of this verdant corner of Kincardine, including, in generations to come, the ministry of its church.

The family crest of the Tailyours of Kirktonhill was a dexter (right) forearm, its hand holding a cross ending in crosslets whose shaft was fitched (sharpened to a point), the motto below it reading: *In hoch signo vinces* ("Under this sign, you shall conquer"). There was earthly power depicted in the thrusting human limb, and piety in the object it grasped. And when a demonstration of royal allegiance was appropriate, the family's heraldic coat of arms was shown emerging from a marquess' coronet. But no effort or escutcheon symbolised the intentions of the Taylor clan in the 18th century more than a great trading ship under full sail, its mass riding low in the water thanks to a bulging cargo.

Robert Tailyour opened shipping offices in Kingston, Jamaica and Lisbon, Portugal, and his son John would find his own fortune in Kingston in the 1780s – but only after he nearly forfeited his life. After being shipwrecked off the Jamaican coast, losing all his possessions in the process except his father's gold watch, John recovered with aid from his rich cousin Simon, then called "The King of Jamaica" by his friends, and joined in enhancing Simon's lucrative Jamaican and Antiguan sugar trading interests. John soon discovered that the sugar business inevitably overlapped with slave trading, and for a time he also served in Kingston as an agent for the "black ivory" brought into Jamaica to toil in the cane fields.

Though Montrose's fortunes were by no means solely dependent on the slave trade, slaves were sometimes part of a triangular trading scheme involving salmon (the primary Montrose export to the Mediterranean) and tobacco (highly profitable in Europe), the human cargo being picked up (along with elephant tusks) in West Africa after the fish was disposed of, with the slaves being the barter in Virginia for the tobacco. Records from the period show as many as 33 Montrose ships engaged in the slave trade (albeit none owned by the Tailyours), with town merchants known to give the wives of slavers' captains a golden guinea as a gift after each successful voyage.

The 18th-century merchants of Montrose were typical in their customary sense of entitlement, with teas, dinner parties, balls, concerts and theatrical presentations filling the seasonal schedules of the area's mercantile families. After Robert Tailyour's death in 1778, his estates at Kirktonhill and Balmanno were sold for £7,000, leaving his widow Jean with a bank account that fed a self-indulgent social calendar. Knowing no other station in life, Jean Tailyour was immersed in idle diversion, even writing of this to her son John in Jamaica on February 16, 1786:

> This town is growing so very gay – that I even am ingaged somenly thrie days in the week paying or receiving visits – last night I was at a Play & came not home till twelve a clok, what do you think of that!

The Montrose town council and its merchant burgesses, including John, had more pressing matters to think about. With slavery illegal within the British Isles since 1772, the rising outcry against any co-ordinated Scottish commerce in slaves – which had centred locally around the slave ships (one of them named *Montrose*) of Thomas Douglas & Company – ensured it had largely ceased by 1773. But there was still strong political pressure to outlaw all such British trade wherever it took place.

In 1788, the Montrose council argued the issue, and after receiving a letter from a committee in Manchester requesting support in Parliament for complete abolition of the slave trade, the council agreed to instruct their MP accordingly. John Tailyour, who had last served on the council circa 1779 but remained an influence through a "faction" composed of his friends, struggled with his conscience, writing to business associates that, "From all the best information I ever had, it clearly appears Slaves live better by far in the West Indies than in Africa and from my own observation I can say they in general live better than the poor of Scotland, Ireland and probably of England."

Strictly speaking, John's defences may have been feebly accurate in a very few of the latter instances, but the momentum of moral and political destiny swept such qualmish rationales back into the dark seas that had borne the pernicious Middle Passage. John, who had already relinquished his role as a slave factor (broker), returned home to Marykirk to conform to a collective change of heart and mind. On March 5, 1792, the Montrose town council met for a final debate on the African slave trade and unanimously agreed to petition Parliament to abolish "a commerce so disgraceful to a free and enlightened nation".

Clearly, much had changed in the forty years since the Tailyours had settled in the village of Marykirk. Intent on regaining clout in Scottish society, John wed Mary McCall, daughter of a Glasgow merchant who abandoned his Virginia and Maryland tobacco lands in favour of Jamaica sugar after he backed the losing Loyalist side in the war for American independence. John Tailyour took some of the new fortune he'd amassed through trading with associates in Glasgow, London, Bristol, Liverpool and Lancaster, and began protracted negotiations to repurchase his late father's Marykirk estates.

During the 1790s John Tailyour bought back the huge Kirktonhill house, lawn park, 220 acres of woods, 2,000 acres of farmlands, and a half-mile of prime salmon-fishing frontage on the left bank of the River North Esk that comprised the estate. He reacquired the adjacent Balmanno house and its acres of grounds a year later. The fee for the properties was a sizeable sum at the time, £17,000, land values having increased during the Napoleonic Wars.

Most importantly, John regained the family's exclusive fishing rights on the West Water, a winding, salmon-steeped capillary of the North Esk which they had controlled since antiquity. It was their earliest commercial and personal link to the region north-west of their original settlement of Forfar, the picturesque wilderness tributary being a gently rolling watercourse on which the clan had subsisted since their name was first known in Scotland. A century later, John's kin would even fight successfully to get the track bed of the local railroad rerouted so the family retained their exclusive access to the West Water. Every river, brook, creek and pond the family's descendants were ever to reside near would be spiritually linked in their psyches to the West Water. In all their creeds and lore, in all their expressive gestures and creative acts, the image of a rolling river would always recur.

John Tailyour elected to simplify the spelling of his surname to Taylor, following the example of the other Marykirk-rooted wing of the family. John rebuilt the main mansion at Kirktonhill for £3,000, and remained there until his death (in 1820), leasing Balmanno to a succession of relatives. Most of John's branch of the Taylor family tree would remain tied to Scotland – a notable exception being his son Patrick, who would settle in Australia, marrying and creating a new offshoot of his bloodlines there.

Meanwhile, John's neighbouring uncle, James Taylor, had moved from Drumnagair Farm to the Mill of Barns estate adjoining Kirkton-hill. But two of James' boys intended to break away from the Angus coast and begin again in the newly independent American colonies; the chief author of this plan was named Isaac.

Isaac Taylor, the sixth of James and Christian Taylor's nine children, was born in July 1763 and christened in the church in Marykirk. Isaac came of age in a household dominated by James, Jr, 10 years his senior and now frequently away in the Caribbean seeing to overlapping Jamaican and Antiguan trading concerns.

The Montrose social whirl was of no interest to Isaac, a smiling, habitually well-dressed young adventurer whose elfin blue eyes burned with purposeful zeal. The parish of Marykirk with its current 1,481 inhabitants, 344 houses, 8 blacksmiths, 5 pubs, 1 schoolhouse, and the mossy remnants of 4 Druid temples, just seemed a drowsy backwater to a well-bred and ambitious gentleman.

So dapper Isaac decided to depart Montrose – the seaport's name later incorporated into his descendants' nomenclature – for the well-known Scottish settlement of New Bern, North Carolina. Isaac, 27, and his 24-year-old brother John, bought a large, two-masted brig and set sail in 1790. It was a trip that would, by degrees, thrust the 18th-century James Taylor's side of the family into the seafaring mainstream, its cultural momentum, and the storytelling songs of America's eastern shores, helping shape the character of each over the next 200 years.

The perils were many, whether from wars, foul weather, risky investments, wily corsairs, misplaced loyalty or unwise affection. These dangers and more would beset the Taylors and their inheritors. Indeed, the full brunt of what lay ahead for the family might have been summed up in a distressingly enigmatic message, scribbled on a scrap of paper in the late 1770s and found in a bottle washed up outside Montrose on nearby Ferryden Beach. Written hastily by the chief mate of a beleaguered brigantine, the missive had the fierce poetry of a farewell note, and the sure metre of a tragic ballad:

> Blowing a hurricane lying to with close-reefed main topsails, ship waterlogged. Cargo of wood from Quebec. No water on board, provisions all gone. Ate the dog yesterday, three men alive. Lord have mercy on our souls. Amen.

3

The Water Is Wide

Many a tipsy or travel-worn seaman striding for the first time up Craven Street from the Trent River wharf in New Bern, North Carolina, during the mid-1790s was literally staggered by the sight of the stately, three-storeyed townhouse of wealthy 30-year-old merchant, ship owner and planter Isaac Taylor. Just as Scottish rye whiskey had replaced rum or peach brandy as the standard cure for a colonial sailor's thirst after 1750, so a resourceful mercantilist from the Aberdeen lowlands had redefined genteel ostentation in the loveliest seaport on Carolina's central coastal plain.

One morning in May 1791, barely a year after Isaac had cruised across Pamlico Sound and up the Neuse River with brother John to where it meets the Trent to form the New Bern harbour, the elder Taylor had purchased lot 50 on the east side of Craven Street as the site for the dream house he built for his intended bride, Hannah Justice. The two were married in New Bern in November 1792, and moved immediately into the handsome Federal-style edifice dominating Craven Street.

The urban mansion, deliberately erected in sight of the water, boasted a façade of Flemish-bond brick, brought from Scotland in Isaac's boat as ballast. He created the perfect merchant-mariner's home to announce his personal and entrepreneurial command of the harbour. The Taylor home also had gable-end parapets, mimicking Montrose-style house construction, plus a huge Diocletian half-circle window at the top of its Southern face, and it was filled with elegant fireplaces and elaborate woodwork. The hand-moulded ceiling cornices, tall-columned mantels, intricate relief sunbursts over the doorways and cresting wave patterns adorning the step-end brackets of its winding staircases were all carved in Carolina's maritime off-season by ship's carpenters.

Such a dwelling represented high civilisation in an America that was still largely wilderness, with settlements to the north such as Pittsburgh, where Conestoga wagons were only just greeting the headwaters of the Ohio, boasting fewer than 400 inhabitants.

New Bern was on the cusp of commercial trading and commercial agriculture in the New World, and the rising prosperity of the port was owed to dramatic fiscal and political developments. As the official and unofficial colonial capital of North Carolina between 1738 and 1792 (when a Wake Country stretch of woods was renamed Raleigh by a special commission), New Bern had regularly hosted aristocrats attending either the Crown's or later the revolutionary colonists' legislative Assembly. Indeed, in the spring of 1791, a little more than a year after North Carolina had ratified the United States Constitution and entered the Union, founding US president George Washington was entertained at a waterside banquet and ball at Tryon Palace, the governor's Georgian-Palladian mansion-turned-state Capitol in the centre of town.

During the War of the French Revolution (1792–1802) and the Napoleonic Wars (1803–15), the Americans of New Bern and other colonial ports were able to rebound from the loss of their privileged British imperial trading terms by marketing vital provisions (pork, rice, corn, flour), raw materials (cotton) and naval stores to the French as well as that European country's shifting coalitions of adversaries (Austria, Holland, Spain, Prussia, and, yes, Britain).

New Bern's population doubled between 1780 and 1800, its civic pride self-evident in the increased "Federal" revisions of the Georgian architecture that preceded it. Isaac Taylor's house was also designed to thank the sea for its mercies. Isaac's brother John was rumoured to have been washed overboard and rescued from drowning during the difficult passage, spending the rest of the trip in an infirm state. Isaac sold the boat used for the Atlantic passage in Wilmington, NC, apparently pleased to be rid of it.

Once John had regained his always fragile health, he returned to Scotland to find another boat for the brothers' thriving trade. On May 16, 1793, he bought a large sloop called the *Rainbow* from a William Clark of Angus county, John registering himself as master five days later in the port of Dundee. The *Rainbow* made regular trips to the Caribbean, often by way of the Firth of Forth, where it would stop at the port of Alloa to drop off a shipment of barley for the local breweries, in exchange for coal and Alloa strong beer, stopping next in London en route to New England, New Bern and then Jamaica.

The *Rainbow*'s last sailing under John's direction was on June 28, 1795, when it left the port of Dundee, fully loaded with barley and ultimately bound for the West Indies. In fact, it was to be John's last voyage, for when he finally returned to New Bern from Jamaica he was seriously ill. In the years since his trauma and resultant sickness on the high seas in 1790, John's physical aspect had varied in degree from hale and game to hampered and grim. Still, he seemed to fare better under sail than on land, as the heat and torpor of the Carolinas and the Caribbean were thought to have been tough on him.

On February 7, 1796, John Taylor died in New Bern, his brother Isaac placing a public announcement in the February 13 edition of the *North Carolina Gazette*:

> Notice
> Is hereby given, to all whom it may concern, that John Taylor, late of Newbern, is dead, and that the subscriber has qualified as administrator to his estate. All persons having claims against said estate are hereby required to bring them forward, as they will not be paid after the time limited by law for bringing claims against the estate of the deceased persons.
>
> All those who are indebted to the estate are desired to make payment to
> ISAAC TAYLOR, Admr.

Like the politically unpopular Highland Scots before him, whose initial 1730–50 mass migration to North Carolina (occasioned by the

Stuarts' defeat in their attempt to regain the Scottish throne) had transformed the territory, Isaac was determined to prevail in America.

He purchased a large plantation located on the Neuse River just outside New Bern called Glenburnie, and did nicely in Caribbean commerce, trading tea, cotton, lumber, pork, corn and other foodstuffs in exchange for sugar cane, molasses and the inevitable rum.

Isaac also conducted trade on the South's inland waterways and up and down the Eastern Seaboard. Isaac Taylor's shops on Middle Street in 1791 and then on Craven Street from 1793 onward were intended to satisfy the needs of locals but also to advertise his inventory of goods to entrepreneurs in the region who might wish for shipments to their locales in exchange for their best wares.

As early as November 1791, "Isaac Taylor's Cheap Store" on Middle Street was advertising in the *North Carolina Gazette* for the sale or barter of imported goods such as "wine, rum, Geneva (gin), Molasses, Pepper, Allspice, Ginger, Salt, Iron, Paints, oil, 7 by 9 and 8 by 10 window glass, Blacksmiths anvils and vices, and a great assortment of crockery and stoneware".

By November 1793, Isaac's Craven Street emporium ran regular notices in the *North Carolina Gazette* that "ISAAC TAYLOR has just Imported from NEW YORK, and has for sale, a general assortment of DRY GOODS, suitable to the season, which he is determined to sell low for cash or country produce. He also has West-India produce of all kinds, which will be sold low for cash only, or country produce, at a cash price."

And on January 14, 1794 an advertising dispatch piously posted in the *Gazette* made it known that "A few copies of the *Book of Common Prayer* according to the use of the Protestant Episcopal Church in the United States of America, published by direction of the General Convention, for sale at ISAAC TAYLOR's Store."

Even a business so upright, however, was occasionally undercut by corsairs, as when the *Rainbow* was seized off the coast of the Caicos Islands on April 2, 1799 by two French privateers. The *Rainbow* was rescued by the famed HMS *Surprise* – a 24-gun frigate.

A portion of the crew of the *Surprise* manned the *Rainbow* and escorted her into Kingston Harbour, Jamaica, where the ship's mate, Ephraim Hackburn, signed a sworn affidavit on April 13, at the office of the Justice of the Peace, stating in protest of his now-impounded vessel that the *Rainbow* had sailed out

> from Newburn on the eighth of February last pastbound to Kingston in this island and on the second of April was taken off the coast of Caicos by two French privateers and on the fourth of the same month was recaptured by his Majesty's Frigate the Surprise . . . The privateer took away with him all the logbook register and all the sloop's papers, their Boats and sundry other things. And that the master of the Rainbow and five of their people were put on board one of the privateers at the time of their capture saith [*sic*] that he arrived here on the tenth of the present month with only one of the seamen and a mulatto, and that the seaman from sickness is not able to join in this protest.

Such were the dire indignities suffered by American merchants and their crews while Britain opposed French aggression during the War of the French Revolution. The French privateers were in the wrong on every score, since their government's authorisation of them as pirates extended only to enemy vessels, especially commercial vessels, in time of war. The *Rainbow* was under the flag of the United States, which was not at war with anyone, least of all the French, and the *Rainbow* bore no arms to either threaten others or defend itself.

For their part, the British saw the *Rainbow* as a sloop forfeited by its owner through a contretemps on the open ocean, and then subsequently "found" by the *Surprise*, thus making the outcome a matter of salvage rather than naval chivalry.

A heated legal battle to regain the sloop was waged by Isaac Taylor, and it lasted until autumn 1800. As Isaac's agent wrote to him from Kingston, JA on September 20 of that year:

> We are truly sorry that the business of the Sloop Rainbow's Cargo has been laying unsettled for so long a time and it is still out of our power to come to a settlement with you on account the Agents of the H. M. Ship Surprise having entered and [*sic*] action against us for not paying them their Attorneys fee which is about 250 dollars – which we are of the opinion would be very unjust. The trial is to come on next Month and you may rest

assured when Settled with them we shall forward you immediately all or accounts.

Lumber and [barrel] staves [i.e. the wooden strips that bind their sides] are now getting in great demand, for the prices thereof and other articles we refer you to enclosed prices.

Isaac's agent in Kingston was struggling to get a fair-market price for the lumber goods (staves, shingles, floor boards) and foodstuffs (corn, lard, pork, etc.) in the *Rainbow*'s hold, but in the end total disbursements in the settlement exceeded the ship and cargo's total worth. And so a beloved craft in Taylor's American trading fleet (and a sentimental link to his bygone brother John) was never coming back to New Bern.

★　★　★

Despite such traumatic reversals, Isaac Taylor's profits were such that he turned the first floor front chamber of his Craven Street residence (situated immediately below a dramatic, second-floor drawing room) into a counting house for his demanding bookkeeping duties. This office was walled off from the rest of the house, with a separate entrance to the left of the front door.

Taylor became an active member of St. John's, the leading Masonic lodge (his forebears having been Freemasons in Montrose), and he was on the building committee for one of the foremost Federal-style public buildings in New Bern, the Masonic Lodge and Theater, erected between 1801 and 1809, which also included a ballroom for public entertainment. Because Masonic philosophy emphasised public service, Isaac was an early trustee of the spired, colonnaded First Presbyterian Church on New Street.

As befitted an educated man of Isaac's cosmopolitan taste and curiosity, his impressive library of books included *Paradise Lost* and *Paradise Regained*, *Don Quixote*, Dryden's *Virgil*, *The Arabian Nights* in two volumes, assorted collections of poetry, fables and essays, books on agriculture, gardening, seasonal planting, fruit growing, arithmetic, household medicine, and a copy of *The Ancient Israelites*.

Isaac and his prominent contemporaries were under the spell of a mode of thinking exemplified by a nationally popular sermon that

Connecticut Governor Jonathan Trumbull had requested from Yale president Ezra Stiles in 1783, a heady mix of chauvinistic spirituality and optimistic cultural proprietorship concerning "God's American Israel". Stiles' sermon was entitled "The United States Elevated to Glory and Honor", and it envisioned a destiny for the new nation of biblical import, led by chief executive (and pre-eminent American Freemason) George Washington – "the only man on whom the eyes of all Israel were placed". Particularly stirring to the new American merchant class was the following passage of this famous and widely republished exhortation:

> This great American revolution, this recent political phenomenon of a new sovereignty arising among the sovereign powers of the earth, will be attended to and contemplated by all nations. Navigation will carry the American flag around the globe . . . The prophecy of Daniel is now literally fulfilling – there shall be an universal travelling 'too [*sic*] and fro, and knowledge shall be increased.' This knowledge will be brought home and treasured up in America; and being here digested to the highest perfection, may reblaze back from America to Europe, Asia and Africa, and illuminate the world with TRUTH and LIBERTY.

A proud product of the Old World as well as the New, Isaac Taylor exhibited in his town and plantation homes two maps of the United States and one map of North Carolina; he had a local bookbinder gather under leather covers nine volumes of the *Edinburgh Review*. Also on prominent domestic display in the parlour of his townhouse was a fine pianoforte.

A standard badge of gentility, most pianofortes cost between three and six hundred dollars, the upper rate representing the price of a small house in the early 1800s. Even a fairly cheap model at two hundred post-colonial dollars would have equalled half a year's wages from a prosperous skilled worker. A preferred 18th-century product amongst cultivated American gentry of British descent were the pianofortes made by Scottish craftsman Robert Stodart, who founded the London firm of William & Matthew Stodart.

In a country accustomed to rural fiddlers, or the fife, drums and brass of male military bands, the subtle tonality of a pianoforte was a revelation, if not a sensation that commonly caused passers-by to pause in the streets to appreciate its overheard lilt. It was considered a woman's instrument in polite society, and Isaac's six daughters were expected to be acquainted enough with it to offer brief recitals for guests. Classical pieces and sacred hymns were the preferred home repertoire, but a few Scottish airs and prim parlour ballads were permitted.

By 1824, Isaac Taylor was openly referred to as a wealthy retired merchant and "one of the most respected citizens of the town", and his spouse and offspring were likewise held in high regard, a whispered exception being his only son Alexander, a bright, handsome fellow with an unfortunate private weakness for alcohol.

Isaac Taylor died on July 4, 1846, leaving most of his bank account, stock in the Bank of New York, Merchants Bank of New York, and Merchants Bank of New Bern, and extensive land holdings – among them 16 choice properties that included a lot on Front Street overlooking "Taylor's Wharf" – to his wife, Hannah. His estate papers for his houses in town listed such worldly goods as two carriages; two milk cows for daily use; three dozen bottles of the finest imported Madeira wine; much fine China, silver plate and crystal; and an array of custom-made mahogany furniture.

Out on the Glenburnie plantation sat 289 barrels of corn harvested from the crop of 1845, plus 5,992 pounds of peas. In the stables and pens stood 9 horses, 12 mules, 65 head of cattle, 72 head of sheep, 105 hogs. And the barn held 32 ploughs, numerous wagons, cultivators and spinning wheels.

Of Isaac's 75 slaves on the Glenburnie plantation – which ranged from an 11-month-old infant named Betty to a 64-year-old man named Bill Foy – they were apportioned amongst his spouse and daughters, two of whom, Janet and Mary, had married, respectively, into the prominent New Bern families of Hollister and Attmore.

Mary Taylor was wed in 1829 to George Sitgreaves Attmore, a lawyer and real estate investor from a Philadelphia merchant family with decades-old business ties to New Bern. In July 1839 Isaac had purchased, enlarged and remodelled a Greek Revival house at 513 Broad Street and presented it as a belated wedding gift for the beloved couple and their two small children.

It was son-in-law George Attmore, along with Isaac's unmarried daughter Phoebe Taylor, whom Isaac had appointed as co-executors of his last will and testament.

Ominously, Isaac's son Alexander was completely left out of Isaac's will, its text curtly inferring that even the land and slaves the son had enjoyed the use of during his early adulthood must now be turned over to the surviving members of the Taylor family, because his father deemed Alexander's drinking habits to be "excessive".

Isaac's house was reconfigured after death, his widow Hannah replacing the office door with a window, and cutting an inside doorway to the former counting house to connect it with the hall, turning that space into a downstairs drawing room. Visiting Hannah Taylor and her maiden daughters were a steady stream of married off-spring, grandchildren and extended family, among them black-sheep scion Alexander, who became a successful physician and wed Sarah Ann Cole, who had two boys, James Cole and Isaac Montrose I.

The Attmores also did well, raising seven children and amassing an estate said in the 1850 census to be worth $10,000. In 1854, two years after mother Mary Attmore died at the untimely age of 45, eldest daughter, Hannah Taylor Attmore, married moneyed New Bern merchant William Hollister Oliver.

★ ★ ★

Back in Scotland, several members of both lingering offshoots of the Taylors of Marykirk followed Isaac's cousin Patrick Taylor to south-western Australia, where Patrick had settled some 200 miles south of Perth, building a fine home on the banks of the Kalgan River in the port town of Albany and raising six children there.

Patrick himself left a personal library of 200 books, chiefly religious, which he gave to the people of Marykirk, Kincardineshire, to form the basis of the parish libary.

The original Kirktonhill House in Marykirk burned down. A new stone mansion was built beside it by later Taylor generations, who stayed on in the village and achieved their own heyday. This second, slightly smaller Kirktonhill complex, overseen in the 1840s by Robert Taylor, Esq. (a direct descendant of the medieval aristocrat who begat Hercules), had a grand entrance hall and subsidiary inner halls, four reception rooms, twelve principal bed and dressing rooms, five bathrooms, business and domestic offices and servants' quarters. The house was so extensive, with two annexes, that it once took two days to give a party for just the household staff. And the nearby Balmanno House was largely unchanged from Isaac's ancestors' days, with its two reception rooms, seven bed chambers, multiple baths, conservatory, and gun room.

For all their public hazards and private heartbreak, the Taylors of Montrose and Borrowfield, Kirktonhill and Balmanno, had amply demonstrated their mettle as migrating gentry. This story might have found a fairly happy ending right here, at midpoint in the 19th century, with the rest of the Taylor lineage fading elegantly away along with the last vestiges of the British Empire.

But America was about new beginnings, whether through war or peace, and the Taylor motto beneath its fisted crest of crosslets was a sign of martial cunning and commercial artistry. A great-great grandson, born in Boston in the 1940s, would one day write a meditative song with friends entitled 'Sugar Trade', which reconsidered such matters, its music a hybrid of a hymn and a hornpipe as it contemplated "the crown and the cross", muskets and chains, and their power to justify both white men's religion and family names. With two centuries of hindsight, who was to blame? The captain, cargo or the bankable sugar cane?

The song also acknowledged that a constant in all this merchantry, wealth and misery was the sea, which retained the right to swallow people up, or let them survive, as well as the means to "heal" them or "steal" them as the fickle trade winds dictated. Hence this unpredictable story, infused with the fluid spirit of all the generations that have thus far inhabited it, was really just getting started.

4

Hard Times

The siege of New Bern by the Union Army began at 7 a.m. on the morning of March 14, 1862. It was almost two years since Confederate troops had fired upon and forced the surrender of Federal troops at Fort Sumter, South Carolina in 1860, signalling the start of the War Between The States – with North Carolina being the last southern state to join the Confederate rebellion against the abolition of slavery on American soil.

By late afternoon, after the Confederate lines of Colonel Zebulon B. Vance had been breached, New Bern fell to Union troops in a campaign by General Ambrose Everett Burnside whose larger designs were the seizure and control of coastal North Carolina. The rebels had burned the railroad bridge over the Trent River to impede the Northern advance on the town. Union shells hit some targets downtown, and there were several days of looting by exultant troops and black citizens, but the greatest damage (the torching of waterfront warehouses and the Washington Hotel on Broad Street) was done by the retreating Southerners.

New Bern immediately became a heavily garrisoned base of operations for the Union forces in eastern North Carolina, with some of the female gentry temporarily taken hostage to insure the safety of Federal officers from snipers. Among them was Miss Mary Attmore, named for her late parent, the daughter of Isaac Taylor. Miss Mary, who remained under house arrest for an extended period, was twice accosted by prowlers, one of whom almost choked her to death before she pulled loose and escaped.

She awoke on another "grey morning", in her words, to find uniformed Yankee scavengers digging up burial sites in her estate's family cemetery in search of plunder.

Running out alone and defenceless into the midst of the macabre scene, she reviled the armed intruders, barking, "Is it possible that you could be guilty of such a dastardly trick as to dig open the graves of our ancestors?!"

Stunned, the body snatchers dropped their shovels, and as neighbours spied the proceedings from a safe distance, they removed their caps in mortification and disgrace. After a prolonged silence under Miss Mary's livid gaze, they began replacing the disturbed earth and hastily departed as dawn broke.

Left alone again, a smock pulled around her nightclothes, Miss Mary fought back tears as she smoothed and patted the soil of the desecrated resting places.

In the days that followed, she was granted greater freedom of movement by Union officials than any other private resident of New Bern. Miss Mary later became a favourite of the occupying troops for her dry wit, keenly eloquent tongue and fearless dignity, ultimately striding into history as a heroine of the North Carolina division of the United Daughters of the Confederacy.

Most of New Bern's white population had fled inland during the Union forces' capture of the town, abandoning their homes and businesses. Union soldiers had commandeered what was then still called the Isaac Taylor House on Craven Street, making it the headquarters for the 45th Massachusetts Regiment. They were astounded to discover Phoebe, Catherine and Frances Taylor – three spinster offspring of Isaac – hiding on the third floor of the mansion. Insisting on continuing to abide on the premises, these maiden aunts of the equally defiant Hannah Oliver refused to interact with the Yankee soldiers, and had their food and supplies raised to their window by a pulley mechanism.

The choice of opposing the Union had been difficult for much of North Carolina, with even Zebulon Vance, a personal friend and political compatriot of the Taylors, pleading initially for fidelity to the Union with "upraised hand". But when word of the events at Fort Sumter reached him, Col Vance wrote that his conciliatory hand fell "slowly and sadly by the side of a Secessionist".

By October 1862, North Carolina Governor-elect Zeb Vance was at odds with the president of the Confederacy, Jefferson Davis, arguing that "the original advocates of secession no longer hold the ear of the people" in his Union-occupied state, which led the South in troop desertions and civil protests.

Mrs Alexander Taylor, whose friendship with the Raleigh-based Governor Vance did not prevent her from also maintaining a cordial relationship with local Union military governor Edward Stanly, was known in New Bern as the "Prison Mother" for her work nursing Confederate inmates. Mrs Taylor was meanwhile spying for the rebels and ran a secret underground mail service, hiding letters to prisoners in special pockets sewn into the insides of her dresses.

She was stopped in the street one day by an unsuspecting Federal officer who mused, "Mrs Taylor, it is very strange, but we cannot find out how or where this Rebel mail comes in or who receives it."

Gripped by panic, and suspecting she was about to be led away to a firing squad, Mrs Taylor swallowed hard and elected to be flippant, replying, "Why I receive it! And at this moment my pockets are full of letters. Would you like to see them?"

The officer regarded her remarks as a dark jest and let her pass unmolested, Mrs Taylor nearly swooning with fear as she moved on with her day's batch of contraband correspondence tucked in the recesses of her skirts.

Hannah Oliver's eldest brother Sitgreaves enlisted as a private in Company F of the 10th North Carolina Confederate troops, seeing battle in 1864 before spending most of his remaining stint as a prisoner of war, dying in May 1865 in a Federal hospital of chronic diarrhoea and fever.

Isaac Taylor Attmore, Hannah's middle brother, joined up with the famed "Beaufort Rifles" of Company I, 2nd Regiment North Carolina Troops and became part of General Lee's Army of Northern Virginia. After fighting at Gettysburg, he was promoted to sergeant and was later killed at Spotsylvania courthouse in 1864.

The youngest brother of Hannah, George Attmore, also took up with the Confederacy, fighting with the rebels at Gettysburg and Spotsylvania. Meanwhile, New Bern stayed in the hands of the Union Army until Southern commander Robert E. Lee surrendered to General Grant at Appomatox courthouse in central Virginia on April 9, 1865. George Attmore was present at Appomatox courthouse but was among those who burned their guns and carriages and left without signing the surrender. George was paroled at Greensboro in '65.

For the last few months of the war, the old Isaac Taylor home on Craven Street saw duty as a Union field hospital but it was restored to the three Taylor aunts after they agreed to sign President Abraham Lincoln's Amnesty Proclamation.

Phoebe and Catherine eventually relocated, but Frances "Fanny" Taylor died in the Taylors' Craven Street house, her iron resolve to remain at the address linked to a tragic incident back in December of 1816, when her fiancé, Lewis Cannon, inexplicably fell dead in a public thoroughfare in downtown New Bern.

As a friend of Frances wrote to her husband at the time:

> There was extreme sudden death on Sunday evening last – Mr. Lewis Cannon drank tea in perfect health, set off for a walk, and dropt [*sic*] dead in the street. He was to have married Christmas morning. When Miss Taylor received the news of Mr. Cannon's death she fainted – poor girl, what a shock it must have been.

From that day forward, Frances refused to leave the Craven Street home in which she'd been born, undeterred by war or its discontents, and supported by her old maid sisters for as long as they could withstand it.

In the century and a half since, it is believed in the town that Fanny Taylor's spectre still sits at a first floor window in the front room of the tall brick house, waiting for the groom who failed to appear for her holiday nuptials. Notorious in Craven County as one of the "ghosts of Old New Bern", Fanny's wan, woeful face is periodically visible to passers-by, who leap back from the narrow sidewalk at the sight of the impossibly sad apparition.

★ ★ ★

"All these matters run pretty deep," descendant James Taylor asserted with a grim face in 1997, "and the Civil War was to change all of them forever."

Speaking in the autumn of 1999, James' brother Livingston, a Civil War buff, concurred. "When I was a kid in North Carolina in the 1950s, the Civil War was still very much an issue," said Livingston. "As a little boy of six or seven I stood at the bedside of my great-great aunt, Grandmother Vernon, who my father told me was born in 1863 – during the Civil War. So I remember actually being next to somebody who was born during what Uncle Charles, my dad's cousin, called 'The War of Northern Aggression'. That phrase always got a laugh, but it was his outlook on the pivotal event that made all of us Americans, because it locked us all into our sense of being part of a *country*.

"The Civil War also gave us the concept that we were now a wide population base that needed the same things," added Livingston. "All mass production was stimulated as a result of the war, because you had troops that needed trousers, underwear, rifles and cannons, whose parts and sizes had to fit everything and everyone. And clearly you had very popular Civil War songs, and the sheet music for them went *everywhere*, just as telegraph and daguerreotype photographs quickly sent news of the battles everywhere and the railways took the troops elsewhere. The unlimited efficiencies of the Civil War made possible both the Industrial Revolution and mass media. We became a country of interchangeable parts – and interchangeable human beings, 'cause if you shot one in battle we discovered there was always another soldier to take his place – the war killed or injured half a million people!

"As for the Taylors in New Bern," said Livingston, "the Union's blockade of Southern ports made it impossible for them to do shipping. And since I'm sure my Southern forebears must have had money tied up in slaves, and the Emancipation Proclamation made owning them impossible for labour, that was capital that would have all been forfeited too. So that was my sense of why the Taylors went inland to the western part of North Carolina to start over."

However, after the Union victory and withdrawal of its occupying forces, several members of the Attmore-Oliver branch of the Taylors held on to their old Isaac Taylor-bequeathed house at 513 Broad Street, raising children and sheltering its elderly inheritors within its walls through Reconstruction, the Spanish-America War, World War I and World War II, until the sole surviving direct Taylor-Oliver heir died at 91 and her nephews sold the home to the New Bern Historical Society, which now uses it as administrative offices.

"But most of my end of the family," observed the modern James Taylor in the late 1990s, "went from being plantation owners after the Civil War – rejecting that way of life – to become professionals; doctors, lawyers and insurance executives. When they moved to Morganton in the western part of North Carolina, they also ran and owned hospital-sanatoriums."

Morganton, situated 200 miles north-west of New Bern, lay in the spectacularly verdant Catawba River Valley at the eastern edge of the Appalachian Mountains. Between 1754 and the American Revolution, the Morganton region of what became Burke County in 1777 was host to waves of Scottish-Irish settlers moving further into the wilderness in what was known as the Great Southern Migration. They discovered an Eden in North America, its piedmont plateau and Appalachian Mountain regions an imagination-humbling immensity of river-marbled luxuriance and eminent promontories.

In the 1820s, Burke County had hosted a gold rush that yielded millions of dollars in ore. And in the early 1830s, the Burke County courthouse was the site of the famed trial of murderess Frankie Silvers, who later escaped disguised as a boy, was reapprehended and on July 12, 1833 became among the few ever females hanged in North Carolina. The lurid tale of Frankie's slaying of her husband, Charles, at the Toe River in 1831 formed the initial basis of the multi-version folk ballad, "Frankie and Johnny" (which saw additional reinvention in 1899 after being interspersed with facets of another crime of passion by a Frankie Baker in the African-American underworld of St Louis, Missouri).

When the focus of gold fever shifted in 1849 to California, the Burke County region grew quiet economically, only to be left nearly desolate by the ravages of the Civil War. A Union cavalry division led by Brigadier General Alvan Gillem had followed Union Major General William T. Sherman's famed scorched-earth policy in western North Carolina, torching factories and mills and pillaging private property in and around Morganton – although his gallant Colonel William Palmer returned a captured trunk of valuables to Mrs Zebulon Vance when she took refuge in nearby Statesville.

Fortunes revived in Morganton during the South's two-decade Reconstruction period, as the resultant industrial development (tanneries, furniture and textile mills) attracted ambitious young men.

The New Bern-born Isaac Montrose Taylor I, one of Alexander Taylor's two sons, graduated from the University of North Carolina in 1879. According to family lore, he was the first student to attend UNC when it reopened after the Civil War, and then he attended the College of Physicians and Surgeons at Columbia University, graduating in 1882, and ultimately bringing his skills to Morganton to practise medicine in western North Carolina. After four years of general practice in China Grove, NC, a small town below Statesville, Dr Isaac M. Taylor I took a post as assistant to Dr Patrick L. Murphy at the Morganton Asylum – officially the Western Insane Asylum of North Carolina and later Western North Carolina State Hospital.

During these years, the panther and grey wolf still prowled the dense Appalachian countryside, and the white-tailed deer, beaver, and wild turkey had not dwindled to where their later reintroduction was necessary. Bald eagles still swooped overhead in the high ground, and shad and small mouth bass abounded in its rivers and creeks. Turkey vultures, woodcock, mourning doves, chickadees, goldfinches, red-bellied woodpeckers, belted kingfishers and dozens of other birds made the hills and meadows their havens.

Spring brought mountain laurel, rhododendron, Catesby's trillium, Solomon's seal, Jack-in-the-pulpit and flame azaleas to the depths of the forests and the banks of watercourses, with the regular populace of mockingbirds, loggerhead shrikes, phoebes, cardinals and ravens mingling in their midst.

Great blue herons, whip-poor-wills, white-eyed vireos and yellow-billed cuckoos arrived each summer with wildflowers of the fields, woods and streams – like Carolina lilies, and three kinds of July orchids.

When autumn cold snaps signalled temperature drops on the eastern slopes of the Blue Ridge, goldenrod and ironweed would give way to the winding, butter-coloured petals of the witchhazel trees, with mallards, bufflehead ducks and red-breasted mergansers descending on the wetlands. Until finally purple finches and hermit thrushes alighted on most bare, wind-knifed boughs, and the appearance of the fox sparrow confirmed that winter was upon the Greater Morganton wilderness.

In total, this was an astoundingly lush province certain to anchor the soul and quicken the amatory impulse. While a physician at the state hospital, Dr Isaac M. Taylor I fell in love with and proposed to a well-to-do young woman of Scottish-Irish lineage named Susan Murphy Evans, the niece of the hospital superintendent, and a descendant of Robert Murphy and Elizabeth Kelso of the Isle of Arran.

The wedding took place in 1889 at Woodland, the bride's family estate in Cumberland County, NC, and she and Dr Taylor would eventually have seven children, including Alexander Taylor II. In 1901, Dr I.M. Taylor I and two other doctors from the State Hospital acquired an old mansion in Morganton and established the Broadoaks Sanatorium on Valdese Avenue, a private institution for the mentally ill, with Dr Taylor advancing from chief medical officer in 1903 to sole owner of Broadoaks. He lived across the street.

Back in New Bern, evidence of the earlier Taylors' great impact on the town grew gradually fainter. Isaac's old Glenburnie plantation grounds were now known as Glenburnie Park. It was the privately run site of a spacious dock for pleasure boats on the Neuse River, as well as a pavilion where dances and concerts were held and a fairground with a steeplechase whose grassy centre ring served as a launching pad for hot-air balloons.

As the years passed, Dr Isaac Montrose Taylor I became a pillar of the community in Morganton, acting as a vestryman at the Grace Episcopal Church, and during World War I he served as medical officer for the town.

★   ★   ★

At this stage, however, the American aspect of the Taylor saga begins to sour, growing downright gothic. James Taylor explains: "My grandfather Alexander Taylor II married my grandmother, Theodosia Haynes, who had come down from the North with Alexander's sister, Sarah, where they had been in school together."

Sarah had been Theodosia's roommate at the Shipley School in Bryn Mawr, Pennsylvania, a girls academy founded in 1894 by Misses Hannah, Elizabeth and Katherine Shipley to prepare its students for the institution that sat directly opposite it: Bryn Mawr College – which the two friends later attended.

While visiting the Taylors, Theodosia, a debutante from a prominent family in Longmeadow, Massachusetts, fell in love with Alexander II. According to grandson James Taylor: "Her sudden marriage came as a shock to the Haynes family." A much greater jolt was to come.

Theodosia Haynes Taylor insisted on her baby being delivered at home by her aged father-in-law, "a psychiatrist", as a family member later noted, "who hadn't delivered a baby in 50 years". And so grandpa Isaac Montrose Taylor became the physician in charge. In a ghastly turn of events, Theodosia died in 1921 shortly after giving birth to her only child, Isaac Montrose Taylor II.

Theodosia had contracted "childbirth fever" – basically a uterine infection – after her incautious and inadequately sterilised father-in-law went in after the placenta. Lapsing into a pain-wracked delirium and then a coma, she perished within two weeks. Naturally, the Haynes family wanted to know how she expired – and was told it had been tuberculosis – but then the truth came out and there was a major rift.

"Theodosia's death was a tragedy," as James Taylor recounts, "and it killed my great-grandfather, the delivering physician, who died about two months later."

The calamity continued to widen in scope, next claiming the inconsolable Alexander Taylor II, who was incapacitated by whisky-aggravated grief. Fortunately, Theodosia requested before her death that Sarah Vernon raise Ike.

"So my father lived nearby to *his* father," James now recalls. "He was raised by his aunt and uncle, Sarah Cole Taylor and her husband, Dr James Vernon. My father's cousins, Taylor, Livingston and Charles Vernon, became like brothers.

"My father's father was pretty much an abandoned alcoholic. If you were alcoholic then, there was little they could do for you. My great-grandfather was left pretty much helpless in those days." So by the end of 1921 James' guilt-ridden great-grandparent, Dr Isaac Montrose Taylor I, was dead.

James Vernon succeeded Isaac M. Taylor I as superintendent and chief medical executive of Broadoaks, having served on its staff for 11 years. At approximately 4.30 a.m. on Thursday, April 3, 1924, a fire ripped through the sanatorium, killing three female patients and one male patient, a J.P. Green, who sacrificed his life while rescuing several of Broadoaks 40-odd resident patients.

Broadoaks itself would survive the deadly conflagration, with Dr Erasmus Taylor, a younger brother of Alexander's, joining the staff in 1925, followed by Dr J. Taylor Vernon in 1951. ("The clan all named themselves with the same names *over* and *over* again," one in-law later commented.) The institution continued operations until its voluntary closure by the Vernon and Taylor families on September 30, 1959. The building was sold off and once again became a private residence. At the close of the 20th century it still stood as a picturesque Morganton land-mark in the National Register Valdese Avenue District.

As for the namesake of the negligent family doctor who had once turned the handsome edifice to its historic purpose, the years would not be quite as kind. From his boyhood onward, Isaac Montrose Taylor II had as much to live up to as he had to live down, and it left him con-sumed by an internal fire he was determined to somehow quell.

"There was some shame involved in how my father was reared, how he grew up with his father nearby but so out of control," his son James now recalls. "So it propelled my dad to succeed from an early age; he felt he had everything to prove."

5

Carolina In My Mind

"Day down" as some North Carolinans call nightfall, is that regular interval when the civilised air of the red clay piedmont, Blue Ridge highlands, and the cypress swamps and piney sandhills of the Coastal Plain is finally exhausted, and a creeping wildness resumes its advance.

About 45 miles down the highway from Morganton, in a sector of the southern piedmont between the tributaries of the Catawba and Pee Dee rivers waggishly dubbed "Scotch-Irish Mesopotamia", lies the Iredell County seat of Statesville. It was here during the years after the Civil War that folks began singing a song after dusk that was named for poor Tom Dula, thought culpable for the death by misadventure of a girl from the county called Laura Foster.

Handsome Tom, nearly six feet tall with dark curls and a gracious smile, was a fiddle and banjo-flailing ex-Rebel in his early twenties, fresh from the disbanded ranks of the 26th North Carolina Regiment. A paroled veteran of a lost cause, he'd come home eager for distractions, and found them with a half-dozen young mountain beauties, at least one being a married woman, Ann Melton, Dula's purported accomplice in the abduction and death of Foster.

Foster's remains were found carelessly interred in June 1866 in a thick local wood of neighbouring Wilkes County known as a lovers' rendezvous, her rotting torso stabbed in the breast, both legs broken to fit in the hole, her remains identifiable by her torn dress and the gold tooth visible in the upper left corner of her static gape.

Former governor Zebulon Vance stood as a character witness for Dula at two 1868 trials in Statesville, for Dula had served bravely under Vance during the fierce Yankee fire at the Battle of New Bern, the rookie private never seeming frightened, nor sustaining even a scratch.

"I have known Tom Dula during years of strain and stress, when a man's soul was tried," Col Vance testified, "and I tell you in all sincerity that never did a better soldier live, and never did one action of his ever lead me to believe him capable of murder."

To Vance, war was a test of character rather than killing ability, and a man fit for valour at the barricades was a man fit for peacetime in the Carolina vale. But witnesses for the prosecution claimed they saw Dula and Ann Melton in rapt conference the day before the terrible deed.

The jury of 12 men was finally persuaded by Dula's accusers, however, and Vance's appeal to the Supreme Court on Dula's behalf had failed.

"You have such a nice clean rope," said Tom Dula on May 1, 1868, standing on the back of a wagon around 2 p.m. on his last Carolina afternoon as he lowered his curl-covered brow to accept the hangman's noose. "I ought to have washed my neck."

The horses harnessed to the wagon were struck with a lash, and they pulled it out from under Dula, dropping him into a stiff, strangling dangle. There was no struggle. His lifeless body was cut down at 2.30 p.m. and buried at day down.

All anyone was sure of were the losses suffered, and how it was noted at the trial that Tom did credit to himself in the war by singing at night to the homesick Rebel boys at the front.

Even before the sad denouement, the deep green Carolina canopy had begun to stir on cool mountain evenings with a folk hymn – like so many that would pour off its front porches and out of its fathomless forests – about the uncertainty of life, the fragile trust of new love, and the fates of men who come back from one solemn engagement with assumptions they can shrug it off and easily adopt another:

Hang your head, Tom Dooley
Hang your head and cry.
Hang your head Tom Dooley
Poor boy, you're bound to die.

Hand me down my banjo.
I'll pick it on my knee.
This time tomorrow evening
'Twill be no use to me.

Western North Carolina is a world of myth and lament, legend and legacy, the land through which Daniel Boone carved his Wilderness Road, the place where future US President Andrew Jackson made his reputation as the "most roaring, rollicking, game-cocking, horse-racing, card-playing" back-county law student in history; the radio market where Jimmie Rodgers, the Father of Country Music, first hit the airwaves in the 1920s via Asheville's new station, WWNC; the hill country where Junior Johnson graduated from bootleg runner to stock car champion; the region in which Congresswoman Exum Clement became the first female legislator in the South, and the political base from whence Morganton judge Sam Ervin emerged to anchor the Senate committees that censured Senator Joe McCarthy and later forced the resignation of President Richard Nixon.

Like its folk songs, the people western North Carolina nurtures simmer with the energy of secret drives and relentless intent; a wildness of the spirit to match the landscape around them. Baptised in June 1921 at the First Presbyterian Church in Morganton, Isaac Montrose II was such a personality.

As the grandson and namesake of the shamed Dr Isaac M. Taylor I, one-time president of the North Carolina State Medical Society, young Ike was determined to erase the stigma of family scandal and tragedy that clung to the memories of his drink-decimated father and grandfather. And while Ike Taylor's heritage also claimed new stars such as cousin Hannis Taylor (1851–1922) former US Minister to Spain, it still saw setbacks like the private auction in Montrose, Scotland on January 14, 1925 of the Taylors' famed 2,314-acre Kirktonhill estate.

After attending the Asheville (NC) School for Boys, an exclusive prep school, Ike was a Phi Beta Kappa and Sigma Ki at the University of North Carolina at Chapel Hill, where he was bestowed in May 1942 with the highest honour on the University campus, being tapped with eight other students for coveted membership in the Order of the Golden Fleece, an award for academic achievement created in 1903. Ike received his AB degree at the UNC-Chapel Hill in 1942, and his MD degree at Harvard Medical School, where he was Alpha Omega Alpha and president of his class for all four years, graduating cum laude in 1945.

While Dr Taylor was in his last year at Harvard he met pert, sophisticated Gertrude "Trudy" Woodard at a 1944 student party in Cambridge. The 21-year-old Woodard was much impressed with the blond, broad-shouldered, intense young med student from the South, who ignited feelings that disturbed the decorum of her quiet, well-structured life.

A graduate of Newburyport High School, in the Massachusetts coastal town at the mouth of the Merrimack River, Trudy was enrolled at The Graduate House, a finishing school run by Katherine B. Child in a brick town house at 20 Chestnut Street on Boston's Beacon Hill. Trudy was also studying to be a lyric soprano at the New England Conservatory of Music on Huntington Avenue. Poised but girlish with light brown hair and a ready laugh, Woodard had been weaned on music, her mother teaching her children her repertoire of World War I songs and Broadway standards, the kids aware that their grandmother's sister was a noted music hall singer named Lottie Collins who'd gone to Europe to make her reputation.

The Woodards were descendants of English seafarers who had landed in New England in the 1600s, coming first to Boston and Gloucester and then settling in York and then Waterboro, Maine, where generations of Woodards dating back to 1792 were buried in the North Waterboro Cemetery. Patriarch Hezekiah Woodard left Waterboro for Newburyport because he preferred the sea to farming, vowing he "was never going to hoe another row of beets as long as he lived". He took his portion of his inheritance from his own parent's 1865 will to live the kind of existence that earned him a ring in one ear – a symbol in maritime circles in the 19th century that one had sailed across the equator.

Hezekiah's great grandson Henry Woodard, born August 12, 1895, was one of the earliest recruits of the US Coast Guard, formed in 1915 when the Revenue Cutter Service that protected US merchant ships (like Isaac Taylor's) against French privateers in the Caribbean was merged with the national Life Saving Service. Henry had married 20-year-old Ellen Angelique "Angie" Knox on September 4, 1916, and when the US entered World War I in 1917, the armed forces declined to draft Henry because he was the sole supporter of his new family as well as his mother's youngest offspring after the recent death of his father.

Henry had been one of 13 children, three of whom died young (one expired in childbirth, one froze to death on the Merrimack in a blizzard, and another perished in a motorcycle crash). Four of the others were taken in by Henry and Angie to raise as their own because the responsibility was too much for his aged mother.

Angie would have five kids of her own by Henry, rearing all the assorted Woodard charges in two houses Henry owned in Ferry Road on Rings Island, located directly across the river from Newburyport. Starting from scratch, Henry Woodard founded a local fishing and boat-building business on Rings Island that sent trawlers up and down the Merrimack and as far out to sea as treacherous Georges Bank, located some 180 miles east of Cape Cod.

Woodard had a small fish market in which to retail a portion of his weekly catch (the surplus usually sold off beforehand in Gloucester). And he regularly built small and medium-sized wooden trawlers (known as "draggers") under contract in his boatyard. To keep his boatwrights busy in between commissions, he also turned out a fairly steady stream of little sailboats and dories.

At the beginning of the 19th century, Newburyport was a leading salt cod port, in strong competition with leading Maine and Massachusetts fishing towns, including Portland, Marblehead and Gloucester, which was the leading fishing port in America by 1866.

Newburyport continued to do well, however, as a distinguished centre for the building of excellent transatlantic steamships like the *Ontario* and the *Erie* of 1866–67 (built for the Boston-financed American Steamship Company), or sloops, cod schooners and other coastal sailing vessels like the renowned three-masted *Cox & Green* and *John Currier* of the late 1800s.

Roughly a decade after Woodard had started his businesses during World War I, many of the men on Rings Island worked for him, and some of them had home mortgages he'd obtained for them during the Depression (often as interest-free or non-refundable loans) in order to keep their cosy island community together. A thoughtful, eccentric workhorse, Henry Woodard was as industrious as he was kindly.

"Fresh fish caught by our own boats," read the slogan on H.H. Woodard's business cards, and so efficient were his trawling nets that he would be credited after his death in 1978 with catching more fish in the Merrimack than any known human on the river – including ancient predecessors in the Pennacook and Massachusetts Indian tribes.

Henry and Angie had "met on the river", as habitués of the Merrimack Valley liked to put it. Both of their social lives, private sensibilities, and public concepts of purpose were inevitably linked to the river and its ancient heritage, whether as a pastoral artery for New England's timeless dramatic unfoldment, or as a practical symbol of the American Industrial Revolution all but born in the mills on its municipal frontage from Lawrence to Lowell.

The Knoxes were an old Merrimack Valley family with kin all along the great inland river from Groveland in its western bend opposite Haverhill, to Salisbury at the Atlantic shore near the New Hampshire border. They were related to John Greenleaf Whittier (1807–92), the Haverhill-born reformist editor and fiery Quaker abolitionist, who pioneered regional writing in such books and poems as *Legends of New England* (1831) and *Moll Pitcher* (1832). After the Civil War, Whittier turned his pen principally to poetry and hymns, mostly evoking New England life and faith, including *Barbara Frietchie* and *The Barefoot Boy*.

Angie Knox's upbringing was marred by the separation of her parents when she was young, which was followed by the sudden death of her dad from heart disease. Having been close to her late parent, who was said to be "able to do anything", from sailing a boat to catching a fish, Angie resolved to be like him and find a beau who followed suit.

In a photo of Henry and Angelique Woodard taken in 1942, the couple are shown poised before a great ship's anchor in front of their market, a knowledge of hard work and a sense of fun in their faces. They had communicated both to the second of their four daughters.

Trudy Woodard was born on November 7, 1922, an election day when the Democrats made gains against President Warren Harding's corrupt Republican majority in Congress. That same year, the 19th Amendment providing for women's suffrage was declared constitutional by the Supreme Court, and the first woman US senator (Mrs W.H. Felton, 87, of Georgia) was appointed. Trudy was a young woman of her era, idealistic yet sensible. She was intrepid enough at 19 years old to insist on going to sea on one of her dad's trawlers, and wise enough never to repeat the experience after spending most of the trip mute with seasickness and wrapped in a tarpaulin at the ship's bow.

During her freshman year in high school, Trudy contracted a chronic upper respiratory illness that curtailed her studies and clouded her attitude towards continuing her education. Walking into the principal's office in the run-down school building one afternoon, the consistent "A" student told him she wasn't going to attend classes any longer. Back home, Trudy explained her feelings to her parents in greater detail, saying she found that the run-down old high school's environs had become intertwined in her mind with her depressing ailments, and she thought it might be better if she just spent the next few months riding her bicycle to the library and pursuing an ad-hoc course of study there.

Since both her parents looked at life as a constant improvisation, the Woodards concurred with their self-motivated daughter and allowed her to do just that. Trudy would not return to regular classes until the following year when, happily, a new school had been built under the Public Works Administration.

The Woodards had been doing their own building in the late 1930s, most notably a sleek fishing craft called the *Sevenovus*, its name a wry tribute to their seven-member household. It was launched in the summer of 1939, several months after the sudden death in the spring of their 20-year-old daughter Ruth from a ruptured appendix. An earlier bout of appendicitis had presumably healed. The tragedy jarred the entire Rings Island community, and the Woodards never got over the loss of their eldest daughter, a fact made plain in weary, late evening musings from Trudy Woodard's diary between January 1 and January 19, 1940:

Monday, January 1:
"New Yrs. Day. Strange, but the coming year doesn't seem to hold anything so spectacular toward us. Ruth died last spring."

Friday, January 19:
"Etta Mae is 12. Doris Jeannie is 7. Henry Woodard, Jr. – 14. Gertrude is 17. Ruth would be 21. Ruth died in May 1939. Her birthday was on August 18th. I shall never forget her radiance, her works, and her lovely charming eyes, hair and teeth."

In between these random reflections, on January 6, 1940, Trudy was registered for voice training at the Conservatory of Music on Huntington Avenue in Boston, taking the shoreline commuter train from Newburyport into Beantown's North Station for her weekly Saturday instruction. Her teacher was Madame Marie Sundelius, who seemed to know what Trudy wanted and needed to learn, immediately encouraging her to purchase a selection of recent Decca, Columbia and Victor recordings, including ones by British contralto Kathleen Ferrier and the glamorous French-Italian coloratura star of the Metropolitan Opera, Lily Pons, especially the latter's famed high F-scaling interpretation of 'Où va la jeune hindoue?' ('Bell Song') in the title role of Delibes' *Lakmé*. In addition, regular piano lessons commenced on January 25 at 2.30 p.m. at the Newburyport home of Julia Finnegan at a cost of one dollar an hour. Once home again, she'd disappear into her bedroom, with its pink and white curtains and blue taffeta bedspread, reading Thackeray's *Vanity Fair* for senior English or doing vocal exercises while waiting out the frequent blizzards of 1940.

The mid-winter tranquillity of such routines was disrupted on March 18, when Henry Woodard and the crew of the *Sevenovus* were reported missing at sea after the ship had failed to return from a morning sail.

Angie Woodard phoned the Coast Guard to request a search party, which promptly departed in quest of the former Guardsman, but high seas and poor visibility impeded their reconnaissance. Angie paced the floor all night, waiting for any word on her husband and his crew.

Twenty hours later, the Woodard's boat was towed back into Newburyport Harbour after having rested distressed for 20 hours off the northern coast of Massachusetts.

This frightening event, plus the recent engagements and marriages of several friends, among them Doris Miller (at whose wedding Trudy sang the 1913 Enrico Caruso hit, 'Because'), engendered an uncharacteristic level of anxiety in Trudy, whose only romantic relationship to date was a "serious longing" for Charles Edward "Hoppy" Hopkinson, her first beau.

At 18, her own checklist of essentials in a proper mate, as set down in April '41, was extensive and particular:

> Through marriage, I would like to gain wealth, happiness, a companion, (an aesthetic companion), a fellow traveler, a nature lover, a Christian, a good citizen, a man who can ride horseback with me, play a short game of tennis with me (and stand my game), a man who will swim, dance, play – then work – with me. A man who will protect and prevent me from working and playing too hard. (Thus far I am an untamed colt – I have never been taught what it means not to have something I really desire; I have had my say always. I am forever winning – never losing. I realise I *must* sometime, and I hope . . . I receive a husband whom I may be proud of).

At least as proud, that is, as she longed to be of herself. By the following year, after her affection for Hoppy had cooled and he went off to World War II service in the Navy. Eligible men of marrying age were few and conspicuous in America during World War II, and people on the home front were particularly sensitised to the onset and aftermath of unexpected emotional pain – although the prime source of late had been letters delivered to neighbours' doorsteps by the War Department, informing loved ones of another fallen soldier scarcely out of high school.

Trudy would hold her senior class spellbound in '41 when she sang in the senior play, *Smilin' Through*, an adaptation of Allan Langdon Martin's extravagantly romantic post-World War I Broadway hit of 1919. Trudy had the starring role of Moonyeen, a girl killed in the crossfire of a suitors' quarrel whose spectre appears on lunar-lit nights to console her bereaved lover. And the show's title ode of undying love remained a showstopper on her lips:

There's a little green gate
On whose trellis I'll wait
While two eyes so true
Come smilin' through.
I'll be there, waiting
Just at the end of the road.

As convincing as Trudy's portrayal of the spirit in *Smilin' Through* had been, the character's hopefulness could not carry over into Trudy's own family life, where such supernatural serenity was hard to sustain. As she confided to her journal on Sunday, May 11, 1941:

My mother is happy, for she has had five children of whom she is proud; she is happy for she had, and has, a great deal of happiness, although she has had strife (mental strife).

We wish that you were here, Ruthie. We know that you see us, but we hope that you don't try in vain to tell us things that we cannot see nor hear. Mother longs for her Ruth, and I should like to see things through your eyes once again, dear. God bless my mother, and keep daddy well, for in him is her strength.

As for Trudy, her own indefatigable strength of purpose and out-wardly confident air could prove at times to be a social liability. The sense of drive and independence she constantly projected hindered her seeming capacity for accessibility, with less self-motivated classmates and potential paramours shying away from the personable but preoccu-pied classical vocalist. Isolated by her keen absorption in her outside interests and ambitions, Trudy often found herself lonely when the frisson of those involvements faded. In her senior-year diary inscription of Friday, May 16, 1941, she paused in her otherwise hectic schedule of music studies to confide:

I do long to go to my Senior Promenade Dance this evening . . . Never did I think that I should ever go through high school without an invitation to the "Prom", but here I am – at home . . . When I reach college days I *do* hope that I may have many friends of the masculine sex – musicians or not!"

49

Smiling through, Trudy Woodard kept to her own dogged course, taking the train into Boston for her vocal lessons at the Conservatory of Music, singing Schubert, Bellini, and lieder, and trying to improve her German and Italian in what little spare time remained. Trudy would once again have the audience in the palm of her petite hand when she accepted the principal's invitation as a senior to sing at the Newburyport High graduation programme, but that occasion had its own capacity to disturb.

During rehearsals for the commencement ceremony, Trudy watched from the stage as another senior girl displayed open annoyance at having to march into the auditorium in two-by-two formation with a black classmate.

Afterwards, the girl went home and told her parents, who complained to the Newburyport High administration that their daughter could not publicly enter the graduation exercise paired with a "coloured boy".

On the day of commencement, Trudy sang as scheduled but stared in dismay and shame as the black student, Frank Cousins, was forced to enter the auditorium alone at the end of the class procession. The world was at war for the causes of freedom and human dignity, yet it seemed in pathetically short supply at a public school in a region of northeastern Massachusetts once known for its abolitionist fervour and agitation for emancipation.

To Trudy's satisfaction, Frank Cousins would one day see his own son hold local elective office (Sheriff and State Representative) in Massachusetts, but social injustices rankled with her and became part of everyday discussion both during and after the inception of the New Deal domestic reform programmes (1933–41) of President Franklin Delano Roosevelt. As the Depression subsided and economic recovery overlapped with defence spending for a war that raged on in Europe and Asia, cocktail debates of these and other societal shortcomings were commonplace at Boston gatherings of college students, with Trudy often contributing sharp insights to the exchanges.

At the medical students' party on the evening in '44 when Trudy first encountered the intense Ike Taylor, she found him to be a liberal-to-left-wing advocate of racial justice and socialised medicine, which pleased her. And the young doctor also possessed some of the essential attributes for husbandhood she had once identified in her diary – but only some. He appreciated music but not in any pronounced sense. And yet, from the instant they'd met, he seemed utterly compelling. The odd merger of his inbred Southern reserve and fierce intellectual hunger formed an alluring alloy, and its smouldering promise felt undeniable to her.

"The minute . . . I saw this man," she later told friends in a tremulous tone, suddenly flushed by an abrupt flood of emotion, "I loved every cell in his body. He brought out feelings I didn't know I had. I said to myself, that very night, 'This is the man I want to have children with.' "

Suddenly Trudy's budding musical career seemed less important, her chic black portable Victrola and the opera records she had revelled in less entrancing, and a future with Ike inescapable. After graduation, Ike served his internship at Massachusetts General Hospital in 1945–46 and was an assistant resident in medicine for a year before being appointed resident. The stillpoints in this hectic schedule were the times he spent with Trudy, and when he advanced the idea of matrimony, she readily accepted. "At the time," she now recalls advisedly, "my favourite song was 'What's The Use Of Wond'rin' ', from *Carousel*.

Isaac Montrose Taylor II and Gertrude Woodard were married in 1946, moving from an apartment in Boston to a big wooden house in Milton, Massachusetts. Trudy gave birth to their first child, Alexander, on February 28, 1947, at the Boston Lying-In Hospital across from the Harvard Medical School, the droll Trudy noting that "the place had a driveway in the shape of a uterus".

Naming the boy Alexander was part of Ike's private determination to remake the past and forge a fresh start in a new century. Alex was a bubbly, blond and headstrong little boy, and he got a brother on March 12, 1948, James Vernon Taylor – "Jamie" or "Jamus" for short – a quiet, self-contained baby, named for the uncle who'd raised Ike when his father could not.

With the appearance of spring and the second child, the Taylors' landlady came by one night and left a blunt, handwritten note in a milk bottle, placing it on the doorstep: "Now I need my house back."

Searching with a nursing James in tow, Trudy traversed greater Boston for a 30-mile radius in her Kaiser automobile until she found their next home in a woodsy suburb called Weston – or at least a plot on which to construct it. The family lived in the house as it was being finished, Trudy describing it to friends as "Cambridge-Bauhaus", with icicles dripping off the roofs. She could visualise gardens situated around the periphery, and tiers of children's records and books strewn about indoors, with selections from the former blaring from a stereo Trudy placed in a hall closet at toddler level: 'Take Me Riding In The Car Car', by Woody Guthrie, Burl Ives and the Andrews Sisters' 'Blue Tail Fly', and Leadbelly's 'Grey Goose'.

The last ode was featured in the pioneering book, *Folk Song U.S.A.: The 111 Best American Ballads*, published on April 2, 1947 by editors John A. and Alan Lomax with voice and piano settings by music editors Charles and Ruth Crawford Seeger. The acclaimed, fast-selling anthology brought authentic folk songs into the mainstream; among its other 100 traditional tunes arranged for mass consumption was a certain Appalachian murder ballad, 'Tom Dooley'.

In 1948, the year Ike was licensed to practise medicine in Massachusetts, he was appointed assistant medical advisor to Harvard University, where for the period 1948–50 he was research fellow in biological chemistry. In 1949, he was named clinical fellow in medicine at Massachusetts General Hospital, which made him chief resident in 1951.

During the few precious breathing spaces in between, a third child arrived on August 15, 1949, their first and only daughter, who was christened Katherine Child Taylor in honour of the founder of Trudy's fond finishing school. "Kate" as she was called was followed on November 21, 1950 by another boy, Livingston "Liv" Taylor.

Ike had his own brood now, and at Harvard Medical School he was a very visible and much sought-after talent on the rise. He was soon approached for a prime faculty position at the University of North Carolina at Chapel Hill – a provocative opportunity for ancestral redemption. "He was a very magnetic, very appealing man," second son James would recall of his dad, reflecting on that turning point in his parent's professional ascent. James added that his father was "A detached person with a lot of animal magnetism. I think he was propelled by his early family situation, whose paradigm was the successful doctor or the successful academic."

Livingston, though, would grow up convinced that even deeper forces were at work within his father and mother, gnawing at them even as they grappled with ties to work and family.

"My father was charismatic," observed Livingston five decades later, "but he was irreparably heartbroken. I think the death of his own mother, and that sense of abandonment he felt, was insurmountable. He was not ever able to overcome that reservoir of sadness, and it continued to drag him down, to drag him back to North Carolina."

As for Livingston's mother, Liv saw Trudy as "competing with the older sister, Ruth, who died of the ruptured appendix. Trudy's mother always spoke of Ruth in really incredible terms. Ruth was a *star*, and Trudy felt driven to compete with the impossibly glowing memory of the favoured sister who died young. ["And trying," in Trudy's own words, "to take on my sibling's responsibilities as 'No. 1'."] So both of my parents would search for things they couldn't find."

Son James Taylor could only shake his head ruefully at the memory of Ike Taylor's decision to resume life in the South. "My father, in moving back to North Carolina, basically re-engaged his family drama," he says. "If I could have chosen for him, I would have said that someone with as promising an academic and medical career as his should have stayed in Boston" – Taylor's soft but tightening voice verges on anger – "and just *let it be*."

But that was not the way that Taylor family leaders behaved when they carried a burdensome legacy. Nor was it consistent with Yankee can-do attitudes, or the method by which Carolina ballads customarily crept out from the dark canopy of Carolina's folk culture.

So Isaac Montrose Taylor II and the former Gertrude Woodard went South, to the land of lost ships and lost wars and ghosts and graves and whisky and wounds. And everything fragile and new in their family trees went south with them.

6

Golden Moments

It was a golden era of academic life and its pleasures at the "Athens of the South". Indeed, the Eisenhower '50s, meaning the period launched in 1953 with the inauguration of US President Dwight D. Eisenhower, would long be considered *the* sublime moment for studenthood on the Chapel Hill campus of the University of North Carolina.

The impeccable sunups and day-downs on the tidy neo-classical campus aptly delineated the charm of its festive formal dances in Woollen Gymnasium, alfresco classes on the new "Polk Place" south quadrangle, hayrides to Hogan's Lake, beer bashes at the Porthole, Brady's, and Edward "Papa D" Danzinger's Rams Head Rathskeller, i.e. "the Rat", plus what one graduate would remember as the "easy familiarity" shared by students and professors. Chapel Hill finally seemed within reach of the goal its trustees had decreed since its charter in 1789: to be as far as possible in every sense from the distractions and perils of city life.

Before this shining idyll could seem complete, however, Chapel Hill had to make its peace with the persistent prejudices of both town and country. In 1950, while Ike Taylor was still a research fellow in bio-chemistry at Harvard, a North Carolina middle district court judge named Johnson J. Hayes handed down a decision denying four black students entry to the Chapel Hill law school. A year later, as Ike was finishing his stint as an assistant professor at the Harvard Med School, the US fourth district court reversed Judge Hayes' ruling on appeal with the US Supreme Court subsequently supporting that reversal.

The parallel efforts afoot to foster separate-but-equal facilities and curriculum at North Carolina's black law school (North Carolina College for Negroes at Durham) as a hedge against impending desegregation were not possible in terms of the state's medical studies programmes, since its sole public medical school was at Chapel Hill. But a 61–14 vote by Chapel Hill trustees on April 4, 1951 in favour of considering student applicants' qualifications "without regard to race or color" soon cleared the way for black medical students' admission to the school. However, at least one University trustee accused the school of "selling out" to Negroes.

Major L.P. McLendon, who'd drawn up UNC's new admissions policy, argued instead that the trustees as a group show its academic and social calibre via compliance, stating, "It is not in the character of the University of North Carolina to say we haven't got the courage to face this issue on the law of the land."

Thus, African-American law students Harvey Beech, James Lassiter, J. Kenneth Lee and Floyd B. McKissick – all state residents – entered Chapel Hill's law school in June 1951, and Dudley Diggs, a World War II veteran currently in pre-med at North Carolina A&T at Greensboro was enrolled for the autumn '51 term at Chapel Hill's medical school.

In the interregnum, the Taylors had moved down from Boston, settling in the countryside, beyond semi-rural Carrboro, named in 1916 after Julian Shakespeare Carr, a Chapel Hill native and UNC graduate who'd been a leader in post-Civil War manufacturing in North Carolina. Carr had been CEO and part-owner of W.T. Blackwell & Company, the source of Bull Durham tobacco and cigarettes, and also established the Durham Hosiery Mills Corporation, whose satellite textile factories in Carrboro employed more than a third of the community (including blacks as early as the 1930s, an unusual exception at the time).

By the 1950s, though, many of Carr's local mills had closed or been absorbed by the acquisitive Pacific Mills wool manufacturing firm. A fair portion of the former mill workers secured jobs at the expanding

UNC-Chapel Hill complex and its reliant local business grid, or subsisted on the same sharecropping that had sustained many of Carrboro's white and black inhabitants since the 1790s.

The resident farmers of central North Carolina had always worked acreage smaller than the plantations of the coastal Deep South, and the predicaments of sharecropping life on the Piedmont were shared by blacks and whites, alike. They often helped each other to get a crop in, and though their children could not attend school together, the farming class mingled in the same streets, feed stores, roadhouses and picnic grounds. Hard work and debt were common experiences – but so was music.

Children's songs like 'Little David Play On Your Harp' (as recorded by the Joe Reed Family) or 'Daniel In The Den Of Lions' (preserved on disc by the North Carolina Cooper Boys) were familiar to adults and kids coming of age in the region during the 1920s and 1930s. The Golden Gate Quartet with Josh White was a familiar presence on WBT radio, a 50,000 watt station in Charlotte, North Carolina, and the group's jubilee gospel style was known throughout the Piedmont for reinvigorating spirituals such as 'Run, Sinner, Run' or such traditional 19th-century fare as 'Old Dan Tucker'. String bands both black and white played these songs and more, including 'John Henry' and 'Boll Weevil', and each forged bonds in North Carolina farming communities that somehow eluded Jim Crow and legalised segregation.

When John A. Lomax and Alan Lomax visited the State Penitentiary in Raleigh, from December 18–22, 1934 and the State Prison Camp in Boone, NC on July 18, 1936 to record the inmates' music for the Library of Congress' Archive of Folk Song, they heard Norman Higgins singing 'Noah And The Flood', Blind Joe's wanderlust ode, 'When I Lie Down Last Night', and Albert Shepherd's 'Pick 'Em Up'. The music bespoke the spiritual, work song, and blues aspects of every poor Piedmont farmer's lot.

In 1940 the town of Cedar Grove near Durham, NC was cited in the census as having 267 white-run farms and 239 black-run farms. Records like 'Cotton Mill Blues' by Wilmer Watts, a local white fiddler-vocalist and mill hand, could unite those growers as if it were a church hymn. These songs and countless others, with their snatches of biblical lore, "let 'em fall down" advice, and images of "a poor boy" with "travellin' on my mind" influenced everybody within earshot, and lingered long in fertile imaginations.

★   ★   ★

The transplanted Taylors found temporary housing in a restored, two-storey white farmhouse with dark shutters set in a wheat and barley field on Old Greensboro Road – a rugged tract to the west of the centre of Carrboro in a watershed that encompassed University Lake. The tall, tree-sheltered home had a sizeable attic, and a shallow, stoop-high shingled porch in front held up by four slender posts suitable for children to swing around on.

Several dozen yards' distance across the level cropland from the Taylors lived the family of Tom Ray, whose bungalow was built at the turn of the century as a rental for mill workers. It then passed amongst his kin, who had been farmers and small shop or boarding house proprietors in Orange County for 100 years.

Trudy was in the parlour of the Taylor house one day when Nancy Ray, Tom's daughter, came by and asked to use the telephone to call her "ma" next door. "I done washed the dishes!" Nancy loudly insisted to her parent as she was concluding her phone conversation.

It dawned on Trudy as Nancy thanked her and departed that she and her children were now in a much different culture from the one they'd previously known, with alien jargon and customs and perspectives far removed from any overheard on Beacon Hill. Her husband Ike had come down to Chapel Hill to teach young Southern doctors how to excel on a par with Harvard's best. But what was his wife expected to teach – and learn – in this strangely contrasting new environment?

Dr Taylor assumed his new duties as assistant professor of medicine at the University of North Carolina School of Medicine. Ike was engaged in teaching and research in body metabolism, he and colleague Evan Calkins having published a highly regarded study entitled *Carbohydrate Metabolism* with the Johns Hopkins Press in 1952. Ike soon became one of 25 men in the United States and Canada to receive a $30,000, five-year grant from the John and Mary R. Markle Foundation as one of the top "scholars in medical science" in North America.

The grant offered both academic security and financial help to faculty members at the start of their careers in academic medicine, and each scholar was selected from candidates nominated by deans of medical schools, with the overall goal, as the Foundation put it, being to spur each recipient's "progress up the academic ladder".

Ike Taylor's days were filled with work and pressure and promise. But out in the high grass of Carrboro, Trudy was a fish out of water, trying to fill the family's rented farmstead with the phonograph-borne sounds of light opera, Woody Guthrie, and The Weavers, the last a popular folk act with former members of The Almanac Singers, an activist leftist group of the early 1940s once composed of Guthrie, Lee Hays and Pete Seeger. Peter was the son of former Federal Music Project musicologist/folklorist Charles Seeger, whose work with second wife Ruth Crawford Seeger (an arranger for Carl Sandburg's 1927 *The American Songbag* book) on assorted New Deal Federal Arts projects helped bring folk music and radical politics into popular view. After Pete and Lee formed The Weavers with singer Fred Hellerman and female lead Ronnie Gilbert, they notched national hits in 1950–51 with Leadbelly's 'Goodnight Irene' and a North Carolina mountain song, 'On Top Of Old Smoky'.

This earthy, unfussy music meshed well with the Carrboro terrain: flat, muddy fields filled with silage crops, a few blue cornflowers and tiny hyacinths peeking out from behind the grain stalks, and pear trees gleaming at grand intervals in the hedgerows.

A black sharecropper, John Hairston, worked the surrounding furrows for the owner, a fellow named Bassett. One morning after the Taylors had settled in, they awoke to the clatter of Mr Hairston guiding a wagon pulled by a team of mules; hitched to the back of the creaky conveyance was a sickle bar that cut down the hay. Following along after him was a hay bailer that Hairston had leased, its operator bailing up what had previously been mowed and windrowed by John.

The sun shone above the treeline of the redbuds shading the rusty Piedmont clay when Hairston steered his haywagon to the circle of the Taylor's driveway. Seated on the back end, her legs dangling, was a middle-aged black woman in a simple dress. The wagon lingered there, neither the driver nor his rider shifting from their resting places.

After about an hour, Trudy Taylor grew curious about the parked buckboard and its passengers. Stepping out of the house, her children clustered around her, she approached the woman who sat silently at the edge of the long, low rig.

"Would you like a drink of water?" Trudy asked, since it was humid and the dense air was still.

"No ma'm," the woman replied, falling quiet again.

There was a long wordless pause, interrupted only by the bustle of a rolling breeze.

"Is there anything I can help you with?" Trudy pressed, her tone both cordial and perplexed.

"*Wayl*," the woman answered, her voice soft but animated with the light-tempered lilt that is the Carolina drawl, "actually I was wonderin' if there's anything I could do for you. I see you have a lot of children and I live just down the way . . ." The last word was uttered in an upward pitch that promised more but trailed off into silence.

In this spare fashion did Effie Hairston, wife of John, introduce herself and request work, having executed her end of the job interview in its entirety. Slowly grasping this mutual examination/transaction, Trudy surveyed the calm-countenanced woman and realised she was quite satisfied. Everyone smiled. And so, for the next 20 years or so, Effie would be Trudy's loved and loving helpmate, arriving each day to help her feed the Taylor babies, prepare the older kids for school, clean the house, complete other tasks at hand and set the basics of dinner in motion before departing shortly after 2 p.m.

Effie became invaluable when Hugh Cole Taylor, Trudy's last child, entered the picture on an exceptionally sultry July 24, 1952 at Duke Hospital in Durham. Hairston liked to hug the happy infant as Trudy introduced him to the neighbours as the "caboose" of her progeny.

Life at the Taylor house followed loosely the tempo of a working farm, since the rhythms of its rural milieu helped shape the mood of each day. The Rays next door were usually up early with their children, doing the chores, as were the Hairstons down the road. The Rays raised feed corn, filling a crib's worth of it for the hogs, and spreading it around the pens for the chickens. There was some tobacco planted in the area and, depending on the season, its broad leaves splayed in thick bouquets in the fields or hung brown and curing in small barns.

The washing machine at the Rays' house was run by a gasoline engine on their back porch, and the use of the former on washdays generated a dual commotion that seemed to shake the muggy breezes that eddied through the foliage. At mealtimes the fare spread out on oilcloth covering the table in the Rays' kitchen reflected the work just finished, with roast chicken placed beside steaming bowls of butterbeans or wax beans, a basket of hot biscuits and a crock of the pudding-like cream gravy that always accompanied them. And on the stove or the window sill rested a cooling fruit pastry – usually the lemon or "chess" (eggs, brown sugar, and milk) pies Effie made for the children to enjoy when they returned from school in the afternoon.

The Taylor kids were sometimes invited by the Rays' daughter Nancy for lunch or dinner, but Ike forbade his children to use the Rays' outdoor privy barefooted. He was afraid of hookworm.

Tom Ray contracted the parasite in his foot one summer, and little James looked on with alarm at Tom's swollen sole, a large worm moving under the skin. Dr Taylor went over to the Rays' house and prescribed a cure.

But while all these things unfolded next door, in the Taylor house the food and the routine and the texture of time passing had a New England flavour, with only casual concessions to Carolina. Trudy cooked lean healthy meals of a meat and potatoes and seafood sort, plus plenty of fresh vegetables obtained from Fowler's Market and local growers, but few of the rich or fatty accoutrements of Southern cooking.

Trudy once asked Florence Vernon, the wife of Ike's cousin, who was visiting from Morganton, how to make biscuits. "Trudy," she said after a pensive swallow, "there's no recipe. You're born knowing how to make biscuits in the South." Trudy somehow learned, with Effie's help, but they were not a staple of the Taylors' dining room.

Yet Southern ways trickled into the tenor of Ike and Trudy's household, leaving their effects. Bees elected to live in the spaces between the floors, and their honey seeped through the plaster to form asymmetrical patterns on the living-room ceiling. In an abandoned smoke house behind the house, a turkey buzzard held court. He could be roused by banging on the walls. From his high chair in the kitchen, little Liv memorised the radio jingle for snuff, chanting, "If your snuff's too strong, it wrong. Get Tuberose." He also had a large repertoire of folk songs.

In the woods beyond the fields there was a makeshift sawmill, a primitive operation at which hardwoods from the immediate vicinity were sliced up for lumber. The afternoon singing of the saw always seemed to be lifted up into the flyway along with cardinals and bluebirds and funnelled across the forest into the eaves of the house.

At sunset the wind would change and the aroma of the air with it, its fragrance slipping from a pine scent into a honeysuckle perfume, as mockingbirds sang sweetly into the depths of night.

"Chapel Hill, the piedmont, the outlying hills, were tranquil, rural, beautiful but *quiet*," James Taylor remembered four decades later. "Thinking of the red soil, the seasons, the way things smelled down there, I feel as though my experience of coming of age there was more a matter of landscape and climate than people. 'Cause there was nobody around!

"Life there was mostly about my siblings and internal things in my family," said James. "I think it was hard on my mother, 'cause she was very isolated down there, out of her element; Carolina in the early '50s was a culture shock for somebody used to Boston, so she focused on us kids."

Eager to contrive a cosier hearth for them, Trudy searched for a proper site in Chapel Hill to build a new house, and she found it on a stretch off Morgan Creek Road, opposite a stand of pines and flanked by meadows and forests. Morgan Creek and the winding trail abreast of it were named after a Baptist Welshman, Mark Morgan, who brought his wife Sarah and their six children from Pennsylvania in 1747 to live in the massive hollow of a felled sycamore tree until he constructed a log cabin; the land Morgan purchased and tilled on either side of the creek embraced most of the original boundaries of Chapel Hill. Morgan later donated 205 acres of his holdings, including the plot now occupied by Carmichael Auditorium, to form the basis for the university campus.

Fish ran in the creek, chiefly small-mouth bass, and Ike Taylor baptised a small skiff he'd begun building in Carrboro in Morgan Creek, fishing at a point 300 feet below the site of the new house.

The home itself was a cypress structure informed by the work of Frank Lloyd Wright and Walter Gropius that Trudy helped conceive, the final effort being an elegant retreat of muted Oriental design – "a Japanese inn", as she called it – with lengthy, cantilevered decks. Its sheathing, beams and joinery were culled from the living timber of the locus: cypress for the exterior, oak and cherry for the innards. Plus a great, lintelled granite fireplace.

Much concrete and steel had gone into its skeleton and under-pinnings, but those industrial materials were skilfully obscured when it was finished in 1953. The smart yet austere home appeared to alight gently, almost floating, atop the gradual slope leading to Morgan's Creek, harmonised with a glen where foxes, copperheads and other snakes lurked after dusk and the atmosphere stayed damp and brisk.

Most of the windows faced south, imbibing the begilded Carolina daylight, and additional warmth later came from the stringed instru-ments Alex (on violin) and James (on cello) brought home from Glenwood Elementary School. Alex's relocation from New England to North Carolina had been hard when the eldest boy left a good buddy named Gregory back in Weston.

James on the other hand was intrigued by the transition, with the move a blur of old images superimposed on new ones. His earliest memory had been of trying to walk on the crust of the snow outside the family's modest-sized contemporary house on Randolph Street in Weston, Massachusetts, feeling its delicacy and then sinking in up to his waist; he was two years old and dressed in a stuffy, quilted, flannel-lined snowsuit, rubber boots and mittens, and a helmet-like woollen hat that itched maddeningly.

"That's the way we were bundled up and thrown outside into the snow," he would joke long afterwards, "looking like you were packed to be shipped a long distance."

James' other hazy memories of Randolph Street were of a stream, with a bridge over it, and a Christmas tree in the living room, and being scolded for eating peanut butter out of a bird feeder . . . and then one morning he was living in North Carolina, looking at the world through three-year-old eyes, watching Alex go off to kindergarten in Carrboro, and seeing his father's laboratory during an informal Sunday tour. He peered at a freezer in the office where hamsters were hibernating, but outside the building the sweltering heat hit him like a body blow.

The bugs were different and more numerous in North Carolina, and the days seemed longer, and there were animal smells everywhere, mixed with floral scents that nearly stung your nose, and stiff gusts that seemed to come from any given angle at any time.

When James was ready to start school, the family was living on Morgan Creek, and he liked to run up and down the white concrete steps in the backyard that led into the woods. At other times, he'd empty the wicker baskets Trudy had put in each child's room, arraying his favourite possessions before a sliding door in the glass-enclosed living room. As he played with his toy cars and read his picture books about cowboys and wildlife, bugs flitted and hopped along the length of the deck.

The family brought 26 sheep onto their 25 acres of property to graze. And there was a shabby old hut in the woods that Ike took on as a project, Alex and James helping him to shingle the roof and putty in new window panes. At weekends the boys ambled inside to lounge about, stringing netted jungle hammocks Ike had bought from an Army surplus store. Then they'd row out on Morgan Creek in the homemade skiff – "a sturdy pram" or working boat, as Ike referred to it – to fish. Returning to shore, they'd gut and clean their catch, fix a blaze in the outdoor fireplace, fry their supper, and then the older boys would cuddle up inside the shack in their sleeping bags, while everyone else retired to the main house.

Years after, when the sons of a local professor sneaked into the shack and slit the sleeping bags with knives, Alex called to complain; the professor listened politely and thanked him expansively for notifying him of the incident. Within days, the Taylor boys were presented with brand-new sleeping bags by the professor while his own vandalistic boys were presented with the slit bags – which they were forced to use from then on. That's how domestic punishment was meted out in the Carolinas, with the culprits compelled to confront those they'd wronged and live with the damage done as a badge of their shame, until such time as outward signs of good works eclipsed bad ones.

This was the code Dr Taylor himself complied with when he accepted an invitation in October 1953 to lecture at a six-week post-graduate course sponsored by the NC State Medical School's Extension Division in Morganton. The prominent article in the September 5, 1953 edition of the Morganton *News Herald*, which featured a portrait photo of Ike, said it all in its banner headline: *Native Son Will Speak*

Here. His "brilliant career" and his heritage were each amply detailed in the story, which reminded readers he was the son of Alexander Taylor and his late wife, the grandson of I.M. Taylor, and a nephew of the Vernons, "in whose home he spent much of his childhood".

All of Morganton would be acutely aware of Ike's mission, and friends, acquaintances and observers would turn out in force for the Wednesday, 4 p.m. session at Grace Hospital and the 6.30 session at the Mimosa Golf Club to see Dr Taylor supplant the errors of the past with the strivings of the present. This was the sort of show-us ordeal and mutual brand of stock-taking that Ike had returned to the South to effect, and there was no backing away from it.

★   ★   ★

No less nerve-wracking, in Trudy's mind, was the racial stratification of the segregationist South. There were no black children in Alex or James' Glenwood School classes, and commercial establishments in the vicinity of Franklin Avenue in the chief shopping district of Chapel Hill had separate facilities for blacks, from entryways to water fountains. White people would pass into the dime store from the front door, and black people from the back alley.

Driving down to a South Carolina beach resort inn on a weekend jaunt with another Chapel Hill parent, Trudy was surprised that the woman brought her black cook along in her car with her kids, expecting the servant to fix home-style meals when they got to the inn. Trudy was more stunned when they stopped at a roadside restaurant for a brief lunch, and the black cook ignored the dining room, detouring to the rear entrance to take her meal with the cafe's black kitchen staff.

"I thought it so strange and sad," she recalled to friends. "She [the black cook] didn't know the people in the back; she only knew the people she was with. But it didn't seem to faze her or anybody. It was just something that was accepted. There are so many instances of things like that happening."

Once all five Taylor children were enrolled in pre-school or elementary institutions, Trudy found she needed assistance shuttling each of them to their respective classes, particularly Alex and James' early-morning string-group rehearsals at Glenwood School. She asked around (since Effie didn't have an auto licence) for a part-time driver.

Ike's family in Morganton recommended a black war veteran named John Micheur who was seeking employment, so John came down from the western part of the state and got a room in a Chapel Hill boarding house. Micheur proved to be a reliable man, piloting the Taylors' green Plymouth station wagon around the town and shepherding the children to assorted activities. Later, Trudy was driving Micheur to his rooming house when she wondered how he'd occupy his evenings as an area newcomer. "Do you know people in Chapel Hill you can socialise with?" she asked.

"No," he said, "but I wish I could go bowling."

"Why, there's a brand new bowling place out on the Durham road," she noted encouragingly, turning off in that direction.

"You don't understand, they don't want me there," he murmured.

"John, I don't believe that," Trudy demurred as she pulled into the parking lot of the bowling alley. "I'm going to go in there and find out."

Entering the building, she asked to see the manager and was directed instead to the owner.

"I know a man in my employ who's dying to bowl," she stated cheerfully. "He's just returned from the Army in Europe, and he's a very good man . . ."

"Oh good!" said the owner. "Bring him in, 'cause we need customers."

". . . and he's also coloured," she finished.

The bowling alley's owner took a couple of steps back from Trudy, eyeing her steadily, and said, "Well, we're not ready for that."

"Ready for what?" Trudy inquired, undeterred. "This employee is out in my car right now and he's really eager to bowl."

"We're not ready for a coloured man in here," the owner stated coldly. "Look, I went to the university. I've gone through it all. We're simply not ready yet."

"Let me know," Trudy rejoined, "when you *are* ready. Here's my phone number." And she left and drove off, never entering the premises again.

"I took Frankie Cousins in my head to North Carolina when I went," Trudy would muse long after the experience. "I saw the most vicious segregation in Newburyport, Massachusetts at my own high

65

school graduation, and so Frankie went with me psychologically to the South to try and make a difference."

Trudy felt the place a difference could and should most readily be made was on the Chapel Hill campus, and she knew that as the wife of a prominent faculty member her actions would carry weight. While serving on an entertainment and cultural committee at Memorial Hall, the university's main auditorium, she listened to accounts of unsold tickets for the previous seasons' concert series, and quickly understood that sales drives had targeted only white students and faculty or white citizens from town.

"Well," she interjected, "has anyone ever approached the coloured community?" Mouths dropped. "Trudy," one committee member advised, "Memorial Hall doesn't *allow* coloured people."

These racist restrictions were removed in the early 1950s, but stubborn pockets of segregation on campus endured. Blacks had been seated in separate sections during some football games in 1951; and when black students were barred from the university pool, black undergrad Floyd McKissick jumped into the water fully clothed so he could say the pool had been integrated.

Many annual parties and fetes had been moved off-campus to elude integration policies. Chancellor Robert B. House balked in 1952 at giving passbooks for athletic events to black enrollees, claiming they were "social occasions", and arguing that "no mixed social functions shall be held on the university campus." The *Daily Tar Heel*, the student newspaper, rallied to the black students' side, editorialising that "There should be no second-class citizens at the University of North Carolina . . . It is regrettable that the university has used such poor strategy in a situation which would have passed with little comment had sounder judgement been used . . . Our task is not to fight grudgingly the new social situation in which we find ourselves but to make the transition as gracefully and smoothly as possible."

In 1953, the (then all-male) medical school's dinner-dance, traditionally organised by the med students wives, was scheduled to take place at the Chapel Hill Country Club, a private stronghold off-limits to blacks. This ploy led to the black spouse of a black medical student being asked to resign from the dance committee. When she refused, she was kicked off.

After this debacle, Trudy Taylor and another faculty wife, Carter Williams, decided to step in and take an active role in trying to dislodge the lingering racist lock-out mentality encroaching on the modern era at the Medical School. Taylor and Williams assumed co-chairmanship of the council for the med students' wives; once installed in this rather public position, the two women organised luncheons at which they informed all interested parties in the university population that they were doing so to get people thinking about integration in a less resistant way.

"We worked very hard at it," Trudy remembered. "We invited outside people in to talk, and I think we really made progress. The wives of the [teaching] staff were certainly for integration; I don't know of anybody in the medical school who felt otherwise."

As for initiatives in the town at large, Trudy openly endorsed integration of lunch counters and other public places, besides voicing her support of peaceful vigils, boycotts and sit-ins. "Every chance I got I spoke up," she reflected. "People knew where I stood, and they were very tolerant of me and my points of view – remarkably so, I thought. But everything I did in Chapel Hill for integration was done in a way that would *not* threaten my children's well-being. I didn't want to lie down in front of bulldozers; I had five small children to raise."

(Half a century later, on New Year's Day 2001, Trudy Taylor phoned Frankie Cousins in Newburyport to tell him how she never forgot or forgave their high school for the racist indignity he suffered at their graduation. "I'm amazed," he confessed, "because you're the only one to mention that in all these years. But it was pretty bad that day; it was so hard for me.")

The neighbours in the Morgan Creek Road vicinity to which the Taylors felt closest were the Perlmutts, Dr Joseph and his wife Helen; they had three children, Louis, David and Martin, who were Kate's, Liv's and Hugh's ages. The Perlmutts were from Savannah, Georgia, and Dr Joe taught at the medical school. The convivial family was a welcome sight at the cocktail get-togethers that formed the social whirl of the university. But other sights, at least to Trudy's knowing eyes, were less heartening.

"At all the faculty dinners and lunches, at the official speeches on-campus and the informal receptions at the house, Ike never had an empty glass," Trudy gradually came to recognise. "It was a prop, at first, as those things are, but then it became more. Alcohol is not a character flaw but a terrible disease, and it can take a wider toll as time goes on.

"Still, Ike was someone of enormous stamina, and even with alcohol and its ravages, the work is always the last thing that goes with those who are afflicted, because it holds their lives together."

In 1953, the Taylors began to frequent Martha's Vineyard, an island off the coast of Massachusetts, on an annual basis. Usually Trudy and Ike would load their red and white Pontiac V8 station wagon with the kids every August. He was on an academic schedule with his vacation not occurring until late summer.

The New England summer ritual provided "a lifeline for my lonely mother – without a question," in her son James' later estimation. "Basically it was her homesickness that had her load us all into her car, but both parents loved it, no question."

The first Vineyard house the Taylors rented was called Summer Cottage, located on South Road in the island hamlet of Chilmark. Next, the family moved up-island to Gay Head, near its landmark lighthouse, for one summer, and then back to Chilmark, where they rented and then bought a simple frame house without electricity or hot water on Stonewall Beach between the small tidal inlets of Stonewall Pond and Quitsa Pond.

But by the start of 1955 there was no fit compensation for Ike Taylor's absences, which had further intensified when he was called to fulfil the military service obligations he'd deferred for medical school. Ike was offered and, feeling he had no way out, accepted an assignment at Bethesda Naval Hospital in Maryland, the posting permitting him to return to Chapel Hill at weekends in the winter and spring of '55. When possible, he'd catch the train from Union Station in Washington, DC at 5 p.m. on a Friday, getting into the depot in Raleigh at 10.15 p.m.

Ike often wrote home during the week to say that his time away from the family in Bethesda "depressed" him, noting in one letter to Trudy, "It's very touching to me that the children really like to have me at home, particularly Hughie and Liv, and I think the older ones really enjoy our Sunday morning walks [along Morgan Creek]."

But then Ike dropped a bombshell, revealing that he had decided to volunteer for Phase I of the much publicised and potentially perilous

Operation Deepfreeze, and was lobbying to join Rear Admiral Richard E. Byrd and 1,800 Seabees and Navy specialists on a fleet of seven ships to be sent to the bottom of the world in October of '55.

The aim of the Operation Deepfreeze convoy (and a small support squadron of aircraft) – collectively to be known as Task Force 43 – was to spend two years and 10 months organising/establishing seven US bases and satellite stations in Antarctica to be occupied by military and civilian scientists between January and July 1957 for the experiments of the 1957–58 International Geophysical Year. The main US bases would be at Kainan Bay and McMurdo Sound, at the edge of the Ross Ice Shelf, and they would form part of a network being jointly created throughout the South Pole by expeditionary forces from Japan, France, New Zealand, Norway, the USSR, the United Kingdom, Australia, Chile, Argentina, and the Union of South Africa.

As assistant professor of medicine at Chapel Hill, Ike had for several years been making a study of frostbite, his research concerning the influence of low temperatures on living tissue. It was this sort of expertise that made him a prime candidate for the post of chief medical officer at the remote McMurdo Sound station, whose encampment on the glacial "ice piedmont" (as it was termed) would hug the foothills of Mt Erebus, the South Pole's only active volcano. Compared with completing his remaining tour of duty in Bethesda as a lieutenant commander in the US Naval Reserve Medical Corps, the exotic opportunity of senior-staff status in an historic military venture seemed like a glorious godsend.

But it came as a rude shock to Trudy, who felt her gypsy husband might be slipping away from her and the family they'd made for good. Since as far back as her pregnancy with Alex, she had feared the normalcy and mundane pace of a conventional home life would be incompatible with Ike's ingrained restlessness. He obviously loved the kids, but he didn't delight in their daily development as Trudy did.

The children's burgeoning interest in music, the outdoors, and family travel, were Trudy's passions – and Ike encouraged them, much as he'd encouraged Trudy to stand at a piano and sing whenever they visited each other's relatives when they were still courting – but Ike's own zeal was for a strict level of self-immersion.

Trudy knew within bounds how to face the world on Ike's terms *and* her own, functioning as the perfect faculty wife while following through as the fully participatory parent. She got more engrossed in raising a family. And each successive child seemed to push Ike further into the middle distance of his own private mission, where he admired the world his wife had made for their offspring but felt little instinctual attachment to it.

The die was cast in a letter to Trudy that Ike penned from the US Naval Hospital on April 4, 1955 – eleven weeks since he'd begun his actual duty in Bethesda – in which he revealed:

> It appears that I shall make the Antarctica trip. I'll know definitely by the end of the week. It's tremendously exciting for me, of course. I really feel it is a momentous opportunity which I cannot refuse.
>
> I'll be away for a long time but it will be worth it, and I'll come home [from Bethesda] to go away from home again. I feel I have to do it, or I'd regret the lost chance the rest of my life. Can you understand?

Trudy couldn't, but she initially tried to conceal it behind a brave show of enthusiasm when Ike came home that weekend. But his stay seemed oddly brief, and Sunday afternoon found him hastily putting his uniform back on again to depart. Writing again as he rode the train back to Washington, Ike tried to reassure them both:

> The fact that over three months – 13 weeks yesterday – has already passed makes me feel that I can stand anything for a limited time . . . If I'm away for a long time I feel like the children will remember me and think about me and be glad to see me when I get back and perhaps be proud of me when I come home.

Another ten days later, Ike wrote Trudy a lengthy letter from Bethesda, waiting until the last three paragraphs of his rambling epistle to disclose its conciliatory point:

> I heard today that I am going to be assigned as staff medical officer to the polar expedition, which will probably mean six months out of the country instead of one year. Won't that be nice?

But the truth of the matter, as became evident in the ensuing weeks and months, was that Ike would be required to serve in the Antarctic expedition for a minimum of fourteen months, with the possibility of more.

The summer of '55 proved a particularly tense and unsettled one, Trudy taking the kids to the Vineyard while Ike's time, except for a few brief visits to the island, was divided between Bethesda and side trips to Boston and to Davisville, Rhode Island, where medical supplies and equipment for Antarctica were being assembled and packed at the Atlantic Fleet Construction Battalion Center. Final preparations neared for his departure to Antarctica on Sunday, October 30, 1955, when he'd sail on the USS *Edisto* (named for an island off South Carolina) from the Boston Navy Yard.

On September 28, Ike wrote to his wife one of the most heart-wrenching letters of their marriage, in which he pointedly reminded her that after his upcoming official leave he would not see his family again until, at the soonest, the spring of 1957. Then he plunged into a well-meaning but brittle summary of all they'd grappled with since their wedding day:

> When you asked me tonight on the phone if I'd be happier if you had insisted that I not go on the trip, I said "certainly not" and I meant it. I really want to have this trip. It's the sort of thing I've always wanted to do, and never had the chance to do.
>
> The only limitation [*sic*] I have about it are these: 1) Do I have the strength of character and purpose to withstand the rigors of the trip with happiness & success. (Answer: I think I do.)
>
> 2) Am I qualified professionally to do the job required. (Answer: I think so.)
>
> 3) Will my darling wife and precious children be safe and well and happy while I'm away? (Answer: They will miss me because they love me, but they will be proud of me and what I'm doing, and my inexpressibly and infinitely competent and absolutely beloved wife will hold all secure while I'm away.)
>
> My dearest, the thoughts of our approaching separation fill me with a tenderness of feeling for you beyond expressing. It has been matched before once that I can remember – when Alex was born.

You came back to your room in the hospital still a little under the effects of the medicine you'd been given and you said I could go away from you at last if I wanted to. And I know then, and I think I told you, that I would love you forever and stay with you forever, and need and want you forever, and never forsake you . . .

Do you remember when we were first married – one time in Newburyport – I suppose you thought I'd leave you soon – you said to me you'd plant two trees together to stand for us for ever in your thoughts? I believe I've reflected on that at least once every day since. Our children are the trees, you know, each one a pair – half you, half me – to stand as symbols of our love.

My darling, love me still as you have loved me before and I'll come back to you safe and happy and full of love to start our life together again.

The unintended message inherent in the letter was that the expedition to the South Pole represented an ending for Ike of the present stage of his marriage, a threshold that would require a new beginning to revive. At 3 p.m. on October 30, he was gone, the *Edisto* slipping out of Boston Harbour en route to New Zealand via the Panama Canal, and then on to Antarctica.

On that same day, Trudy left the Chapel Hill dream house on Morgan Creek, whose much-delayed finishing touches had just been completed, and she went to the local 5 & 10-cent store to buy her children Halloween costumes. Based on her purchases, Alex would be a black cat, James a clown, Kate a leopard, Liv a skeleton.

"Turn out the lights!" Liv yelled that night after he'd tried on his costume, "skeletons have to have dark!" And darkness was what Liv, and the rest of his family, got.

"I think it was an escape from the harness of his shamed existence in Carolina," James would one day conclude of his father's fateful decision to leave his family behind for two years. "Ships and planes can't reach the Antarctic most of the year, and there were no phones, so we could only communicate by a periodic mail packet.

"At one point in 1956," James added, "my mom took a photo of us kids on the porch of our house, saluting dad, just so he knew what we all looked like. It was tough for us, who missed him a lot, and very rough on my mom that he had even decided to do this. And for him, there was nothing to do up there but work, avoid fatal frostbite, and drink."

7

Daddy's All Gone

Cape Evans, Antarctica

Dear Alex and James:

Can you imagine what I'm doing right now? You would love it if you were here. I'm in my tent at Cape Evans, waiting for my breakfast to cook. This place is where Captain Scott lived before he started to the South Pole – his house is near my tent. We came here a week ago to get ready to build our winter camp. Seven of us came in two tents, four in one and three in the other – mine. We are camped on a small beach of black gravel and sand formed from the lava of the volcano, Mt. Erebus . . .

This morning at eight my alarm clock went off and I woke up. The tent was dark and cold but I'm used to that now. I unzipped my sleeping bag, reached for my hat and gloves on the ground beside me, and put them on. Then I pulled on my wool shirt which was also nearby. Then I lay down in the sleeping bag again to let the shirt warm up . . . I must wake the radio operator so he can report to the ships as we do twice a day that we are all right . . .

As always, Antarctica had room and forbearance for everything – except human life, which it fitfully accommodated only by ignoring most of its needs and frailties. The crude, shack-like quarters built in

1911 by British Captain Robert Falcon Scott that Ike Taylor and his Navy compatriots camped beside were Scott's final shelter before he set out southward in November of that year, never to return. When Scott arrived at the South Pole he discovered he'd been beaten in his race to be the first man there by Norwegian Roald Amundsen; to add dire calamity to disappointment, Scott and four companions perished in March 1912 while trying to return to their base camp.

Little had changed at Cape Evans in the forty-odd years since, including the perfectly preserved foodstuffs (English cocoa, curried rabbit) left by Scott and by Sir Ernest Shackleton's 1915–16 party – which the Deepfreeze workcrews sampled before sealing the cabin as a memorial to Scott and Shackleton. Ike also wrote to his family that "I have been lucky enough to find some candles left here by Captain Scott" and he often lit and propped them in tin cans as reading light after shutting his opaque tent's flaps against the Polar summer's midnight sun. It was these kinds of ironic compromises and fragile reinforcements of prior modes of existence that made the Pole so ineffably desolate.

As a consequence, those who went to the South Pole to forget something immediately reversed gears, straining to recall anything that reassured them that memory and the human scale it honours still mattered. And if someone stayed in Antarctica from 1955 to 1957 to escape a rut or a bad habit, he found himself burrowing into that rut or clinging to that habit, because it seemed an entitlement of things past, a vestige of the relative benevolence and indulgence of the civilised world so rashly left behind.

Although one was cramped by the conditions of mortality at the Pole, one was equally unencumbered by any pressures beyond duty and survival. While a very few men cracked under the strain of the isolation, most who went to the Pole confessed a curious joy there, because all the ways and means by which most adult human beings are measured or judged were missing. Thus the freedom to be insignificant was unsurpassed.

Under the frigid polar plateau of Greater Antarctica were mountains as lofty as the Appalachians, and this gigantic sweep of depthless terrain – hosting 95 m.p.h. gales of routine 50°-below-zero briskness – existed primarily in a realm of the unequivocal: either piercing daylight for a round-the-clock span of "summer" or perfect darkness for month after immobile "winter" month. The continent contained 90 per cent of the planet's ice and 10 per cent of its landmass, and it experienced no rain and scant snow, enduring mainly as an ultra-cold desert of inert hydrosphere.

But in Lesser Antarctica, the south-western underside of the South Pole that was separated from the far larger portion by the steep, semi-circular vertebrae of the Transantarctic Mountains, there was substantial regular snowfall, and variable winds ranged from a low 10 m.p.h. to a more customary 25–35 m.p.h. Flesh exposed here to high gusts would freeze in mere seconds, the grip of its tissue-killing frostbite often lethal.

It was in these precincts, at the desolate edge of the Ross Ice Shelf – a buoyant ledge of glaze the size of France that hunkered 125 feet above the water line and 750 feet below – that the Deepfreeze military organisation helmed by the US Navy re-established its initial bivouacs inside McMurdo Sound. Ike moved between the two encampments: one was at the Cape Evans camp erected on the permafrost and the other at the Hut Point Base at the tip of Ross Island – where, 14 miles away, stood the 12,444-foot Mount Erebus, plumes of steamy smoke oozing from its craggy top. Even for its size, the restful volcano was a feeble sentinel in the face of the chalky haze that frequently obscured the horizon around McMurdo to create the formless "Big White" that could warp the mind with its seamless sense of a wild void. As it was, a dense overcast blocked the sun 60–65 per cent of the time.

The best time to venture into this coldscape of deadly extremities was between mid-October and late February, when an unceasing sun beamed down and the mean temperature was 23° Fahrenheit (or minus 5 Celsius).

The USS *Edisto*, Ike's assigned ship, was an icebreaker of the Wind class, and its voyage from the East Coast via the Panama Canal Zone to the lower Pacific and Antarctica took over a month. By December 10, the *Edisto* had departed New Zealand, its last link with civilisation, and was scheduled to cross 2,230 miles of ocean and pack ice to reach McMurdo Sound a week before Christmas of '55.

On December 16, the *Edisto* penetrated the Ross ice and was heading into McMurdo Sound to a point where the crew would prepare an ice runway for the squadron. At 4 p.m. on December 19, the *Edisto* radioed Admiral Byrd and Rear Admiral George J. Dufek on the icebreaker USS *Glacier* that the airfield was ready to receive aircraft, which began landing the next day.

Admiral Dufek's ties to the exploration of Antarctica dated back to November 22, 1939, when he sailed out of Boston on the *Bear*, a former seal-fishing boat originally built of Scottish oak in 1873–74 in the Dundee shipyard of Alexander Stephen & Sons and then purchased by Admiral Byrd in 1932 to be refitted as a barkentine (boosted with a 600 h.p. diesel auxiliary engine) for Byrd's earlier polar journeys.

Thus, Dufek was familiar with the South Pole when the Navy Department made him commander in August 1954 of the most ambitious polar project in US history, and he was ordered to assemble a crack team from the cream of its volunteers, which included the only doctor who would serve at McMurdo base during 1955–57 operations, Lieutenant I.M. Taylor II.

On the evening of December 20, Ike Taylor ate a midnight steak dinner aboard the *Edisto* with the recently arrived fliers and the rest of the crew, and then got a restful night's sleep aboard ship – his last for some time.

The following morning Ike and the rest of the team he was detailed to care for as base physician disembarked from the *Edisto*. The 29 officers and men from the US Naval Mobile Construction Battalion and the senior staff of the overall Task Force that first hit the ice to begin operations had to build their base as soon as possible in order to facilitate the reception of more men and materials. On December 22, a 10-man tent at the Hut Point Camp on Ross Island was pitched on snow (with no deck to cover the inevitable slush) and assigned to the medical department for use as a sick bay. A diesel fuel-burning stove was provided for heat, and a gasoline lantern for light, but they were either hazardous or inadequate, since the former contributed to the snow-melt underfoot while only raising the inside temperature to an inadequate 37° Farenheit for treating patients, and the latter didn't fully illuminate the windowless tents. Three days later, sick bay was moved to another tent on a plywood deck with plastic window panels and it remained there until prefabricated buildings were ready for occupation starting January 21, 1956.

Ike and company were hastening to get settled in their primitive quarters on December 22 when one of Deepfreeze's support squadron Otters (a single-engine aircraft on fixed skis, with a flight range of 1,000 miles) was reported crashed on the bay ice. Packed with passengers and supplies bound for Hut Point, the Otter had stalled out immediately after take-off, sinking like a stone from an altitude of 75 feet. It landed tail-first on the icepack in McMurdo Sound, midway between the ice airway and Ross Island. Although its fusilage was a formless wreck, there were no fatalities.

A "weasel" snow vehicle at the crash site transmitted an SOS to Hut Point, and a Neptune (P2V) plane was sent to the ice edge to bring the seven injured Otter crewmen back to the Hut Point tent settlement. The worst hurt were an enlisted man with treatable back trauma and officer George R. Oliver, who suffered knee and ankle fractures. Ike could only give first aid, since most of his medical instruments weren't yet unloaded and he and his team had not yet completed work on the permanent, prefabricated sickbay facility for the base.

Despite the special Arctic training Ike had received at Bethesda in preparation for the trip, he remained a research physician rather than a medic. And while he had to keep his letters home open-ended and circumspect for security reasons, he tried to convey the gist of his own extemporal but game outlook on his polar mission in his epistles to eight-year-old Alex:

> I am the only doctor . . . and I have to do all there is. I have been sewing up cuts and opening boils and things like that which I did not do at home, and I find that I enjoy it very much.

Meanwhile, the since-departed *Edisto*, which had exited McMurdo to rendezvous as an escort with the arriving cargo ships, was ordered to reverse course and to assist in the removal of the Otter crew for further medical treatment onboard. It was Christmas when the ship returned to the edge of the McMurdo ice port, but 50-knot winds prevented the *Edisto*'s rescue helicopter from taking off to retrieve the injured fliers at Hut Point.

Thirty-three hours later, the 'copter was able to lift off and land at Hut Point, Ike helping the injured into its loading bay, but the chopper had no sooner taken off again when it was trapped in the onset of a dreaded white-out, all signs of the ground, sky and horizon disappearing in the milky, amorphous haze.

As 'copter pilot Lt John Bacon later recalled, "I felt like a fly trapped inside a ping-pong ball." Bacon kept his nerve and his static position, however, and managed to avoid crashing himself as he held steady and inched along, waiting for the unnavigable conditions to dissipate.

On the ground, Ike worked diligently along with the Seabees during the short Antarctic summer of January–February to complete construction at the main Hut Point staging area. Speed was essential, since principal work had to be finished by the time the sun would set on April 22, its reappearance impossible before August 22. During the four-month interregnum there would be total darkness, interrupted only by starlight, with temperatures outside too extreme for much activity.

On Friday, January 6, 1956, a 30-ton D-8 tractor was hoisted from the cargo ship *Wyandot* onto the bay ice for its 50-mile drive to the base. Driver third class Richard Williams climbed into the cab and was steering the vehicle over a bridge spanning a fissure in the ice when it suddenly gave way under him. Although the doors of the cab were open, the massive tractor dropped so fast Williams was unable to jump out, and it carried him 600 feet down to the bottom of McMurdo Sound. As Ike delicately put it in his January 10 note to Alex and James:

It was planned at first to unload the ships by sled trains drawn by tractors, but a huge tractor fell through the ice to the bottom of the sea and this plan has been abandoned.

Three months later, the McMurdo base would be renamed Williams Air Operating Facility USA-1 in honour of the dead driver, but at that moment in January '56, there was nothing for Ike and the rest of the men to do but silently resume their toil. Ike's subsequent notes back to Alex and James in Chapel Hill that winter supplied regular updates:

We won't be here at Cape Evans many more days, for the site for the winter camp has been changed again to Hut Point and we are to return there as soon as helicopters can fly us back . . .

When you get this letter it will be near your birthdays and I wish I could send a present for you. I'm enclosing for each a pound in New Zealand money. If you need to buy something in the United States, Mother can have the pounds changed to our money at the bank . . . Remember, dear sons, that though I am half a world away from you I think of you and your mother and brothers & sister all the time and will be very happy when I come home. One thing that is good is that I've really learned how to camp out and when I come home we can, if you like, buy some equipment and camp out together.

Much love from your
Devoted
FATHER

The learning curve in the South Pole regarding the navy's own equipment was taking its human toll. The *Glacier* had scarcely departed McMurdo Sound, leaving behind Ike Taylor and 92 other Americans for duty during the long upcoming April–August Antarctic night, when a radio bulletin passed from the base to the ship. The message read: TRACTOR TRAIN LAYING FUEL CACHE LOST TRACTOR IN CREVASSE AT CACHE NUMBER TWO. DRIVER MAX R. KIEL KILLED. BODY NOT RECOVERED.

On March 5, 1956, Kiel had been part of a tractor train traversing a previously marked trail as it was stockpiling fuel in a remote outpost for use in future operations. The leading tractor driver noticed a crumbling of the snow – a tip-off to hidden crevasses – and explosives were used to settle the snow in suspicious areas. Afterwards, Kiel was using his own tractor to fill one known crevasse with snow in order to bridge it; while backing up, his vehicle instantly fell into another hidden fissure, plunging one hundred feet downward and killing Kiel instantly.

Rescuers descended by rope in an attempt to retrieve the body but could not extricate it from the mangled machinery. The failed effort was so frustrating the rescue workers afterwards sat slumped next to the crevasse and wept. Later, a memorial service was held and a flag planted to mark the grave site, and the airfield at the 73-man Little America operations site near Kainan Bay (the sister operation to Ike Taylor's McMurdo Sound outfit) was renamed Max Kiel Airfield.

As winter set in for the crews left in Little America and McMurdo Sound, temperatures dropped to 78° below zero and blizzards roared down upon the bases, whose buildings were connected by tunnels of chicken wire covered with burlap. Fresh air was pumped in every-where by massive ventilators, with all vents and glass windows constantly cleared of snow. Water was supplied by massive snow-melting machines; it was clear and palatable although it contained volcanic ash, and Skua gulls bathed in freshwater ponds in warmer seasons. Heat, light and communications equipment were monitored round the clock, and in case of fire, escape was through a series of rooftop hatches.

Days began with 7 a.m. reveille and ended with taps at 8 p.m. The hours in between were filled with camp maintenance and repair, and preparations for next season's assault on the South Pole plateau, an elevation of 10,000 feet, 780 miles away, where the central new South Pole Station would be constructed. Also planned was a more extensive airfield at McMurdo, where ski planes were equipped with emergency propulsion rockets to blast their runners free whenever they froze to the frigid landing surface. The material and planning necessary for these tasks was mammoth and kept all hands well occu-pied – except for the notorious "long" stretch that commenced with the two-hour rest and relaxation period following dinner and ex-tended after lights-out until one finally succumbed to sleep.

Each barracks also had a lounge for reading, as well as a library and record players equipped with earphones. But certain officers were per-mitted to bring such possessions to the Pole for use in their private quarters.

"My dearest Kate," Ike wrote to his daughter in March 1956, "I am listening to the phonograph – the one I bought just before I left home. Do you remember? The music is beautiful and makes me think of you and home. How I wish I were there. The record I am playing is a waltz – one of the kinds of music we played at home when I'd pick you up and dance all over the living room and then dance with Mother and the boys would cry 'Stop! Stop!' What happy silliness . . . Remember that I love you more than any girl in the world."

Of all possible activities, letter-writing was often considered the pre-ferred option, since it offered the illusion of immediate contact with the outside world. Meanwhile, in the surreal remoteness of Antarctica, any-thing posted from its precincts could not be "mailed" until a long-awaited ship (or, occasionally, a plane) was available to transport it.

Snapshots cleared by commanding officers were also frequently sent to loved ones and just as often found their way into local newspapers, with the *Chapel Hill News Leader*, the *Chapel Hill Weekly*, the *Charlotte News*, the *Charlotte Observer*, UNC campus outlet the *Daily Tar Heel*, and various newspapers in the Raleigh, Durham, Asheville and Morganton areas reprinting shots of Dr Taylor watching passing ice floes from the deck of the *Edisto*, or examining the throats of sailors in sick bay, or sterilising surgical instruments in his makeshift dispensary.

Ike became a celebrity around the State, with editors from the dailies and the wire services asking permission to quote from his letters and cables for pieces such as a feature that ran in the *Chapel Hill News Leader* under the headline, DR TAYLOR RELATES ADVENTURES NEAR SOUTH POLE.

Those adventures included frequent headaches, induced by the effects of long-term cold on the body, and enhanced the affliction of South Pole insomnia – a dreaded condition. Disoriented by the months-long winter night, one's mental and metabolic instincts frequently resisted normal restful reflexes. As Admiral Dufek later wrote of time in the sack in the Antarctic, "Recurring thought patterns refuse to let the mind relax, and sleep is long in coming . . . Even after a hard day of twelve hours' work, the men would go to their bunks and stare up at the ceiling . . . They wandered around – they washed their clothes, went to the galley for more talk and coffee. Then someone painted a picture of a big eye and posted it on the bulletin board of the mess hall. From then on when the men couldn't sleep they said it was the 'big eye'."

For Ike Taylor, the restless post-taps onset of the "big eye" was fuelled by the relative inactivity during his average day. Working with two male "corpsman" nurses, he oversaw a base medical department equipped with hospital-level facilities and a substantial medical library.

Neither rust nor dust exist in the Antarctic, and because it's too frigid for germs, colds and respiratory ailments are few. In fact, barring injuries in the line of duty, troops seldom got ill. The one Navy man who did developed "a frank psychosis", according to Ike's official medical report, "and for most of his stay in the Antarctic was unable to work." Otherwise, "most individuals suffered mild depressions with homesickness and feelings of frustration: . . . Absence of mail was keenly felt."

Due to thorough briefings, no cases of serious frostbite occurred, although Ike had to treat a mild condition on the hand of a man who'd immersed it in cold gasoline. Ike and his colleagues performed a few appendectomies, pulled a few teeth, set some broken bones, healed a fractured skull and sewed up a few bad cuts – and as Ike wrote to James in September '56, one steel worker had a spark fly down his ear while working with a welding torch, painfully burning his ear drum. Such treatment was complicated when a shipment of X-ray tubes proved to be nothing but empty cartons, so the winter of '56 passed without the benefit of X-ray diagnosis.

But too often Ike's sick bay was dull, or entirely devoid of patients.

Naval regulations prohibited the consumption of alcohol aboard ship at any time at sea or in port, and spirits could only be administered by a medical officer to a man recovering from exposure. But drinking was permitted ashore at Antarctica, albeit under the general supervision of the commanding officer. In traditional practice that supervision was nominal, with only clear insubordination-level over-indulgence bringing reprimands or appropriate punishment.

As explained in Ike's own official medical report of the two phases of Operation Deepfreeze, "Beer was sold through the Ship's Store in a ration of one case (24 cans) per man every two weeks. On Saturday evenings, a party for all hands was held in the mess hall at which spirits from the medical supplies were distributed to all who desired them."

Since Ike was himself formally ranked as Base Medical Officer, Lieutenant Commander, and "you automatically got a certain amount of rank in the service if you were a doctor", as son James later put it, his fellow officers and crew were very deferential towards him and regularly allotted him the privacy of mind and person he usually appeared to prefer.

Radioman First Class Thomas Montgomery of Vineyard Haven, Massachusetts gave an account to *Vineyard Gazette* reporter Colbert Smith in the spring of '57 regarding Antarctic basemate Dr Isaac Taylor. Described in the article as "a Vineyard visitor in recent years, who was the chief physician on Operation Deepfreeze", Ike's exploits and those of other South Pole colleagues of Montgomery's were illustrated with a photo of Ike hopping up to croon to the accompaniment of an accordion, its caption reading, "Dr. Isaac Taylor bursts into song, demonstrating yet another talent for which he became famous during the operation." The article went on to detail other activities at McMurdo for which Dr Taylor was a central figure:

> He was one of the main proponents of the regular Saturday night shindig. He styled himself, to the delight of the men, as 'the president of the bald-headed contingent at McMurdo'. And it was he, at a time when refreshments were low, who concocted a delightful punch, consisting of medical alcohol and various fruit juices, having obtained permission from the government beforehand to dispense the solution for what, if you stretched the point a bit, could be called medicinal purposes, since it instigated and maintained a feeling of general well being. Mr. Montgomery said that the doctor carefully rationed out his punch to the men, seeing to it that they did not get too much to be harmed."

In his polar naval medical report, Ike stated that "At NAF McMurdo, medical department liquor was dispensed periodically – usually at Saturday night parties – to all who wanted it, at the direction of the Officer-in-Charge. Experience showed that serious abuse of liquor so provided did not occur." However, Ike added that "Control of the distribution of liquor is properly a function of the command rather than of the medical officer." He also wrote in his report that "the provision of alcoholic beverages free of charge by the command seems fundamentally unsound in that responsibility for its use is removed almost entirely from the individual. In a sense, such dispensation may be considered to imply encouragement by the command and the medical officer of imbibing. On the other hand, liquor dispensed through properly organised messes and procured and paid for by the individual user is taken much more directly upon individual responsibility, and, though with the command's consent, certainly without a hint of encouragement. It is recommended, therefore, that spiritous beverages be made available to personnel in isolated bases by purchase through properly authorised messes and that the medical supplies of spirits not be used for social and recreational purposes, but rather reserved for medical prescription."

In retrospect, Ike was deeply uncomfortable being in the ironic position of regulating the alcoholic intake of his fellow recruits, regardless of their rank or personal inclinations. As "an alcoholic but in a very controlled way" in son James' words, the physically imposing and extremely fit Ike was nonetheless quite able while in his thirties to drink according to the informal rules of naval camaraderie and still maintain a high level of professional performance, even excelling at all his duties.

Indeed, he received a special commendation for "endless hours" of caring for survivors after a Neptune P2V plane crashed at McMurdo in October 1956 as weather conditions deteriorated, killing the pilot and two crew members and leaving five other crew seriously injured. Several days later, one critically injured officer died. The other four were airlifted on stretchers to New Zealand, where they recovered.

Climatic and psychic gloom immediately descended on McMurdo after the P2V crash, with a funereal snow squall enveloping the base and prompting an urgent radio dispatch to the outside world: VISIBIL-ITY ZERO. TOTAL WHITEOUT BLIZZARD COVERING RUNWAY AND WORKING AREA. DO NOT SEND ANY PLANES UNTIL FURTHER WORD.

Two days later, the weather cleared, and by the end of October a giant Globemaster transport plane made the first airdrop in history at the South Pole. Morale at the base saw a sharp upturn, but it had no parallel in North Carolina, where word from home had a raw urgency to it, Ike's children growing unsubtly alarmed by the length of his time away.

On Tuesday, November 6, 1956, James, now 8, wrote to his faraway father:

> Dear Daddy: I hope you are well. I wish you wear [*sic*] at home. It wold [*sic*] be so good to have you back. I am in school and it is so good too [*sic*] sit down here and write you a letter. We miss you vere [*sic*] much and the children in my room do too. A boy in my room named Elmer is writeing [*sic*] you a letter to [*sic*].
>
> Wih [*sic*] love, James.

In December 1956, as summer again seeped into the Antarctic, the five miles of ice between the McMurdo base and the returning supply ships turned into a swirling swamp of slush under the metal treads of transport tractors and smaller weasel vehicles. One weasel with five men aboard suddenly vanished below the marked ice trail a scientist had recently referred to as "Russian roulette". Four of the men managed to push through the vehicle's narrow escape hatches and swim to the surface of the freezing sea, but one Ollie Bartley from Kentucky could not get free, and divers in insulated suits found his body hours later.

Operation Deepfreeze and the International Geophysical Year would go on to become huge scientific, diplomatic and military-logistical successes, but Ike was disappointed when he learned he himself would not accompany any of the teams of men sent to the South Pole proper in the central objective of the expedition. The news from home accentuated his acute sense of time and events passing him by.

Letters, poems, notes describing trips to Rings Island in Newburyport, and watercolour scenes by Trudy of Quitsa Pond in the Chilmark section of Martha's Vineyard were always dependable cargo in the sporadic mail planes, each artefact illuminating another vacation he'd missed or the transitional achievements the children were experiencing without him. Kate, who had just begun kindergarten when Ike left Chapel Hill, was now finishing second grade, and Livingston had evolved from a playful toddler into a literate personality. "I can hardly believe that you can write," Ike wrote back to Livingston on January 4, 1957 after getting mail from the boy.

As the final months of his two-year stint in Antarctica inched by, Ike's mood darkened, as indicated in his missives home, with passages like "We're in a lonely place here" set down amid many crossed-out lines. His obligated span of Navy duty formally expired on January 16, yet he agreed to an extension of some two months, which would cover a concluding 10 days of mop-up activities on the base plus the time his return voyage on the USS *Curtiss* would require.

Trudy was aware of her husband's anxieties, and attempted to respond to them in a tenderly candid note dated January 21, 1957, which began, "Dear Heart":

> In a few days you'll be on the Curtiss (I hope) and ready to start another phase of your huge journey. Bon voyage. Imagine leaving such a year behind. How will it be in retrospect, I wonder. All along I've been thinking of how nice it would be to meet you somewhere but my mental pictures were Boston or somewhere other than Raleigh-Durham Airport. We'll take a trip after we

collect you, and be off by ourselves somewhere – where I can LOOK at you (by myself) again . . ."

As the note continued, Trudy's own anxieties rose to the surface regarding the children ("They all need a steady kind of love and attention") as well as her, and she elected to share the depths of her trepidation with her spouse:

> Everyone seems to have an adjustment to make in being out of the service, I hear. Will you, I wonder. I'm more interested in whether we can all appreciate each other – I want you to be happy with me and us, and I want us to face situations that may be unpleasant to each other and do things about them instead of steaming, stewing and brewing. I said once that "life is short" and you thought me silly but it really CAN be short. And it can be lovely . . . And I want you to love me AND like me."

As his departure for the US approached, Ike himself seemed to fear the possible nature of the reception he might find in Chapel Hill. In his final note to four-year-old Hugh Taylor before shipping out of McMurdo on Wednesday, January 28, Ike framed his affection with a sense of apprehension that bordered on defeat:

> I'm glad you dreamed about my ship coming up Morgan's Creek. That's not really the way I'm coming home though. I'm coming in a ship much longer than your house. It can sail only in oceans. So when it gets to the edge of the land – in California – I'll get off and come to North Carolina by airplane or by train. You can come to meet me at the station in Durham or at Raleigh-Durham Airport. Mother will tell you when it is time to get in the car to come meet me.
>
> I hope all of you will come. But of course you don't have to if you don't want to.
>> Your loving
>> FATHER

8

Isn't It Nice To Be Home Again

The prevailing wind over North Carolina emanates from the southwest, its speed somnolent after sundown, but it starts to pick up around sunrise, reaching its maximum strength around mid-afternoon. During the winter, low-pressure storms move farther south, but by March and April, the northerly path of the sun heats the territory above Virginia, and so cold air masses from Canada seldom migrate as far as the Carolinas. Spring weather in the Raleigh-Durham portion of the upper Piedmont is thus an uncertain sequence of warm periods and sudden cool spells. Such were the forces in play climatically and emotionally as Ike Taylor headed home to his family in Chapel Hill.

Tucked in a letter he received from Trudy in February 1957 while aboard the homeward bound USS *Curtiss* out of New Zealand, Ike found a lock of her hair enclosed, its strands of silver mingling with the honey brown of her days at Katherine Child's Graduate House. The snip of hair was accompanied by a page of flowing script in which she recalled an amorous night they had once spent as newlyweds in the sleeping car of a train. Ike wrote back in kind, confessing to his care-worn wife, "Your inflammatory recollections of us in a Pullman berth got an immediate rise out of me. I may bust the buttons of my trousers this minute."

The exchange was a mutual search through former times for the residue of a romantic spark that could see them through the next few anxious weeks of their clouded future. Trudy was emphasising to herself as much as Ike that, at 35, she was starting to age in fact as well as spirit, the tender gesture of her lock of hair tinged with anger for lost time that couldn't be reclaimed. Ike was insisting for them both, in his earnest fashion, that his years away had changed nothing. But the need for both parties to express such sentiments accentuated the distance they represented.

Here was loneliness at its most enervating, when the simultaneous pangs of loving and loss were two aspects of a living thing that had begun to expire. Down the line, some 14 years later, their son James would sing in 'Long Ago And Far Away' about just such a situation, in which "a young man sits" and "plays his waiting game" amid "slowly passing" ships, the lyric acknowledging that things are "not the same" as former lovers find themselves stuck between what "might have been" and what "has come to pass".

The singer bore witness in the composition to a strain of disappointment fettering generations of the seafaring Taylor family. Given his own nebulous perspective, the central phrase James placed in the chorus to exemplify dismay with such setbacks was surprisingly apt: "Where do those golden rainbows end?"

In a previous century an Isaac Taylor had forfeited his beloved *Rainbow* sloop when a merchant's career venture turned into a confounding misadventure. Now his 20th century namesake had wagered all he held dear on an equally exotic risk, and was slowly discovering the outcome hadn't been worth the hazards it entailed. Contemplating the latter-day Ike, the son who watched all this happen to his parent would not soon forget either the folly of such a gamble or its sad aftermath. In fact, it cast a pall over most every path James Taylor ever trod, and helped pattern the needful songwriting by which he'd earn his keep.

" 'Long Ago and Far Away' is a simple song," James would confide, "about how things don't turn out the way you planned for them to. The most coherent part of that song is probably the second verse, with the line, 'Love is just a word I've heard when things are being said.' It's a musing on the nature of expectations, and how they don't last."

Ike's return voyage from Antarctica to the United States deposited him in San Diego in March of '57, and he made the last leg of his journey by rail, his train met only by Trudy as it pulled into the Durham depot. She knew the moment she saw him that he had not overcome his drinking habit, the first signs being his puffy, markedly weary features and flushed complexion.

The rest of Ike's homecoming rite was borne on jagged waves of energy, the core sense of relief and contentment Ike might have exuded at finally returning outweighed by an odd, overly effusive comportment.

"He was full of himself," Trudy would admit afterwards, "in an enormously agitated, almost swashbuckling way that was very frightening."

Confronted with this relentlessly boisterous parent for the first time since 1955, four-year-old Hugh Taylor turned with alarm to his mother and exclaimed, "That wild Indian is not my father!"

All Ike's gestures and expressions seemed outsized and overplayed, as if he were still holding court among his Navy buddies in the improvised saloon of a polar No Family's Land. Once the gallant sole physician for thousands of miles of impenetrable Antarctic territory, now Ike was once again just one of many prominent, grey-suited research MDs in a well-regarded Southern medical school. He even guiltily indicated that the delicious freedom he'd tasted may have ended too soon. However, the big welcome he got at the University was public recompense. And since it stood in sharp contrast to the tense silences he found within the dogwood-shrouded house on Morgan Creek Road, Ike immediately showed a preference for the celebrityhood found on campus, which had been well-primed for his reappearance.

A May '56 presentation at the Morehead Planetarium on the UNC-Chapel Hill campus was titled "From Pole To Pole", and featured panoramic photos taken by Ike during the early stages of Operation Deepfreeze. Moreover, as was publicised at the time, "Harvey W. Daniel, one of the Planetarium narrators . . . read excerpts from a score of graphic and interesting letters Dr. Taylor has written to his wife and two sons, Alex and James." Other semi-academic overtures followed, and now that Ike himself had reappeared on campus, he was deluged with requests for Antarctica lectures. He eagerly assented, devising huge slide shows drawn from his personal collection of photos during his entire tour of duty. Once he had obliged close friends and colleagues, his seminars were expanded as events for the Faculty Club, various strata of Chapel Hill's student body and local fraternal organisations.

"At first it was quite a novelty to have him home," Trudy told friends, and she was willing to share her husband and his experiences with the outside world. "But," she admitted, "when all the slide shows and lectures went on and on, I resented it after a while."

When Ike wasn't in his research lab or teaching, he was away on school business, and when he was at home he was preparing a talk to an explorers' club or a travellers' organisation, or doing interviews with newspapers in the Carolinas and New England. He spoke across the state, from Morganton to Charlotte, and as far north as Martha's Vineyard's West Tisbury Congregational Church – any place to escape the searching looks at home.

"His re-entry after a couple of years was difficult," son James would say of his errant father. "There were some difficulties for him just living in his own skin. Then he came from a world of men in authority to a world of women in authority – because by that time it was my mother's house. On some level he never really got back into the house, or our lives, or his marriage."

The house was devised by Trudy to be low-maintenance and efficient for active children. Each of the kids' rooms was simple in design, airy and easy to tidy up, the catch-all baskets in Liv's room filled with the rocks he liked to collect. Sun poured in the glass walls and beckoned the four boys and their sister outside. As a counterpart to the boys' clubhouse, Trudy hired a carpenter and spent $200 creating a little house in the yard for Kate, with two windows, a front door she could shut for privacy, and a bed on which she could nap.

"It was my little club house in the woods: Kate's Place," Kate later enthused. "It was just 300 yards from the house; this was when I was 8 until I was 13. I had a couple of cots and would have a friend over, Maryanne Lasley. You'd hear the wind and the creaking at night, and Maryanne and I would sneak out and prowl around town and come back. It was *almost* like camping out in the woods."

Ike's pledges in his South Pole correspondence to take his offspring on camping trips when he returned were quietly forsaken. "It was not really his style," according to Trudy. "Once he was out of the Navy for good, he preferred a good hotel room and his dinner sent up from room service."

So his wife became the co-ordinator of such alfresco endeavours, arranging for Alex and James to attend Camp Sequoiah in Weaverville, NC, near Asheville from June 12 to July 17 in the summer of '57. Thereafter, in the sultry late-spring and early summer weeks before she and the kids would head up to the Vineyard, Trudy began taking the kids to a rural compound north of Morganton in Burnsville, Yancey County, which the Taylors and Vernons had jointly owned for generations.

Located just beyond the Quaker settlement of Celo in the South Toe River Valley between the Black Mountains and the Blue Ridge range, the compound had been the primary summer vacation spot for Ike as a youth. He'd spend 6–8 weeks there annually with the Vernon cousins with whom he was reared as a brother: Charles, Livingston and J. Taylor Vernon.

Known for its wild flower fields and rhododendron forests, the family encampment offered a cool respite from the oppressive Carolina dog days. Though the adjacent Toe River was too rocky for boating, it was a nice site for Ike's fishing or an icy plunge for the kids. But native folklore lent a forlorn flavour to its flow. According to legend, the river was named for Estatoe, an Indian princess who drowned herself there after her lover was murdered.

To reach the Taylor/Vernon compound, one had to ride across the open fields of a simple North Carolina farm, and then slip through a gateway of hemlock hedges. Inside were rough-hewn cabins in open ground, each panelled with wormy chestnut and warmed by fireplaces of river stone.

Low-key family reunions were a staple of the Vernon and Taylor summers during the 1940s, '50s and '60s, but the Celo area was tinged with less light-hearted memories after Ben Vernon, 15-year-old son of J. Taylor Vernon, was killed one night in 1968 in an automobile crash on a narrow pass near Mount Mitchell when returning from a party. The friend driving the car in which Ben had been riding wasn't familiar with the tortuous upland roads and misjudged a turn, hurtling into a telephone pole. Ben died instantly but the car's driver survived unscathed. J. Taylor Vernon, who also had two daughters, never got over the loss of his only boy.

"I didn't have much fun at Celo," Trudy herself confessed later, since, as with the Vineyard, Ike was often too busy and the visits were short. "It was a long way for me to drive from Chapel Hill with five kids, some still in diapers, and no washing machine. I had to lug all the food up there. Cook and wash. I didn't have the connections with the local people that Ike's family had, and I didn't have the leisure to find out about these people. Often we'd go up there and there'd be no one else there; to me the attractions were the beautiful trees and plants." On hikes, Trudy imparted her love of nature to her children, combining it with exposure to handicrafts and home-made music common to the region.

"Liv was always inventing things," Trudy recalled. "He and James would make a stringed instrument out of a gourd, or a gut-bucket bass from a broom pole and a washtub, or a flute out of garden hose, or drums out of cans."

More and more, music was becoming an integral part of the Taylors' lifestyle. "Mom and dad would pull out the old show tunes every so often, like 'Some Enchanted Evening'," says Kate. "Dad was known to put out a few BTUs," she adds impishly, using the acronym for British thermal units to describe his singing, "but mostly he played the harmonica and the wooden recorder flute. It was never an official concert when we were very young but when my parents were feeling light-hearted they'd break into song."

Impromptu family singalongs were also a way for Trudy to preserve a sense of cohesion while Ike was away, and had led, through opportunities in the local school system, to her children playing stringed instruments. James showed promise on the cello, taking lessons for four years, and he played with other guest students in the travelling North Carolina Symphony when it came to Chapel Hill.

Trudy had a cellist friend from Philadelphia named Mary Mukle who often visited Chapel Hill to play, and at one point Trudy asked Mukle to find a better cello for James in Pennsylvania. Mukle selected a darkwood cello at the well-known William Moennig & Son shop in its brownstone on Locust Street in Philadelphia, and had it shipped south.

Besides James' cello, Alex's violin, Kate's dulcimer (obtained by her mother from a friend in the Western part of the state) and the upright Knight piano on which a UNC graduate student would give Kate lessons, more rustic musical tones seeped into the Chapel Hill household by means of accordion, harmonica and banjo, the last of which was bought for Liv after it was advertised in the university newspaper's classified section.

Toni Gauer, a family friend from Switzerland, showed the children how to yodel by spinning a silver dollar in a resonant creamery bowl, its ceramic bell shaping a tone against which their wobbly warbling could be gauged.

In James' words: "We sang African songs, union songs, folk hymns and radio jingles. Leadbelly, Pete Seeger, Woody Guthrie and The Weavers were the records we most listened to. There were also various cast albums of Broadway shows around the house. I remember listening to Aaron Copland a lot, too," including Copland's 'Old American Songs' – two sets of choral music, written in 1950 and 1952 and scored for orchestra several years later, whose pieces included 'The Boatmen's Dance', 'Long Time Ago', 'Simple Gifts', 'At The River', 'The Golden Willow Tree', and the traditional children's song, 'I Bought Me A Cat'.

Since the Taylors' Morgan Creek redoubt was far out in the countryside, with even fewer young companions for the kids in the vicinity than they'd encountered while living in Carrboro, Trudy realised they needed diversions to occupy them after school, before supper, and during clean-up duties prior to homework and bedtime.

"There wasn't much on TV before '56," to James' mind, "and after that the viewing was still pretty slim, although Porter Wagoner had a programme [Wagoner appearing first on Red Foley's *Ozark Jubilee* on ABC-TV, which débuted on January 22, 1956, and later on the syndicated *The Porter Wagoner Show*, which began in 1960]."

Among the normal weekday fare available in the South were morning children's programming like CBS's *Captain Kangaroo* and its animated episodes of *Tom Terrific*. After 1954 afternoon viewing was highlighted by the televangelical tent sermons of Pentecostal faith healer Oral Roberts. Weekends after sunrise the kids could catch Jay Ward and Alexander Anderson's witty syndicated cartoon serial, *Crusader Rabbit*.

Friday nights before and after Ike's mission to the South Pole, as James recalls, the man of the house crouched before the box for *The Gillette Fight Of The Week* bouts telecast as part of NBC-TV's *Cavalcade Of Sports* programming. When a featured match failed to go the distance, Ike was just as thrilled to view the *Greatest Fights Of The Century* filler segments.

Alex was the first to discover the pleasures of rural radio, with Ernest Tubb, Loretta Lynn, and Patsy Cline sweetening the airwaves in the morning. At night, WLAC from Nashville brought black music like Slim Harpo and Howlin' Wolf, on which Alex thrived.

For James' tastes, "The radio played Hank Williams, white gospel, *The Grand Ole Opry*, and jingles for Valleydale Smoked Ham, Penrose Pickled Pork Sausage, Toddy Time Jerusalem Artichokes." Kate liked Raleigh's Top 40 radio station, WKIX-AM, but also loved R&B belter Etta James.

One evening while fixing dinner, Trudy turned to her kids as they dawdled around the stove and held up a tin of vegetables, saying, "Why don't you invent an ad jingle about this can of food?" Alex, James and Livingston took up their banjo, cello and harmonica and began to improvise some musical sloganeering as Kate and Trudy joined in.

By this casual means were conceived the "kitchen concerts", as Trudy christened them, that would be a major family outlet until the kids were old enough for secondary education at boarding schools. Sometimes Ike was present, piping in with a snatch of melody on his grammar school recorder, but mostly it was just the children and their mother. Their audience was the family dog, which Ike named Hercules, never informing his brood that the animal's heroic moniker mirrored that of a distant Scottish forebear.

Folk music was on the rise in the nation, and a few stories examining its American and British roots were materialising in the popular press. Riding the crest of the wave was the West Coast-based Kingston Trio, whose chart-topping hit in the autumn of 1958 was 'Tom Dooley'. The song had finally filtered down from the North Carolina hills in June 1938 by means of Frank Proffitt, a mountaineer from Pick Britches Valley, Tennessee, who sang it for folk-song scholar-collector Frank Warner, a graduate of Duke University in Durham.

Proffitt's grandparents had known both the murderer and his victim, and Proffitt's father Wiley had taught him to play the grisly ballad on a home-made banjo. Although it had been recorded for Victor Records in the 1920s by G.B. Grayson, a blind fiddler from Tennessee whose ancestor had arrested Tom Dula, it was the version of 'Tom Dooley' that Proffitt related to Warner that would become the most famous. Warner, later the author of the 1963 book *Folk Songs Of The Eastern Seaboard: From A Collectors' Notebook*, and a board member of the Newport Folk Festival, taught the song in the 1940s to colleague Alan Lomax, who included it in his compendium, *Folk Music U.S.A.,* published in 1947.

It was in a copy of Lomax's book that lead singer Dave Guard of The Kingston Trio found the song, its arrangement adapted from its Appalachian rudiments by Ruth Crawford Seeger. Guard had been inspired to pick the banjo in 1954 after attending a Palo Alto, California concert by Ruth's stepson Pete, and Guard learned picking techniques by reading Pete's 1948 manual, *How-To-Play The 5-String Banjo.* For Pete's part, he "fell in love" with the instrument while accompanying his musicologist father Charles on a 1935 song-gathering field trip to Asheville, North Carolina, where they attended a combination square dance and ballad festival.

America's youth culture in the late 1950s had become cross-pollinated with the rich lode of folk culture first mined in the 1920s, the former's curiosity for grassroots folkways aiding the resurgence of the latter. Yet it was the mammoth, breakthrough acceptance of The Kingston Trio's Capitol Records–issued version of a North Carolina murder ballad that awakened both the Tar Heel State and the world to the enduring significance and commercial potential of folk music forms.

Besides the publicity 'Tom Dooley'/Tom Dula earned, there was much debate in music circles regarding issues of authenticity. Who had a right to sing what songs? How should the material be recorded or performed to ensure artistic trustworthiness and credible attention to custom? Who spoke for the common people, and who courted mere popular acclaim?

Some observers felt The Kingston Trio's rendition of 'Tom Dooley' was too basic and unproduced to appeal to the mainstream, while others distrusted its college-boy brio and lack of rusticity. In the end, the Honolulu-born, Stanford-educated Guard and cohorts Bob Shane and Nick Reynolds won out. Tempering their sound in Stanford hangouts like the Cracked Pot and San Francisco clubs like the hungry i and Purple Onion, before bringing it East to the (Greenwich) Village Vanguard, The Kingston Trio performed the cautionary murder ballad as they felt it – gravely but with galvanising power – and acknowledged the studious modus by which it had found its way into their repertoire. 'Tom Dooley' sold 2.5 million singles during its primary 1958–59 chart life, and the mainstream embrace of folk music was confirmed.

Among the beneficiaries of this reawakening were folk-singer and famed south-eastern country ragtime guitarist-banjo picker Elizabeth 'Libba' Cotten, the composer of 'Freight Train', 'Shake Sugaree' and other Carolina folk-blues standards. Cotten was born in Chapel Hill circa 1895, and came to prominence with the support of the Seeger family, who hired her as a housekeeper after Cotten returned a lost Peggy Seeger to her mother Ruth while Cotten was working in a Washington, DC department store.

Libba (Peggy's pre-adolescent nickname for Cotten) was in the Seeger's employ for several years before she disclosed her gifts as a guitarist-singer, and Peggy's performer-brother Mike produced an acclaimed album of Cotten's distinctive tunes and folk interpretations in 1958 for Moses Asch and Marian Distler's Folkways Records label. Also under the encouraging spell of the Seegers was young Joan Chandos Baez, who had attended the same Pete Seeger show as Dave Guard. Similarly affected by what she heard and saw, Baez made her own stunning début in 1959 at the first Newport Folk Festival. (The headliners included Seeger, The Kingston Trio, and Sonny Terry & Brownie McGee.)

In the Taylor household, interest in music continued to escalate, with Trudy's involvement in the arts and concert committee at UNC-Chapel Hill's Memorial Hall helping to bring an intriguing array of performers into campus. These ranged from mimes, choral groups, and classical pianists, to folk music preservationist-singer Jean Ritchie, who, like many of the people Trudy booked, would stay at the Taylors' Morgan Creek house during her UNC stint.

The author of the 1955 book, *Singing Family Of The Cumberlands*, Ritchie was a native of Viper, Kentucky, who wrote of how her own knowledge of folk music had been passed down from blood relations in an unbroken line dating to the earliest wave of colonial emigration from England, Scotland, Wales and Ireland. In 1768, her great-great-great grandfather, James Ritchie, and his son, Crockett, carried such traditional songs from England as 'Lord Bateman', 'Killy Kranky', 'Old Sally Buck' and 'Nottamum [i.e. Nottingham] Town'. In 1959, Ritchie's Folkways album with Oscar Brand and David Sear, *A Folk Concert*, brought her to national prominence.

★ ★ ★

Intent on exposing the children to European as well as American culture, Trudy decided to take four of them (Alex, 11, James, 10, Kate, 9, Liv, 8) to Europe one June, sailing to Rotterdam on the *New Amsterdam*. Proceeding to Venice, they absorbed its art and architecture, along with the canal-bisecting boatmanship of the gondoliers, and James and Kate would always remember feeding the swarms of pigeons in St Mark's Square. Pressing on to Switzerland by rail, they visited Ike's distant relatives on his late mother Theodosia's side of the family, Ike rendezvousing with Trudy and the kids for the return passage on the *Ile De France*.

Periodically, Trudy would also treat one of the children to a trip to New York to see a Broadway show. James was 12 when his turn came, and Trudy got tickets for composer Frank Loesser's musical entry at the Alvin Theater for the 1959–60 Broadway season, *Greenwillow*. Based on B.J. Chute's novel and starring Anthony Perkins and Ellen McCown, the production was an evocation of bygone rural America, focusing on the reluctance of Perkins' young character to court his girlfriend (McCown) because he worried he was doomed to inherit his family's penchant for wanderlust. The musical and its show-stopping number, 'The Music Of Home', earned mixed reviews and a run of only three months, yet "it definitely had a powerful effect on me," as James told his parent.

So powerful, in fact, that when James was asked on that trip what he wished for that Christmas, he replied he wanted a guitar, so he was taken past Schirmer Music on 43rd Street to window shop. He "tingled at the sight" of the Fender electric guitars hung up inside the store, being thoroughly smitten with Elvis Presley, whose current hit during his stint in the Army was the number one smash, 'A Big Hunk O' Love', but James and his parent earmarked a nylon-string acoustic as most appropriate for the moment.

That winter, not long after James got his first guitar from Santa Claus, the mountingly mischievous Alex, now 14, decided to spray paint it blue – including its insides and the strings. "I think he was looking," commented the customarily laconic James, "for the expression on my face."

For 13-year-old James, life at home was both cozy and claustrophobic – cozy because his immediate, quietly stimulating environs were a crystalline creek, an unblemished knoll that gave way to a pine grove, a meadow grazed by two dozen pillowy sheep, and 25 acres of woods; and claustrophobic, because the sleepy beauty around him was inevitably being spoiled by the dejection at its core: his parents disintegrating relationship.

Pondering the strains of the period, James said, "For me there was an element of having a parent who was away a lot and another who was upset a lot, and that's hard for kids. There was also a lot of stress between my mother and my older brother Alex. That particular dynamic, especially when my father was away, was hard. Alex used to turn around and fight with the next [child] down the line, because he was frustrated. It's just typical sibling stuff."

There were tensions in North Carolina that transcended family ties. Back in 1954, Greensboro (48 miles north-west of Chapel Hill) was the South's first city to comply with the Supreme Court's anti-segregation decision in *Brown Vs. Board Of Education*. Greensboro now hosted the first "sit-in" of the Civil Rights movement when four young black males from North Carolina Agricultural and Technical College entered the local Woolworth's on February 1, 1960, sat at its lunch counter seeking service, and declined to leave until they got it – thereby igniting the student phase of civil rights activism.

A Bi-Racial Human Relations Committee in Chapel Hill had achieved little when black students from Lincoln High School held a sit-in on February 18, 1960 at the Colonial Drug Store on West Franklin Street. More sit-ins and picketing erupted, prompting town aldermen to request a 30-day trial integration of all restaurants and lunch counters. Twenty-seven local ministers bought a full-page ad in the *Chapel Hill Weekly* on March 24, 1960 pledging support to "peaceful picketing", and hundreds of townspeople, black and white, responded. While still careful not to put her children into physical jeopardy in the highly charged environment, Trudy pushed hard for integration of the area's public schools and businesses. By mid-April the Student Non-Violent Co-ordinating Committee had formed in Raleigh to support desegregation.

"My children and I, we discuss everything at the dinner table,' Trudy told her friends in the North. "Everyone in North Carolina is very political, and the university is state-run, so everything is political here. Every night, five minutes before the national news comes on [Senator] Jesse Helms comes on with his editorialising [on WRAL-TV, from Raleigh] about 'Communist Hill', which he calls Chapel Hill, and calls us names for our progressive Civil Rights views. It's amusing, and leaves you incredulous."

Meanwhile, Trudy discovered friends from Boston and the Vineyard were willing to march in Selma, Alabama – "It was *safe* for them to march in Selma, they said – and other parts of the South, yet not on Boston Common."

Trudy and Ike were open champions of North Carolina gubernatorial candidate Terry Sanford, whose opponent in the primary run-off was segregationist I. Beverly Lake. After Sanford's election, the Taylors were visitors to the governor's mansion in downtown Raleigh. In his inaugural address, Sanford declared that "no group of our citizens can be denied the right to participate in the opportunities of first-class citizenship."

Sanford had his work cut out for him in the Ku Klux Klan-influenced state, where there were no black members of the 600-man highway patrol, no black employees in the local federal government offices more lofty than its elevator operators, only 24 black employees in the 7,000-person state government civil service above the rank of janitor or messenger, and no blacks among the 11,000 North Carolinans on the $5 million National Guard payroll. Sanford devised a network of Good Neighbor Councils (named for former US President Franklin Delano Roosevelt's Good Neighbor Policy toward Latin America) to encourage employers to hire blacks and "set us free from the drag of poor people, poor schools, from hate, from demagoguery."

But change came slowly. The Carolina Theater was picketed in January 1961 for barring black patrons from a mostly black *Porgy And Bess*; it conceded in December of that year.

"Like my mother," Kate said, "by 9th grade my friend Maryanne Lasley and I were political activists, and would march in Civil Rights demonstrations in Chapel Hill and peace rallies in Washington. There were some scary moments in Chapel Hill, but there was that feeling you were doing something right. I was in one march in Chapel Hill, walking down Main Street with a big crowd, when somebody fired guns, maybe in the air. All I heard was the *pop! pop!* in the distance. Nobody got hurt; we just kept marching."

As their offspring grew, Ike wanted them to attend private boarding schools as he had; Trudy assented but preferred liberal co-educational schools. Alex, becoming more overt in his obstinacy to his father's designs for high achievement, was allowed to remain at Chapel Hill School (as was Hugh, when his time came), but Livingston would be sent to the Westover School in Pennsylvania, and Kate was destined – after two years at Chapel Hill High and summer school at both Ecole Arcadie in Bar Harbor, Maine and at Philips Exeter Academy – to board at the Cambridge School of Weston (Massachusetts). The sedate and deferential James, increasingly described as the "good" boy to Alex's "bad", yet still too different from his imperious father to be comprehended by him, was nonetheless adjudged the brightest academic and social hope by default, so he went on to the eminent Milton Academy.

"I was a good kid," as James interpreted his parents' viewpoint, "and Alex was a bad boy; he probably wasn't allowed to be a good boy. I was, and I was allowed to find a way to accommodate my parents and do what I thought my parents wanted me to do. But I was disillusioned with the feeling of being far from home at Milton Academy."

Named for the moneyed suburb of Boston in which its stately brick buildings had long stood, Milton was the Brahman institution where future President Franklin D. Roosevelt had delivered his renowned "Whither Bound" address to the graduating class of 1926. Sidestepping the ritual solemn tone of seasoned adult authority and dutiful admonishment, the 44-year-old FDR had instead used that May '26 occasion to relish the excitement of an as-yet undefined new century and its sweeping capacity for "sudden changes". Roosevelt noted that people of his own father's age had been "brought up in a Victorian atmosphere of gloomy religion, of copybook sentiment, of life by precept; he had lived essentially as had his fathers before him."

But now, FDR assured, "steam was replacing sails, sputtering arc-lights were appearing in the comfortable darkness of the streets, machine-made goods were forcing out the loving craftsmanship of the centuries . . . Men were speaking of new ideals." And thus, "In government, in science, in industry, in the arts, inaction and apathy are the most potent foes." Roosevelt viewed "the solidarity of the opposition to a new outlook" as a dangerous element which "welds together the satisfied and the fearful."

In May of 1961, as James faced three months of leisure on Martha's Vineyard before leaving the company of his family to confront his future at Milton Academy, 40-year-old Ike Taylor was worried about his second son's seeming satisfaction with the world as it was. Yet Ike misjudged James, who actually dreaded the world around him for what he knew it could never be: a ready source of solutions for sorrows such as those within his own family.

Like FDR at the Milton Academy commencement, James craved genuine inner and outer change. Ike was packing James off to a seat of privilege in hopes he'd be inspired by the new ideals of which Roosevelt spoke, yet Ike never guessed how James would actually embody any of them.

"The secret of life," as James would later sing, "is enjoying the passage of time" – not denying it. In order to dislodge his family from its fixed path, Ike's son would turn away from every hidebound thing his dad held dear. As a Roosevelt friend once wrote to a cousin of FDR's in reference to the well-born President's unlikely role as the architect of the New Deal, "Responsibility is a winepress that brings strange juices out of men."

9

You've Got A Friend

There is a special summertime bond between a boy and his throwing knife, as 15-year-old Danny "Kootch" Kortchmar was pleased to demonstrate for an envious new acquaintance, Jamie "Stringbean" Taylor.

The two had just met behind the up-island post office in the heavily wooded Martha's Vineyard hamlet of Chilmark, where the broody Kootch, perpetually dressed in black (his other nickname was "Happy") was perfecting the angle of release for his weighted pocket lancet. Born on April 6, 1946, the second son of machinery-parts manufacturer Emil Kortchmar and his author-wife Lucy, Kootch grew up with older brother Michael in Larchmont, New York, and summered every year in Chilmark, which his mom enjoyed for its community of vacationing intellectuals and his dad prized for its placid fishing spots.

"James was into my knife and eventually we each bought four or five knives apiece, throwing them at anything that didn't move," Kortchmar assured with a laugh. Things lightened up for both boys when James pulled out his harmonica, and Kootch proposed they hitchhike to his folks' cottage to get his acoustic guitar, on which Kootch showed James some 12-bar blues progressions in G and E.

Kootch was one of a loose aggregation of avid young musicians who frequented the coffee houses and folk parlours in Vineyard Haven and

Oak Bluffs, chief among them the Unicorn Cafe on Circuit Avenue in Oak Bluffs, a regular haunt of the Reverend Gary Davis and other blues players and an offshoot of the Unicorn in Boston where Tom Rush was a regular attraction. The other top club in Oak Bluffs was the Mooncusser, where Jim Kweskin's Jug Band was a seasonal regular and the Charles River Valley Boys often appeared. In '60 and '61 the Vineyard was part of the Cambridge-Boston folk axis, such performing couples as Debbie Green and Rolf Cahn, and Richard Farina and first wife Carolyn Hester spending the summer there to recharge.

Back on the mainland, Joan Baez, who would also make it out to the Vineyard to play, was still living at her family's house in Belmont, Massachusetts, playing on a steady basis at the Golden Vanity near Boston University and in rotation with a roster of other acts at Mount Auburn Club 47 And Gallery (later simply Club 47) in Cambridge that encompassed Eric Von Schmidt, Tom Rush, The Charles River Valley Boys and (Bill) Keith & (Jim) Rooney.

James was well aware of all these goings-on and wanted to gain musical entree as something more than a mere spectator.

"Within the first half-hour of meeting James and the rest of the Taylors, I knew they were a completely unique family," Kootch later admitted. "They had their own rapport with each other, a secret language of nods and gestures and expressions that came from living so close together and in such self-imposed isolation in the South. But James' lack of conventional social grace worked in his favour, and attracted people to him."

At Kootch's house, James and Danny began to jam on guitars and mouth organ, while listening to John Lee Hooker's 'Crawlin' Kingsnake'. They clicked as an informal musical duo and, sandwiched in between softball games, began toting their instruments to the houses of other friends – particularly girl friends. Cathy Cameron's family had a place in the fishing village of Menemsha, just over the hill from Chilmark, and there was a tent rigged up in her backyard where Jamie and Kootch would strum, sing and flirt with Cameron and her equally cute female pals.

Martha and Susan Lafferty, who resided off South Road near Lucy Vincent Beach, were two other pretty girls worth impressing, and their mother Louise also liked Jamie and Danny, frequently fixing them lunch or dinner and letting them crash in the house after parties that ran late.

Few teenage boys were as welcome in female company that summer as Jamie and Kootch, the latter a darkly handsome, kindly but self-contained boy whose acquired knowledge of Delta, Texas and Chicago blues from Howlin' Wolf and Lightnin' Hopkins to Muddy Waters guaranteed a certain cachet. His buddy Jamie was a raw-boned, yet wiry, muscled beanpole with a chiselled face canopied by his dark, wing-like eyebrows, his clear-eyed gaze blending keen intelligence and a kindly diffidence. Whenever he began to sing in his nasal, medium cool croon, it parted the clamour of the noisiest barbecue or bonfire roast like a ship's prow slicing through fog in the shoals. Everybody cocked a head (especially the females), shut their mouths, and listened willingly.

It was a pleasure for Kootch to accompany James on guitar, knowing his own arpeggios and articulate licks would always fall in synch with his chum's impeccable sense of vocal metre: "From the first time we sang together on old blues stuff, and I heard his natural sense of phrasing, every syllable beautifully in time, I knew James had that *thing*. It was really a gift he had, and he was smart enough to know *what* to sing and when."

July and August of '61 were a magic time on the Vineyard, during which every local kid was humming along to the 19th century folk plaint 'Michael (Row The Boat Ashore)' as recast by a folk quintet from Connecticut's Wesleyan University called The Highwaymen. Everybody's parents were meanwhile lolling on the beach reading Harper Lee's *To Kill A Mockingbird*, which had just won the Pulitzer Prize, or passing evenings clustered on porches sipping vodka gimlets and discussing the Wimbledon women's doubles title won by Karen Hantze and Billie Jean Moffitt, or the suborbital flight of Capt. Virgil "Gus" Grissom in Project Mercury's *Liberty Bell Seven* space capsule, or Federal Communications Commission Chairman Newton Minow's recent assertion that television was "a vast wasteland".

After Labour Day, James was installed at Milton Academy, waving goodbye in corduroy slacks and a rumpled Oxford shirt, his cello beside him, as the rest of the Taylors returned to Chapel Hill. Later that autumn, Trudy went up to Milton to see James act in an eighth grade play. Afterwards, James' English teacher took Trudy aside and mentioned that James had recently murmured to him that he was thinking about leaving the school.

Trudy did not broach the topic with James, judging it was just a bout of homesickness. After she returned home James phoned and said, "My cello has been in a locker for six weeks. Could I sell it and take the money and buy a guitar?" Trudy said, "Yes, and buy a good one."

Sports were the chief social currency of the school, but routinely James shunned them, staying in his room in his free hours to master his guitar. Four years of classical cello instruction had got him "thinking in the bass clef", and his strong, thin, unusually dexterous fingers and skill at banjo brailing and thumping sister Kate's keyboards all combined to mould an uncommon approach to his instrument: "My style was a finger-picking style that was meant to be like a piano, as if my thumb were my left hand, and my first, second, and third fingers were my right hand."

The sound was so distinctive and lyrical it made him popular at school out of sheer respect for his deft air of individuality. At weekends, he often fled Milton to return to the Chilmark beachhouse his parents owned, bicycling on the empty, leaf-strewn back lanes during the autumn.

At 14, he wrote his first original song on guitar, a strangely beguiling hymn that seemed to evoke Morgan Creek, the tidal pond of Menemsha, and an age-old vision of the West Water beyond Marykirk in a single, vivid stroke:

> Roll river roll, long as you can be,
> Longest river I've done seen, rolling to the sea.
> When I was a little boy, I played along her side
> Built myself a raft of reeds, and on her I would ride.
>
> Then one day I left my home, and down the river bound,
> Sit back on my raft of reeds, I float past fields & towns.
> Now the river is my life, and it's coming to the sea
> And the ocean is the biggest thing that I will ever be.

Part sea shanty, part personal lament, the song's theme could have been the ruminations of a Taylor at any point between Montrose,

New Bern and Boston over the last three centuries. It was a song of departure but also of arrival, regretful but optimistic, grand in its purposefulness but grave in its belief that time and nature are the ultimate ignoblers.

"It never took any work for me to play the guitar from the moment I got it," James would explain. "It was just a release and an outlet, and it was a delightful thing to be able to play. And somehow I felt as though if it had taken any kind of discipline, any effort or will or strength of character for me to develop a musical style, it never would have happened. It's just that it fed itself, and had its own momentum. It was lucky for me – it actually saved my life."

What would always set James apart from most of his privileged lineage was a lascerating degree of self-knowledge, enforcing a humility that melded simple gratitude with a survival instinct. The shadow that sometimes fell across his youthful stare when he would force himself, in conversation or in song, to recount his family torments and exploits was perhaps the grim certainty that nothing guarantees anything, but people are still worth depending on.

For himself, James found almost overnight that he needed his song-writing to help make sense of his feelings, and that his knack for the craft came instinctively. "I wish I weren't so self-centred or self-referred with the stuff I write," he admitted, "but for some reason that's the window I utilise."

The most remarkable thing about the view from that window was that, somehow, over the next forty years, in an equally unconscious, subliminal fashion, James would also survey and reconsider his entire ancestral saga, to where an innocent observer rediscovering his music three hundred years from now might presume that this was his primary intent. And yet, eerily enough, he had never been told most of the tales he was retelling. If James and his kin had the burdens of their bloodlines – the melancholy, the intemperance, the longing for the sea and the restlessness it certified, the humiliations of wars and the upheaval they ratified – perhaps they came with a deeper inheritance that comprised a memory bank embedded in the nucleic acid of their Scottish chromosomes.

What's certain is that everything that had happened before to the Taylors was fated to recur, entangled this time with young Jamie

Vernon Taylor's destiny, whose detours compensated for the roads not taken so long ago.

By the summer of '62, James had bought his first electric guitar, purchased with money earned washing dishes at the Home Port Restaurant overlooking Menemsha Habor. The Cambridge–Boston folk scene had widened in terms of fanbase, venues and outreach, with five coffeehouses or clubs in Boston (the Golden Vanity, the Turk's Head, The Salamander, Cafe Yana, the Ballad Room), the Unicorn and Club Mt Auburn 47 in Cambridge (where Bob Dylan had played between sets for free during '61 in order to say he'd sung at Club 47). There was an increasing spillover of talent from the mainland to the Vineyard, with Mississippi John Hurt, Ian & Sylvia, and Sonny Terry coming by ferry. Keith & Rooney also spent the summer on the Vineyard.

Back at the University of Massachusetts in Amherst, where Bill Keith was still a student, he met Manny Greenhill, Baez's manager, who helped Keith create the Connecticut Valley Folklore Festival (partially inspired by the first Indian Neck Folk Festival organised by Yale students in May 1961) in order to book an Odetta concert at U. Mass. The event attracted other U. Mass talent, notably a transplanted Canadian of Native American Cree extraction, Beverly "Buffy" Sainte-Marie, and a folkie (and animal husbandry major) from Springfield, Massachusetts, christened Henry Fredricks but called Taj Mahal, whose first and only guitar teacher was a man from Durham, North Carolina named Lynwood Perry. Afterwards, Taj began playing the Club 47 on Hootenanny night.

Baez moved to California in the autumn of '61, but the following summer James and Kootch often played her *Joan Baez, Vol. 2* album, particularly the track 'The Banks Of The Ohio'. Another beloved record of their's in summer '62 was Ray Charles' 1961 Atlantic LP, *Do The Twist!*, "a marketing-theme album", in Kootch's words, "of hits you could dance to", like 'I Gotta Woman (Part One)', 'I'm Movin' On', 'Heartbreaker', 'What'd I Say (Part 1)', and 'Tell The Truth'.

"James' brother Alex had initially gotten James into Ray Charles and Elvis," according to Kootch, and everybody on the Vineyard knew Alex could really sing rock and roll. He would hang around the coffee houses on Circuit Avenue and just burst into it.

"Alex had a different look from all the other Taylor kids – he was closest to Ike in his big build and broad shoulders, and he had the same dominant personality. But whereas Ike had the bulk and bearing of an ex-Navy officer, Alex was determined while still a young man to be the biggest and the baddest."

In this sense, Alex fitted in somewhat more easily in the boisterous down-island port towns of Vineyard Haven and Oak Bluffs than he did in subdued, cerebral Chapel Hill. The seminal settlers of Martha's Vineyard, the Wampanoag branch of the Algonquin tribe, saw their 100-square-mile home as "Noepe", meaning "in the midst of the sea", and they liked the fact it was an isolated spot, difficult to get to, and problematic to live on.

Normans landed on the island as early as AD 1000, and European ships brought metals to the Wampanoags early in the 14th century. After British explorer Bartholomew Gosnold claimed the grapevine-draped island for the Crown in 1602 en route to Virginia (he named the "vineyard" in honour of baby daughter Martha). Gosnold returned to Falmouth, England with talk of the island's wild charms, the romantic scuttlebutt prodding William Shakespeare to use such an outpost as the setting for his play, *The Tempest*.

Massachusetts Bay Colony merchant-missionary Thomas Mayhew bought the island from the British for £40 in the mid-1600s; he pacified the native tribes by decreeing no land of their's could be taken without their consent. (The Wampanoag people still control parts of Gay Head today, now renamed Aquinnah.) Farming, merchant sailing and whaling became the mainstays of the economy, the island's dairy products prized as exports, while the perilous whaling trade reached its commercial apex between 1820 and 1860, when Edgartown was home to over 110 captains of whaling vessels and petroleum had not yet eclipsed whale oil as lamp fuel. The Civil War saw Confederates sinking numerous New Bedford and Nantucket whalers, and heavy freezes in 1871 crushed many vessels stranded in the icelock.

By 1860 the retired whaling captains who'd built Edgartown's fine homes had shifted into hotel and real estate development, while the Methodists had a 25-year-old camp-meeting community in Oak Bluffs. Such spirituality and gentrification found an uneasy stand-off with the swabbies, shipwrights and rough waterfront element that would continue to animate the recesses of after-hours Vineyard Haven and Oak Bluffs. Alex, with his brusque manner and bristly blond adolescent chin whiskers, often seemed to blend in with the townies guarding their dockside turf against the vacationers.

"Alex liked to exert himself," Kootch recalled, "and he normally meant no harm. But as he got older he'd sometimes be under the influence of one thing or other and it affected his judgement; he would pick fights with other guys, although what he meant to do was just joke around and project what was a big personality. His potent style would work against him, but if you knew him and he knew you, those issues never came up, and he could be protective, generous, a real big brother and very funny and warm."

Alex's short fuse and fitful impulses seemed an outgrowth of his father's more latent tensions, which in Ike's case manifested themselves in his itch to impart his prideful knowledge of various pursuits to his sons, notably sailing. Ike learned to sail as a boy while visiting his Aunt Winkle, the sister of his mother Theodosia, at her home in Owl's Head, Maine. When James showed an interest in the hobby and its skills at age six, Ike responded by taking him out in a 15-foot white skiff, plywood with a canvas deck, which he rented on the Vineyard for that purpose in the summer of '54.

In the free time he allotted to the Vineyard after his stint in Antarctica, Ike resumed tutoring Liv, James and Kate in how to tack, using the Chilmark sail races held on Menemsha Pond every Wednesday and Saturday as a motivation.

"Some people would take it more seriously than they should," James observed of the quaint boating contests, "and my father would be one of those. He really loved that sailboat race, and somebody would get a little trophy."

The Taylors also rented a 3-horsepower motorboat each season from Earl Vanderhoop, a Menemsha neighbour descended from an old Vineyard family. At one point in the summer of '62 while Ike was on the pond with Kate and preparing to participate in the usual race, James came tooling by on his way back from Menemsha and Stonewall Pond, the Johnson outboard engine on his sluggish craft puttering spunkily. When James saw his father in the sail boat with his sister he pulled up alongside.

"Jamie!" Ike barked. "Go back and get me a pack of cigarettes and bring them back out to me *here*!!"

His son obediently spun his motorboat around, skimmed home to fetch his father a pack of Parliaments, and was about to hand them off to Ike as the race was about to get underway. James decided to toss them to his dad while motoring past. The Parliaments landed in the pond. Ike was "really pissed" at his son for his clumsiness, insisting the cigarettes immediately be retrieved. "We laid them out at the deck," as James told it, "and they dried out enough so he could have a smoke."

What made the incident memorable was that Ike's will was not to be questioned. He wanted what he wanted, from a prompt start in the weekly sailing races to dry cigarettes as he tilled his rudder, and all obstacles must be surmounted, regardless of effort or inconvenience.

By his late teens, James had his own sailing skills perfected, and thereafter for him the activity meant freedom from care rather than subservience to a curmudgeonly mentor. His ability to enjoy sailing for itself was yet another trait that set him apart from his demanding parent.

James had a similar attraction to music, which is why he and Kootch got along so well. In 1963, Danny graduated from Mamaroneck High School in Westchester County. His father Emil was at the foot of his bed at 7.30 a.m. the next morning, rousing him with the order, "Get a job!"

Danny felt he had a job already, playing music, but his dad disagreed. During their '63 respites on the Vineyard, James and Danny tried to demonstrate to their respective parents that they had more direction in life than they were being credited for by lining up gigs at the island's coffee houses. A short set by the twosome consisted of Lightnin' Hopkins' 'Custard Pie' and 'Rocky Mountain Blues', Ray Charles' 'Hallelujah I Love Her So', and Hoagy Carmichael's 'Circle Round The Sun'.

Appearing at the Unicorn Cafe, they were initially billed on a typographically challenged poster as "Jamie & Kotch". Soon accepted as promising new faces, they shared a bill with the Reverend Gary Davis, and went on to win a folk contest that was supposed to earn them $50 and a chance to play the main Unicorn coffee house in Boston. Given the shaky reputation of the Vineyard branch's manager, Kootch doubted they'd see their payment or their prize – especially after hearing that blues singer Jessie Fuller had to pull a pistol on the box office bursar in order to get paid. Kootch showed typical prescience on both scores.

That summer, Kate Taylor was a waitress at the Galley in Menemsha, where she made her public singing bow. At the Mooncusser club were the Simon Sisters (Lucy and Carly), whose début LP in '64 for Kapp Records would notch a minor hit, 'Winken, Blinken And Nod'.

A strong influence on both James and Carly was a male folkie who'd also cut 'Winken, Blinken And Nod' – David Gude. An associate of folkie Jim Kweskin (they co-compiled *Festival: The Newport Folk Festival/1965* live album for Vanguard Records), Gude was featured on Vanguard's *New Folk* sampler album of the era and was a sound engineer for the label. David's family was friends with Lee Hays and other members of The Weavers, and the Gudes were among the intelligentsia who mingled at The Tavern, a Chilmark barn that was the main site of summer square dances and folk concerts in the late '50s and early '60s before the Chilmark Community Center was built. Bill Keith and Jim Rooney performed there, as did Gude. Those who came by to kibbitz included Vineyard cultural figures like publisher George Brasiller, songwriter Edgar "Yip" Harburg, puppeteers Bill and Cora Baird, and painter Thomas Hart Benton's daughter Jessie, who married Gude.

Leaving this fertile milieu in September for his junior year at Milton, the gangling, loping Jamie – known around the hallways as "Moose" – started strongly by playing some small-scale concerts, backed up in one case by students from Milton's girls school. But Taylor couldn't get himself in synch with Milton's "high-powered" college prep programme. Petitioning his mother, James was allowed to go home to North Carolina for a breather, finishing the remaining semesters at Chapel Hill High.

Alex Taylor had formed a band in Chapel Hill that he named The Fabulous Corsairs (initially misspelled Corsayers) as a droll commentary on the bygone exploits of privateers in his father's side of the family tree. The group, with Alex on vocals, plus organist Cam Shinnon, guitarist Vic Lipscomb and a drummer, was R&B-based. James bought a Fender Duo-Sonic guitar and lent his rhythmic chords to the cause, their business card touting them as "The Sound That Abounds In Musical Style".

The Coasters' 'Searchin', Bobby "Blue" Bland's 'Stormy Monday Blues' and assorted R&B hits of the era by Sam Cooke and Ray Charles formed the essence of The Corsairs' attack, with Alex belting most of the lead vocals. They worked a circuit that included sock hops at surrounding secondary schools like Fuquay-Varina High, plus junior high sock hops and beer bashes along fraternity row in Chapel Hill. The group's standard stage costumes were turtleneck shirts and tweed sport-jackets – "an outfit that was hot as hell in North Carolina," James knew, "but we thought we looked pretty collegiate."

Alex's ambitions were wider than winning adulation from either students in the college orbit or graduates employed at the state-funded Research Triangle of scientific, health and business firms set in the Durham, Chapel Hill and Raleigh industrial park nexus. "Often on Saturdays," as Trudy remembers, "he'd say, 'Mom, drive us to Raleigh to cut a record.' How could I take it seriously?" Ushering the Corsairs into Jimmy Katz's two-track studio in Raleigh – a teeny establishment with egg cartons stapled to the walls as sound baffles – the group cut a single in '64 of Alex's 'You're Gonna Have To Change Your Ways', with a tune their guitarist wrote, 'Cha Cha Blues' on the flip side.

James felt The Corsairs were fun after the sun went down and the gigs got underway – and never more so than at frat houses, with flirtatious young co-eds showing a lot of interest and the beer kegs beckoning. But the next day's hangovers throbbed with other overlays of discomfort – notably Ike's critical morning-after estimation of Alex, who would be blue-faced and bent forward at the breakfast table beneath his dad's glowering stare. Ike knew Alex intended after his senior year to linger around the hometown hoping for a record deal – while also leading young Jamie further into music.

James, however, felt his father was programming his older brother for failure: "The main thing about kids growing up, especially at that adolescent age, is that they be given the sense that there's something that they can do well. A little success goes a long way at that age.

"Alex was just trying to cope with everyone around him telling him they were unhappy with him because he was fucking up," James reasoned. "He was trying to cope with what was not a very good situation. And he started acting out, started going bad, staying out late, running with people my parents felt he shouldn't spend time with. He got into trouble in school and just wasn't doing well; he was a black sheep, and it was hard on him."

Being home with only Alex's band as an outlet grew just as hard in its own way for James, because it heightened the sense of estrangement he felt from all his former Carolina chums, most of whom were now away at prep schools and on track for university acceptances and pre-ordained careers. He'd "lost touch with friends in Carolina", James confessed to himself with a shudder, thinking, "What the hell, finish boarding school and aim for college, because the past has nothing more to offer."

James re-entered Milton for his senior year, the academy happy to have the popular guitarist back since his scholastic performance had always been more than adequate. But James soon descended into a murky depression and was taken out of the dorms, being given a small private room in the headmaster's residence. By the eve of Thanksgiving vacation, his grades were a shambles and he was sleeping twenty hours a day.

Back in Chapel Hill for the holidays, James hobbled about under a cloud of qualms and anxieties, reluctant to announce his resolve to drop out of Milton for good. Not long before the moment came to lift his luggage to leave, he visited a Cambridge, Mass. teacher, the husband of Trudy's best friend, named Stan Sheldon. "Stan," he murmured, "if I go back to school I'm afraid I'm gonna take my own life."

Stan suggested a certain psychiatrist, and James took his advice; he broke down in the shrink's office and heard him say, "Listen, I'm gonna put you under observation for a while."

"It actually was probably typical adolescent stuff," James would say in retrospect, "but people around me put me into a mental hospital for a spell – about 9 months." That hospital was McLean, poised solemnly on manicured slopes 15 minutes west of Boston, where James officially committed himself. Coincidentally McLean was the institution where James' hero Ray Charles had once gone to detox.

Trudy was philosophical about her son's distress, explaining, "A psychiatrist told me many adolescents go through depression but some have it worse than others. So Ike and I took it very seriously. I was frightened and we kind of turned it over to McLean and they almost never talked to the parents. A doctor there said, 'You must understand that your child is not depressed because of anything you've done.' We knew some of Ike's aunts had severe depressions."

However, in James' eyes, his entry into McLean "was my exit from the family agenda, as I perceived it."

He completed his senior year at the Arlington School, McLean's own exclusive lyceum, and received a diploma. The nine numbing months until graduation consisted of daily medication, drab meals eaten with plastic forks (confiscated afterwards) and weekly consultations with therapists who interrogated him while he stared out of the 2000-pound-test security screens bolted to the windows.

Getting a summons from the Selective Service, James was escorted to the Boston's Kendall Square draft board by a McLean attendant named Carl and a burly associate, both of whom wore white suits and stern miens as they answered all questions posed to their suitably sullen, uncommunicative charge. It was a great performance by Taylor and his willing confederates, and James received the "crazy papers" he sought, certain he'd never again have to face either the Milton faculty or the Army.

Keen to avoid the 3-days-in-a-locked-ward observation period that preceded a voluntary AMA (Against Medical Advice) discharge, Taylor hid in a Dodge van driven by a friendly accomplice named Dave Barry and fled with his record collection (Joseph Spence, Vaughan Williams, Frederick Delius, Miles Davis, Irma Thomas, Stones, Beatles, and *Music Of The Ituri Rain Forest*). James got a job at the Bort Carlton Handbags bindery on Washington Street in South Boston. Hating the gig, he dialled Kootch.

"Let's start a band!" said Kortchmar – and James instantly showed up at Danny's door – a walk-up apartment on 65th Street between York and First Avenue that Danny shared with first wife Joyce Helfer.

It was 1966 and Kootch had undergone his own share of changes. After succumbing at last to his father's pleas, Danny had taken a day job in the autumn of 1964 as a mailboy at MPO Films, a small New York ad agency specialising in commercials that was located at 44th and Lexington near Grand Central Station. Danny quit after three months and formed a blues-rock band called The King Bees with Mamaroneck

High buddy Richard "Dicky" Frank on rhythm guitar, Kootch on lead guitar, Joel "Bishop" O'Brien on drums and Johnny "John-John" McDuffy, a Harlem-bred teenage friend of his Larchmont housemaid, on piano.

A shakedown shift for the summer of '65, at the Raleigh hotel in the Catskills, enabled a confident King Bees to audition for and get the slot as the house band at Arthur, the chic discotheque in Manhattan's East 40s. The Bees replaced The Wild Ones, whose leader, Jordan Christopher, had just wed Arthur's owner, Sybil Burton (ex-wife of actor Richard Burton).

Despite the grind of five nightly sets between segments of turntable dance music, it was a glamorous gig, with established artists like The Young Rascals, Herman's Hermits, Brian Jones of The Rolling Stones and John Hammond, Jr stopping by to party and jam.

After nine months of the dusk-to-dawn regimen – plus side dates at rival clubs like Harlow's – Kootch was burnt out. He quit the Bees and took Joyce with him to the Vineyard for the first time in two years. On the island he jammed on folk-blues with fellow Vineyard songwriter Joel Zoss, all the while wishing Jamie Taylor would resurface – which finally occurred when Taylor rang Kootch in July '66.

After hugging Stringbean hello, Kootch announced the band he'd proposed should be called The James Taylor Group – "after The Spencer Davis Group." James recoiled from such billing, and they negotiated a compromise in which James became lead vocalist of a combo called The Flying Machine. Joel O'Brien was available to drum, but they had no bassist. It was decided they'd teach boyhood Vineyard friend Zachary Wiesner the bass parts to McLean-inspired material of James' like 'Knocking 'Round The Zoo', 'Don't Talk Now', and 'The Blues Is Just A Bad Dream'.

James crashed at a flat on 84th and Columbus when he hit Manhattan; then he and Zack lodged in the Albert Hotel on University Place between 10th and 11th Streets in Greenwich Village. The hotel's upper levels were gutted from a recent fire and Taylor and Wiesner registered for cut-rate digs on a floor burnt out except for one room. Groping to it in the dark each night was a "charred experience" for James but at least the rodent and cockroach community had been deterred by the blaze.

The Flying Machine rehearsed in what Kootch liked to call "the rat-infested, shit-box basement" of the Albert. Gigs at the Cafe Bizarre were a humble prelude to a peach hire replacing The Lovin' Spoonful as the staple act at the Night Owl Cafe on West Third Street off MacDougal Street. Many evenings prior to the opening set, James and Kootch went into the back dining room of the Minetta Tavern Restaurant, a showbiz/ left-wing bistro at the top of Minetta Lane, where they swapped set lists and toasted their fortune. James wrote a song called 'Night Owl' to celebrate, and The Flying Machine stayed aloft there for eight months.

Noodling on their guitars that summer of '66 in their girlfriends' flat on Fourth Street, James and Zack got to talking about The Rolling Stones' hit, 'Paint It Black'. James observed that people can be drawn to sadness, saying 'Paint It Black' was about seeking the solace or company of something "very blue, very dark, as if you wanted to draw the shades and keep the light out because it matches your mood." He added that it does no good to try to cheer up someone in this state; what they need to do instead "is go down, all the way to the bottom."

Once The Flying Machine began performing the resultant 'Paint It Black'-triggered song Taylor and Wiesner wrote, namely 'Rainy Day Man', fellow musicians assumed it was about heroin, which was then infesting the Village folk-rock scene. "No," Taylor averred when questioned directly, "but that would be a reasonable interpretation." Because James had begun using heroin.

"Joel O'Brien had been doing heroin," Kortchmar knew, "and then one day I realised James was, too."

"I think if I had been a better friend I'd have found a way to intervene," Kootch would later confide to others, "but I was a square, never used heroin, and we got into a schedule where I didn't see James each night until it was time to play – because of the dope. Both he and Joel hid it from me. James was ashamed for me to know, but it still hurt. He had shut me out, never let me see him doing it, and it put a veil between us that remained for years."

The Flying Machine was expected to do three to four sets a night on a 6.30 p.m. to 2 a.m. shift in between stands by The Turtles, Lothar & The Hand People, and an act called The Ragamuffins. Pay was $72 per band per night, plus a dinner of burgers, salad and fries, or tuna fish sandwiches with potato chips on the side. Things seemed on an even trajectory in terms of esprit de corps within The Flying Machine until the act made the mistake of trying to cut a record late in 1966 – a single of James' 'Night Owl' backed by his 'Brighten Your Night With My Day'.

Singer–songwriter/producer Chip Taylor (no relation to James; the brother of actor Jon Voight) caught The Flying Machine's shows, and got a tape of James' songs from Kortchmar and Bishop. Chip had issued a single of his own in 1965 on the obscure Mala label called 'Angel Of The Morning', which was a sizeable hit two years later when recut by Seattle-bred singer Merilee Rush. As a writer with April-Blackwood Music, Chip had also penned the Hollies' 1966 chart success, 'I Can't Let Go', and 'Wild Thing', a number one hit in the summer of '66 for Andover, England rock quartet The Troggs (and further immortalised in June 1967 when Jimi Hendrix performed it at the Monterey International Pop Festival).

Chip and fellow producer Al Gorgoni brought The Flying Machine into Select Sound Studios in New York and cut what the group considered to be demos of 'Night Owl', 'Knocking 'Round The Zoo', 'Rainy Day Man', 'Brighten Your Night With My Day', 'Something's Wrong', and an instrumental of Danny's called 'Kootch's Song'. Gorgoni added harpsichord on a few tracks. During the session, which lasted barely three hours, James was running a temperature of 102. Jay Gee Records, a subsidiary of the Jubilee label, rushed out a single of 'Night Owl' backed with 'Brighten Your Night With My Day'. The A-side got airplay in the North-east, but Jubilee passed on funding further recording.

"The people involved wouldn't spring for the money for a whole album of James' songs," Kortchmar would observe bitterly. "So it seemed terrible years later [in 1971] when the same people put out the *Flying Machine* album [on the Euphoria label] of those few sessions."

The group had meanwhile secured a manager in the belief that more exposure would boost their stock as a recording act, but the dates they secured were lousy, among them a Grand Union supermarket opening in Union, New Jersey. The best of the worst was a United Jewish Appeal fashion show whose models for the evening happened to include jazz great Charles Mingus' daughter. Mingus approached The Flying Machine in mid-set and asked to sit in; he stood an electric bass

James, at Milton Academy, Milton, Massachusetts.
(*Taylor Family Archive, courtesy Trudy Taylor*)

The original Isaac Taylor, in the 1790s.
(*Taylor Family Archive, courtesy Trudy Taylor*)

Isaac Taylor's only son Alexander, in the 1830s.
(*Taylor Family Archive, courtesy Trudy Taylor*)

FRESH GOODS.
Juſt imported, and opening for ſale at
ISAAC TAYLOR's CHEAP STORE,
In *MIDDLE-STREET,*
between *Mr. JOSEPH OLIVER's and*
the CHURCH ;

A GENERAL aſſortment of DRY
GOODS, Hard ware and Cut-
lery; ALSO Wine, Rum, Geneva;
Molaſſes, Pepper, Allſpice, Ginger,
Salt, Iron, Paints and oil, 7 by 9 and
8 by 10 window glaſs, Blackſmiths
anvils and vices, and a neat aſſortment of CROCKERY and STONE
WARE. All which will be ſold very cheap for Caſh or Country Pro
duce.

A FEW COPIES OF
the BOOK of COMMON PRAYER
according to the uſe
of the
PROTESTANT EPISCOPAL CHURCH
in the
United States of America.
PUBLISHED
By DIRECTION of the GENERAL CONVEN-
TION,
For ſale at *ISAAC TAYLOR's* Store.
January 11.

Advertisements placed in the *North Carolina Gazette* by Isaac for dry goods and prayer books available at his shop
on Middle Street and Craven Street, New Bern, NC., on November 5, 1791 (*left*) and January 11, 1794 (*right*).
(*Timothy White Collection*)

The front of Kirtonhill Manor House, Marykirk, Scotland, the family seat of James Taylor's ancestry, as it appeared circa 1920. (*Taylor Family Archive, courtesy Trudy Taylor*)

Taylor's Close in Montrose, Scotland, 1998. (*Timothy White Collection*)

Isaac Taylor's house, 228 Craven Street, New Bern, NC, as it is today. (*Timothy White Collection*)

The Taylor-Attmore House, 513 Broad Street, New Bern, NC. (*Timothy White Collection*)

Isaac Taylor as a virtual orphan, early 1920s, Morganton, N.C.
(*Taylor Family Archives, courtesy Trudy Taylor*)

Ike Taylor, James' father, on the porch of the "1st House", outside Carrboro, in Orange County, NC, in March, 1952. (*C. Gottschalk/Taylor Family Archive, courtesy Trudy Taylor*)

Isaac Taylor in 1945.
(*Taylor Family Archive, courtesy Trudy Taylor*)

Ike in Antarctica.
(*Taylor Family Archive, courtesy Trudy Taylor*)

Henry and Angelique Woodard, Trudy Taylor's parents, outside the family's commercial fishing business, Newburyport, Mass, 1942. (*Taylor Family Archive, courtesy Trudy Taylor*)

The Woodard family boat, *Sevenovus*, at Newburyport, Mass, 1939.
(*Taylor Family Archive, courtesy Trudy Taylor*)

Gertrude 'Trudy' Woodard, 17, in formal evening dress she sewed herself: "I made all my own dresses. In this one I was trying to look very grown up." (*Taylor Family Archive, courtesy Trudy Taylor*)

on an amp, holding it erect like a string bass, and played Little Richard's 'Lucille' with the band.

The nadir of the nadir for The Flying Machine was a booking in the Bahamas at a failing nightspot called the Jokers Wild Club in Freeport; after three weeks of bad food and no pay, the group used their return plane tickets to flee. They disbanded once their flight landed in New York.

Sadder still was Taylor's horrifying descent, just before The Flying Machine had hit career turbulence and begun to lose altitude, into full-blown heroin addiction.

"I just fell into it, since it was as easy to get high in the Village as get a drink," James would admit, and subsequent revelations would demonstrate this deluge-level influx of the drug in urban areas in the 1960s had not occurred by accident.

As disclosed in investigative reports circa 1972 by journalist Frank Browning and the editors of *Ramparts* magazine, as well as inquiries by authors Alfred W. McCoy (*The Politics Of Heroin In Southeast Asia*, 1973) and Henrik Kruger (*The Great Heroin Coup*, 1980), unscrupulous CIA personnel in opium-steeped South-east Asia became enmeshed in the drug trade during the years (1961–75) of the United States' direct involvement in the Vietnam War.

As it was, 15 per cent of US troops who saw action in Vietnam returned home as heroin addicts (with the Federal government forced to allocate funds for their treatment); and for eight years, the opium derivative that is heroin was brazenly smuggled back to America in the corpses of servicemen killed in action. The drug was then sold in ghettos and bohemian neighbourhoods in New York, Detroit and other cities through a contraband network controlled by corrupt police and mobsters also active as CIA operatives.

Such disclosures caused an uproar in the late '60s and early '70s, with indignant denials and moral outrage spewed in all directions. *New York Times* editor C.L. Sulzberger was particularly incensed when prominent beat/hippie poet Allen Ginsberg personally attacked the CIA for heroin trafficking, but Sulzberger later relented in a remarkably gracious letter to Ginsburg dated April 11, 1978, writing, "I fear I owe you an apology. I have been reading a succession of pieces about CIA involvement in the dope trade in Southeast Asia, and I remember when you first suggested I look into this I thought you were full of beans. Indeed you were right."

Back in the mid-'60s the serious problem of heroin use by middle-class and upper-class American youths, which had been building for two years, was becoming an overt crisis and a national issue. The teenage James Taylor found himself in the centre of the rising gale. It had enveloped him as quietly as a breeze across Washington Square Park, where it was as easy to score heroin as share a match with a cigarette-smoking bystander. The start was that casual, a gesture extended by street people who hovered around James when he'd choose a bench for himself, keeping depression at bay by strumming his guitar. Soon he was passing out on those same benches, or letting junkies, barmaids, debauched runaways, and striptease dancers crash at his apartment.

As Taylor told this writer, "I had fallen in with some people who could have done me some harm if I'd stuck with them. There were warrants out for these two guys staying at my place. I knew them by no other names than Smack and Bobby, and they were robbing people for a living. I was addicted. I was beginning to get desperate."

Broke, James went to his former manager's office one weekday after-noon. Sitting down heavily, strung out on speed he'd taken to alleviate the somnolent side-effects of smack, James asked for financial assistance.

The manager pulled something wrapped in wax paper out of his desk drawer. "Here," he said, "have a sandwich," offering a wilted corned beef on white bread. James began to cry, and left, finding his way back to his pad.

That Friday night, James dialled the Taylor house in Chapel Hill, lifting the telephone receiver as near to his ear as he could bear, hoping his physician father was home.

Ike and Jamie were "not terribly close, especially in those days" as his son knew. Yet he was also aware that his father, once openly disheart-ened by James' musical aspirations, had lately taken to telling people, just after the 'Night Owl' single had come out, that when James was two years old, Ike fetched a wire recorder he'd bought in 1950 – this was in the days before tape recorders – and had Jamie sing along with him on 'Little Red Wagon Painted Blue'.

"James was still crawling on the floor," Ike would explain. "And I said, 'Come on, Jamie, sing with me! And he started going goo-goo-

goo in time, along with me.'" He'd say it was James' first recording, right? And then, sometimes, he'd sheepishly lament he'd "since lost that damn recording."

When Ike heard the phone jingle down on Morgan Creek Road, he answered it on the second ring. James took a laboured breath and spoke, haltingly, getting out a few muddled nasal statements, saying just enough that his father had the sense his misguided pop star son was now in some terrible new predicament.

There was a short silence. Then Ike said, "STAY PUT. WHAT'S YOUR ADDRESS? I'LL BE RIGHT THERE."

After James hung up, it suddenly occurred to him, even through the haze of his addiction, that no father of a Taylor boy may have ever made such a selfless promise to his son before.

10

Never Die Young

"It was a dreadful, stressful situation James got into when he was 17," according to Dr Ike Taylor. "When you're 17 years old and playing music and nobody pays any attention, you learn ways to try to get that attention and settle for the results."

But young James was never markedly demonstrative in terms of notifying the outside world about his innermost dilemmas – which is precisely why his sudden phone call from New York left his hapless parent panic-stricken. Ike was also seized by a morbid fear that family heredity was once more playing cyclical havoc with descendants' lives, drawing its familiar dark cloak of addiction, psychic suffering and personal isolation around a new generation.

Ike went immediately to Raleigh-Durham Airport, catching the next plane to New York. He rented a station wagon at a Hertz outlet in the LaGuardia terminal and drove to Greenwich Village and his son's apartment building, where he found James in sorry physical and emotional condition. Distraught, Ike wavered and then clicked into his Navy-bred Chief Medical Officer mode and began to organise, pack and load all his son's musical equipment and personal effects into the wagon as if they were a swabby's duff for sea duty.

Once he got James and his possessions into the rental car, Ike decided it would be wisest to drive all night to deliver them both back home by daybreak on Saturday. James slept most of the way, saying little, and Ike restrained himself from lording it over the boy, being anxious that anything less than kindly forbearance might alienate him further and accelerate his heroin-fuelled descent. But the truth was the son was so startled and touched that his father actually cared enough to drop everything and come to his aid that he was at a loss for words.

"I wasn't calling home very often in those days," James would comment in recollecting Ike's stunned reaction to his beseeching call, "so he had a sense that I was in *trouble*. It was a solid thing he did."

Heading out of Manhattan on US 95, Ike glared at the road as he sped south, sometimes stopping for coffee at a roadside rest area and periodically glancing over at the dozing James, who seemed a long way from the toy trucks and cello practice that had once been his chief pre-occupations. Ike barely knew the boy Jamie had been, let alone the young man James was becoming.

These and other unsettling realisations were sufficient to keep Ike awake as the station wagon moved on through the deepening night, hurrying along the outskirts of New Jersey, Pennsylvania, Delaware and Maryland to link up to US 85 and cross into Virginia. It was 1967, and Dr Taylor was in his third year as dean of the School of Medicine at UNC-Chapel Hill. As the seventh dean in the school's history, he was currently overseeing the establishment of Medical Research Properties, Inc., a corporation designed to provide funds for erecting new laboratories and faculty office facilities while assuming responsibility for the school's capital debt, its construction loan to be repaid from rental fees from federal grants and other sources.

UNC's School of Medicine was the first educational institution in the nation to utilise such innovative financing, and Taylor played a prime role in its success. He had also played a key role, in terms of impaired bloodstock and brooding personal reserve, in the drastic predicament of his emotionally neglected son.

"I must admit James and the other children never showed any interest whatsoever in the medical profession," Ike ultimately conceded. "One of the problems of being a doctor is being away travelling. It makes you feel so removed from family so often. Looking back, I wish I had found some kind of work that could have kept me at home. I really think it's too bad. When I was a young doctor I was ambitious in academic medicine and I remember that on Sunday mornings I made a *point* of taking the children to my laboratory for two to three hours to see what I did all week.

"I was doing experiments with heart tissue, and I had a colony of hibernating hamsters. I feel sure James and the other children enjoyed seeing them. It was just a conscious attempt to get closer to my children."

But James had chosen the music world Trudy openly embraced over the academic life Ike stubbornly esteemed; thus, James was steadily pulling away, as Alex had, from the will of their father. The saddest part was that Ike himself had no firm opinion on the matter beyond a reflex disapproval – since popular music bore no clear benchmarks for advancement and accreditation – and he was oblivious to the personal goals on which contemporary musicians might set their sights, like probative self-expression and relief from the sting of private compromises and defeats.

For the rest of the Taylor kids – who were each seeking their own release from the unravelling household – music also represented fond communion with loved ones and friends, whereas academia symbolised a stark insularity.

"It's funny," as James saw it, "that my father was such an academician, and none of his children – not *one* of us – went to college."

Most of them went to McLean instead, with Livingston destined to follow James into the mental hospital as a self-committed occupant. Kate also arrived voluntarily not long after Liv, seeking treatment for self-inflicted burn wounds.

Since Livingston had gravitated to guitar and Kate had been singing in the Cambridge School's glee club, both got friendly with McLean's music therapist, who pushed Liv to compose songs, and induced Kate to assume lead vocals in a Top-40 cover band she convened, Sister Kate's Soul Stew & Submarine Sandwich Shop.

During the course of sporadic visits back to Chapel Hill, the troubled Taylor offspring accepted that the widening rift between Trudy and Ike was beyond repair. Ike couldn't seem to discover or invent a convenient route back into the fraying fold, and Trudy didn't sincerely know how to compel a man suffering the stubborn illusions of alcoholism to accept the obvious exit from his own trap. He simply wouldn't, or couldn't, curtail his drinking, and so work and the toll of his disease left him little time or stamina for much else.

Yet the latent lieutenant commander within Ike could still respond to the call of other people's emergencies and crises of the spirit, just as the little boy inside Ike knew the true signs of desperation, having felt them himself after being orphaned by his mother's tragic death and his father's fatal melancholy. So Ike instantly deduced James' phone call to be a cry for help that demanded a dramatic rescue mission.

"If he had just sent me a plane ticket," James admitted afterwards, "I definitely would have just sold it." Probably to buy drugs.

★ ★ ★

As Ike steered the station wagon carrying him and James down into North Carolina in the dusky pre-dawn, accelerating onto US 158 near the textile manufacturing outpost of Henderson, his thoughts meandered from the V8 drone of the monotonous drive to the real origins of James' music career, each of the father's memories frustratingly fragmented and incomplete.

"I remembered when James was seven or eight and his mother bought him a cello and he took lessons," Ike later recounted. "Then at 10 he wanted a guitar. He found college students to teach him, I think.

"One of his qualities as a youngster was he was always organising little shows. Once – I didn't go to see it because I was too busy – he was in a school play at 12 or 13, and Trudy said she couldn't believe his presence. Yet he wasn't a show-off. As a child, he was very intent, very intense." And very aware of who was and wasn't interested in his hobbies and unguarded passions.

"He's fundamentally a shy, retiring person," Ike would rationalise of James, "who wants and is able to be in meaningful contact with other people. At the one-on-one level, that shyness interferes. Paradoxically that shyness disappears onstage."

To the degree he was capable of such self-awareness, Ike had once been the same – except James had the courage to reject the harness of the Taylors' ancestral dictates. One day James would achieve a plateau of self-display that didn't require doses of artificial courage.

The station wagon sped west on Route 15, Ike gunning it from the old tobacco town of Oxford into the misty morning shadows of

Creedmoor. As bleary-eyed father and slumbering son crossed freshly tarred stretches of Route 15/501 that led from busy Durham (headquarters of Lucky Strike cigarettes, Duke University, Rev. Gary Davis, Sonny Terry and Brownie McGhee) and into the hushed tranquillity of Chapel Hill, Ike hoped there might yet be a chance to redirect James, to win him over to a Carolina teaching doctor's old-tie outlook on duty and destiny.

But that conquest required much focused effort, and Ike couldn't muster nearly enough of it. "You know, I tell friends, in jest," he would confide, "that I didn't want James to be a doctor and that I'd tell him to get on back to his guitar and practice, because that's where his future would lie. But that's not true, really. I didn't do that."

James would also find himself without the musical tutelage his brother Alex once afforded. The elder sibling had cleared out of Chapel Hill a few months after his tardy attainment in 1966 of a high school diploma. Alex had adjudged a post-graduate stint on a local bakery 3 a.m. to 9 a.m. graveyard shift to be too damned grim, so Ike advised his eldest son to reconsider higher education.

Alex enrolled at the University of North Carolina – Wilmington near Wrightsville, North Carolina, a port town on the southern coast of the state that was widely known for its welcoming beaches, year-round resorts, and myriad motels catering to collegiate packages for fun-seeking weekend matriculants. Alex pronounced Wilmington a "dynamite place to go to school but not much for studying." True to his synopsis, Alex amassed a mere 25 credit hours over the next two years.

Back on the upper Piedmont, James felt lost in his mother's charming but cloistered Japanese-modern quarters beside Morgan Creek. After six months of treatment, care and tentative recovery (he also underwent a throat operation "because I screamed my vocal cords into a bad state"), James heeded an inner voice much stronger and enticing than the lofty hopes of his dad or the light-hearted impulses of his older brother. He bade farewell to the Chapel Hill lifestyle for good, this time bound for the land where the Taylors had made their initial fortunes and first big mistakes: the British Isles.

11

One Man Parade

"I saw that North Carolina was no longer an anchor for me," James told friends. "Somehow, I had to create a future for myself. I decided I'd like to travel around a bit. And I don't know *why*, under the circumstances, but my folks thought that was a good idea!"

Ike and Trudy staked James with money his fraternal grandmother had left him, which was enough to get him to England and to buy a car. "So I hit London," James exulted, "and stayed with a friend from the Vineyard named Alby Scott, who was married and had a new baby. I was getting used to working as a solo act and wanted to play in the streets."

England in the last days of '67 and early months of '68 was edging into an intense new era of cosmopolitan transmutation, even though the March '68 issue of *Life* magazine insisted " 'swinging London' is dead." It had been *Life*'s competitive sister publication, *Time*, which had anointed the English capital as "Swinging" in its April 15, 1966 issue. The 2,000-year-old metropolis had since shaken off the trite celebrity of its Carnaby Street tailors, Mod photographers and art-school Mersey stars in pursuit of a municipal modernity surpassing the trendy surfaces depicted in films like *Darling, Alfie* and *Blow-Up*.

The London County Council and other civic agencies were busy plotting urban planning and redevelopment schemes, creating high-rise housing estates, office blocks and voguish concrete bunkers called "conference centres".

Luckily, many '68 proposals like the demolition of two-thirds of the quaint Covent Garden neighbourhood were scrapped, but the soulless designs of architect Richard Seifert for Telstar House, Centre Point, Royal Garden, Univac House, the National Westminster Tower and other highly visible public spaces succeeded in marring by comparison much of what Christopher Wren (1632–1723) once wrought on the elegantly grandiose London skyline.

More worthy in its transformational profile was London's varied immigrant influx of the '50s and early '60s, with tens of thousands of Irish, Greek Cypriots, West Indians and South Asians (mostly from the Bengal and Punjab provinces of British India) recasting the character and pulse of civic life. The scents and styles of Eastern mysticism, alloyed with citrus-shaded 'psychedelic' trappings and Jean Shrimpton's ribbed sweater slinkiness, quickly flooded King's Road from Sloane Square to World's End, as sitars and acid rock interwove with "tighten up music" (named for Trojan Records' rock steady/early reggae LP series spawned by the '68 Untouchables hit, 'Tighten Up').

Coinciding with these cultural convergences were increasingly cheaper air travel, the 1967 devaluation of the pound sterling, an inflationary US economy and prosperity in Europe, which together triggered the multi-million-person boom in (largely US) tourism that propelled James V. Taylor across the Pond just as he was turning 20.

In Ike's optimistic eyes: "James went to Europe to seek his fortune." And, with almost alarming dispatch, this fatherly prediction came to pass.

James had originally flown over late in '67 with street singing in mind, bringing along a folk guitar he'd bought in Durham when he was 14, and he indeed "played in a couple of underpasses and looked for whatever work I could."

He felt "totally free – for *sure*" for the first time in his life, but travelling across Europe wasn't as effortless as he'd presumed: "You had to have papers and had to worry about immigration."

Except for erratic side-trips, James lodged mainly in London, living first in Notting Hill Gate, a burgeoning hippy enclave. He also stayed in Pont Street Mews in Belgravia with a girlfriend from New York,

Margaret "Maggie" Corey, daughter of comic monologist Professor Irwin Corey and sister of Richard Corey, also a close friend. James also stayed in a small basement flat on Beaufort Gardens in Chelsea, where he was alternately amused and chagrined by a coin-operated gas heater that ran, albeit in brief bursts, on two-shilling pieces.

Among new confrères James found in London was Judy Steele, who worked as a set designer at the BBC and knew people in the music business. After hearing his songs, Judy told James, "You really must record these things." It was at her urging that he began to audition for record companies, at first proffering crude tapes and then purchasing 45 minutes worth of proper demo time in a Soho studio for eight quid.

At the Soho session, he cut 'Something's Wrong', 'Knocking 'Round The Zoo', 'Something In The Way She Moves', and several other songs for a 30-minute acetate.

★   ★   ★

At this stage of Taylor's personal and professional passage there were marked parallels with the previous advances of American singer-songwriters.

Peggy Seeger, first daughter (born in 1935) of Charles and Ruth Crawford Seeger and sister of singer Pete, went to London at the urgent invitation of folklorist Alan Lomax in 1956 to complete a folk ensemble he'd organised for BBC-TV. Seeger met future husband Ewan MacColl in a basement-flat audition site in Chelsea at 10.30 in the morning on March 25 and promptly fell in love. The Scotland-born MacColl would later compose 'The First Time Ever I Saw Your Face' for Seeger, a classic ballad also covered by Joan Baez, The Kingston Trio, and Peter, Paul & Mary. MacColl and Seeger performed together throughout Great Britain and Europe until MacColl's death on October 22, 1989.

Known on both sides of the Atlantic for such compositions as 'The Battle Of Springhill', 'I Support The Boycott', and her feminist folk standard, 'I'm Gonna Be An Engineer', Seeger also partnered with MacColl and BBC producer Charles Parker to mount the famed 1958–64 *Radio Ballads* documentary series that commenced in July 1958 with the tragic railway saga, *The Ballad Of John Axon* and featured subsequent instalments on British seafarers (*Singing The Fishing*), indigenous gypsies (*The Travelling People*), and troubled teens (*On The Edge*).

"We look for pride in ourselves in this individualistic country here," Seeger later told this writer regarding America, "but pride that goes outside yourself I think is very necessary. Pride in your children, of course, is natural. But pride in the principles that you have when you live with other people I think is extremely important. That would be one of the main messages of these [radio] ballads. Even pride to survive. We're talking about what we produce, we're talking about people who are like US. We are community."

Such wise, fiercely felt words held the spirit of a bold brand of public songcraft gathering disciples at midterm in the 20th century, and such thinking had a magnetism that lured others from America to England. Paul Simon sojourned in London in 1964, some four years prior to Taylor and over a decade after Seeger made England her base (until 1994, when she came back to the US, settling in Asheville, North Carolina). And like Seeger, Simon found the ready acceptance in England that had likewise eluded him at home.

Simon was born in Newark, New Jersey on October 13, 1941, the son of professional orchestra/studio bassist Lou Simon and his wife Belle, who taught English at the elementary school level. Paul grew up in the Kew Garden Hills/Forest Hills section of Queens, New York, and as an adolescent he was infatuated with the doo-wop vocal style of Jamaica, Queens group The Cleftones ('You Baby You', Gee Records, 1956).

At 15, Simon had formed a vocal quintet called The Peptones with neighbourhood friends Artie Garfunkel, Johnny Brennan, and two girls, Angel and Ida Pellagrini. Their first demo was of a song Simon wrote with Garfunkel, 'The Girl For Me', but it found no takers.

A year later, as seniors at Forest Hills High, Simon and Garfunkel clicked commercially with 'Hey Schoolgirl', a song co-authored under the pseudonyms – Tom Graph (for Art) and Jerry Landis (for Paul) – that underlined their stage name, Tom & Jerry. Done for Sid Prosen's Big Records label based in the Brill Building at 1619 Broadway, it rose to number 49 on the *Billboard* Best Seller singles chart in '57, with Tom & Jerry issuing other less auspicious singles for Big/King, Hunt, Ember and ABC-Paramount.

In 1958, Paul released a solo single, 'Teenage Fool'/'True Or False', on Big Records under the name True Taylor.

While in Queens College as an English major, Simon sang on other people's demos (among them 10 songs for Burt Bacharach and Hal David) at $25 a side and also cut roughly a dozen tracks – penned by himself and others – as Jerry Landis ('Anna Belle', 'Just A Boy', 'I Wish I Weren't In Love', 'I'd Like To Be The Lipstick On Your Lips', 'It Means A Lot To Them', etc.) for the MGM, Warwick, Canadian American and Amy labels. Simon also struck up a friendship with fellow Queens College undergraduate Carole King (born Carole Klein in Brooklyn, New York on February 9, 1942).

"Carole was good at math, and doing friendly tutoring but not charging me," Simon would explain, "because she'd made records when she was a kid, too." Like 'Goin' Wild', and 'Baby Sittin', her 1958–59 singles for ABC-Paramount.

King and Simon duetted on the demo version of 'Just To Be With You'; it became a minor 1959 hit for The Passions on Audicon Records when they aped the King/Simon demo's vocal modulations. In 1961, as Tico & The Triumphs, Paul charted at number 99 in *Billboard* for Madison Records with 'Motorcycle'.

Paul graduated from Queens College in 1962 with a Bachelor of Arts degree, then decided to pursue a law degree at the same school. His outside activities continued, however, and in 1963, he climbed to number 97 as Jerry Landis with a song for Amy Records titled 'The Lone Teen Ranger.'

By the summer of '63, Paul and boyhood chum Art Garfunkel (who'd been recording solo as Artie Garr) were reunited due to mutual interest in the folk boom fuelling the success of acts like The Kingston Trio. Simon & Garfunkel began playing as a folk duo in such Greenwich Village clubs as Gerde's Folk City. In '64, Simon met Columbia Records staff producer Tom Wilson while toiling as a song-plugger for E.B. Marks Music and secured an audition for himself and Art that led to a Columbia deal.

Recording began in March '64 for Simon and Garfunkel's début album, *Wednesday Morning, 3am: Exciting New Sounds In The Folk Tradition*, and Simon dropped out of law school. A few months later he went on a summer sabbatical to England and France. Paul was in Paris at midpoint in his hitchhiking/busking itinerary when he read in a newspaper that Andrew Goodman, a student in his Queens College acting class, had been killed on June 21, 1964 along with two fellow Civil Rights workers in Mississippi by Ku Klux Klansmen.

The decomposed bodies of the missing Goodman and the others were found on August 4, buried in an earthen dam on a farm near Philadelphia, Mississippi. " 'He Was My Brother' was written about Andrew Goodman," Simon told this writer in 1997. "We knew each other from class. I didn't even know he was going down to Mississippi that summer, but I was in Europe when I read about it and I was shaken."

Simon had been inspired by the rising activism of Goodman – whose interest in theatre and politics while at Queens College landed Andy a small part in the Greenwich Village show *Chief Thing*, while also luring him to the March On Washington in August, 1963 – but Paul's verses weren't vespers for Goodman. Art Garfunkel recalls Simon writing 'He Was My Brother' in June 1963; it appeared on Tribute Records in the US under the name Paul Kane; in 1964 the UK Oriole label released it as a Jerry Landis single.

The "Singin' " martyr in the 'Brother' lyric was three years older than Goodman and was shot by an "angry mob". Andy, 20, and his two co-workers were slain on a back road by the KKK after local cops had stopped their car and jailed them.

'Brother' had first gotten Columbia producer Wilson interested in Simon and Garfunkel. The duo cut its track of the ballad on March 17, 1964 for *Wednesday Morning, 3am* and the album hit the shops two months after the deaths of Goodman, Michael Schwerner and James Chaney were confirmed. 'He Was My Brother' became what it foretold: a funeral requiem.

Simon & Garfunkel's first album (also containing 'The Sound Of Silence') met with commercial indifference in the States after its October '64 release, so Art resumed his Masters programme in architecture at Columbia University and Paul returned to London. While playing in a Soho club, Simon was heard by social worker Judith Piepe, who had an ally in the Religious Broadcasting Department of the BBC, the Reverend Roy Trevivian. Piepe invited Simon to join a kind of folk salon centred in her East London flat; Paul sang, played and stayed there with emerging local talents like Al Stewart and Sandy Denny.

Clergyman-deejay Rev. Trevivian taped 12 songs with Simon

during a one-hour solo BBC session on January 27, 1965. The reverend picked four of the batch to broadcast in May '65 on *Five To Ten*, a regular "thought for the day" slot. It aired five minutes prior to the BBC's highly popular *Saturday Club* programme; millions of BBC listeners heard Simon perform an acoustic suite consisting of 'The Sound Of Silence', 'I Am A Rock', 'A Most Peculiar Man' and 'Bleeker Street'. Letters poured in afterwards, the radio audience eagerly inquiring how Simon's music could be obtained.

The CBS UK label (a Columbia affiliate) responded to the clamour by issuing an EP containing songs culled from *Wednesday Morning, 3am*. Next in '65 came a solo acoustic LP CBS UK commissioned, titled *The Paul Simon Songbook*, which was recorded at Levy Studios on Bond Street for a 60-minute session fee of £60. During this period Simon was exposed to the waterfall-like finger-picking techniques of gifted British folk guitarists Davey Graham and Bert Jansch which helped enhance his own approach. He also learned Martin Carthy's version of the traditional 'Scarborough Fair', and co-wrote the ditty 'Red Rubber Ball' with Bruce Woodley of The Seekers.

When Garfunkel visited East London in '65, he and Paul cut their own highly stylised adaptation of 'Scarborough Fair'. As Garfunkel later commented, "Those lovely English ballads with their sweet folky changes, they really got to me and Paul," adding that, "The [Francis James] Child ballads [collected between 1882 and 1898 by that folk scholar for his landmark *English And Scottish Popular Ballads* anthology] were already part of American folk music, via the Appalachian tradition" – of which North Carolina balladry was central.

In America, Columbia staff producer Tom Wilson had just finished Bob Dylan's *Bringing It All Back Home* album, and he decided to nudge the absent Simon & Garfunkel in the folk-rock direction Dylan was favouring by overdubbing electric guitar on the original 1964 Columbia studio version of 'The Sound Of Silence'. On November 20, 1965, Wilson's new edition of the song, retitled in the plural as 'The Sounds Of Silence', entered *Billboard*'s Hot 100 at number 80, where it would ascend to number one by New Year's Day.

Released in February 1966, the subsequent *Sounds Of Silence* included fresh material Paul had developed in England like 'Kathy's Song', 'April Come She Will' and 'I Am A Rock', plus a recasting of

Davey Graham's guitar instrumental 'Anji'. Simon & Garfunkel hits of '66 included singles 'Homeward Bound' (unavailable on an album until November's *Parsley, Sage, Rosemary And Thyme* collection), as well as 'I Am A Rock', and a number two cover version of Simon and Woodley's 'Red Rubber Ball' as recorded by The Cyrkle, a Pennsylvania pop quartet named by John Lennon and handled by The Beatles' manager, Brian Epstein.

Simon & Garfunkel's US support was echoed in the UK, where many folk observers felt (in the words of a reader of England's *Folk Scene* magazine) that of all "visiting singers", Paul Simon was the most popular in English folk circles.

★   ★   ★

That is, until James Taylor arrived. Uncertain at first what to do with the demo that resulted from his half-hour in a Soho studio, Taylor got on a trans-Atlantic phone line and located Danny Kortchmar in the States, who advised James to contact singer Peter Asher, one-half of the highly successful British pop duo Peter & Gordon (Waller) that mutually dissolved in 1967. Kootch explained to James that Asher had just taken a position as head of A&R for The Beatles' new Apple Records label, and was in the market for signable acts. Kootch gave James a number for Peter, urging him to call.

"I'm listening to everything!" Asher responded cordially when Taylor rang him up, and James was encouraged to submit some tapes.

And as Taylor was finding his footing as a Carolinan/New Englander/ Scots folk mongrel on the London streets, an Asheville, North Carolina-born R&B singer named Roberta Flack was still a year away from recording her own hit-destined version of the MacColl/Seeger perennial, 'The First Time Ever I Saw Your Face'.

An historic conversation between two diverse cultures was expanding. But for now, it was the forlorn Taylor's ripe chance to submit his own hybrid brand of American songcraft to the British public.

As a rising studio musician and an avid reader of the *Billboard*, *Cashbox* and the other US and overseas music trades, Kortchmar kept up on movements in record label hierarchies as well as artistic circles, and he had given his adolescent buddy a timely tip.

Kootch knew Asher, a former child star who appeared with

Claudette Colbert and Jack Hawkins in *The Planter's Wife* (1952), because The King Bees had once toured with Peter & Gordon, who'd charted fourteen Hot 100 singles in the States between 1964–67, including hit covers of Del Shannon's 'I Go To Pieces' and Buddy Holly's 'True Love Ways', as well as the number six release 'Lady Godiva' and the chart-topping '64 smash, 'A World Without Love'. The last song, and three subsequent Top 20 singles ('Nobody I Know', 'I Don't Want To See You Again', 'Woman'), were all written by The Beatles' Paul McCartney, then dating Asher's sister Jane.

Asher was impressed with Taylor's acetate, which he played for McCartney – who eagerly gave the go-ahead on an album.

"I heard his demos – Peter played them for me – and I just heard his voice and his guitar and I thought he was great," as McCartney remembered for the author in March 2001. "And then Peter brought him around, and he came and played live, so it was just like, 'Wow, he's *great*.' And he'd been having troubles; Peter explained to me that he'd just got clean off drugs and was in a slightly difficult time in his life. But he was playing great, and he had enough songs for an album. Peter said, 'I think it'd be good to sign him.' So I said to the guys [The Beatles], 'We should sign him.' "

By this unlikely scenario did James Taylor become the first non-British artist signed to Apple Records, whose roster also boasted Beatle finds Mary Hopkin ('Those Were The Days'), former Under-takers vocalist Jackie Lomax ('Sour Milk Sea'), the John Foster and Sons Ltd. Black Dyke Mills Band brass ensemble ('Thingumybob'), plus promising classical composer John Tavener ('The Whale', 'Celtic Requiem').

Taylor and Asher placed ads in the *New Musical Express* and *Melody Maker* seeking backing musicians. Respondents were sent to a four-storey brick building at 94 Baker Street that The Beatles were using as temporary headquarters for the Apple Corps holding company, of which Apple Records and Apple Music were subsidiaries. On the top floor were vacant rooms commandeered for auditions in which James listened to and jammed with various keyboard players and bassists; the open slots were quickly filled, respectively, by Don Schinn and Louis Cennamo. Former King Bees/Flying Machine drummer Joel "Bishop" O'Brien came over from the States to man the drums.

More material needed to be generated for the album, and James strained to apply himself amid the excitement and general hedonism of the period: "The whole thing was like a swirl. I stayed a lot of different places, I lived with a number of different women, writing a lot of songs like 'Carolina In My Mind' and 'Taking It In', and forming, and breaking off, and exchanging volatile romantic attachments."

Taylor was equally combustible in other realms of recreation. An evening acid trip with a friend turned into a pyrotechnic misadventure, during which a matchstick cabin built around a burning candle became the catalyst for near-disaster: "Pretty soon the wax was vaporising inside the cabin and giving off a nice light." Gripped by a dangerous degree of euphoria, James suddenly clambered out of the window of the apartment building he was in, swinging from fire escapes, jumping from rooftop to rooftop.

"I used to get crazy from this drug," he later allowed, since his escapade escalated: "I walked along a ledge, storeys and storeys up, and jumped into a tree in a park along Baker Street. I climbed out of the tree, hopped into my car, a [Ford] Cortina GT, and blasted around the West End, doing about eighty – just screaming. It was a golden time, and I was right *in the pocket*."

When he got back to his friend's apartment, re-entering by way of fire escape and window, Taylor learned that the burning match cabin he'd left behind on a wax-filled plate had "become a nova and blown up", with shards of crockery and gobs of molten wax flying in all directions as the superhot explosion blew a hole in the table and the ceiling overhead. The regular occupants of the apartment were standing about, "spooked and dragged", as James surveyed the damage. "I later thought of that as being pretty irresponsible," he said of his actions.

Taylor tried to settle down and concentrate on his composing, but additional fanciful forces soon intruded: "I remember writing 'Carolina In My Mind' in three different places. I stayed with Peter and his first wife [Betsy] in their flat on Marylebone High Street. Then I went on vacation for five days to Formentera, an island next to Ibiza, just off the coast of Majorca in the Mediterranean. I spent about two days on the island, drinking Romilar [cough syrup with codeine] and riding a bicycle, just chanting. It was a hypnotic, anti-psychedelic experience. It was nice.

"One night, a girl I met there named Karen and I took the boat over to Ibiza for the day. We missed the last boat and spent the night in a cafe that was closed down, and I wrote the rest of it" – meaning 'Carolina In My Mind' – "on a piece of paper that was lying around there."

In February '68, rehearsals began for Taylor's début Apple album and lasted three months. During run-throughs for basic tracks, James' song bag was whittled to 12 selections. (One of them, 'Something In The Way She Moves', had been heard in pre-release form by Tom Rush when Taylor visited Elektra's offices in late '67 to perform his wares. Being Boston/Cambridge folkie cohorts, Rush and Taylor had conferred after James' audition. "We sat down on the floor of a vacant office," Rush recalled three decades later, "and he played me some songs. I ended up putting 'Something In The Way She Moves' on the record" he was then assembling for April '68 release on Elektra – *The Circle Game*.)

As for Taylor's own project of the same era: "We recorded at Trident Studios between July and October of '68 and sort of worked around The Beatles," he explained, "who were in there doing *The White Album* [aka *The Beatles*]. I would usually be coming into the studio as they were beginning or finishing a session, and so I'd hang around and get to hear a playback of the material, listening to early versions of 'Hey Jude' and 'Rocky Raccoon'. I also heard them re-cutting 'Revolution' in the Abbey Road studio."

Once Taylor's formal recording was underway, Asher and McCartney brought in young British arranger Richard Hewson, who had previously embroidered the rudiments of a song on a forthcoming album for 17-year-old Welsh singer Mary Hopkin. Destined to be an international hit, the piece was 'Those Were The Days' – a melody, with original lyrics by Gene and Francesca Raskin, that the Raskins had adapted from the Russian folk song, 'Dear For Me'.

Hewson had done an effective job recasting both the original Russian textures and the Raskins' cabaret-style lyricism in a polished pop context, and McCartney thought Taylor's meditative material warranted similar contextual touches. Everyone at Apple had been struck by the simplicity but also the indelible emotional stamp of James' work, which had the immediacy of a personal meditation but also the plaintive, worldly wise polish of Stephen Foster's best parlour ballads.

As the essential tracks for the Taylor songs were assembled, Asher delivered them to Hewson, who conceived additional instrumentation that strove to augment or complement them with aural embellishment. Also composed and/or inserted were connective interludes. Occasionally it worked well enough, as in the solo guitar variation on the traditional 'Greensleeves' (originally composed by King Henry VIII) that Taylor plucked after 'Don't Talk Now', a ballad about the brittle romantic break-ups James was experiencing.

More ponderous was Hewson's string prelude to 'Knocking 'Round The Zoo', a song based on Taylor's rehab at McLean. String and harp passages by the Amici String Quartet and harpist Skaila Kanga were efforts at ornamenting a basic demo of 'Sunshine Sunshine' that Taylor had given to Hewson. To James' alarm his rough pass at 'Sunshine' wound up as the final template for the track; he had wanted to re-record the raw take but instead found himself playing guitar overdubs around orchestration conducted by Hewson, a weird conjunction the disconcerted singer-songwriter critiqued as "confining".

As the record progressed, Hewson's touches grew still more intrusive, his string interlude for the otherwise unadorned 'Taking It In' lasting a full 40 seconds before the main track was allowed to start.

Don Schinn's harpsichord "link" (as most such musical intervals were officially billed) prior to 'Something In The Way She Moves' was charming but unnecessary. As for the song it was intended to introduce, 'Something In The Way She Moves' was unquestionably Taylor's finest performance: spare in presentation, poignant on its own eloquent terms.

(The song was so arresting it left a subliminal mark on George Harrison, who unconsciously borrowed a bit of its title for the opening line of a love song he'd conceived at a point when rehearsals of June/July '68 at London's Trident Studios for *James Taylor* had overlapped with Jackie Lomax's Harrison-produced sessions. Conceived as a Ray Charles-type torch song, Harrison actually wrote the bulk of 'Something' in an empty Studio 1 at Abbey Road Studios while cutting *The Beatles*, and did tracks in February '69 for the final version of 'Something' on the Beatles *Abbey Road*, doing the vocals, guitar parts and piano alone. George's song had a fourth verse not used on the finished release ["That woman of mine/Need her all the time . . . What I'm telling you/That woman don't make me blue"] whose rhyme scheme resembled Charles' style, and Ray himself later recorded it, much to Harrison's delight.)

Next on *James Taylor* was 'Carolina In My Mind', the late-adolescent ode to Southern homesickness that was the album's quiet masterpiece. An earlier version cut with a 30-piece orchestra was shelved. The somewhat overproduced edition preserved on the Apple record got a deft bass line by McCartney and backing vocals by Taylor, Asher and an uncredited Harrison. But Hewson's strings in the verse before the bridge were close to cloying, and the orchestration at the bridge and thereafter were superfluous. (A superior studio take of the song would not see tape until an October '76 *Greatest Hits* session in LA.)

"It was The Beatles, by the way," Taylor later explained, "that I was referring to on 'Carolina In My Mind', when I sang about the 'holy host of others standing around me.' At the time, it made me think back to a girl I'd once tried to make it with when I was in boarding school at Milton Academy in Massachusetts. She and I were in her bedroom, engaged in this light-hearted adolescent wrestling match, and I wanted it so bad, and she wouldn't because, as she said, 'I don't feel strong enough about you.' I said, 'Well, who would I have to be? Suppose I got to meet The Beatles, suppose I *knew* them – and introduced you to a Beatle?' She smiled and said, 'You bet!' As I was completing the album, I recalled that girl in Massachusetts and thought, '*Damn.*'"

The brass ensemble at work in the link after 'Carolina In My Mind' and then inserted in 'Brighten Your Night With My Day' sounded fidgety and tacked-on, dishevelling an open-souled lyric. When the brass parts were also incorporated into what resembled a Broadway overture for 'Night Owl', the gesture was ungainly. In fairness, brass was used better in the body of the 'Night Owl' track.

'Rainy Day Man' was exquisite in its simplicity but harsh echo effects placed on the backing vocals sounded like an error in the mix. Fortunately, the melody was indestructible, as all subsequent recordings and performances of the song made clear.

A lush string piece lent a dawn-like prefiguration to the opening verse of 'Circle Round The Sun' – an obvious yet enticing touch – but Hewson's inability to see this humble Hoagy Carmichael tune for its intrinsic, Taylor-shaded strengths was head scratchingly odd.

Hewson's subsequent string-brass-harp link was effective on its own but had little to do with the lone voice-and-guitar grandeur that followed, as James guided listeners through the disturbing 'The Blues Is Just A Bad Dream'. The mordant junkie soliloquy didn't need the surreal strings that rose up under it near the close. As before, the bare piece had sufficient power to forego Hewson's faux-classical flourishes.

Taylor himself had no such pretensions, the suit he wore for the album cover's photo session with Richard Imrie was picked up for the occasion in a second-hand shop, the pictures snapped shortly afterwards in a park in south-east London. The music presented on *James Taylor* as a pleasant young fellow's balladry was actually deathly dark and highly unpredictable in its denouements. What some young female fans soon took to be a boyish troubadour worth fawning over was, to more discerning eyes, a big talent to watch carefully – and with a degree of concern.

"My life remained in disarray," Taylor said, "and I was racing around changing houses every two weeks – usually because of high rent or having made too much noise – while I tried to keep to the recording schedule and fulfil Peter and Paul's faith in me."

But such demands pushed the fragile artist to the brink of his capacity to cope, and on many of the principal sessions for *James Taylor* the man himself seemed, by his own admission, to be curiously "sleepy". Taylor had slipped back into junk, and was addicted again by the mid-point of recording the Apple album – James being "stoned for most of the sessions", as he admitted to *Rolling Stone* in 1971. Finding the hard drugs in London uncommonly pure and potent, he was shooting speedballs of smack and methadrine.

Driving through London, strung-out, with Joel O'Brien one night after recording, James was startled by the sudden appearance in a darkened thoroughfare of a drunken pedestrian, who darted in front of his car. Careening off the bumper of the Cortina, the inebriated chap was tossed some eight feet into the air and then tumbled rag doll-like into the gutter. Miraculously, he was unhurt but for a bruised hip. Two policemen who witnessed the entire, terrifying incident were more grateful than aggravated, since it was the drunk's flight from their arrest that had sent him into the path of Taylor's vehicle. And because the drunken pedestrian had fiercely pummelled the two constables before breaking into a fumbling run for several blocks, they were pleased to see his frantic escape thwarted.

Taylor accepted with good grace the huge dent in his auto, having dodged the crimp in his reputation that a drug bust-cum-reckless driving charge could have caused.

Others were not faring quite so well. The Apple album was complete and in its concluding production stages when Taylor learned of the death of Suzanne 'Susie' Schnerr, a chum of James, O'Brien and the Coreys who'd regularly hung out with them in New York in 1966–67.

"I knew Suzanne well in New York," James reflected, "and we used to hang out together and we used to get high together; I think she came from Long Island. She was a kid, like all of us.

"But she committed suicide sometime later while I was over in London. At the time I was living with Margaret, and Richard was around a lot and so was Joel O'Brien. All three of them were really close to Susie Schnerr. But Richard and Joel and Margaret were excited for me having this record deal and making this album, and when Susie killed herself they decided not to tell me about it until later because they didn't want to shake me up."

During an alcohol-fuelled wee-hours huddle in London with O'Brien, the truth finally came out, the liquor giving Joel the courage he needed to divulge something he felt James deserved to know. Within a week and a half, Taylor had fashioned the outline of a lament called 'Fire And Rain'. Sweet-sounding at first blush, with its chiming guitar, throbbing bass and plunging drums, the song was actually pop at its most pessimistic. Its tune seemed so delicate yet the tale underneath it was a pitch-black essay on ruined lives, the harrowing disjunction of smack, a dear friend's dismay as sudden death supplies an ugly awakening.

The first verse of 'Fire And Rain' declaimed in clipped phrases Taylor's reaction to the reality of Schnerr destroying herself, but its blunt, next-day aftertaste of anger and hopelessness later troubled him.

"I didn't find out until some six months after it happened," he observed of Suzanne's suicide. "That's why the 'They let me know you were gone' line came up. And I always felt rather bad about the line, 'The plans they made put an end to you,' because 'they' only meant 'ye gods', or basically 'the Fates'. I never knew her folks but I always wondered whether her folks would hear that and wonder whether it was about them.

"But like all of these things," he mused, "the lines just show up as they will. That song really tapped an aquifer." Taylor started to write the song in his basement flat in Chelsea. The rest of the inky psychic pool for which 'Fire And Rain' became a tap concerned Taylor's efforts to kick heroin in England before returning to the States. He entered a programme utilising visepdone, the British version of methadone, and the song's "look down upon me Jesus" verse was real in its plea for "help" to "make a stand" against his secret scourges. Not long after his flight back to America, James was hospitalised in Manhattan and he sketched the second verse of 'Fire And Rain' in his room while an in-patient.

Depression over the obstinate monkey on Taylor's slender back became severe, summoning up demons described in the song's third verse from his days before and after McLean as summarised in the image of "sweet dreams and flying machines in pieces on the ground".

Leaving the Manhattan hospital, Trudy went with him, James driving, and he committed himself to Austen Riggs, a 44-year-old private psychiatric clinic on Main Street in the postcard-pretty Berkshires village of Stockbridge, Massachusetts.

Situated a short diagonal stroll from the quaint block-long stretch of town immortalised in Norman Rockwell's 1967 painting, *Main Street Stockbridge At Christmas*, the subdued grey and white complex of mansion-like Austen Riggs' handsome halls and annexes resembled the campus of a small college. The institution was affiliated with Harvard Medical School and Cambridge Hospital, with a seminal contributor to its Austen Riggs techniques (as well as a subject for a Norman Rockwell portrait) being renowned Germany-born US psychoanalyst Erik H. Erikson. Emphasising the significance of cultural, social and historical factors in the development of an individual identity, Erikson helped formulate the therapeutic centre's philosophy: "To facilitate change in the individual's capacity to work, play and love by helping the patient acknowledge and come to terms with psychological and biological impediments to growth, development and self-esteem. Most patients at the center suffer from personality disorders or have experienced major trauma, often complicated by mood disorders, anorexia/bulimia, substance abuse, or psychosis. Patients who have not been helped in other settings often benefit from a more sustained treatment that reduces the likelihood of hospitalisation."

In its comfy but sterile quarters, the mentally and physically exhausted Taylor finished the third verse of 'Fire And Rain'.

Then he penned a deceptively upbeat, skiffle-flavoured shuffle called 'Sunny Skies' about a person much like himself at that time, who "weeps in the evening" and "doesn't know when" to sleep or rise as morning approaches.

In 'Sunny Skies' the narrator glances outside to see traffic puttering along Main Street, noting also the snow and trees outside his window, and then figures he ought to throw the rest of his waking hours away in medicated oblivion, because he feels he hasn't a friend in the world.

London and his recent accomplishments seemed far removed to Taylor, and he was unsure, as he admitted in 'Sunny Skies', if where he'd been was worth the things he'd been through. It was an open question, impossible to answer from inside a privileged holding tank like Austen Riggs.

After recuperating from the severe nervous and physical fatigue that led him to Austen Riggs, and fed up with his own fretful lassitude and leering demons, James loaded his bag into one more station wagon and left yet another sanitarium associated with the lineal travails of the Taylors.

It was the last time James would allow himself to give in to giving in. No more nut houses for a young man too sane for his own good. Taylor would hereafter leave the pieces of his former life where they had fallen, resolving to erect something new upon the wreckage of the old.

★　★　★

The *James Taylor* album was released by Apple in the UK on December 6, 1968, arriving just after the November 22 issue of *The Beatles*, but Taylor's record sold poorly, its tepid commercial reception owed to James' initial promotional absence from England due to his stay at

Austen Riggs for detoxification. A single from the album, 'Carolina In My Mind' b/w 'Taking It In', appeared in February 1969. The single failed to chart.

In the States, *James Taylor* was issued on February 17, 1969, with its British single scheduled by Apple for a March 3, 1969 US release, but that single was cancelled – although test pressings were widely circulated – in favour of 'Carolina In My Mind' with a different B-side, 'Something's Wrong', issued as Apple 1805.

'Carolina In My Mind' entered *Billboard*'s Bubbling Under the Hot 100 chart on April 12, 1969 and lingered for just two weeks, climbing to number 118. (A 1970 re-release reached number 67.)

In July 1969 Taylor, who began his solo performance career during his teens with a forgotten gig at a bygone Vineyard Haven boite called Cafe Moscow, was booked for his first appearance alone on the stage of the legendary Los Angeles folk club, the Troubadour. Sixteen-year-old future singer-songwriter Karla Bonoff ('Someone To Lay Down Beside Me', 'Lose Again', 'Tell Me Why'), a graduate of Los Angeles' University High (alma mater of Jan & Dean, and Randy Newman) felt fortunate to catch James' set.

"I was about to walk out the door," she said, "and this guy said, 'No you should wait, this guy is really cool!' James got up on stage and played 'Carolina In My Mind' and four other things from that first record. It was like something clicked in me, and I felt this was *the* guy. I've never felt that ever since that moment."

Shortly afterwards, Taylor suffered a motorcycle crash on the Vineyard after "borrowing" a stolen bike the local Police Chief had stowed in the woods until the owner could be found. Taylor didn't grasp how damaged the motorcycle was until he opened its throttle while ripping down a rural fire lane doing 50 mph; he was in third gear as he hit a dip in the road with the throttle stuck, brakes gone, and trees dead ahead.

Taylor broke both hands and both feet, getting plaster casts on all four limbs. A few days following the accident, he dropped mescaline, had a friend help him down to the ocean's edge, and chose a rocky vantage point that seemed restful for a man sporting four casts. Reclining there and listening to the sea, James thought he heard a snatch of harmony in the breeze rushing past his ears, a kind of wind chord, and the words it bade him sing were: "Mescalito has opened up my eyes, mescalito has set my mind at ease." (Years later, he cut the little chant for his 1972 *One Man Dog* album.)

It would be months before James could pick up a guitar again, but he continued moulding songs, some silly (two more songs about acid and another on peyote) and some serious stuff like 'Country Road', begun at Austen Riggs and polished during Vineyard wiles with Kootch in the summer of '69.

'Country Road' was a rustic hymn of resurrection, proclaiming the chance discovery of avenues leading beyond the encumbrances of his upbringing. James knew his family had little faith in what he felt was now unfolding for him musically ("Mama don't understand it/She wants to know where I've been") but the message was credible to fans of his generation simply because they wanted to believe in such a believer.

At Apple Records in London, however, confidence in the future was rapidly eroding. The Apple Corps was in fiscal chaos. The Beatles had been without real management since the death of Brian Epstein in August 1967, and there was no consensus in the group as to the best choice for an overseer. John Lennon had hired former Rolling Stones manager Allen Klein in January 1969 to handle his personal affairs and was pushing the other Beatles to take him on as management, too.

McCartney resisted, knowing Klein was on the outs with the Stones and preferring reputable show business attorney Lee Eastman, father of his wife Linda. Although Paul was outvoted regarding the Klein hire at an Apple board meeting on February 3, 1969, he won a crucial concession: the Eastman and Eastman law firm became the Beatles general counsel on February 4.

Klein was nonetheless authorised to conduct an audit of Apple's corporate finances, and became the Apple business manager on March 21. Klein moved quickly to eliminate excess staff and unprofitable wings of Apple (of which there were many, among them Apple Retail). At one point Klein even fired The Beatles' boyhood friend, Neil Aspinall (arguably the most honest and capable organisational presence in the Beatles camp, as time would reaffirm), but the group balked at this outrage and Klein relented. Veteran Beatles press officer and informal staff historian Derek Taylor was also retained.

Among those who resigned from Apple of their own accord was Peter Asher, who briefly served as A&R chief at MGM Records UK, and gave a statement to the British music paper, *Disc And Music Echo*:

> "When I joined Apple the idea was that it would be different from the other companies in the record business. Its policy was to help people and be generous. It didn't mean actually I had a tremendous amount of freedom; I was always in danger of one Beatle saying, 'Yes, that's a great idea, go ahead,' and then another coming in and saying he didn't know anything about it. But it did mean that it was a nice company to work for. Now all that's changed. There's a new concentrative policy from what I can see and it's lost a great deal of its original feeling."

Returning the favour of two years earlier, Asher next approached Taylor and said he'd like to manage him.

"Let's give this thing a try," James remembers Peter suggesting, and it was done. The first order of business was gaining Taylor's release from his Apple deal, and Asher asked McCartney if he'd consider tearing up James' contract, much as The Beatles had simply given away the apparel in the bygone Apple boutique when it was closed.

"So James Taylor came," McCartney recalled of their meeting, "and he and Peter said, 'We don't want to stay on the label. We like you, we like the guys, but we don't like this Klein guy and we don't like what's going to happen.' "

Klein was against a no-strings release of Taylor, insisting there at least be a sizeable payment made. McCartney refused, as did the other Beatles, who felt, as Paul put it, "We should just give him his contract back."

"Klein said, 'We should keep him!' " as McCartney recalled ruefully for this writer in March 2001. "But I said, 'Look man, we're artists here, this is the idea of Apple. We should let him go. He's given us a great album, he's made money for us, why do we need to keep him in a slave thing?'

"So I think he [James] was grateful for that," added McCartney. "I hate to see artists keeping each other to contracts, it's not cool."

(While Klein would prove effective in renegotiating The Beatles' deal with Capitol/EMI, the relationship remained turbulent, with eventual lawsuits culminating in a January 1977 settlement of $4.2 million to Klein, who left Apple. Aspinall became the company's head administrator, a position he retains to this day, and Apple prospered.)

Asher swiftly lined up a deal in the autumn of '69 with Warners Bros. Records executive vice-president and general manager Joe Smith; final details of the contract were negotiated between October 10 and 15. The plan called for Taylor and Asher to convene in Los Angeles and begin recording Taylor's first Warner Bros. album in December of '69. "The deal," Smith summarised, "was they got $20,000 going into the studio, and $20,000 when they finished."

Tired of lolling beside the ocean in the Vineyard, Taylor was raring to go. "Both my hands and feet were in plaster for a long time," he recollected. "I think it built up a lot of energy because as soon as I got out of the casts I went into Sunset Sound in LA and it was explosive, the album went so fast."

Certainly Taylor had a backlog of fine material, including 'Fire And Rain', 'Sunny Skies', 'Country Road', and a lilting ballad called 'Blossom'. And then there was this "cowboy lullaby" he'd conceived for the toddler nephew who was his namesake.

12

That's Why I'm Here

"**S**weet Baby James," whose proper name was James Richmond Taylor, was born on May 16, 1967, the first son of Alex Taylor and his bride of four months, the former Brent Blackmer. Alex and Brent were hometown sweethearts who wed in January '67 and the going-steady innocence of their six-year romance acquired a less casual tone when she had to accompany Alex to UNC Wilmington as his young bride. Suddenly every step they took seemed to *matter*.

Alex abruptly quit the school in outrage after an English instructor accused him of cribbing a paper on birth control from a magazine article – Alex called her "a narrow-minded Southern bitch" and stalked out of the class.

Alex and Brent moved to Atlanta, Georgia, living there for a year and a half as Alex became acquainted with the recording scene in nearby Macon through his brother Livingston. At this point, Liv had been playing music in public for payment since 1963. At 13, Liv had been in a folk trio in Chapel Hill with guitarist Paul Collins and singer Kim Packer, their biggest gig being a set at the local country club in which they covered Kingston Trio and Peter, Paul & Mary hits. Liv was also briefly in a rock combo at Guy B. Phillips Junior High.

"I was in that junior high when Jack Kennedy was shot," Livingston recalled in the spring of 2000, "and Jack Kennedy was really disliked in the South – it was visceral. And I'll never forget a classmate saying, 'Jack Kennedy shot! Heck, I'm not crying 'cause'n he's shot, I'm crying 'cause I didn't get to him myself!'

"It wasn't said out of hate," Liv advised, "it was just a 13-year-old mimicking the world around him there at the time." Still, it was greatly at odds with the liberal world-view in the Taylor household as well as Liv's own idealistic heart.

Since '66, while he was completing his secondary school education at McLean's Arlington School, Liv had been making progress in his own musical objectives. Liv's first serious attempt at songwriting was an awkward effort – "A terrible song," he admitted almost immediately – "called 'I'm Searching For A Miracle'." But Liv's second try proved an eloquent plea for brotherhood and quality companionship called 'Good Friends'. He added the latter song to his repertoire as a fledgling folkie, and it stayed in his sets for the next four decades.

After Liv's parents saw his grades at the Arlington School, he said they "pointed out that there were other things in life aside from academics." Liv took that as a signal to seek acceptance in the music industry rather than a college or university.

"It became very clear to me academia was not going to be an option," he recalled in 2000. "When I was going to Arlington I was boarding with a family in Boston named O'Neill, and I'd go up to my room in the attic and take my inexpensive Gibson guitar and get down and work on my songs. Then I'd go down to these clubs on Charles Street like The Sword In The Stone, which was run by a fellow named Mark Edwards, and there'd be 15 other people competing with me at an audition to play there. They usually looked, played and sang better than me, but the only difference was they didn't *want* the job as much as I did. I played there half-a-dozen times.

"And then I sent a tape to Manny Greenhill, who had managed Joan Baez for a while and was active in the folk scene, and he was enthusiastic and got me into a show at a YMCA in Worcester and that led to some shows at Boston University. All this happened in 1968."

Liv had been turned down for record contracts by Elektra Records and Atlantic Records, as he struggled to establish himself performing at hoot nights and open-mike stints on the Cambridge-Boston folk circuit, a high point being a well-received slot on a Boston University bill with Joni Mitchell. The latter night was a direly needed restorative for the nearly disheartened Liv, who was beginning to spend as much time on his table hockey habit as on his largely unheard songs. "When I saw people having a good time and enjoying themselves as I played my music," he wrote months afterwards of the enthusiastic reception as an opener for Mitchell, "I knew this is what I wanted to do for a time, regardless of whether I did well or not."

A strangely encouraging childhood image etched in his Liv's head was of father Ike, his arms outstretched in the Chapel Hill kitchen as he sang convincingly (despite a sketchy grasp of the *My Fair Lady* score) that "with a little bit of luck one can get it all – and not get hooked", while Trudy responded with *Porgy And Bess*-implanted wisdom that "it ain't necessarily so." Such tableaux reminded Liv music was the stuff of pluck, demanding an industrious heart, a healthy self-deprecation and the resolve to protect one's ego from easy punctures.

Noted Boston music critic Jon Landau, who met Liv through the McLean music therapist and became a fan, counselled the singer to persevere, telling him his literate songwriting merited a major label deal. Landau's suggestion to approach the Macon, Georgia-based Capricorn studio and record label outfit proved fortuitous.

The Capricorn organisation was run by Phil Walden, former manager/ booking agent of Otis Redding and Sam & Dave, current career guide for The Allman Brothers and the architect in '69 of the Capricorn Records label he'd formed 50 miles from Atlanta with Atlantic Records' vice president Jerry Wexler.

"Phil was working out of Macon, Georgia," Wexler would remember, "and had this big management company. He said to me, 'Would Atlantic back me in a studio in Macon?' I said, 'Better than that, let's set up a label and we'll distribute it.' We called it Capricorn Records because that was our astrological sign – which I don't believe in, but it was a handy rubric."

Walden believed in Livingston Taylor, even if the parent Atlantic office in New York City had passed, and he added him to a roster that included the Allman Brothers, whose début Capricorn album, *The Allman Brothers Band*, would appear in stores at the end of '69. Liv formed his own publishing company, No Exit-Taylor Made, for his songs, and signed with the powerful and progressive Broadcast Music

Incorporated royalty and rights administration organisation.

"Jon Landau had asked me to fly down along with him to Macon in 1968," said Liv, "because he was researching an article on Otis Redding, who had died" – on December 10, 1967 in a plane crash in Wisconsin – "and Macon was a sleepy, sleepy town. Phil was a bit of an outcast and a wild man who had a little studio and management office on 235 Cotton Avenue, in a downstairs office with a sad-looking secretary and some bad fluorescent lighting. But he liked me, and there it was: we were in show biz!"

Walden had a top-tier group of session players at Capricorn Sounds Studios for his recording, with Pete Carr on guitar, Paul Hornsby on keyboards, Robert Popwell on bass and Johnny Sandlin on drums. Landau was producing the eponymous album, which was scheduled for release in the summer of 1970.

"We made a lot of the album in Macon, and then we came up to Boston to finish off a few vocals," Liv later reflected, "and then we mixed it in Detroit because Jon was recording an album with a group called MC5."

The songs on *Livingston Taylor* sounded optimistic in their tunefulness but were scathingly honest in their lyrical content, a good example of a sweet cradlesong with a searing subtext being 'Hush A Bye', its verses concerning boyhood let-downs and fallen idols. Liv sang how he "did pray to be like you, to be part of your life" about a man he once looked up to, only to accept at length that he was "lost to richer lands, your friends to foot the price."

Familiarity with the verses moved Ike Taylor to avouch to *Rolling Stone* reporter Timothy Crouse that he "felt it was addressed to me."

Dr Taylor was correct, but the rest of the Taylor family could tarry no longer around Ike, waiting for attention and inclusion that never came. As for Ike and Trudy's marriage, it was over; the Taylors legally separated in '69, Ike moving into a small ranch house not far from the Morgan Creek Road home while Trudy, feeling extremely lonely, stayed on in the Japanese Modern "inn". There was no longer a single rallying point for Taylor reunions. As individuals the family membership was undergoing a kind of forced separation from each other coupled with a widening search for purpose outside the ties that bind.

Alex had tried to get permission to do some demos at Capricorn Sound Studios, but he continued to come away dejected. Seemed people there all liked the bearish, affable, R&B loving fellow but couldn't take him seriously as a recording artist.

The eldest Taylor son was still ferreting about for a niche for himself, and his latest strategy was to move his own family to the Vineyard permanently, with the intention of opening a record store on the island in the summer of '70. His relationship with wife Brent appeared stable, having been with her for a cumulative six years, but at 23 (and he looked ten years older) with a child and no visible vocation, matters were becoming worrisome.

The frustrated Alex and his new family were in North Carolina visiting his parents when brother James contacted them to say he wanted to come from Massachusetts to see, for the first time, the little boy named after him.

James had just retrieved his 1968 Cortina GT (shipped trans-Atlantic from England) at the docks and was tickled to be reunited with the same car in which he'd well-nigh terrorised Swinging London. Stimulated by the liberty of his newly cast-less hands and feet – plus the open road and the controlled substances he'd imbibed to assist in completing the 20-hour journey – James suddenly got a notion for a song as he was motoring south on Route 95.

The melody took shape just outside Richmond, Virginia. It would be a cowboy tune, but also a lullaby, intended as a loving keepsake for Alex and Brent's two-year-old boy. Staring at passing headlights as he ground his teeth in chemically fuelled concentration, the first line fell out of the night sky in a synapse-sized flash: "There is a young cowboy, who lives on the range . . ."

Besides coming face to face in Chapel Hill with the adorable, blond baby James, Taylor also confronted the withered state of his parents' bond as a result of Ike's overwork and dipsomania.

Ike had aged drastically, his features furrowed and bloated, with deep creases leading from the corners of his eyes to the edges of his cheeks, and his jowls marked by sharp folds on either side of his mouth. His thick walrus moustache was neatly trimmed but accentuated the often sombre set of his jaws. Friends were shocked to see his haggard appearance in a press conference photo with Democratic Congressman Hugh

Johnson in the May 1, 1969 edition of the *Raleigh News-Observer*, Ike shown leafing through a report from a committee on the Physician Shortage in Rural North Carolina. The report put North Carolina "near the bottom of the list" in its supply of qualified physicians, with only 69 doctors per 100,000 persons, compared with the national average of 97.

Among the report's recommendations were construction of new hospitals and increasing the output of the state's three medical colleges, with the emphasis away from specialisation and towards general practitioners better suited to care-giving in rural areas. To effect these changes, the expansion of the medical school at UNC-Chapel Hill was called for. What this meant in real terms for Dr Ike Taylor was a great deal more stress as dean of the medical school.

Addressing the medical school Senior Banquet sponsored by the Medical Alumni Association at the Carolina Inn on May 30, 1969, Ike seemed so stiff, stilted and vacant-eyed that a visiting colleague leaned over to Trudy Taylor and said, "Tell me, what is the matter with Ike?" His wife waited until after the ceremonies to confide the truth: the advance of his alcoholism was finally affecting the one thing that still held his heart: his job.

It was by the unwritten laws of such Piedmont-bred civility that Ike Taylor's alcoholism was tolerated – even within the precincts of one of the nation's top medical schools – until it brought him to the very threshold of personal and professional ruin. For even as Ike was preparing for the divorce Trudy requested in '69, he was also in preparation for his premature retirement at the age of 50 as dean of the medical school. Despite a brilliant mind and bold administrative talents, his private afflictions had hurt his job performance and damaged his standing in academic circles.

"Alcoholism is a nasty disease," Trudy would fret, "and as *early* as 1964 I could tell Ike was losing control of his judgment – yet he still became dean. I would have never considered divorcing him except for his alcoholism, but his problem was a very severe one, and I didn't know how to help him or keep the family on course in the face of it, it was so upsetting.

"His father and his grandfather struggled with alcoholism," she added, "and they didn't fare well. To make matters worse, Alex started drinking earlier than my other children, and that became a new problem."

Alex's excessive drinking and good-time instincts could be dismissed as a mere carry-over from his college days, given the hands-off, "Do Your Own Thing" philosophies of the time, so he was viewed benignly as still enjoying an elongated late adolescence. Trudy knew better, but her attention was also divided.

Notwithstanding the break-up, Trudy still had many enduring responsibilities as a faculty wife, and she changed her personal stationery to reflect the awkward new situation. The new letterhead identified her as "Mrs. Isaac Taylor", with the usual Chapel Hill address set in smaller type below. As missives began to course through the mail under this new heading, they looked at first glance like the correspondence of a widow.

Many of Trudy's letters were addressed to Washington, DC in protest of the steadily expanding United States troop commitment to civil war in the post-colonial US client state of Vietnam – divided during 1954 into a Communist-ruled North Vietnam and nominally democratic South Vietnam. Since 1961, America had sent soldiers to defend the South against the Communist-led guerillas (the Viet Cong) seeking to overthrow a corrupt regime propped up by the US government. After North Vietnamese gunboats allegedly attacked US destroyers, President Lyndon Johnson asked Congress to pass the Tonkin Gulf Resolution requesting more troops – 550,000 by 1969 – and his successor President Richard Nixon regarded it as his own mandate to escalate (until it was repealed in 1970).

"I was a letter writer," Trudy acknowledged, "at the beginning of the Vietnam War – much to Ike's chagrin – who did *not* want me to write letters because he had a state job. Still, I wrote every two weeks to someone in government. I wrote to Lyndon Johnson, [Vice President] Hubert Humphrey, and Lady Bird Johnson, one or the other, during the whole Vietnam War. From the very beginning I knew it wasn't right, and I got very upset with the whole Tonkin Bay thing. I knew it was a fake, and that they had manufactured this scenario to get us deeper in.

"Johnson didn't want that Vietnam War any more than anyone else did, but we were already committed when Jack Kennedy died.

[President Kennedy was assassinated by gunfire in Dallas, Texas on November 22, 1963.] Johnson wanted both guns and butter, but you can't do that; you've got to pay taxes to support a war, and our deficits were all tied up in what we paid for that war. Johnson in his heart of hearts wanted to usher in an era of egalitarianism in our society. Jack Kennedy came in [to the White House in 1961] with a strong push from his father [Joseph P. Kennedy]. But when he made his brother Attorney General I saw the dynastic thing he and his family were into, and they're still doing it. It cost them terribly."

Trudy's outspoken perspectives on the Vietnam War, her distaste for political families with dynastic inclinations, and her sense of urgency towards social equality were all stances that chafed against Southern attitudes. "But people around us in the university appeared to share our ideas," she recalled.

Like her own parents, Trudy was a rugged individualist who admired original aspirations, original strength, original achievements. But progressivism in the New South as epitomised by North Carolina prized sure manners and ritualistic deference over substantive action. One could be tolerant of new ideas, and kindly towards the less fortunate, but civility was the virtue that surpassed all others, and open personal conflict was its nemesis.

Liv had decided to maintain a respectful distance from the rest of the other Taylors, rattled by the unspoken rivalries taking shape as he and his siblings picked music as their guiding light and lodestone. Shunning the South as a locus for his adult life and chary about the Vineyard's remoteness, Liv and long-time girlfriend Margaret "Maggie" Shea found a cottage surrounded by fields and orchards in a quiet, semi-rural corner of Weston, Massachusetts, yet still convenient to the Massachusetts Turnpike for touring purposes.

In Kate Taylor's case she also declined to continue living in Carolina, opting for the Vineyard, where in 1970 she shifted her few things from her mother's Chilmark beach-front house (which became Trudy's permanent northern residence after her divorce from Ike was signed three years later) and into a one-time bakery storefront on the Vineyard that was converted by an island sculptor into a single-room artist's studio complete with Franklin stove.

Kate gleaned some songwriting and performing insights during a brief enrolment at Boston's Berklee School of Music, and signed a recording deal through Peter Asher after auditioning for him outside London (with James providing accompaniment) during what she termed an "impromptu trip there in the summer of '69; we just stayed with a friend in London and just prowled around. James and I went out to Peter and Betsy Asher's country house outside London. They had an empty swimming pool, and James and I sat down in the bottom of the pool and just sang together.

"A few months later, at the end of the summer," as Kate recollected, "I got a call from Peter while I was still living at home in Chilmark with my mom, and Peter asked me if I would like to make a record. I said, 'You bet!' Then I went out to LA and we got a record deal with Atlantic-Cotillion."

But recording for the venture had been repeatedly plagued by false starts due to what Kate called "nerves".

She was due back in Los Angeles early in 1970 to begin serious recording for Atlantic's Cotillion subsidiary – on which the forthcoming soundtrack record from the recent Woodstock festival of August 15–17 ("Three Days of Peace and Music") was also slated to be released. The Ashers, who also had a home in Los Angeles, had asked Kate to stay with them during the recording process. Peter was now serving as her producer as well as her manager, and he thought Kate would feel more comfortable living under his roof as the album progressed rather than in the less impersonal environment of a hotel.

As for the soft-spoken, sandy-haired Hugh, who was and would remain the child closest to Trudy on a daily basis, he now lived with his girlfriend in a Vineyard bungalow without plumbing or electricity that was reputed by local lore to have been owned by a harpooner on a whaling ship that speared Moby Dick. (Actually Moby Dick was mythical, but *Moby Dick, Or The White Whale* (1851), by Herman Melville, an American novelist of Scottish descent, drew from Melville's own harsh 1841–42 experiences on the New England whaling ship *Acushnet*, as well as the spectacular sinking of the Nantucket whaler *Essex* in 1822 after it was charged by a massive rogue whale.)

While fond of boats and fishing, and open to performing with his siblings whenever asked for assorted community benefit shows, the skinniest and shyest of the Taylor offspring was concentrating on learning carpentry from a master tradesman on-island named Emmett Carroll.

★ ★ ★

The Taylor clan was changing, shifting, and all the while peeking out of the corners of their respective eyes at James, who had somehow become the most independent and self-reliant pup of the litter. With a $40,000 record contract to his credit, a new spring in his loping step, and Tom Rush's rendition of 'Something In The Way She Moves' already a staple on New England radio beside Rush's interpretations of work by rising new singer-songwriters like Joni Mitchell ('Circle Game', 'Urge For Going') and Jackson Browne ('Shadow Dream Song'), James was considered by his own kin to be the musical Taylor most likely to succeed.

"During '69, in her house overlooking Stonewall and Quitsa Ponds, Trudy used to have this poster on her wall," recalled Danny Kortchmar in Martha's Vineyard in the summer of 2000, thinking back on something that spooked him over 30 years before. "It was a store-bought poster, a photo of a lonely young man with a guitar strapped on his back. I remember standing in the house looking at that picture and I thought, 'That's what James will become, that image.' And he did become it."

But Kortchmar felt that consequence was less a matter of calculation than of desperate forces colliding: "Young kids always want somebody close to their age to admire. James seemed like the perfect guy for the time. As a young man in his early twenties, his aura was of somebody who was sensitive but not feminine, handsome but not too macho. He had that air of Southern gentility but also the New England look of a fisherman or a farmer.

"But when fame was thrust upon the Taylors through James, it changed the family dynamic completely," Kortchmar decided. "The idea that all the Taylor kids had been headed straight into music isn't accurate. I watched that happen, and it didn't come about naturally. What happened was that the break-up of Ike and Trudy was tearing the family apart – since it was because of Ike's drinking problems and he had been the leader and the most respected Taylor. Now that had turned dark, too dark to deal with it.

157

"With James' fame the hierarchical clout that Ike had was over-turned, it was over," said Kootch. "James became the leader, and the fact he didn't want any part of that only made it more attractive to everybody, inside and outside the family. James didn't want that power, so giving it to him – making him take it – almost seemed generous or noble to do. James was so confused by all this that over time it would almost destroy him. But at the start all the other Taylors, including Trudy, obviously felt that James' way was the way to go. Either they followed James, or they turned toward Ike and the darkness around him. So James' path of escape automatically became the new plan.

"But it was even heavier and weirder than that," Kootch assured. "Ike was a doctor, a man of medicine, and people coming up to James began to act like James was some sort of preordained healer, like his dad, instead of a guy in deep need himself of some healing."

During the interval between Thanksgiving and Christmas, James had an appointment in Los Angeles and a lot of expectations to fulfil. Peter Asher and Joe Smith, the staff of Warner Bros. Records Inc. were waiting for him to begin an album to be christened *Sweet Baby James*.

Luckily, so was Kortchmar, whom James had solicited for help on the sessions scheduled at Sunset Sound studios, since Danny had already been living in LA for some time.

Kootch had joined a group called The City that issued an album on Lou Adler's Ode Records in 1968 called *Now That Everything's Been Said*. The City included drummer Jim Gordon, and bassist Charles Larkey, the latter originally introducing Kootch to his lady friend, the chief vocalist and songwriter of the group, who was about to start cutting her first solo album at Hollywood's Crystal Sound facility with Danny's assistance. This 26-year-old female singer-songwriter, a native of Brooklyn, NY who attended Queens College and did extra-curricular vocal demos with schoolmate Paul Simon, was better known by her writing nom de plume as co-author (with ex-husband Gerry Goffin) of such hits as 'Will You Love Me Tomorrow', 'Up On The Roof' and 'Go Away Little Girl' – namely, Carole King.

13

Migration

Carole King bought a quaint, castle-like stucco home below Wonderland Avenue on winding Appian Way in Laurel Canyon. The pointy round tower dominating the centre of the house rose over a high stand of hedges like a vision out of a fairytale, and it epitomised the charmed existence many musicians from the East were convinced they'd find in the booming pop music marketplace of Los Angeles. (It was also just a stone's throw from Blue Jay Way, site of the spectral sonnet to jetlag that George Harrison wrote in August '67 for The Beatles' *Magical Mystery Tour*.)

After a full career writing songs for other artists, King was eager to get her second wind as a performer of her own output – a path presaged by The Beach Boys and The Beatles, whose members now wrote, arranged and often produced their own material. (Although The Beatles had rendered Goffin-King's 'Chains' back in '63, besides covering the Luther Dixon-Wes Farrell song on the B-side of The Shirelles' 'Will You Love Me Tomorrow', a piece of Brill Building teen pop personified: 'Boys'.)

Previous steps by King in a more autonomous direction had been a short-lived indie label she founded with New York journalist Al Aronowitz, Tomorrow Records, which issued a King single, 'A Road To Nowhere'/'Some of Your Lovin' and then an album by band The

Myddle Class, whose bassist was Charlie Larkey, who became her second husband after her '68 divorce from Gerry Goffin was finalised. The Myddle Class saw sporadic airplay for singles 'Don't Look Back' and 'I Happen To Love You', but nothing to justify sustaining the act, which broke up.

The subsequent self-titled album by The City was an effort by King to reconsolidate musical friendships from New York in the fertile terrain of Hollywood. Reunited inside Armand Steiner's Sound Recorders facility in Hollywood, Kortchmar and Larkey knew each other from The Fugs, with whom Kootch played for about six months, including work on their 1968 *Tenderness Junction* album, the outrageous rock 'n satire act's first LP for Reprise. Afterwards, Kootch was part of Clear Light, a folk-flavoured LA psychedelic band led by vocalist Cliff DeYoung that Doors producer Paul Rothschild signed to Elektra Records. Kootch joined just as Clear Light was nearing its fade-out.

Next, Kootch entered The City, whose studio dates marked his initial legitimate recording experience, while DeYoung shifted to television acting (and later solo recording), and Clear Light keyboardist Ralph Schuckett became part of the Gary Usher-produced Columbia Records act, The Peanut Butter Conspiracy ('It's A Happening Thing', 'Then Came Love'), when they cut their third album in '69 for the Challenge label. Clear Light's two drummers were Michael Ney and Dallas Taylor. Taylor later enlisted with Crosby, Stills & Nash, playing on prime cuts on their Atlantic début LP (released May 20, 1969), like 'Suite: Judy Blue Eyes' and 'Long Time Gone'.

The latter CS&N song was penned by former Byrds charter member David Crosby, who had composed it in the early hours of June 5, 1968 after Democratic presidential candidate Robert F. Kennedy was shot at 12.15 a.m. in a Los Angeles hotel following a speech proclaiming his victory in the June 4 California primary. Like The Byrds, whose seminal soldering of folk and rock transformed LA's musical landscape, CS&N were turning out intricate, acoustic-based pieces whose heady harmonies and ringing guitar filagrees belied an acrid aftertaste of disgust with America's squandered ideals.

The aim was to create a canon of contemporary, socially conscious songs that had the resonance of America's classic folk statements. And The Byrds had first set the pace; between 1965 and early 1970 they covered folk material both old- and new-fangled: Pete Seeger's 'Turn! Turn! Turn! (To Everything There Is A Season)' – which Seeger had adapted from Ecclesiastes and cut in '62 after his publisher begged for another song as popular as Pete's revision with The Weavers of Leadbelly's 'Goodnight Irene' – or Seeger's '58 arrangement of Welsh poet Idris Davies' 'The Bells Of Rhymney'; also large chunks of Bob Dylan's catalogue, most notably 'Mr. Tambourine Man', 'Chimes Of Freedom', 'All I Really Want To Do', 'Spanish Harlem Incident', 'It's All Over Now, Baby Blue', 'Lay Down Your Weary Tune', 'The Times They Are A-Changin', 'My Back Pages', and 'Nothing Was Delivered', as well as work by Woody Guthrie ('Pretty Boy Floyd', 'Deportee [Plane Wreck At Los Gatos]') and such favourites by traditional North Carolina country folk artist Doc Watson as 'Black Mountain Rag/Soldier's Joy'.

Even after Crosby left The Byrds for CS&N, the remaining Byrds (Jim McGuinn, Chris Hillman, Michael Clarke, Clarence White) continued to cut a wealth of world-weary allegorical hymns, such as 'Goin' Back' and 'Wasn't Born To Follow', recorded for 1968's *The Notorious Byrd Brothers*, with the latter track also incorporated into the soundtrack of the hit 1969 film *Easy Rider*.

However, those last two songs were penned by Gerry Goffin and Carole King, with The City's drummer Jim Gordon playing on 'Goin' Back' – just as he had when the song had earlier seen release on The City's *Now That Everything's Been Said*.

The high, hip visibility of these songs constituted a crucial turning point for the Goffin-King team, who seemed in grave peril of falling permanently out of vogue as pop reinvented itself in the late '60s. The couple had been a potent creative force in pop since marrying in 1958 after meeting at Queens College and placing their first big hit, 'Will You Love Me Tomorrow' with The Shirelles in 1960 via Don Kirshner and Al Nevin's Aldon Music publishing firm in New York's fabled Brill Building. (Columbia Records chief Mitch Miller had nixed the piece as ill-suited for mannered pop crooner Johnny Mathis.)

The husband and wife songwriting alliance thrived throughout the early '60s after Aldon was sold in 1963 to Columbia Pictures/Screen Gems and Kirshner became president of the corporation's Screen Gems music division, with Goffin and King giving The Chiffons' a Top 5 smash that very summer with 'One Fine Day'.

The two songsmiths were now well-seasoned and interested in bypassing teen pop clients for the earnest, sober-sided and more thoughtful sounds of the British invasion and California rock. Goffin–King songs were cut in the mid-'60s by Manfred Mann ('Oh No, Not My Baby'), Herman's Hermits ('I'm Into Something Good') and The Animals ('Don't Bring Me Down'), and one of their last and finest major hits strictly as a writing duo – with assistance from producer Jerry Wexler – was 1967's '(You Make Me Feel Like) A Natural Woman' for Aretha Franklin. But Goffin and King's tentative foothold in the sophisticated West Coast scene was typified by 'Pleasant Valley Sunday', a saccharine '67 effort that nevertheless became one of the Screen Gems-spawned Monkees' brightest hits (number three on the Hot 100).

Thus the acceptance on a serious rock plateau that The Byrds' pair of covers represented came as a welcome relief to Goffin and King. And as their private and professional paths began to diverge (with Goffin and former Electric Flag keyboardist Barry Goldberg co-authoring early '70s hits like Gladys Knight's 'I've Got To Use My Imagination'), King found she could gain credibility alone in contemporary spheres on the strength of her solid, do-it-yourself musicality.

The owner of Ode Records, The City's label, was Lou Adler, who'd co-written songs with Herb Alpert for Jan & Dean ('Baby Talk') and Sam Cooke ('Wonderful World'); since his time as a west coast executive at Aldon/Screen Gems, Adler formed business ties with King while building his Dunhill label with the *Easy Rider* soundtrack and acts like The Mamas and The Papas. After serving as one of the sponsors of the Monterey Pop Festival, Adler sold Dunhill to ABC Records and founded Ode, launching it with a roster anchored by Los Angeles group Spirit (who scored a number 25 *Billboard* hit in '69 with 'I Got A Line On You'), and The City. But The City's ability to tour was hampered by King's early stage fright and a record distribution snafu; when Ode switched its distribution agreement from CBS to A&M, the well-reviewed album's fortunes stalled as Adler hesitated to reservice it. "I pulled it back from CBS," he said of *Now That Everything's Been Said*, "but decided against re-releasing it on A&M."

Publishing-wise, The City's best songs were not allowed to languish, though, and another Goffin-King track on *Now That Everything's Been Said*, 'The Old Sweet Roll', became a number 14 hit in 1970 for Blood, Sweat & Tears under its original parenthetical subtitle, "Hi-De-Ho".

All of these issues and obstacles helped foster the climate for King's trial by fire as a solo act. Determined to forge a second act in the ongoing drama of her artistic growth, King worked on her vocals and the warm, almost conversant aura of her piano figures at the Appian Way house, which she shared with Larkey and her young daughters by Goffin, Louise and Sherry. In addition, she wrote more direct, emotionally incisive material, some of it still with Goffin but increasing amounts of it with new collaborator Toni Stern.

With over a decade in the music business, dating back to her late-'50s writing/arranging experiments as part of a vocal group at Lincoln High School called the Co-sines, Carole King was adept at the whole-souled art of presenting a song for make-or-break approval, pounding out its percussive and passionate essence to demonstrate its value as a vehicle for imparting personal truths. That's how songs were sold to publishers in the Tin Pan Alley modus carried on in the Brill Building. And now, on the threshold of the '70s, as artists sought to eliminate the middlemen and surrogates between audiences and originators, she realised she was uncommonly equipped for the task. ("People in the biz had treasured her demos for years," as James Taylor himself knew.) And so, at long last, King prepared to make her inaugural album under her own name.

But first she had agreed to assist Kootch's chum James complete his send-off project for Warner Brothers. It was a transitional period at the label, when new, more musically attuned leadership in President Mo Ostin and jocular cohort Joe Smith (the pair known with affectionate regard around Warners' casual West Coast offices as "Mo & Joe, The Gold Dust Twins") was supplanting a stilted corporate regime under former chief executive Mike Maitland.

Through the efforts of Ostin, Smith, and an A&R staff of Richard Perry, Ted Templeman, Russ Titelman, Lenny Waronker, Andrew Wickham and others, Burbank, California-based Warner/Reprise Records replaced an ageing roster whose decade high point was the 1966 Grammy Awards, wherein Frank Sinatra (who founded Reprise in 1960 and sold it to Warners in '63) copped Album of the Year honours for *Sinatra, A Man And His Music,* and Record of the Year and Best Male Vocal Performance for 'Strangers In The Night', while The Anita Kerr Quartet earned Best Performance By A Vocal Group for 'A Man And A Woman', and Bill Cosby clinched the Best Comedy trophy for *Wonderfulness.*

In April '67 Ostin signed Arlo Guthrie, Woody's son, to Reprise, sending him into the studio to hatch his storytelling *Alice's Restaurant* album. Later in April Ostin brought Jimi Hendrix to Reprise and issued Hendrix's 'Hey Joe' single in the US. On August 15, Waronker coaxed Randy Newman into the fold, and Ostin and Wickham inked a Reprise deal with Joni Mitchell in December. Neil Young, formerly of Buffalo Springfield, joined Reprise in July 1968 and Van Morrison arrived in September, followed a month later by Jethro Tull.

While managing with folk veterans Peter, Paul & Mary to reap concluding gold (*Peter Paul And Mommy,* 1969) and double platinum LPs (*10 Years Together/The Best Of*) with the label, the 11–year-old recording subsidiary of Warner Bros. Pictures (incorporated as Warner Bros. Records, Inc. on March 25, 1958) found its best sellers on the eve of a new decade were tepid stereophonic patio fodder like the Association ('Cherish', 'Windy', 'Never My Love'), Sinatra's daughter Nancy ('These Boots Are Made For Walkin', 'Sugar Town', 'Somethin' Stupid' with her dad); and the spoken word dreck of sad-sack poet Rod McKuen and collaborator Anita Kerr (whose joint concept *The Sea* went gold in December '68). Holding up the bottom line was a crinkle-eyed, martini-tilting infantry comprised of Sinatra's Las Vegas 'Rat Pack', particularly woozy-voiced Dean Martin (who earned four gold albums between 1967–69, including *Welcome To My World,* two *Greatest Hits* volumes and *Gentle On My Mind*), and self-dramatising male saloon diva Sammy Davis, Jr (who issued a hit '69 collection, *I've Gotta Be Me*).

The same month James Taylor was signed, Canadian folkie Gordon Lightfoot (whose 'Early Morning Rain' and 'For Lovin' Me' were hits for Peter, Paul & Mary) was also courted and acquired; *Alice's Restaurant* went gold; and Joe Smith got The Grateful Dead into the Warner Bros. stable. In short order were added Ry Cooder, The Youngbloods' Jesse Colin Young, Frank Zappa's Bizarre/Straight label (himself, alone and with The Mothers Of Invention; The GTOs, Wild Man Fisher, Alice Cooper, Captain Beefheart), and groups Fleetwood Mac, The

Beach Boys, Black Sabbath, Deep Purple, Earth, Wind & Fire, and The Doobie Brothers, who all clambered onto a less moribund bandwagon with Bugs Bunny as their wisecracking mascot.

Where once there had mostly been novelty records, post-War ginmill Muzak, and bad poetry on Warner/Reprise, with Francis Albert Sinatra barring rock and roll in his capacity as "Chairman of the Board" – an honorific title bolstered by his one-third interest in the music firm and a three-picture pact in '63 with the film division for merging Reprise with Warners – now the rejuvenated record company was poised to make a more competitive dent in the real appetites of the music marketplace as informed by the nation at large.

Richard Nixon was still in the White House, vigorously prosecuting a Vietnam War much of America's citizenry considered immoral. A crowd of 250,000 anti-war protesters staged a single-file "March Against Death" in Washington, DC in November '69, with news breaking days later of the My Lai Massacre in which a US troop unit slaughtered a reported 450 unarmed South Vietnamese villagers, many of them defenceless women and children. These developments, plus charges of an illegal war being waged in Laos, contrasted with the peaceful assembly of 400,000 young people in August for the Woodstock Music and Art Fair in upstate New York. Increased public pressure pushed Nixon to pledge a Vietnam troop cut by April 1970 to 434,000 (a total reduction of 110,000 since he took office).

The economy was faltering, and morale was poor at home, where Ronald Reagan would soon begin his second term as the California's conservative Republican governor. Los Angeles County was an amazing hive of industrial vitality with a staggering 3.6 million registered passenger cars on its freeways, and Southern California's employment was pointed upwards, as Lockheed and McDonnell Douglas committed themselves to building airbuses designed to carry 250–350 persons. Such craft were in demand locally, as 20.8 million annual air passengers surged out through the long custard-coloured corridor of Los Angeles International airport, each of them longing to experience the sprawling empire of the sun.

One such pilgrim, a scarecrow-skinny, broad-shouldered wraith attired in bell-bottomed jeans, denim shirt and a ratty pea-coat, seemed a nasal-throated cross between populist folklore's young Abe Lincoln, popular literature's Icabod Crane, and parlour music's Stephen Foster. This was 21-year-old James Taylor, ambling through the pre-Christmas crush in the main LAX terminal en route to the Chateau Marmont Hotel, and whether anybody liked or fully understood it, he was gonna be a brand new kind of pop recording star.

Folk-rock was peaking on the band level, but it had broadened its base and raised its volume to where it had taken the electronics of the jet age and made them part of the studio mix, the concert draw, and the promotional scale surrounding them both.

Long before Crosby, Stills & Nash became high-decibel superfolkies in the wake of their Woodstock set, Dylan had already decisively electrified the folk agenda on July 25, 1965 at the Newport Folk Festival when he strapped on a Fender Stratocaster to hold forth with members of The Paul Butterfield Blues Band on 'Maggie's Farm', 'Like A Rolling Stone' and 'It Takes A Lot To Laugh, It Takes A Train To Cry' (then titled 'Phantom Engineer') as the crowd complained either for reasons of aesthetics (i.e. purism), auditory quality (i.e. a pathetic PA mix), or entertainment value (just three over-amped songs, Bob?).

Peter, Paul & Mary urged Dylan to sate the surly crowd by offering an unrehearsed one-man acoustic encore. Using a borrowed folk guitar and harp, Dylan's reluctant gesture yielded adequate readings of 'It's All Over Now, Baby Blue' and 'Mr. Tambourine Man'. But it was too little, too late. Both latter numbers would pervade either end of the decade as facets of The Byrds' repertoire, not Dylan's.

History is mostly unavoidable accidents made in public, and Dylan had handily antagonised a supposedly fragile form of music into an irreducible aural upheaval.

At a 1965 symposium in New York on the American folk revival, Ewan MacColl's Scottish temper got the best of his critical judgement and he attacked Dylan's poetry as "cultivated illiteracy". A nonplussed Phil Ochs politely advised MacColl that there were two authentic revolutions in popular music, and *neither* of them involved traditional folk music.

One revolution, Ochs assured, was an emphasis on "perceptive" songwriting, some of it with "protest" in its "poetry". The other revolution was the deepening integration of rhythm and blues and country-and-western idioms as spawned by Hank Williams, Chuck

Berry, Elvis Presley and Buddy Holly into the rock and roll ferment that had drowned out the quaint proprieties and studious musical chops of ageing big band adherents.

Folk could revive itself all it liked to genuinely winning effect, but traditional folk was still a scenic blue highway lying off the main drag, where in 1964, The Beatles had six US number one hits, with five more to follow in 1965.

Dylan himself knew all MacColl's moot arguments about poetry, which he never really claimed to dispense, or politics, which he'd always largely left to Pete Seeger, Dave Van Ronk, Tom Paxton, Tim Hardin, or Ochs.

But Dylan had little patience in discussing this vexatious mid-'60s cultural vectoring with Ochs himself when Ochs told him he initially thought Bob "could become Elvis Presley . . . Essentially he could physically represent rural America, all of America and put out fifteen gold records in a row . . . What happened then was The Beatles got in the way. Dylan wrote the lyrics, and The Beatles captured the mass music."

As Dylan barked back at Ochs, "The stuff you're writing is bullshit, because politics is bullshit. It's all unreal. The only thing that's real is inside you. Your feelings. Just look at the world you're writing about and you'll see you're wasting your time. The world is, well . . . it's just absurd."

In effect, Dylan was warning that Ochs was flattering himself for waiting at the station for a mystery train he couldn't comprehend, one that was bringing a far more personal style of songwriting and self-exposition – one whose exponents would protest the impersonal and counter the absurd by simply telling the bone truth on themselves. And this coming style, by the way, was one which Dylan had not (and would never) master, even though he made fitful attempts in 1969–70 with his sparse-selling *Self-Portrait* and *New Morning* albums.

This, then, is exactly where Taylor came in as he headed towards Hollywood's Sunset Strip, with Carole King, Danny Kortchmar and Peter Asher awaiting him, each happy to do all he or she could to help James' cause.

★　★　★

The musicians who congregated or got called into Sunset Sound for the two weeks and $8,000 worth of recording necessary to get *Sweet Baby James* on tape were a well-picked covey of kindred players. The majority of the tracking was done by a nucleus of Taylor on guitar and vocals, Kootch on second guitar (usually electric) as he doled out rhythm and his characteristic arpeggio-laden leads, and King on her crisply expressive piano.

Arrayed in concentric circles around this trio for various songs was a gathering of astute instrumentalists. Pedal steel ace Red Rhodes, who appeared with The Byrds on 'Goin' Back', supplied all the sinous sighs and whines on the songs, commencing with opening cut 'Sweet Baby James', while Chris Darrow did the nimble fiddling. Bass was contributed at one juncture or another by Poco's Randy Meisner, with assistance from Robby West and John London. Jack Bielan did the subtly Stax-Volt inclined brass charts, and the marvellously astringent drum textures and sticking accents were the bounty of brilliant session percussionist Russ Kunkel. Everyone chipped in on back-up vocals as the urgency arose, and the final menu resembled nothing so much as a shimmering country-pop strain of chamber music.

The songs owed less to conventional folk than to 19th century parlour ballads, the melodies condensing the sparkle of the music hall and the sonorities of the village band box into airy near-classical cadences appropriate to a drawing room recital. The rhythms weren't marches or jigs but rather swaggering walks that invited singalong participation.

'Sweet Baby James', already earmarked as the album's maiden single, was everything a child's cowboy lullaby should be, but it also sounded as if it was meant to soothe a full-grown cowpoke, its passages about a snowy "turnpike from Stockbridge to Boston", with "ten miles behind me and 10,000 more to go" obviously alluding to higher personal hopes than a good night's sleep.

'Lo And Behold', the second track on *Sweet Baby James*, began with a metred thigh slap that signalled a relaxed temper, but it quieted in the second verse as those slaps became the precise timekeeper of the piece, whose down-home spontaneity was redolent of a musical break in an old-time medicine show. But the couplet James snarled evenly near the song's close – "You just can't kill for Jesus, let it be", was a sign the song's underlying anti-war message was hardly ad-libbed.

'Sunny Skies' was a more formal acoustic guitar piece, almost skit-like in its narrative clarity, its tempo between a sashay and soft-shoe, but the concluding assertion that its nicknamesake "hasn't a friend" shattered its calculated reverie.

Before it was recorded, 'Steamroller', a whimsical guitar blues, was always introduced in clubs with a brief burst of expositional patter by James about The Flying Machine. Quoted from a live show of the period is an example of the ritual precis absent from the album track:

> We played this 8-month-long gig at a place called the Night Owl Cafe down in Greenwich Village in New York; it used to be at MacDougal and Third but it might have moved since then, I don't know. But anyhow, at that time there were a lot of so-called blues groups in New York City, you know, and they were making a lot of noise. They weren't very good, and they were mostly white kids in from the suburbs with electric guitars and amplifiers that their parents had bought them for Christmas and for birthdays and stuff. And their idea of soul was volume; they'd just crank it up, you know. And they were singing all these heavy songs like 'I'm A Man', or 'I'm A Jackhammer', or 'I'm A Steam-ship', or whatever – 'I'm The Queen Mary', [*crowd laughter*] or 'A Ton Of Bricks'.
>
> We weren't to be left out of all of this, so I wrote this next song, which is the heaviest blues tune I know ladies and gentlemen. It's called 'I'm A Steamroller'. [*crowd laughter*]

The obvious send-up that ensued was punctuated from the second verse onwards with deadpan comments from Taylor like "Pick it, James", "Get on it man", "Um-um-um, my-my-my", "Look at those magic fingers boogie up and down them silver frets", and "I don't know nothing but the blues."

But then the last verse caught Taylor's draft-age patrons off-guard with a sure dose of post-modern blues, James voice edged with tension as he shouted out, "I'm a napalm bomb, baby, guaranteed to blow your mind!"

Spectators' chilled surprise with this stern stanza was always palpable, as it jogged their synapses with glimpsed TV images of My Lai carnage or the latest Saigon body counts, messily intermingling them with their own secret ideas of mortality. Taylor's bulletin–like bit of dark jest was a grim device, making a humbling point; and crowds always applauded warily at the song's end, out of either respect or relief.

'Country Road', the fifth track on *Sweet Baby James*, exulted in the simple pleasures and sensations that constantly beg for our attention, each one capable of "taking us to church" as Taylor once expressed it, if we'd only let them into our purviews. The sentiments of the song made it sound as if it came from a more innocent era; it had the same sad, dreamlike character of 'Sweet Adeline', originally composed in 1896 by Somerville, Massachusetts musician Henry W. Armstrong, who'd first titled it 'My Old New England Home'. Lyricist Richard Gerald, a friend of New York Mayor Jimmy Walker, added the love-smitten words in 1903 and 'Sweet Adeline' became a fixture of minstrel shows and barbershop quartets.

That 'Country Road' dissolved so effortlessly into Taylor's spare, guitar-and-voice turn on 'Oh Susannah' indicates how compatible were the two slices of Americana. The latter song was introduced in Pittsburgh by famed American composer Stephen Foster on September 11, 1847 at the opening of a fashionable ice cream parlour/music hall, the Eagle. Often called the first great popular songwriter in American history ('Camptown Races', 'Hard Times', 'Old Folks At Home') Stephen Collins Foster was born on the Fourth of July, 1829, in Lawrenceville, Pennsylvania, and was a studious musician who wrestled with alcohol problems and poor business acumen to immortalise a South he visited only once on his honeymoon.

'Oh Susannah' was simultaneously homespun and cosmopolitan, with Foster's first mention in song of the banjo. He depicts it as if posed on the knee of a European serenader, but the player of this rustic string instrument is plainly an Alabama rounder destined for Louisiana. The confused meteorological extremes of his trip ("It rained all night the day I left/The weather it was dry") attested to the clashes of wild frontier and advancing technology then transfixing travellers across America. The seminal lyric spoke in hellish terms of electricity, steam-boats, and the telegraph, but Taylor deleted such topics (set down in stereotypical black dialect) to stress its true theme: the torment of homesickness – a word not coined until 1798, when English poet

Samuel Taylor Coleridge (the co-publisher with William Wordsworth of *Lyrical Ballads*) wrote that "Home-sickness is a wasting pang."

Sweet Baby James had more such pangs to explore. 'Fire And Rain' was cut as if a re-enactment of daybreak on the day after Taylor heard the awful news of Susie Schnerr's suicide. There was a slow, unsteady feel of half-awareness in the opening moments' subdued music, the piano very carefully measuring out its tolling chords as the dazed singer begins to remind himself of what he's learned.

The drums gradually engage with the track's preoccupied trundle, as if the speaker is pulling himself from his bed and out through a doorway, flurries of guitar, snare drum and cymbals indicating the rapid, passing movement of a disinterested outside world. This abrupt exposure to the onrush of commonplace light and din – i.e. all the normally ignored accoutrements of feeling alive – is the saddest possible confirmation of what's now gone missing, and a clumsy, self-pitying prayer leaps to the singer's lips.

He hears himself asking, selfishly, for help for his body's aching addictions, anxiously fretting "his time is at hand" and he "won't make it any other way." But one can hear his fear is even greater than that, because it toys with the knowledge that if Susie can die and he can die, then *all* he'll ever see and feel can die, too.

The singer trembles, shakes off his chills, and the phobia of death seems to dissipate as he moves on through the day – until he suddenly blurts, at the very instant an icy waft raises the hair on his bare neck – "Lord knows when the cold wind blows, it'll turn your head around."

With this statement, the singer acknowledges he will only be able to forget his friend's untimely end when he himself is dead. His acute and unwelcome sudden awareness is that time is borrowed – a loan from the friend whose extinction awoke him to life's terrifying brevity.

As recorded with Kunkel's dark dashes of tom-toms and cymbals at its conclusion, 'Fire And Rain' evolved in the studio from a classic Carolina death ballad into a far stormier and more pointed parable about the senseless damage we do to ourselves and each other in the pitifully short span we're allotted. The ultimate lyric line, "But I always thought I'd see you again", is an effective attention-grabber. Yet it's the last cast-off remark that is the song's true clincher: "There's just a few things coming my way this time around now." The singer is telling himself, aloud, for anyone alive to hear, that he damned well better appreciate whatever he gets between now and the grave.

'Blossom' and 'Anywhere Like Heaven' are short, pretty pieces that seem intended to clear the morbid air, James asking a lover in the former song to "melt his cares away". Interestingly, 'Blossom' was hung on a winding guitar lick James knew he'd borrowed from an earlier, then-unrecorded song by brother Livingston called 'Good Friends'.

"Liv is the one who influenced me on that," James admitted of 'Blossom', noting, "It's a D fingering with a descending bass line," as in 'Good Friends'. And Liv's song is also about asking for and accepting "love and kindness", as well as the loyalty that strengthens them.

'Anywhere Like Heaven' was another sonnet to homesickness, with the singer amazed that he's comfortable anywhere. But he retains a figmental vision of a "pasture in the countryside" in North Carolina that serves as a home in his head whenever he needs a ready refuge.

'Oh Baby, Don't You Loose Your Lip On Me', a bluesy flight hearkening back to his formative days with Kootch, reinvoked an adolescence when they used the blues they were learning to measure their own emotions against worldlier pronouncements from Howlin' Wolf or Elizabeth Cotten.

Sweet Baby James culminated in the full-band frivolity of 'Suite For 20G', which drew on all the respective gifts of the studio ensemble, James showing how his guitar chords could unfurl like piano figures, while Carole King demonstrated a guitarist's versatility on her instrument. Jack Bielan's horns switched from being a scrim of gauzy atmospherics into a punchy foreground soul-review, and Kootch played spiky leads that part the way for what becomes a rollicking R&B jam. For all its twists and diversionary tactics, it was gladdening to James how well 'Suite For 20G' worked as the finale of his 10-track parlour recital and medicine show.

"Ultimately we didn't have the last tune," he explained, "and I had a lot of fragments of various other things, so I strung them all together and we named it after the balance of record company cash waiting for us when we delivered the finished product: 'Suite For 20G'."

14

Fanfare

The song 'Sweet Baby James' never got within hollering distance of the Hot 100. Unlike 'Carolina In My Mind', which also failed to make the chart (until reissued in 1970) but at least bubbled under it at number 118 for two weeks in April of '69, Taylor's introductory 45rpm single release for Warner Bros. in April 1970 (with 'Suite For 20G' as its B-side) may have been too potent in its lulling intentions because it apparently put radio programmers to sleep.

The progress of *Sweet Baby James* was also slow, the record opening at number 90 in the *Billboard* Top LPs sales chart on March 14, 1970 and hovering in its middle reaches. It wasn't until the release of the second single, 'Fire And Rain' (backed with 'Anywhere Like Heaven'), first sighted on the Hot 100 on August 12, that the album's commercial reception began to accelerate.

Taylor was busy during March and April of 1970 at Crystal Sounds studios in Hollywood, where Carole King was making *Writer*, her album initiation into a solo orbit. Among the record's most tempting tracks were a new Goffin-King piece called 'Child Of Mine' about the divorced couple's daughter Sherry (born in 1963), King's own rendition of 'Goin' Back', and a vulnerable, meditative modification of 'Up On The Roof'.

When The Drifters made 'Roof' a number five hit in 1962, it was a landmark in pop realism, extolling an urban perch whose worth as a spiritual oasis was steeped in class consciousness. So it was a revelation for a generation reared on Jerry Leiber and Mike Stoller's glossy, upbeat Atlantic Records production of the song to hear the Goffin-King classic re-imagined by King herself, her piano cosseted by the chiming torsion of Taylor's acoustic guitar.

The freeform/progressive music formats of FM radio – as pioneered in California in 1967 by KMPX-FM disc jockey Tom Donahue and emulated in New York City that autumn by WNEW-FM – were a breeding ground for artful juxtaposing of multiple incarnations of classic songs. Programmers on both coasts found King's 'Up On The Roof' track on their own and gave her stripped-down *Writer* presentation of it special attention (at first in tandem with The Drifters and then alone) to help spread the news that Carole was out from behind the scenes with an ear-grabbingly honest sound. (New York deejays also liked to remind listeners that King had done two popular 1962–63 singles on Don Kirshner's Dimension label with 'It Might As Well Rain Until September' and 'He's A Bad Boy'.)

Kortchmar and Larkey were the linchpins of King's studio combo on *Writer*, with Joel O'Brien sitting in on drums and Ralph Schuckett on organ. Producer John Fischbach played a Moog synthesiser in spots on the album, and though King layered most of her vocal harmonies herself, Abigale Haness and Delores Hall supplied some back-up singing. Gerry Goffin mixed *Writer*, which was released on September 21, 1970. When the album didn't chart in its first few months of issue, an undaunted King resolved to make a sequel.

During the interim, her musicians had numerous commitments. Some of the principal contributors to *Writer* – Kortchmar, O'Brien, Larkey, Schuckett and Haness – had been signed to Atlantic as a group Kootch christened Jo Mama. "The name was a gag," he explained, "and was taken from the first half of a current 'knock-knock' joke: 'Knock-knock.' 'Who's there?' 'Jo' mama!' It was dumb but funny, and then it just stuck."

Haness, who would become Kortchmar's second wife, was Jo Mama's lead singer, and its self-titled album saw release in 1970. Jo Mama's recordings became known in the industry as the outside endeavours of "Carole King's band".

As King's stock rose on radio and she outgrew her greenhorn touch of onstage nerves, she ripened as a performing artist of great garrulous zest. Taylor, however, was still getting accustomed to life as a work-a-day musician, public figure and performer – roles he'd not fully envisioned for himself.

Once his pastoral 'Prince Valiant' pose was selected by Warner Bros. art director Ed Thrasher as the best portrait from photographer Henry Diltz's *Sweet Baby James* jacket cover assignment, Taylor's piercing gaze and angular features loomed in every dorm room in Christendom. Guys preferred the firelit visage on the back cover because it made Taylor look as if he'd been interrupted in the midst of some faintly suspicious act, but the immediate recognisability of either shot ensured they were widely silkscreened on T-shirts by unlicensed college capitalists. The improvised marketing of the man mistakenly called Sweet Baby James was underway.

"The popular music world was becoming more of a business," Kootch would later rule, "but James hadn't gone into it with that mindset. He wasn't innocent, none of us were, but our values were different. He and the rest of us wrote songs for their own sake, because something was burning inside and you had to let it out.

"Growing up as James and I did, you didn't see popular music as part of mass consciousness. Popular culture as it was accepted in the '50s and early '60s still had the emphasis on the word *culture*. In mass-media TV terms, that meant something like the *Omnibus* programme, hosted by Alistair Cooke on Sunday afternoons, with excerpts from plays and operas, and it meant Leonard Bernstein's *Young People's Concert* specials. Later in the '60s, you'd see maybe a two- or three-minute snatch of a pop band on *The Ed Sullivan Show*. And then in 1964–65 came the *Hullabaloo* and *Shindig* TV shows, but that was still mostly Top 40 stuff, not John Lee Hooker, or Dylan, or The Fugs and people we hung with.

"So the idea of James or I telling our parents we'd earn a living with an electric guitar always seemed insane to them. They'd ask why we didn't at least try a classical instrument. And even when the guitar band stuff began to happen, it wasn't very logical or organised for us. I know for James it was a very hard adjustment, because of having to break away from his family to play music full-time, and then having to

175

break away from drugs to keep the music going. Then he needed to break away from people, including all the women who were chasing him after checking out his album covers.

"I mean, James liked meeting chicks like all of us, and that's a big part of playing in bands when you're young. But he never wrote his music just to make money, and now he had a record company saying he had to do that! And finally, he had his own family, who hadn't fully understood what was up with The Flying Machine and the rest. Ike had felt like Alex probably got into bands to embarrass Ike in academia – which may have had some rebellious truth to it. But even Trudy, who loved music, once phoned me after The Flying Machine broke up to say, 'Don't you think James has spent enough time on this and should go back to school or maybe get a more serious profession?' I didn't really answer her, because there was no point.

"Now, two years later, 'Fire And Rain' was becoming the biggest song in America and England, and every word in it was just James telling the blow-by-blow truth about how he felt. Even the line when he sings that he wrote down this song, and he 'just can't remember who to send it to' had to do with the fact he'd signed a contract with a new publishing company, Blackwood Music, and he didn't know who he was supposed to send his stuff to!

"If you look at it through our lens," said Kootch, "and our idea of fun and time well spent in the context of that early-to-late '60s period, and *then* what it suddenly became because of corporate forces, you'll at least understand how we all had our troubles handling it. Everything changed overnight, it all became *business* and James was constantly told he had the most responsibility! No wonder he wanted to hide out sometimes."

Recording for Carole King's second solo album commenced in January 1971 at A&M Studios in Hollywood, the sessions taking place on the 4th, 8th, 11th, 12th and 15th at studios B and C in what had been the old Charlie Chaplin Films lot on LaBrea Avenue off Sunset Boulevard. A homey, cloistered throwback to a moment when Hollywood was still a cottage industry, the lot felt like a tiny neighbourhood and workspace filleted from a company town in the 1920s. Carole had worked hard inside the sunlit piano room in her Appian Way atelier, whose comfy, cat-prowled hallway window seat was immortalised in the cover photos Jim McCrary took for a record that was to be called *Tapestry*.

There were lead sheets spread out at A&M studios for some thirteen songs whose titles were: 'I Feel The Earth Move', 'So Far Away', 'It's Too Late', 'Home Again', 'Beautiful', 'Way Over Yonder', 'You've Got A Friend', 'Where You Lead', 'Will You Love Me Tomorrow?' (with its rarely used question mark in the formal title), 'Smackwater Jack', 'Tapestry', '(You Make Me Feel Like) A Natural Woman', and 'Out In The Cold'. The last song, a funky, Sweet Inspirations-styled slice of testimony about female infidelity, was ultimately trimmed from the album's final running order. Eight of the songs had words and music by King alone; 'It's Too Late' and 'Where You Lead' were co-written with Toni Stern; the rest were Goffin-King, with the exception of 'A Natural Woman', which Jerry Wexler aided.

This baker's dozen was pounced on by Carole, James and the Jo Mama line-up – which had expanded to include drummer pal Russ Kunkel, long part of the house band at the Whisky A Go Go and a regular backing musician on the albums of ex-Kingston Trio member and hit songwriter John Stewart (Stewart wrote the Monkees' '67 hit 'Daydream Believer') – as well as flautist/tenor saxophonist Curtis Amy, backing singers Merry Clayton, Julia Tillman, and the (Joni) Mitchell/ (James) Taylor Boy And Girl Choir, plus a top-flight string section.

That one of the biggest-selling (over 24 million units worldwide) and best-loved albums of modern times was knocked out in five days is a tribute to all concerned, including *Tapestry* producer Lou Adler and engineer Hank Cicalo, who helped uphold the nonchalant solidarity permeating the whole enterprise.

The featured guitar parts conceived by Taylor, now sporting a feathery moustache and goatee, were on 'So Far Away', 'Home Again', 'Way Over Yonder', 'Will You Love Me Tomorrow?' and 'You've Got A Friend'. And the casual, all-for-one/one-for-all ethos governing the proceedings was so pervasive it spilled over into parallel sessions in Hollywood for Kate Taylor's début Atlantic/Cotillion album (on which Kate cut 'Home Again' and 'Where You Lead' with Carole and company playing on the tracks). This repertoire company of players also invaded the feverish record-making taking shape at nearby Crystal

Sound between January 3 and February 27 for James' second album, whose recording dates drew Kootch for James' own edition of 'You've Got A Friend'.

Despite all the mutual support in evidence, the unaccustomed pressure on Taylor was mounting, with the need to conceive another album's worth of material in a fraction of the three-odd years in which he'd composed the last batch. Other than slipping off for sanctuary at girlfriend Joni Mitchell's Laurel Canyon address – a one-storey wooden house erected on rock piers – where Joni was writing 'A Case Of You' and other lovesongs for a record she was carrying in her head called *Blue*, Taylor had few places left to run.

But one new locale Taylor was offered as a change-of-pace hideout was the on-location seclusion of a movie shoot. As 1970 intensified he thought he could really use a breather, since sudden fame was sucking the oxygen out of every public and private corner of his customary environments.

It was inevitable that movie directors would come calling, but Monte Hellman got in ahead of more logical choices and hooked a great white hope. Hellman was born in Greenpoint, Long Island to parents who were visiting from the Midwest. After studying drama at Stanford University and filmmaking at UCLA, he came under the wing of Roger Corman, a master of mid-tier horror movies (*Attack Of The Crab Monsters, The Pit And The Pendulum*), teen exploitation thrillers (*Sorority Girl, The She-Gods Of Shark Reef*) and sundry other '60s nailbiters (*Bloody Mama, The Trip*).

After Cormanesque work on *The Beast From Haunted Cave* (1959) and *Back Door To Hell* (1965), Hellman fostered a cult following with two refreshingly off-beat Westerns in 1966, *The Shooting* and *Ride In The Whirlwind*, which he made together in the Utah desert on a combined brown-bag budget of $150,000. *Two-Lane Blacktop*, from a bleak screenplay by Rudolph Wurlitzer (later known for *Pat Garrett And Billy The Kid*) and Will Corry, was a 103-minute moodpiece about two drag-racing drifters in a '55 Chevy and their episodic attempts to hustle suckers into cash-stakes shutdowns.

In their first and last screen-acting roles, Taylor was induced to assume the part of "The Driver" and Beach Boy Dennis Wilson was cast as "The Mechanic". *Two-Lane Blacktop*'s cinematography was washed out and grainy, its settings often overcast or nightlit, and the storyline was a tad slow in stretches but its plot development had the real-time melancholy of a fateful decline.

As the film begins, an unsubtle triangle arises at a roadside stop when a pug-nosed, dishevelled blonde hippie-nymph in jeans and moccasins (played by Laurie Bird) eases herself into the backseat of the Driver and the Mechanic's Chevy with a wordless hubris that is accepted on sight. The deeper implications of this hot-rod hejira are established soon enough as stringy-haired James and unwashed Wilson pull the gun-metal Chevy (which boasts a 450 block and a four-speed transmission) into the Stygian gloom of King's Cafe, a late-evening dragger's haunt, as Jerry Lee Lewis' 'Hit The Road, Jack' squalls from tinny dashboard radios.

"How much bread we got?" asks Taylor, hunched over the steering wheel as they wend their way through the parking lot.

"We got 300 racing bread," answers Wilson, "and twenty to spend." The girl in the backseat is silent, watching.

Static-laced strains of The Doors' dreary 'Moonlit Drive' from the group's 1967 *Strange Days* album leaks into the morose, fluorescent-streaked scene, as Wilson scans the lot for beatable funny cars (i.e. draggers whose racing chassis and engine components are encased in the bodies of standard street vehicles). "They got some muscle here tonight," Dennis decides.

Armed with this judgement, Taylor halts and leaves the Chevy, wandering over to a pompous looking guy poised next to his flashy heap, James telling this likely mark that his car is "A clean machine."

"Clean enough," the guy snaps back, saying Taylor must have wheels he wants to challenge him with.

"Well, ordinarily I'd jump at the opportunity," JT/The Driver drawls, "but the thing is I'm just not in the habit of seeing a Chevy work against a two-bit piece of junk."

"Okay," says the insulted sucker, bristling, "let's make it $50."

"Make it three yards, motherfucker," Taylor snarls – as an onlooker exclaims, "Hey, this guy just bet 300 bucks!" – "and we'll have an automobile race."

Taylor wins the shutdown, the Chevy escaping the scene of the race just a few lengths ahead of several siren-wailing highway patrol cars.

The sullen, taciturn triumvirate (Taylor, Wilson, Bird) check into a cheap motor hotel. James withdraws from their company to get drunk alone in a bar and returns to overhear Dennis and Laurie having sex in the one room the three could afford, so he sleeps outside the door.

A day or so later, after she and Wilson are tired of each other, Taylor snags Bird's straying attentions with a coarse pick-up line: "You hear the cicadas? . . . Those are some freaky bugs . . . They come out of the ground every seven years, and they live underground the rest of the time. And the only time they come out of the ground is to fall out of their shells so they can grow some wings so they can fuck, and then they die. But before they die, they manage to lay some eggs."

"We got a lot better life, haven't we?" says the irritated Bird, who was expecting something more romantic, and she stalks off in a huff, their mutual attraction confirmed.

An inauspicious distraction in this mating dance is a rootless scamp (played by actor Warren Oates) in a banana yellow Pontiac GTO. Encountered at several successive gas stations, he gets hustled by the Driver and Mechanic (with the girl's wily assistance) into wagering with the Chevy for an all-or-nothing cross-country peal-out, with the first car to reach Washington, DC having to surrender its "pink slip" (ownership papers) to the victor.

"You stay on the country roads," Wilson warns Oates as he shows the route of the backroads race on a map. "Less heat that way. Never say you're racing, or they'll bust you for it."

"Here's to your destruction," says the grizzled Oates as he nips from his flask.

"Same to ya," Taylor retorts.

The rest of the movie chronicles an unexpectedly touching rite of unblessed bonding as all four characters mistrust, misjudge, then miss each other's signals entirely, due to an inability to admit their inevitable attachments to each other. The film ends with Taylor, who's just been deserted by the vagabond girl, gripping the wheel of the Chevy as it awaits the start of another drag-for-cash dalliance on the outskirts of another drab town. The starting flag comes down and Taylor floors the accelerator, his features exhausted and almost skeletal, as he hurtles towards a sadly drama-less oblivion.

Their Lives Begin At 140 M.P.H.! screamed the theatre trailers promoting the Universal Pictures' film's March 1970 opening, when it was billed as *The Far-Out World Of The High Speed Scene!*

But *Two-Lane Blacktop* was better and more piteous in its tenor than the average rods 'n bods potboiler, and its pop-existential foreboding feel had stomach-tightening relevance for young draft-age viewers fully aware they could be inducted any day to die in some rice paddy outside Hue or Da Nang.

Esquire said *Two-Lane Blacktop* was, "Our nomination for movie of the year," and in March 1971 Jay Cocks of *Time* called it, "One of the most ambitious and interesting American films of the year." Since Cocks was also surveying the early stages of what would be a field of odd, outré, uncompromising, and overwrought '71 cinema fare such as *A Clockwork Orange, Sunday Bloody Sunday, Hospital, The French Connection, The Last Picture Show, Klute, Carnal Knowledge, The Garden Of The Finzi-Contini, Shaft, McCabe And Mrs. Miller, The Conformist, Nicholas And Alexandra, Fiddler On The Roof* and *Summer Of '42*, he was entitled to take a rain check on the rife cynicism of the era and give flawed sincerity the benefit of the low-budget doubt. Moreover, the release of *Two-Lane Blacktop* coincided with Taylor being featured on a March cover of *Time*, so the publication had chosen to rally round the troubadour and his refuge-seeking sidetrips.

Taylor had many more burdens, appointments and promises to keep during 1971. *Tapestry* was released on February 10, and was an immediate success on the strength of its initial single, 'It's Too Late' backed with 'I Feel The Earth Move'. The double A-sided 45 became a dual smash, although 'It's Too Late' retained a slight airplay edge that made it the official number one side of the single for five straight weeks.

The *Sister Kate* album entered *Billboard*'s album chart on March 27, 1971 and FM radio jumped on 'Home Again' as the favoured track, especially at New England stations like Boston's WBCN. And a 27-city tour was booked for a package of James Taylor, Carole King and Jo Mama, with bassist Lee Sklar and Russ Kunkel also on board. But before this band of gypsies left LA, James had to finish his own follow-up album.

"He was freaked out, as we all were," Kootch remembered, "but most of it was on his shoulders, and he was still battling old demons, too, and was trying desperately to find ways to keep everything light.

181

James was always coming up with silly names for himself and the band, the silliest things he could think of to call us. One of them was Mud Slide Slim and the Blue Horizon.

"It was meant as a little joke. We all laughed, but time was running out on getting the new album done. James decided to make his funny name for all of us the basis of a song about what he was going through. Next thing we knew, that was also the name of James' next album. So that's pretty much how *Mud Slide Slim And The Blue Horizon* got its title."

James, alias Mud Slide Slim, 1971. (*David Gahr*)

Gertrude 'Trudy' Woodard, Newburyport High School, 1941. (*Taylor Family Archive, courtesy Trudy Taylor*)

Trudy Taylor, spring 1942. (*Taylor Family Archive, courtesy Trudy Taylor*)

Headmistress Katherine B. Child (*front row, centre*) and enrolee Trudy Woodard (*front row, far right*) at Child's The Graduate House finishing school, 20 Chestnut Street, Boston, Mass, mid-1940s. Years later Trudy's daughter Kate would be named for Child. (*Taylor Family Archive, courtesy Trudy Taylor*)

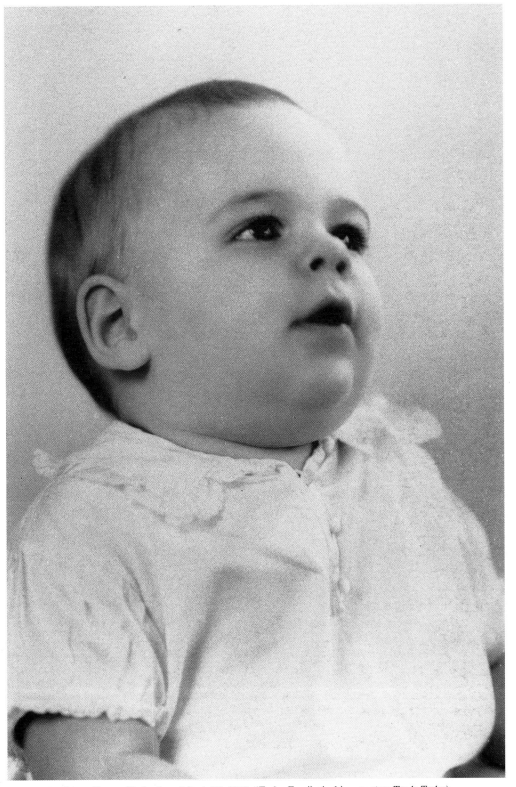

James Vernon Taylor, born March 12, 1948. (*Taylor Family Archive, courtesy Trudy Taylor*)

Ike Taylor with his children, left to right, Alex, James, Kate and, in his arms, Livingston.
(*Taylor Family Archive, courtesy Trudy Taylor*)

The five Taylor siblings at Morgan Creek House, Chapel Hill, NC. Left to right, Alex, James, Kate, Liv and Hugh.
(*Taylor Family Archive, courtesy Trudy Taylor*)

Alex and James playing cowboys. (*Taylor Family Archive, courtesy Trudy Taylor*)

The Taylor children salute their father Ike,
away in Antarctica, from the back porch of
their Morgan Creek home, 1956.
(*Taylor Family Archive, courtesy Trudy Taylor*)

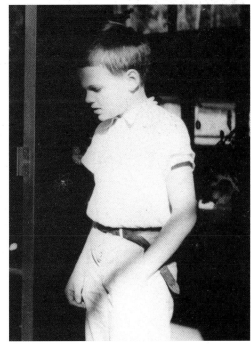

James on the porch of the Morgan Creek house, 1957.
(*Taylor Family Archive, courtesy Trudy Taylor*)

The Taylor House at Morgan Creek, Chapel Hill, NC, mid-1950s. (*Taylor Family Archive, courtesy Trudy Taylor*)

"I miss my lovely mother… " Trudy Taylor, late 1950s. (*Taylor Family Archive, courtesy Trudy Taylor*)

"… and I love my lonely father." Ike Taylor on Martha's Vineyard, late 1970s.
(*Taylor Family Archive, courtesy Trudy Taylor*)

James, 10, and Kate Taylor, 9, feeding the pigeons
in St Mark's Square, Venice, Italy.
(*Taylor Family Archive, courtesy Trudy Taylor*)

"Long ago, a young man sits and plays his waiting
game." James, 9, in the Morgan Creek house.
(*Taylor Family Archive, courtesy Trudy Taylor*)

James Taylor, 12, (*front row, centre*) in his school orchestra, Chapel Hill, NC.
(*Taylor Family Archive, courtesy Trudy Taylor*)

"Essentially me and my guitar." James Taylor, Milton Academy, Milton, Mass.
(*Taylor Family Archive, courtesy Trudy Taylor*)

15

Hey Mister That's Me Up On The Jukebox

"Sweet misunderstanding, won't you leave a poor boy alone," sang James Taylor in the studio in February 1971 in a song about his new life as a hard travelling and poorly comprehended cynosure from a family suddenly producing similar victims. The misunderstandings pertaining to Taylor were too incessant to list, but a typical one concerned 'Fire And Rain', for which, as James detailed, he'd been getting "a lot of response from fundamentalist Christians about the second verse" – ("Won't you look down upon me Jesus," etc.) – "thinking that I was a kindred spirit."

As for the catalysts for keeping Taylor highway-bound, they were manifold. During the first full week of recording for *Mud Slide Slim And The Blue Horizon*, Taylor found he had three albums in the *Billboard* charts. The old *James Taylor* record for Apple and something called *James Taylor And The Original Flying Machine–1967* (a slapdash disc of the substandard Chip Taylor demos) were both clutching the lofty commercial coat-tails of *Sweet Baby James* as if it were a "Nantucket sleigh ride" – as Massachusetts whalers once called the triumph-or-tragedy wintertide rush of harpooning the amphibious mammals and holding on 'til either the poor sperm whale grew tired enough to die or the skiff carrying the harpooners capsized and sent them to a likely demise in the North Atlantic's frigid depths.

But James was not alone in his quasi-peril as the Moby Dick of contemporary troubadours; he had plenty of close-knit company. Brother Livingston's first album had been on the charts since July 1970, with his 'Carolina Day' getting extensive airplay, his own tour bookings abounding, and four appearances just taped for British television programmes. Sister Kate was taking to the road to promote her album, and Alex Taylor had given up asking Capricorn Records to give him a shot, only to have label chief Phil Walden contact him in the summer of 1970, saying, "Hey Alex, you want to be a star?"

"I'd been trying to get in the studio there for two years to do a fuckin' demo and they wouldn't even turn their heads around," Alex told *Rolling Stone*'s Timothy Crouse. "Then James' [first Apple] album took off again and Liv's album was doing really well and so they said, 'Hey, we'd better get a hold of this guy whether he can sing or not, the name's there.' I knew that, I knew the name was worth somethin'.

"Like, I don't think I'm hung up at all about bein' James Taylor's brother," Alex added with the unqualified frankness that was among his most admirable traits. "I'm gonna capitalise on it. Liv's all torn up tryin' to deny it. I'm not."

As a consequence, Alex's *With Friends & Neighbors* enjoyed two weeks on the tail end of the charts in March 1971, the boisterous album praised in print for its raucous romp with Jimmy Reed's 'Take Out Some Insurance', a Corsairs-inclined spin with Bobby Womack's 'It's All Over Now' (previously cut by Womack with The Valentinos, and covered by The Rolling Stones), some country-rock toe-tappers by the songwriting team of Talton and Boyer, and a steady-rocking version of 'Night Owl' in which James played guitar. *With Friends & Neighbors* also has the distinction of containing the earliest released incarnation of 'Highway Song', which James had concocted in 1970 and was only just getting around to cutting himself.

Besides its "sweet misunderstandings" passage, 'Highway Song' was notable for the leitmotif of its opening lyrics, in which a son implores his father to build a boat and sail away because there's nothing left for his parent in his current locale. Then the son bids his brother join him in throwing their lot out "upon the sea" to try to make a living from it, reminding him that "it's been done before". The implied message, as addressed previously in the "take to the highway" exhortation of

'Country Roads', was that this restive Taylor-style means of resolving problems by sailing off on the supposed clean slate of a steel grey ocean had long been a family mainstay.

Other songs written in 1970 that got used on *Mud Slide Slim And The Blue Horizon* were 'Riding On A Railroad', 'Long Ago And Far Away', and 'You Can Close Your Eyes', the last one formulated in a hotel room in Flagstaff, Arizona. Each was composed, as James would recall, "very fast, back when music was still very much a hobby for me." He saw 'Long Ago And Far Away' as "a sentimental song, but good" and felt 'You Can Close Your Eyes' was "a secular hymn".

But the act of writing was turning from internal solace into external toil. "When I made my first and second albums," Taylor explained, "it was basically unknown terrain, and I was still working, somehow, from a very pure place. After *Sweet Baby James* I knew what it felt like to work for a living and be this sort of hypothetical entrepreneur with a record company, agent, manager, whatever."

Hence, despite the presence on the album of more recent material presaging a retreat from the multitudinous fans' woes for which he was fast becoming a human mailbox ('Love Has Brought Me Around'), and his self-described "sticky" memories of unresolved romances and fleeting friends ('Places In My Past'), *Mud Slide Slim* was at bedrock a nonbinding brief on Taylor's right to leave ('Let Me Ride') and return as he pleased ('Isn't It Nice To Be Home Again') from periodic self-exile. After all, he was unmarried, unfettered by anything more legally binding than a record contract, and convinced, as far as non-musical links, that he was temperamentally unready for much more.

"He was under the gun to write material," said Kortchmar with a shudder, "and he was on heroin" – having fallen off the hard drugs wagon again given the rattling stress of Warner Bros.' unrealised demand for product – "and he was a total cult hero. Parents would bring their children back stage, all these rich girls contemplating his songs for meaning, as if he knew all the answers to mysteries and was a shaman. But he still had a drug habit!"

Kortchmar sighed heavily at the memory of such dilemmas. "I don't know how he got through it," he said, "but he was *not* happy at that time, and *not* having fun."

Which is how the forlorn frankness of 'Hey Mister That's Me Up On The Jukebox' surfaced. "It was exactly how he felt," said Kootch. "Like the song says, he knew he was spread thin and needed time alone to get better again."

"You know, I'm a little bit embarrassed to have written that kind of song, which seems to be sort of ungrateful about what I've been given," Taylor would acknowledge. "That was just an early song complaining about the thing turning sour for me by going to the marketplace. Anyone who becomes professional and who has some amount of success, there's a loss of innocence and shift of motivation. It becomes less pure and then it becomes more worldly and I think that was my first real sense of that."

But James was too close to the subject while making *Mud Slide* to separate truth from either tact or tacit careerism. At the time, Kortchmar was also feeling bruised and ambivalent about ironies in his own backyard. "My first wife Joyce had left me, just as things with music were starting to go well," Kootch admitted. "I had sad feelings and regrets, and at the time I was reading a paperback book called, I think, *Gangsters Of The 1930s And Their Molls*. The combination of the two things made me write a song about an outlaw and his personal life, called 'Machine Gun Kelly'."

Memphis, Tennessee-based gangster George "Machine Gun Kelly" Barnes was a hoodlum involved in one armed transgression too many when, as Kortchmar's song relates, he became part in July 1933 of a ring of kidnappers who abducted Texas oilman Charles Urschel and demanded $200,000 in ransom from Urschel's family – which was duly paid, with Urschel released unharmed nine days later. However, Urschel was a shrewd cuss of the sort not crossed without consequences. Despite being blindfolded and driven around rural Texas during his ordeal, the oil heir gleaned scraps of details from his captors, by asking innocuous questions – like the time of day as he heard a plane pass overhead – or by mentally cataloguing the surrounding sounds of farm animals and objects like a squeaky well – and was able to establish later the site of his captivity (near Paradise, Texas) by merging the data. The FBI raided the abductors' lair and thereupon traced George "Machine Gun Kelly" via telegrams sent by confederates; he was caught and sentenced to life in Leavenworth Prison, where he died.

Kootch and Jo Mama recorded 'Machine Gun Kelly' in 1970, so the riff was well-practised when, during a regenerative half-hour jam session with James at Crystal Sound, James and Danny and the other musicians skipped from Bobby Darin's 'Splish Splash' and other narrative pop outbursts to the catchy hook of 'Kelly'. The embittering plight of "a simple man" spurred into crime by frustration and bad advice seized James' imagination. A no-frills formal take by Kootch, Russ Kunkel and Taylor, with James and Peter Asher on backing vocals was attempted, then essayed with pleasure by James during playback in the control room, and immediately locked into position on the *Mud Slide* master tape.

The other departure on *Mud Slide* from themes of love, friendship and the non-committal allure of a nomad existence was 'Soldiers', a one minute and 12-second rock haiku whose aggrieved lilt lay halfway between a slow march and a waltz. The single verseless stanza related the sight of "nine lucky soldiers" from a platoon of twenty who were returning from war, the wounded men "barely alive" as they stepped by drumbeat across the sandflats of a coastal plain. Intoned as if "out of a dream", the pathetic image envisioned in the brief piece might easily have been a dour description of the homeward trek of James Taylor's Civil War ancestor George Attmore.

The sole survivor of three brothers who fought against the Union, George and his "Beaufort Rifles" contingent torched their arms and carriages at Appomatox Courthouse after the Confederacy surrendered in April 1865, the wretched soldiers returning to New Bern, North Carolina on foot after declining to sign the Federal troops' capitulation documents.

'Soldiers' could also have served as a tragic 19th century ballad for George Attmore's eldest brother, Sitgreaves, the Confederate private of Company F who perished not gloriously on a battlefield but rather undeservedly in a Federal hospital, dehydrated and delirious from fever and acute diarrhoea, while still a prisoner of war – with all fighting in the War Between The States having ceased the month before.

What's certain is that James himself was in poor physical condition and feeling all but overcome by forces he'd set in motion for *Mud Slide Slim* as he stared down his own spectre of defeat. Yet something inside Taylor prevented him from giving into the usual pattern of crashing and burning – possibly a ripple of pride mixed with anger, largely with himself for his weaknesses. He would submit himself once again to out-patient treatment for his insistent addiction.

All the while, Taylor's thoughts always strayed to a house he was designing and hammering together himself in a thicket outside the town of Vineyard Haven. It was a tall barn-like hostel that illustrator Laurie Miller would wishfully depict as finished, with smoke content-edly spiralling from its chimney, on the back cover of *Mud Slide Slim And The Blue Horizon*, which was released by Warner Bros. in April 1971.

"I was building my own house on the Vineyard, and my career as well," James later synopsised, yet both were only half-formed in any substantive sense.

"After *Sweet Baby James* being such an overwhelming success," explained Taylor, referring to the record that was certified a million-seller on October 16, 1970, "I guess with the strength from that previous record but still being the people we had been before, we just barely managed to get through *Mud Slide Slim.*

"But after that, it was time to adjust to what the new agenda had become, which was that now I had a *career* that received a lot more attention and was taken much more seriously. To me, I'd been very sheltered by the fact my music had once been very rogue and maverick to make. It was an alienated thing to run off and make music! When suddenly that became, from my family's point of view, so central and a point of *pride*, it achieved for me the very opposite of what I had gone into it for. I was threatened by the degree of success I'd gotten and was really confused about it.

"That was the beginning of a long adjustment to a different sort of phase. Once music had been part of my *flux*. Now it was part of a band, a contract, a manager, a growing concern, and the alienated music soul you'd always been was now simultaneously the most responsible figure in this new realm!

"It's an *odd* turnaround. You're also more aware of how the songs are going to be heard than what they express. They're not being pressed out of you anymore – they're being pulled out of you."

And the highway was exerting its own familiar pull, the Taylor/ King/Jo Mama touring package ready and waiting to take their collective music to the concert hall. The cavalcade commenced with King opening for Taylor, a billing she liked because she could warm up along with the audience, yet the sheer repetition of touring was new and disquieting to Carole.

"One of the things I dislike about performing, at least under those circumstances," she volunteered in a conversation taped with Adler during the period, "is that you lose the spontaneity after doing it once or twice.

"I mean, you gotta go and take the same show on the road, and somehow you do manage to get some spontaneity just because it's a new audience every night. But sometimes you can see it in James when he's been working too hard – and some people will put him down for it – *between* numbers you may show that you're dragged. But somehow, when you start singing a song, you just get lost in it, and the fact that you've done it before doesn't really matter. It's just that I don't like the part between numbers."

James didn't like the part between the shows themselves – when fans, well-wishers, hosts and hangers-on all sought him out, and took his soft-spoken nasal sonority and bred-in-the-bone politeness to be evidence of an otherworldly avatar.

"People were treating him with kid gloves," said Kootch, "whispering around him like he was Montgomery Clift or a saint who knew everything. And he was being pursued by every chick, everybody around, to where it was painful. By the time he got to Chicago in '71 he was in bad shape and we'd wonder if he'd make it through the next show."

On April 6, 1971, during a break in the tour regimen, Taylor was back in Los Angeles and sitting in the audience at the Troubadour, where singer Cat Stevens was booked for three nights based on the national commercial clout of his second Island/A&M Records album, *Tea For The Tillerman*, and its number 11 hit, 'Wild World'.

James was in attendance, however, to cheer on buddy Russ Kunkel, who'd been asked to play drums for Stevens' opening act, a female singer–songwriter with one solo album out on the Elektra label, and a single that would appear in the Hot 100 a week later called 'That's The Way I've Always Heard It Should Be'. The artist's name was Carly Simon, and Taylor had a fuzzy idea she was one of the Simon Sisters who used to gig in Provincetown and on the Vineyard in the early '60s. He hadn't heard her latest music.

After the show, Simon met "Jamie" Taylor face to face for the first time, a passing encounter she never forgot – although James did. Carly would later admit how during her teens she and her Vineyard girl-friends always regarded Jamie and Kootch as part of the "cool" adoles-cent set she could never penetrate either musically or socially.

Making small talk with the lanky, handsome Jamie backstage, she found she was attracted to him and flirted impetuously as they parted, her come-on half mothering and half minx-like. "If you ever want a home-cooked meal . . ." she said.

"Tonight," he answered.

But their retinues of friends drew them apart moments later with incompatible sets of post-Troubadour plans.

Simon was soon off to other cities, continuing her opening slot for Stevens (with whom she was briefly involved, having written a song in '71 based on their first date, titled 'Anticipation'), and landing a string of dates second-billed to Kris Kristofferson.

'That's The Way I've Always Heard It Should Be' became a Top 10 hit, and Carly was now a beguiling pop star who'd begun dating a big film star, Warren Beatty, whose work in *Bonnie And Clyde* (1967) and the current *McCabe And Mrs Miller* had made him a favourite with the same adolescents buying Carly's new album.

Taylor was likewise one of the hottest music figures on the map, his placid, reassuring 'You've Got A Friend' becoming his first (and only) number one smash in the summer of '71. The follow-up hit, 'Long Ago And Far Away' (backed by 'Let Me Ride') reached the Top 30, with Joni Mitchell's harmony refrain and King's piano on the single's A-side.

The behind-the-scenes bonds enjoyed by Taylor, Mitchell, King and other musical colleagues became a buffer for the intrusions of success. One of the nicest moments in which James participated in the summer of '71 was the night of Friday, June 18, when King headlined at Carnegie Hall. With husband Charlie Larkey beside her on bass, she introduced a new song at mid-concert (written for her *Music* album, due in December) called 'A Song Of Long Ago', noting it was "Not to be confused with 'Long Ago And Far Away'," and then laughed and said, "You see, I wrote this under the heavy influence of James Taylor."

Seven songs later, King paused and said, "I'm gonna be right back," and ran into the wings, returning with a white suited Taylor, who she drew by the hand amid ear-splitting screams and applause. "Surprise!" she said, as James padded towards the footlights like a bashful beau.

"We'd like to do a little tune for you," King continued, taking her seat at the Steinway as Taylor lifted an acoustic guitar. "Maybe even a big tune."

They launched into a mutually revised vocal arrangement of 'You've Got A Friend' that intermeshed their individual recorded versions. Taking their musical companionship a step further, King and Taylor duetted next on a transporting medley of 'Will You Still Love Me Tomorrow', 'Some Kind Of Wonderful' and 'Up On The Roof', her reedy treble planing against his nasal pitch with such warm resonance that she was plainly at the point of tears as 'Tomorrow' veered into several bars of 'Wonderful' and then the main verses of 'Roof'.

Speechless with emotion afterwards, King managed to say, "Well, well, well," collected herself again, gulped hard and finally whispered, "Thank you." Then she closed the concert with '(You Make Me Feel Like) A Natural Woman'.

June of 1971 was a fortuitous time for Taylor's female compatriots. Joni Mitchell's superb *Blue*, released late in the month, was an immediate platinum success, duplicating the sales might of her equally revered *Ladies Of The Canyon* album of 1970. Besides his guitar on *Blue*'s 'A Case Of You', Taylor also played on 'California' and 'All I Want' and he and Mitchell did a joint BBC special, "just trading songs back and forth" as he noted affectionately. Career demands soon diminished the time spent in each other's company, however, yet they would stay close, appearing on each other's albums for the next 15 years. As Carole King sang of the whole unsettled era: "So far away/Doesn't anybody stay in one place anymore?"

On June 30 in Chapel Hill, Dr Ike Taylor stepped down as the dean of the UNC School of Medicine. After six months leave, he was expected to return to the medical school classroom. During Dr Taylor's seven years as dean, blacks and women had joined the student body, 11 new department chairmen and 100 new full-time faculty staff had

191

been appointed, and there was an increase of medical students from 264 to 320, with the number taught going from 2700 to 3300. Research and training grants expanded from $4.2 million to $10.6 million. Taylor was praised for his activity in community health, including the creation of teaching units in community hospitals. He also set up new UNC-Medical School departments like the Office of Medical Studies. Since his "most highly visible accomplishment", according to a spokesman for the UNC faculty, was his energetic building programme, a new facility housing additional office and laboratory space was dedicated on October 6 as Isaac M. Taylor Hall. Final accomplishments by Taylor that were cited were "support of new and growing programmes in problems of great social importance, such as neurobiology, child development and reproductive biology", and "the creation of a Department of Family Medicine."

Trudy would reflect afterwards on her role as a one-time faculty wife, saying, "Ike and I entertained 10,000 people during his years as dean."

Autumn was pungent in the cool, quickened air along the Eastern Seaboard, with many things entering phases of maturity, mellowing, or a last blazing intensity before the onset of decline. Carly Simon's infatuation with Beatty had dimmed after three to four months. Not long afterwards, Carly re-encountered Taylor and was formally introduced. The common attraction was more powerful than before, and of course they had the Vineyard in common, too. But she was hurt he was still unfamiliar with her songs – even after having sat through her Troubadour set.

Stranger still, months later, after Taylor had already moved in with Simon – who was promoting a second hit album called *Anticipation* – James had an embarrassingly unaccustomed reaction when he first spied the cover of the initial *Carly Simon* solo release.

"Hey, that's a fine-looking woman," he told a friend.

"That's *your* girl," the friend advised.

"What?"

"That's Carly!"

"Oh," said Taylor, looking closer. "*So it is.*"

16

There We Are

Evidence of love. It is the strongest asset, finest achievement and most lasting legacy of any relationship. Without it, there is no peace, no satisfaction, no resolution, no getting close in generosity, or letting go in joy. The greatest relationship of all is the family, because it is the only organic school capable of teaching all the modes and means of unselfish love.

Without evidence of unselfish love, one has family in name or façade only, and within such families, one tastes the bitterest fruits of human existence: maturity without true growth, materialism at its most piteously grasping, and the betrayal of trust in its most vulnerable places.

In the presence of unselfish love, there is a kind of music. With evidence of unselfish love, there is the possibility of more such music. But without such evidence, there is only, at best, the sound of someone else's music, echoing in an empty place. And that is something very different indeed. Carly Simon grew up hearing her father Richard playing someone else's music on a grand piano in their gracious Riverdale home, and it still reverberates down through the decades. Repeating and repeating.

Richard Simon was one of five children born to Leo Simon, a well-to-do manufacturer and importer of the silk flowers and marabou (West African heron) feathers that were leading decorative elements in hats, dresses and fashion accessories in America and Europe between the 1830s and 1930s. While Richard's father permitted musical instruments in the family brownstone on Manhattan's West 87th Street and had no quibbles with weekly visits for himself or his children at the New York Philharmonic, he forbade Richard from pursuing his dream of a career as a classical pianist.

Entranced by Frederic Chopin and marathon practice sessions, Richard had natural talent and the vigorous hands and long tensile fingers ideal for the keyboard. He was wont to put his full six-foot-four-inch frame into the full-pressure grandeur of Chopin's mazurkas, ballades, nocturnes, concertos, polonaises, and solo études. It was his first love. But his parent said playing the piano, even with the Philharmonic, was unsuitable as a source of income for anyone hoping to provide for a family.

Richard might have cultivated an ally in his mother, Anna, but she died when he was 18. So Leo Simon's domineering word held sway in the household on 87th Street, where he invited his wife's best friend, a Swiss woman named Jo Hutmacher, to come to live and act as surrogate mother to Leo's younger children. This, Miss Hutmacher did. She also became the secret paramour of tall, insecure teenager Richard, initiating him into sex.

This near Oedipal trysting was still in place in the 1920s, as Richard, now a graduate of Columbia University, was making his way in a profession that was a pale substitute for his heart's desire; he was a piano salesman for the Aeolian company, in whose West 42nd Street building Richard met trade magazine publisher Max Lincoln Schuster.

Schuster's dad ran a stationery shop in Harlem but he was a bright, resourceful man and a voracious reader. Among the books on Schuster's desk the day Simon called to sell him a piano were a biography of Beethoven and several novels, including *Jean Christophe* by Romain Rolland. A chat about these books disclosed a common admiration for music and literature, and led to other chats, which led to their partnership in the new publishing firm, Simon & Schuster, its financing being personal loans totalling $8,000.

The real seeds of Simon & Schuster's success were in a faddist realm no other publishers took seriously: crossword puzzles. An aunt of Simon's was an ardent crossword enthusiast, and Richard was intrigued to learn adherents of the diversion were dependent on daily newspapers to feed their habit, i.e. crosswords were not available in bulk. Simon & Schuster arranged with the crossword editors of the *Sunday World* for a book-length collection of 50 puzzles. The first edition sold 40,000 copies in 12 weeks, with 375,000 copies moved the first year.

A natural marketing mind who let his Muse skip wherever its erratic tendencies took it, Simon absentmindedly did piano exercises on table tops during meetings and passed daily through a forest of flip monikers for office associates whose names he never learned or rarely recalled. One such acquaintance was Andrea Heinemann, a one-time sales girl from B. Altman & Co. who'd got the switchboard job at Simon & Schuster in 1934. A petite and darkly pretty woman with a tomboyish style that drew greater than normal attention to her sensual femininity, Heinemann had grown up poor in Philadelphia.

"Hello, little woman," he'd greet her in the morning.

"Hello, big man," she'd answer with a grin.

Blessed with a theatrical knack inherited from her mother for glamorising her humble past with winking wives' tales about far distant royalty, Heinemann adopted the style and manner of nominal lookalike Katharine Hepburn, literally from the moment that the young actress was an unqualified hit opposite John Barrymore in the 1932 film, *A Bill Of Divorcement*. But unlike Hepburn, Heinemann was not from a distinguished New England family of surgeons and suffragettes; her father deserted the family when she was three, and her mother Maria Heinemann refused to divulge anything about him to Andrea and her two younger brothers.

Richard Simon didn't care about the Heinemann pedigree; Andrea exuded the natural verve and audacity he lacked, and he proposed – but only after a year of coyly amorous office banter and the disconcerting encroachment of rivals. Their 1936 Hawaiian honeymoon went badly; the marriage was not immediately consummated. Out of his Manhattan element, Richard lost all poise and elan, and he began cabling Jo Hutmacher daily, while requesting Andrea sleep in a separate bed.

Once back in New York, the relationship would not take its natural course until Andrea agreed to an unnatural contingency: "Auntie Jo" would become an official part of the extended family. Shaken but proud, Andrea stood by as Richard installed her own mother and

Auntie Jo in a rented apartment together, as bizarre a pair of room-mates as the crestfallen young wife could have imagined.

When Andrea was pregnant with Richard's first child, he insisted on naming her Joanna – an amalgam of Auntie Jo and his own mother, Anna. This drive to put the optimum spin on anything from which he derived comfort would also serve Simon's ends in business. A creature of capricious instinct, Richard scored next for Simon & Schuster with a text by fellow card player Charles Goren on contract bridge, a social craze in which the Simons indulged. It became one of the best-selling hobbyist books of all time.

With amateur camera buffs proliferating, and Simon himself an avid shutterbug, he issued his own guide in 1937, *Miniature Photography From One Amateur To Another*. Simon & Schuster was brainy and brash, with nearly 50 volumes of crosswords in print by 1939. Less frivolous titles in the back catalogue were texts by Albert Einstein and the best-selling popular history series by Will and Ariel Durant that began with *The Story Of Philosophy*.

The next step for Simon & Schuster was the admission of another partner into the firm, the accountant Leon Shimkin. Such moves mandated more strategic thrusts, and a decision was made to get into the trend in publishing: inexpensive paperback books. Penguin Books had done well with them in England since 1933 and that company was due to introduce them in the US in 1939. Paperbacks weren't entirely new in the States, however; colonist-publisher John Bell instituted a 190-volume series on British poets in 1777, and its final edition appeared in US shops just a few years before Isaac Taylor sailed into New Bern in 1790 and began trading in both domestic and imported books.

In an effort to get an edge on Penguin as well as the new Red Seal/Gold Seal/Blue Seal brand paperbacks being published by New York's Modern Age Books, Simon & Schuster started Pocket Books, a collaborative enterprise between Robert DeGraff (who coined the name) and the three directors of the hardcover Simon & Schuster company, namely Simon, Schuster, and Shimkin. The first Pocket Book DeGraff lined up was *The Good Earth* by Pearl S. Buck in September 1938 – Buck then won the Nobel Prize for Literature. Pocket Books' trademark was a kangaroo wearing glasses, with books in hand

and in pouch; the studious marsupial (called Gertrude) earned artist Frank J. Lieberman $50 and was one of America's best-known logos. Pocket Books first top-ten list encompassed James Hilton's novel *Lost Horizon*, Dorothy Parker's light verse, *Enough Rope*, and *Five Great Tragedies* by William Shakespeare.

But the idea that ensured Pocket Books fortunes was DeGraff's concept in July 1940 to issue a paperback of one of Simon & Schuster's hardback staples, Dale Carnegie's *How To Win Friends And Influence People*. The parent company feared the paperback would cannibalise hardcover sales, but DeGraff stocked the title in outlying drug stores and five-and-dime outlets rather than urban bookshops and other traditional retail outlets.

Huge sales (five big printings by November) of the paperbound edition of *How To Win Friends And Influence People* opened the eyes of Simon, Schuster, and Shimkin. It also made one wonder if the three men had ever availed themselves of the advice Carnegie offered their readers:

* ★ SIX WAYS OF MAKING PEOPLE LIKE YOU.
* ★ TWELVE WAYS OF WINNING PEOPLE TO YOUR WAY OF THINKING.
* ★ NINE WAYS TO CHANGE PEOPLE WITHOUT GIVING OFFENCE OR AROUSING RESENTMENT.
* ★ PLUS: SEVEN RULES FOR MAKING YOUR HOME LIFE HAPPIER.

Any of these entries might have aided Richard Simon or his household, which was a big, broad-winged brick colonial on a hilltop in the upper-middle class Fieldston section of Riverdale, New York. At the piano, Richard still played to amuse family and business friends like Oscar Hammerstein II, George Gershwin, Arthur Rubenstein, and Benny Goodman, with the three Simon daughters, Joanna, Lucy, and Carly often called upon to sing such Broadway tunes as 'A Real Nice Clambake' from Rogers & Hammerstein's 1945 Broadway hit, *Carousel*. By her teen years, the Simons' living room cabaret had gone to Carly's head, since it was the one area in which the gawky "ugly duckling" of the daughters was allowed to shine. Relatives remember

Carly gesticulating on the lawn as she sang, with her best pre-teen torridness, "All I want is loving you and music, music, music!"

One of Richard's brothers, George T. Simon, was a band drummer and respected critic/editor for *Metronome*, which in 1943 celebrated 60 years of covering American popular music – with an emphasis on big band, contemporary jazz and swing, from Duke Ellington, Count Basie and Benny Goodman, to Coleman Hawkins. George's "Simon Says" column in the anti-censorship, pro-integration minded *Metronome* was must-reading amongst jazz fans of all social and political backgrounds. Simon was a founder of the New York chapter of the National Academy of Recording Arts & Sciences and later earned a Grammy Trustees Award for his career.

Music overshadowed even publishing in the Simon pantheon. On the one occasion when Andrea herself tried to tread with any degree of seriousness into the domain of her husband's first love, the effort stumbled. Her rendition of 'Summertime', delivered in front of guest George Gershwin, wilted under Richard's curt correction from his place at the keyboard.

During the 1940s, there was increasingly grave conflict within and without the Simon's grand house (and a collateral country estate in Stamford, Connecticut). As Hitler's Nazis made initial headway in conquering Europe, and World War II began to envelop the entire world, Pocket Books wanted to impress the portability factor of its lightweight, softbound texts on the public's mind. So when a fan letter arrived in the mail from a buck private stationed at Camp Edwards, Massachusetts, it was quickly appropriated for promotional ads; the text was positioned below a list of Pocket Books' 1943 List of Titles In Print:

> I want to tell you how much my buddies and I have appreciated your books. We have just returned from two-months manoeuvres in North Carolina, where everything we owned we carried on our backs. Consequently, reading matter was something of a problem, except for the fact that Pocket Books were easily carried in hip pockets.

After the Japanese bombed Pearl Harbor on December 7, 1941, the war came home to America, where Richard Simon not only had to cope with periodic paper rationing but also waning troop morale in the face of the Allies' protracted battle in Europe and Asia. As Simon & Schuster's primary marketing and idea men, Richard and Pocket Book's DeGraff were unfailingly patriotic in their perspective, participating extensively in the non-profit Armed Services Editions series distributed to combatants in the war zone. The slogan that accompanied them: *Books Are Weapons In The War Of Ideas. Our Men Need Books, Send All You Can Spare.*

Pocket Books went even further with its regular editions, setting up the "POW Service" to send books to American prisoners. By 1943, Simon was serving on the government's Managing Committee of the Council On Books In Wartime. To encourage pass-along patriotism from regular patrons, Pocket Books also printed a black box on the back of every wartime paperback in which was stated either "Send this book to a boy in the armed forces anywhere in the US" or "Share this book with someone in uniform."

Andrea Simon appeared to take the latter back-cover credo somewhat personally by embarking on a clandestine existence outside the Simon household. Unbeknownst to her husband, she joined a uniformed volunteer corps at a nearby Army base and drove a jeep as a civilian aide for officers throughout the war. It was an exciting alternative outlet that freed her from Richard, mother Maria, Aunt Jo and all the high-toned houseguests to which she felt inferior, and it put her squarely in the company of men, which she always extolled to her daughters in a distinctly open-ended manner as "wonderful!" But Andrea was always careful to return home by 4.30 p.m., changing back into suburban mufti to relieve the nannies in the nursery just before Richard got home. Carly recalled watching in bewilderment as a toddler as her mother told her father: "The children have kept me busy all day."

The children at this point were eldest daughter Joanna (nicknamed Joey) and younger siblings Lucy, born May 5, 1940, and Carly, who says she was born on June 25, 1945.

In 1944, Simon was pressured by his partners into selling Simon & Schuster to the retailing empire of Marshall Field, the tactic attributed at the time to the wartime dip in regular sales as a result of the Pocket Books acquisition. It was a dubious decision at a discount price: a comparatively paltry $3 million, equally divided between the three partners. The step initially exhilarated but then severely depressed Simon, who was shunted aside internally for opposing the buyout.

In 1947, Simon's only son, Peter, was born, but by then Richard was a sullen, chronically downcast and increasingly uncommunicative man; the all but defeated father whom his son would never get to know.

"I consciously blotted him out, my memories of him," Peter would say afterwards; still, when he later discovered his father's darkroom and camera equipment, it led Peter to become a professional photographer.

In 1952, the mountingly mercurial Simon was marginalised within the Simon & Schuster fold by being accorded an imprint, New Ventures Books. But Simon didn't go quietly. New Ventures published many clever and consequential titles ranging from photographer Philippe Halsman's influential *Jump Book* to novelist Sloan Wilson's epochal bestseller, *The Man In The Gray Flannel Suit*.

A year later, 44-year-old Andrea hired 20-year-old Ronald Klinzing, ostensibly as a companion for her six-year-old son Peter, claiming that her husband was too old and busy and growing too infirm to be a proper companion for her son. Indeed, Richard Simon was ill-equipped to run in the park with his little boy; he would suffer two heart attacks and several strokes during the 1950s. But the real reason, her daughters would deduce, for Klinzing's enduring presence in their Riverdale and Stamford households was that within six months Andrea began an affair with Klinzing. And when Joanna Simon finally confronted her mother she admitted it.

Carly has repeatedly recalled "convoluted" emotions when handsome "Ronnie" Klinzing – whom she often compared to Rock Hudson – entered the Simon's life in 1953. This was also the year she says she developed a near-crippling stammer, a nervous problem she later attributed to the bizarre unfolding of Klinzing's relationship with her mother.

As Carly faltered more frequently in her everyday discourse, Andrea Simon advised the girl that a good way to elude halting speech was to "Sing it". The habit of singing to ease her stammer led Carly to songwriting and the impulse to project her personality by utilising the two practices. Meanwhile, the sad web of infidelity, denial and deception was apparent to others, among them frequent visitor Irwin

Shaw, an author friend of Richard Simon's who used the Simon family's disturbing vortex of disloyalty as an element of his novel, *Lucy Crown*.

Thus gawky, stuttering, socially inept Carly came of age in a house of intrigue, watching her mother slip off to a double life that gathered increasingly in dimension as her dad became an invalid.

In her late pre-teen years, Carly was sent to her first psychiatrist. She was excused from school each Tuesday and Thursday for her appointments, and the disruption in the classroom routine became a matter of mortification. It was the 1950s. Psychiatry was for misfits and malcontents. She felt she was indelibly stigmatised. "There were teachers who explained to the kids that I was more *complicated* than the other children, as opposed to sicker," she told this writer in 1981. "Of course, I knew it meant that I was sicker."

She also felt ridiculed for her "unusual" looks and her awakening interest in the opposite sex. "It seemed like a very long period in my life where I felt ugly," she says, noting in 1981 that she still felt homely one day out of every three. "It was in sharp contrast to the way I saw my two older sisters, which was as great beauties. People would come to the house and say, 'Oh Lucy, you've gotten so *beautiful*. And Joey, you look so *elegant*.' And then they'd turn to me and say, 'Hi, Carly.'"

Her father's blunt criticism and caustic wit did little to alleviate this notion of her undesirability.

"He could be very thoughtful but he could also be very cruel," said Carly. "One day I said, 'Daddy, do you have any good-looking friends who could come to the house?' because I was reading *Gone With The Wind* at the time and was in love with Clark Gable" – who of course had starred opposite Vivien Leigh in the 1939 screen version of Margaret Mitchell's book. "He said, 'There's a man coming today who, in fact, looks just like Clark Gable!' I was so excited and got all dressed up, put on make-up, did my hair, the works. When the dinner guest showed up, I came down the stairs Scarlett O'Hara–style, and he was just a little old man with glasses. I saw my father laughing at me, and I was crushed."

In 1955, when Simon had his first heart attack, Andrea was in Europe with Klinzing, who had been drafted into the services. Perhaps resentful (as Carly later surmised) for all the years she shared psychic space with Auntie Jo Hutmacher in Richard's affection, she did not deign to return to care for her husband.

In 1956, when Marshall Field died, Richard Simon was in Florida resting from a second heart attack. Field's estate decided to divest itself of its holdings in publishing. Leon Shimkin, who had engineered the original sale, stepped up and asked Schuster to join him in the buyback from the Field estate of Simon & Schuster – but Simon was not invited to participate.

Simon was in fragile health and spirit, and he could have contributed little to the publishing house that still carried his name as co-founder, but it would have been a nice gesture to include him (and by extension his heirs) in some small fiscal aspect of the deal. It didn't happen.

When Simon learned of this, coupled with the behaviour of his wife, of which he apparently had both knowledge and silent acquiescence, he took it to be the last piece in a long, star-crossed puzzle of personal betrayals. Feeling conflicted and misunderstood all his life, a guest in his own career, in his own business, in his own home – where Andrea now lived openly with Klinzing, sharing a room together in another part of the house – Richard Simon had lost the strength or the will to keep fighting the demons within and without. Bouts of delirium grew more frequent; after a third heart attack, he died on July 31, 1960.

Carly was informed the next morning of Richard's passing by her mother; his daughter remembers being too numb to cry. She had never been able to get to know her father, to find common ground or draw his attention away from her more self-assured and conventionally pretty sisters. Other than the two years – "1952 and 1953" – that Carly was invited to keep her father company at Dodgers home games at Ebbett's Field, driving out with him, they shared little.

For her, it was an effort to find a way into his heart; but for her father, though she couldn't grasp it at the time, her little brother Peter would have been far more logical company given the accepted male chauvinism of the era. Yet Richard Simon took her out to the ball game – until his health was too precarious to make such fond excursions.

Carly had continued to suffer from nervous disorders, her stammer turning into a "worry lump" she couldn't swallow, and then developing palpitations that plagued her through late adolescence and early adulthood. She developed agoraphobia and began seeing a psychiatrist.

A relatively even-tempered college experience at Sarah Lawrence, which Simon left without graduating, was a prelude to four costly years of Freudian analysis ("I spent all my inheritance," she told the author in 1981). But still Carly's bouts of anxiety reoccurred. The clammy, heart-pounding tremors were blamed on food allergies, even wine allergies, or some chemical or hormonal complication.

As her brother Peter would reflect, "It never surprised me that performing became such a terror for Carly, a source of tense disorientation. Her need to perform, the tremendous expectations she has when she does, and the fear she feels, just seem logical extensions of her having to perform for my father to get the slightest reaction from him. As time went on, her performing became more articulate. For some crazy reason – a manifestation of his craziness – he completely rejected her as his daughter. He was in a worsening state of insanity."

Carly insists she never planned a career in music, that it had been Lucy who dragged her, over the course of Carly's summer before college, into the spotlight. (They hitch-hiked to Provincetown and got a gig at a bar called The Moors as a folk duo.) However, Carly herself studied with Pete Seeger, an association she emphasised early-on in her folk career.

Carly feels her primary vocal influence was Alabama-born folksinger Odetta, whose bestselling album was the 1963 RCA release, *Odetta Sings Folk Songs*. Other acknowledged female vocal heroes of Carly's echo a childhood and adolescence in the 1940s and 1950s rather than the '60s: Peggy Lee, Ella Fitzgerald, Annie Ross of Lamberts, Hendrix and Ross.

Lucy and Carly's folk career as the Simon Sisters was sufficiently well established by the early '60s that the two women – often mistaken for twins at this ripening stage of Carly's allure – were opening on the Greenwich Village coffeehouse and folk cabaret circuit for such hip comedic draws as Woody Allen, Bill Cosby and Joan Rivers. Their break as recording artists arrived when Dave Kapp of Kapp Records heard them at the Bitter End and signed them to his label.

The Kapps had entered the record business a generation earlier with Kapp's Imperial Talking Machine Shop on Madison Street in Chicago. Jack Kapp, a son of the store's owner, was hired by Brunswick Records in 1925 to guide its so-called "race records" wing and became general manager of Brunswick Records, whose roster boasted Bing Crosby, The Mills Brothers and bandleaders Tommy and Jimmy Dorsey. In 1934, E.R. "Ted" Lewis, founder of the British Decca Record Company, gave Jack Kapp $250,000 to launch the American Decca division, with Lewis as chairman and Kapp as president. Jack's younger brother Dave, who ran a record and mail order business in Chicago, moved to New York in 1935 and joined his brother at Decca.

Dave was brought on to strengthen Decca's stable of country acts – whose music was then described as "hillbilly" or "old time" or "sacred" music. He and a staff engineer began travelling in the South and Southwest making portable wax-disc field recordings of regional talent or cutting them in small studios in San Antonio, Dallas, Houston, New Orleans, and Charlotte. An informal advisor/supporter in such matters was Pulitzer Prize-winning poet/troubadour Carl Sandburg, a family friend from Chicago who also wrote a poem for Dave's son Michael (nicknamed Mickey) called 'Arithmetic'.

"I was having trouble with math in 7th grade," Mickey Kapp now recalls, "and Sandburg told me he was supposed to go to West Point but had flunked the math test. So he wrote me a poem about how numbers can fly in and out of your head." Sandburg's way with numbers improved, with songs and the income underlying them destined to linger in the psyches of Carl and the Kapps. At the time, Sandburg was still reaping the benefits since 1927 of his successful Harcourt, Brace Jovanovich, Inc. book, *The American Songbag*, but would make albums in the 1950s for the Lyrichord and Columbia labels, while the Kapps were profiting from the post-Depression boom in American popular recordings.

Etho-musicologists John and Alan Lomax were also comrades of the Kapps and their paths often crossed as they sought out native talent of a rustic type. Early Dave Kapp discoveries were Red Foley, Jimmie Davis, and Ernest Tubb, whose seminal Kapp Records release of 'Blue Eyed Elaine' spurred cowboy film star Gene Autry to do a cover version and make Tubb enough money to leave his job as a salesman at

Western Mattress Company in San Angelo, Texas.

Jack Kapp did the first Broadway cast album in 1937, George Gerswhin's *Porgy & Bess*, and the first complete original cast recording of a Broadway score in 1943 with *Oklahoma!* Decca would also get Ella Fitzgerald, The Ink Spots, Louis Jordan, The Mills Brothers, Webb Pierce and Kitty Wells under contract.

Jack Kapp died in 1949, and Dave stayed on at Decca to oversee A&R for the main label and its Brunswick and Coral subsidiaries, the latter the home of Buddy Holly. In 1955 Kapp formed Kapp Records, finding success in pop with pianist Roger Williams, in teen hits like Jerry Keller's 'Here Comes Summer' (1957), Johnny Cymbal's 'Mr. Bass Man' (1963) and R&B quintet Ruby and The Romantic's number one hit in '63, 'Our Day Will Come'.

The Kapp label's catalogue retained its ties to folk music in the 1960s with such titles as *Alan Lomax Presents: Folk Song Saturday Night* (1961), *The Many Voices Of Miriam Makeba* (1962), and Lomax's *Raise A Ruckus And Have A Hootenanny* (1964). The Makeba release was licensed to Kapp via Belafonte Enterprises, a production company run by Harry Belafonte, the Harlem-born folk singer ('Banana Boat (Day-0)', 'Jamaica Farewell') of West Indian heritage.

Also brought into the Kapp roster via Belafonte Enterprises was The Chad Mitchell Trio, a folk-pop outfit from Spokane, Washington's Gonzaga University which issued a hit album for Kapp in 1962, *Mighty Day On Campus*, recorded at Brooklyn College. The Mitchell group's follow-up that year, *The Chad Mitchell Trio At The Bitter End* – featuring future Byrds member Jim (later known as Roger) McGuinn on second guitar – also sold well, as did a 1963 album titled for their cover of the Bob Dylan classic, *Blowin' In The Wind*.

The Simon Sisters had evolved a tight, close-harmony folk-pop sound at the point Dave Kapp encountered them, and their Kapp recordings reflected that experience. Lucy, with her slightly higher voice, was the lead in the Simon Sisters, with Carly adding the low harmony. They were managed by Harold Leventhal (former manager of the Weavers and Woody Guthrie) and Charlie Close. In February 1964, they released their first album, *Winkin', Blinkin' And Nod – The Simon Sisters*, whose title track (with 'So Glad I'm Here' on its B-side) rose to number 73 in the Hot 100 in April of that year.

Lucy Simon – whose name usually appeared before Carly's in credits – wrote the music for 'Winkin', Blinkin' And Nod', and the song's lyrics were an adaptation by her of a children's verse from a poet whose work her father often read aloud from at family readings – Eugene Field. The single caught the ear of Jac Holzman, 33-year-old owner of the Record Loft on West 10th Street in the Village, and the founder in 1950 of Elektra Records. Despite its humble hit status as a regional (East Coast) folk-pop flash in the pan, 'Winkin', Blinkin' And Nod' became a personal favourite of Holzman's.

In 1966, the Simon Sisters issued another LP on Kapp, *Cuddlebug*, a collection leavened with public domain material like 'Motherless Child' and 'If I Had A Ribbon Bow', whose first single was the title track, with the flip side being the downbeat, 'No One To Talk My Troubles To'. Tracks featuring Carly included 'Dink's Blues', one of innumerable variations on the traditional folk song 'Wings Of A Dove'. Little came of the second album, or a third for Columbia Records, *The Lobster Quadrille And Other Songs For Children*, which appeared in 1969.

★   ★   ★

Lucy quit the act to compose on her own, get married to physician David Levine and start a family. Circa 1968, Carly had got up the courage to cut her first solo demo, an assertive guitar-and-vocal volley of womanly folk-rock called 'Play With Me', in which she half-shouted, "You can have your fun/But only with me". It was simple but sure in its evocation of passionate yearning, and good enough that it could have easily made a space for itself three years later on her 1971 *Carly Simon* début solo album.

But during the late '60s Carly was still hoping she could be a Carole King without the concert facet that was to come. Simon spent a lot of time writing jingles for clients like J.C. Penney's, and sending demos to other artists, including Judy Collins and Cass Elliot of The Mamas And The Papas.

"She and I grew quite close for a span of time," Peter recalled, "and when she had to go solo and project herself alone in order to gain acceptance from record companies and the public, she became very down on herself, awfully negative and depressed. Between 1967 and 1969 or so she was just bouncing around New York, recording commercial jingles and demos and being very depressed. I've always been curious why she's never talked much about that gloomy era. I used to hang out with her a lot, supporting her when she had to go to auditions and recording sessions. It was just a rotten time for her. Very difficult to break through her depression. Really, it was very serious, really bad."

Carly also held a job as talent co-ordinator for a live TV show, *From The Bitter End*. Bob Dylan's management office, run by Albert Grossman and partner John Cort, tried to redirect Carly artistically. Dylan rearranged Eric Von Schmidt's 'Baby Let Me Follow You Down' for her, and she cut it with Mike Bloomfield and some members of The Band, but Columbia, Dylan's label, refused to issue it. Cort and Grossman also had the notion of pairing Carly with Richie Havens, calling the act Carly & The Deacon. She also served an uneasy six-month term as co-lead singer in '68–69 with Elephant's Memory. She dated director Milos Forman and had a small part in a film about auditioning, *Taking Off*.

The turnaround arrived, by increments, after meeting *New Yorker* writer and professional lyricist Jacob Brackman while she worked as a counsellor at a summer camp. They began to write material for Simon, including his own lyrical interpretation of what life might have been like for Carly as she came of age in the same house with her distant father: 'That's The Way I've Always Heard It Should Be'. Carly's then-manager Jerry Brandt proffered a cassette in 1970 to Elektra Records chief Jac Holzman, who took it because Carly had been one of the singers on 'Winkin', Blinkin' And Nod'. After listening to her demos while on vacation in Japan, he phoned Brandt and signed her.

While Carly did not take her 1971 'Heard' hit literally, it captured the pessimism of the times in the wake of the Vietnam build-up, the assassinations of John Kennedy, Malcolm X, Robert Kennedy, and Martin Luther King, the shooting of four campus war protesters by the National Guard at Kent State, the government lies and the surveillance of its citizens, and the rising, sceptical sense that Simon's generation would never inherit a semblance of normal adult life after so much cultural despoliation during its formative years.

★　★　★

On November 3, 1972, Carly Simon married James Taylor in her Murray Hill apartment on East 33rd Street. "I remember," said Trudy, who attended the modest nuptials, "that Carly had a small apartment then, and her mother Andrea had brought chrysanthemums from her garden. Carly's friend, Jacob Brackman, whose whole face was bearded, was unable to speak – he was 'in a speechless phase,' someone said. Carly was barefoot. James was calm. The judge who married them said to me, "It's a ceremony of hope."

James played a concert that night at Radio City Music Hall and announced the happy event to the audience. "A post-concert party planned for three a.m. at the Tower Suite was suddenly a wedding party," recalled the jocular Joe Smith, the newly appointed president of Warner Bros. Records (Mo Ostin was now Chairman), "with the aristocratic German-Jewish Simon family on one side and the Taylors from Carolina, complete with everything but livestock, on the other. I was asked to give the wedding toast, which touched me, because James was very vulnerable and you always wanted to repay that trust with sensitivity."

This was to be a public toast to a public relationship that needed more privacy than either partner realised. Meanwhile, others understandably saw it as a kind of artistic partnership. Among them, officials of their respective Warner (James) and Elektra (Carly) record labels, who had been joined just a year and a half before in a new corporate configuration, the Warner/Elektra/Atlantic Group (or WEA, for short) which had only just become fully operational.

Everyone laughed and smiled and hugged in the Tower Suite. But some of those present recalled how, just the year before, the Atlantic and Warner labels had been locked in what Atlantic vice president Jerry Wexler had been quoted in *Billboard* as calling a "healthy competition" to see if Atlantic's Donny Hathaway/Roberta Flack duet version of 'You've Got A Friend' (released slightly before Taylor's own single) could trounce James' edition on the charts.

"Even though Warner Bros. is a sister label, we're going ahead full tilt," said Wexler in an article headlined LABELS IN 'UNFRIENDLY' FAMILY FEUD OVER 'FRIEND', "just as we would in a battle with any competitive label."

In the end, the Hathaway/Flack track rose no higher than number

29 in contrast to Taylor's chart-topping triumph, but a certain tone was reaffirmed: all's fair in the record business. It was not, however, the tone Joe Smith wanted to set for the Simons or the Taylors.

But it was getting harder to tell whether or not you've got a friend or not in a world of war and assassinations, of upfront competition and backstairs betrayals, of open auditions and anxious performances. And the two families who mattered most in that room on the night of November 3, 1972, were only toasting one thing: evidence of love.

17

Don't Let Me Be Lonely Tonight

"It was a full day," James said of his nuptials with Carly and its collateral public ceremonies, and he had many such days and nights ahead of him. He was undergoing methadone treatment to hammer away at heroin's grip, even as he drove nails and sawed planks to finish his farm house outside Vineyard Haven near Lamberts Cove Road.

"At this point the house wasn't fully built," he said. "This was an early timber structure my friends called Wood Hinge or Shingle Mountain. It was at that point a very odd, narrow, tall house, just stuck in the middle of a wood lot *way* back in the woods."

Due to his marriage and his need to complete his third album for Warner Bros., due for release in late November, Taylor had tried to minimise touring and sidetrips other than to New York. He was now sharing Carly's Central Park West apartment until he got the Lamberts Cove house into inhabitable condition.

As that task had lagged, Taylor had been struck months earlier with the idea that recording much of his next record on the rustic site of his Vineyard house would speed the completion of both. And so, sandwiched between periodic New York recording with producer Phil Ramone at A&R Studios (where 'Back On The Street Again', and short pieces 'Fanfare', 'Hymn', 'Dance' and 'Jig' were cut) and work on all principal vocals with producer Robert Appere at Clover Studios in Los Angeles (where 'Nobody But You', 'Fool For You', 'Instrumental I', the old British folk standard 'One Morning In May', and a cover of John McLaughlin's 'Someone' were done), the demoing, basic tracking and most significant toil had taken place at James' Vineyard place-in-progress just prior to his wedding, with Peter Asher getting it on tape and supervising the integration of all the rest into a uniform statement. Quite often, in a glen deep in the Tisbury woods, the trucks coming and going on the meandering gravel road to the construction site were hauling cement, lumber, sound equipment or mixtures of both.

The songs that came to fruition on a portable recording console in the general disarray of the house's bare wooden shell were 'One Man Parade', 'Chili Dog', 'New Tune', 'Woh, Don't You Know', written by James, Kootch and bassist Lee Sklar, 'Instrumental II', 'Little David', 'Mescalito' (the chemically sparked chant James conjured at the beach while still in his hand and foot casts), and 'Don't Let Me Be Lonely Tonight', the first single from the album, which he'd been contemplating calling *One Man Parade*.

"Before that," said Taylor, 'I'd briefly considered *Farewell To Showbiz* and *Throw Yourself Away*. Then *One Man Parade*, but it got changed for no particular reason." The new title was *One Man Dog*, in reference to his shepherd dog, David, who earns a mention in the song. The corresponding photo on the front of the album – showing James gliding in a rowboat with a guidepole, his canine at his feet – resulted from an impromptu visit Carly and James paid her photographer brother Peter in the summer of 1972 while Peter was living on a commune outside of Brattleboro, Vermont.

"Carly and James were driving around the countryside," said Peter, "and they showed up in a huge, blimplike Winnebago and stayed all afternoon. We lived down this dirt road, with a pond on the property. I asked James what his next album was going to be called. He said, "*One Man Dog*." So I got him out in the pond with his dog, David, and I shot the picture from the shoreline. He wore the tie for a bizarre effect: the isolation of a man and his dog against the world, but subconsciously so. It was a lot of fun."

One Man Dog had a handsome but remote feel to it, from its compilation of suite-like miniatures and songlettes to the cover image of him surrounded by raw timber in his Vineyard hideaway. Principal players on the sessions were Kootch, Kunkel, Sklar, Craig Doerge on keyboards, with Bobbye Hall on congas and percussion. Kate, Alex and Hugh Taylor supplied most of the backing vocals.

But Carole King and Kootch's wife Abigale Haness of Jo Mama sang on 'Fanfare' and harmonised with James on 'Mescalito'. Carole and James were pleased to be recording together again; they'd each got Grammys back in March 1972 for 'You've Got A Friend', James winning in the category of Best Pop Vocal Performance, Male, and King getting her trophy for Song Of The Year. King won three more *Tapestry*-related Grammys for Album Of The Year: Best Pop Vocal Performance, Female for the 'Tapestry' song and Record Of The Year for 'It's Too Late'. At the same ceremony, the Best New Artist award went to Carly Simon, who would join King and Haness in James' house to furnish harmonies on the song, 'One Man Parade'.

Faces old and new assisted on the rest of *One Man Dog*. Mandolinist Dash Crofts of the duo Seals and Crofts joined John Hartford on fiddle and banjo and Red Rhodes on steel guitar for James' sprightly two-minute-and-seven-second hoedown on 'Dance', which sounds like it was tossed off in a hayloft but actually got taped with Phil Ramone in Manhattan, and contained the aforementioned "throw myself away" line that abided for some time as a working album title.

Ramone also brought horn players Art Baron, Barry Rogers and Brecker Brothers Randy and Michael into the New York sessions, with Michael dubbing the aching tenor sax solo on the final version of 'Don't Let Me Be Lonely Tonight'.

The spell of the record was in its sequencing, its disparate cuts of lovesickness and the exigencies of emotional attachment meshed together in the truly natural way Taylor's Apple album never achieved, with all musical segues and ligaments flexing in deference to each other on the basis of rhythmic ease and forward flow.

Advancing deadlines led to a production style sanctioning the line of least resistance; if James got an idiosyncratic idea at home while the carpenters flailed away, he would hasten into the attic room under the eaves where Asher and Jock McLean sat on boxes and rocking chairs, mixing the day's work, and asked for assistance in exploring it. If there were spare microphones and a quiet corner left for experimentation, off James went.

"We miked a chain saw and did a rhythm track with construction tools – you have a lot of chutzpah at that point," Taylor explained regarding his own eleventh-hour instrumental contributions to 'Little David', with workman Mike Paletier credited on the track for 'Cross Cut Saw'.

More traditional methods were employed for the dulcet 'One Morning In May', on which Linda Ronstadt was invited to sing the backing vocal. The song was a mutation of 'Soldier, Soldier, Won't You Marry Me?' as preserved by English musicologist Cecil Sharpe when he visited North Carolina during the years 1916–18. The more modern version of the song resembled in its chorus the ancient children's song, 'I Went Out One Morning In May', as later transcribed in North Carolina by song researcher Fletcher Collins and recorded in 1958 on Richard Dyer-Bennett's Folkways album, *Songs With Young People In Mind*.

Dyer-Bennett's many records (15 in all, preserving English ballads and American folk songs) were represented in the Taylors' Chapel Hill record library and he was a subtle but definite impact on the Taylor children's song sense. The version of 'One Morning In May' that James cut for *One Man Dog*, however, was an arrangement conceived by Cambridge/Martha Vineyard folkies Jim Rooney and Bill Keith, who put it together while still students at, respectively, Harvard and Amherst. Rooney had found the song in Carl Sandburg's revised 1955 edition of the landmark 1927 anthology in which Ruth Crawford had participated, *The American Songbag*, where it was paired with its Appalachian offshoot, 'The Troubled Soldier'. Rooney took the 'May' version, turned it into a waltz, and devised a new melody that Keith strummed on an autoharp he was learning to play. Rooney and Keith took their vibrant new arrangement of 'One Morning In May' on the folk circuit, from shows with Joan Baez at the Dartmouth Winter Carnival to festivals in Asheville, North Carolina and then at Club 47 off Harvard Square in Cambridge.

A Cambridge folk classic, the Rooney-Keith melody also confirmed the song's status as a beloved British transplant, and Taylor gave the Massachusetts duo full credit for the wonderfully winsome folk air he ignited with Ronstadt about a heartbroken young maiden and the musician/soldier she sees off as he sails away to London and the wife and children he'd left behind.

"I love that version," Taylor said of the track, adding that the entire *One Man Dog* project "arrived in cooperative pieces." And since James was, at times, "walking on eggshells," as Kootch put it, because of the medicinal shock methadone had on his system, he was openly appreciative of the loving care his musician friends brought to the tiring *One Man Dog* endeavour.

" 'Woh, Don't You Know', with Kootch and Lee Sklar, was surprisingly the only song I've written with Lee," said James of his resplendently bearded bassist. "He's so gifted and he could and does play with everyone you can think of" – including Linda Ronstadt, Jackson Browne and Emmylou Harris – "but he has always made it clear that he'll drop everything and move Heaven and Earth to come out on the road with me, as long as I give him a month's notice or so. It's not for the money; he's just a solid, solid guy. Happily, I had a lot of solid people around me then."

Encapsulating one of the more harried records he would make, Taylor concluded, "That record's got 18 songs on it, and some of them are little bitty things" – the shortest being 'Mescalito' at 29 seconds – "but they hold up, and I like 'em a lot. 'Don't Let Me Be Lonely Tonight' was the obvious highpoint, writing-wise." But when that single was released in October of 1972, two months ahead of the record, the reaction was a delayed one, the song not rising on the Hot 100 until the first week of December. It eventually peaked at number 14, but subsequently became one of the biggest recurrent radio tracks of Taylor's career, yet the rest of *One Man Dog* did not maintain a comparable pace.

The album went gold, cresting at number 4 on the US charts, in contrast to *Mud Slide Slim And The Blue Horizon*, which had a lock on the number 2 slot in '71 for four straight weeks. And *One Man Dog*'s second and third singles, 'One Man Parade' b/w 'Hymn' (number 67, February '73), and 'Hymn' b/w 'Fanfare' (March '73), each failed to see the Top 40. Whereas Taylor's wife's *No Secrets* record – which was released in December 1972 and also went gold – would spend five weeks at number 1 on the *Billboard* album chart, fuelled by the biggest hit (three weeks in the top spot) of her career, 'You're So Vain'.

Simon had cut *No Secrets* during September and October of 1972 at Trident Studios in London, site of James' work for his Apple début. James sang back-up on 'Waited So Long', on which Carly saucily declared, "I'm no virgin!" *No Secrets* was produced by Richard Perry with arrangements by Elton John collaborator Paul Buckmaster. Taylor also appeared along with Kootch on tracks Carly cut with Buckmaster during 1972 that were not released at the time, including a version of John Prine's 'Angel From Montgomery' and a song of Carly's called 'I'm All It Takes To Make You Happy'.

But the backing vocal on 'You're So Vain' – a song which Carly said was partially informed by her relationship with old beau Warren Beatty – was provided by Mick Jagger.

Commenting on the enormous attention *No Secrets* elicited for Carly, Taylor said that the album, "really broke things open for her. I guess the two of our successes amounted to a lot, and it was a very public kind of marriage. I found the attention difficult, but also gratifying and flattering."

During the span between the success of *Mud Slide Slim* and the matrimonial media blitz heralding *One Man Dog* and *No Secrets*, Livingston and Alex Taylor had both issued albums. *Liv*, produced by Jon Landau for Capricorn Records, was done at Intermedia Sound Studios in Boston and arrived in stores in November 1971. A single, 'Get Out Of Bed', climbed to number 97 on the Hot 100, while *Liv* itself stalled at number 147 on the album chart after 10 weeks. The record also featured an inventive, plain-spoken version of 'On Broadway' that was widely admired.

Alex's *Dinnertime*, his second album for Capricorn, was cut at Muscle Shoals Sounds Studios in Alabama and issued in February 1972. It didn't chart, despite notable radio response in the South and North-east to a radiantly soulful barrelhouse blow-out written by Alex, Jimmy Nalls and Chuck Leavell called 'Change Your Sexy Ways'.

Upon receipt of *Liv* and *Dinnertime*, critical observers often preferred the hearty brio and brisk, live-sounding acuity of Alex's album. Alex was plainly singing with skill and conviction on precisely arranged covers of Randy Newman's 'Let's Burn Down The Cornfield', Scott Boyer's 'Comin' Back To You', 'Four Days Gone', by Stephen Stills, Jesse Winchester's 'Payday', Howlin' Wolf's 'Who's Been Talkin', and

'Who Will The Next Fool Be', by Charlie Rich.

As produced by Johnny Sandlin, each track on *Dinnertime* was polished but pungent in the manner of a tight, armed-to-the-teeth road band and the whole eight-song package progressed from a simmer to a boil as it closed with Bob Dylan's 'From A Buick Six'. Whether or not Alex would ever find stardom, he earned grudging respect with the dandy *Dinnertime*, which gained him credibility in the South and Midwest as a bluesrocker, and was a cult favourite for decades to come.

Livingston ended 1973 (and his Capricorn contract) with *Over The Rainbow*, an album that entered the sales charts in November but proceeded no higher than number 189. However, *Over The Rainbow* got him a decisive airwaves edge throughout the decade with the exuberant, radio-friendly 'Loving Be My New Horizon', a fun single from the record that featured James and Carly on harmony vocals, in addition to the title track, which had been a concert crowd pleaser of Liv's for several years prior to its availability on vinyl. He would not issue another album-length project, however, for five years.

★ ★ ★

Carly, pregnant with first child Sarah Maria Taylor (who was born on January 7, 1974) portrayed her beaming pride in motherhood as she sat in an expanded white cotton gown for the Ed Caraeff photo on the sleeve of her next album, *Hotcakes*. Among her best and most straightforward records, it addressed the summits and ravines of everyday life without pretence or hauteur. Produced by Richard Perry, who started the project in Los Angeles in September 1973, it was completed during October and November of that year at the Hit Factory in Manhattan.

Hotcakes featured husband James' vocals and guitar throughout, notably on the record's most memorable tracks: 'Mind On My Man', 'Older Sister', 'Just Not True' and 'Misfit' (all penned by Simon), as well as the Carly and Jacob Brackman-co-authored 'Haven't Got Time For The Pain', and Carly and James' high-energy duet on 'Mockingbird', which was adapted (with additional lyrics by Taylor) from Inez and Charlie Foxx's rhythm and blues-fangled 1963 take on an old folk chestnut. (Kate Taylor and James had often sung 'Mockingbird' at home in Chapel Hill.)

As a 15-year-old R&B fan, James was first exposed to the song in 1965 while at the Apollo Theater to see a Southern soul revue. On the bill that night were James Brown, "Fat Boy" Billy Stewart, Joe Tex, Lee Dorsey, Gladys Knight & The Pips – and also Inez Foxx and her brother Charlie, former gospel singers from Greensboro, North Carolina, who wowed the crowd with their signature song, 'Mockingbird'.

"It was a very springy, leggy kind of thing," Taylor recalled of their performance, "and it made a dent in my brain thereafter. So, Carly was in the studio recording with Richard Perry and Richard said, 'We've got to do this one.' So I wrote a second verse and we nailed it. Dr John [aka Mac Rebbenack] played great organ on it, but the main thing about it was the great rhythm guitar part by Robbie Robertson. He really glued that one together."

'Mockingbird' became *Hotcakes'* smash, the single soaring to number five and going gold even as the album did (both hitting the *Billboard* charts simultaneously on February 2, 1974).

'Haven't Got Time For The Pain' proved a worthy follow-up when it bounded to number 14 after its release that May. Meanwhile, the rather theatrical 'Misfit', prominently placed at the start of side two of the album, disclosed the pain the former song seemed to dismiss, the song's narrator asking her partner to "come home", while stewing that not every man seeking fulfilment necessarily has "a boat to catch", even if "the water is wide".

It's only hip to be miserable, she also admonished, when one is "young and intellectual".

Intriguingly, the finest song on *Hotcakes* enjoyed neither a featured place on the album nor single status. 'Forever My Love', co-written by Simon and Taylor in the prayer-like waltz tempo James often favoured, was a movingly forthright assessment of love and its possibilities between the newlyweds, Carly wondering if "lovers born in May" might grow "bitter and jealous" in a media corona of stardom and impossible expectations. Her voice was raw, flawed and unconfected, as if she'd sung the words wholly without rehearsal or premeditation, engaging the lyrics aloud at first glance.

Direct in its doubts, 'Forever My Love' was also humble regarding the prospects ahead, Carly admitting what she'd found with Taylor was far from "another lovers' game". She also acknowledged that whatever preliminary value the first sparks between them had, it wouldn't be "the way I act" that would carry her and Taylor "through the years intact".

Openly unsure of what to say next to sustain the intimacy of real caring after pillow talk and whispered confidences drift away, Simon saw she would not be able to bid for her partner's attention like she had her father's, i.e. by approaching bonding on a mere pass/fail basis.

In order to love, the song suggested, Simon would have to somehow forget herself and in the process find if she was capable of giving rein to an unrecoverable trust.

As she reached the third verse of 'Forever My Love', Simon sang with an imperceptible tremble while Taylor's acoustic lead guitar rang behind her, her voice catching for an instant when she confessed she was warily looking forward "to looking back", from further "down the track" in hopes she and James would still be "together in fact".

It was arguably the loveliest song ever to appear on a Carly Simon album, and the fact it was a cooperative effort with Taylor was surely a vital part of its power.

Yet 'Forever My Love' was lacking in one crucial respect: it expressed only Carly's side of the equation, with no substantive scrutiny of James, as if she could somehow understand their union without fully comprehending his role in it.

Simon's view of her husband was tender but tentative, romantic but from a distinct remove. She was, of course, older than Taylor, having been born during the war-time heat of Franklin D. Roosevelt's terms as president, whereas James was winter's child, emerging in the chill March months of 1948, as FDR's successor Harry Truman was fighting to win the peace as well as his own re-election that autumn. Thus the distance was becoming more emphatic between a war baby weaned on the big bands of Glenn Miller and Tommy Dorsey, and her younger mate, born into the heyday of Nat "King" Cole's suave jazz, Louis Jordan's jump blues and the crisp uncertainties of the Cold War.

And you could hear that chary distance, that cloudy incomprehension, quite clearly on *Hotcakes*. Somewhere between the surface judgements of 'Misfit' and the searching projections of 'Forever My Love' lay a dark, rutted pathway Simon seemed to avoid addressing, even as the man striding along it was slowly disappearing down its winding length. As Taylor himself quipped in a sombrely "self-defining" new song he'd written as another winter descended, "Say, who is this walking man?"

18

Walking Man

Winter came in December 1973 with its numbing inevitability, but this time its chill wind seemed to be whistling through every hidden crack in American society, from its compromised political institutions, and self-deluding culture of hedonism, to the daily lives trapped in the dreary undertow.

Any relief felt with the Vietnam peace agreement of early 1973 had been sadly undermined as the year wore on by the Watergate scandal engulfing the Nixon White House, in which a burglary of the Democratic Party headquarters at the Watergate hotel back in June 1972 had revealed itself, by monthly degrees, as symptomatic of the smarmy rule-by-flimflam in which Nixon and his cronies specialised. Top White House officials were indicted in September for complicity in Watergate, while in a side-scandal Vice-President Agnew resigned on October 10 after pleading *Nolo Contendere* to a charge of income tax evasion. Attorney General Elliot Richardson quit on principle on October 20 after refusing Nixon's order to fire special Watergate prosecutor Archibald Cox, and then Deputy Attorney General William D. Ruckelshause was dismissed by aides loyal to Nixon for the same reasons. At the end of October, eight impeachment resolutions were introduced in the House of Representatives, setting the Republic squarely in the headlights of a Constitutional crisis.

Meanwhile, Max Yasgur, on whose Sullivan County, NY farm the Woodstock Festival had occurred, was dead of natural causes. America had its first black mayor of a major Southern city, Maynard Jackson of Atlanta, Georgia. The National Commission on Marijuana and Drug Abuse urged treatment for drug users and recognition that alcohol was also a drug problem, but the nation's strongest drug law went into effect in New York State, imposing mandatory life sentences for those convicted of trafficking in hard drugs.

The nation felt unloving and unloved as 1973 ended; crime was up, especially violent crime, and the birth rate was reported at 1.98 children per couple, below the 2.1 rate needed for zero population growth. The CIA had overthrown the elected government of Chile president Salvador Allende Gossens, a Marxist, and murdered him. The Middle Eastern oil exporting countries put an embargo on the US for support-ing Israel, and US plans for a trans-Alaska oil pipeline were approved. Pro sports salaries increased but attendance for basketball, baseball and football declined, as O.J. Simpson of the Buffalo Bills set a new National Football League rushing record of 2003 yards.

In early January 1974, subpoenaed White House tapes made surrep-titiously in the Oval Office by Nixon were revealed by Watergate investigators to contain deliberate and repeated erasures, and Nixon resisted pressure to be the first US president in history to resign. Feeling the trickle-down effects of all these matters and more, James Taylor walked into The Hit Factory on the West Side of Manhattan and began recording a fourth Warner Bros. album to be named *Walking Man*.

"*Sweet Baby James, Mud Slide Slim* and *One Man Dog* were still very whimsical, very unself-important and not taken very seriously on my part," said Taylor, "but by *Walking Man* I was being very affected by my sense of my position in the world, and the difficulty of continuing things in as free and light-hearted a way as I had been before.

"I felt things closing in on me, and that inevitability," he mused. "And then you find a way around that – a way to deal with it, or to make a deal with it."

The chant-tempo songs Taylor was writing bespoke the dismal dis-position of his countrymen, as the rhythms of everyday America took on those of a menial drudge – one who labours slavishly in tedious routine, his superiors unworthy, their leadership aimless. In the

Scotland of James' ancestors, dating from the 17th–18th century heyday of their textile weaving and trading, the cloth workers of Marykirk, Montrose and the Angus coast would sing a partially improvised form of Gaelic song as rhythmic accompaniment to their tasks – most notably the practice of beating wet woollen tweed (soaked in human urine) or other cloth in order to ensure a close-knit durability. Seated at a lengthy trestle table, male or female teams would thump the cloth with fists and wooden hammers until its resultant *waulking* (shrinking) was sufficient, the pounding treatment for each stretch of a bolt of cloth being roughly thirty minutes. In good times the messages in waulking songs were passionate ("Get me a sweetheart soon") or practical ("Move o-ho to the cloth of the lads"), but in bad times they were anxious laments ("They are coming upon you/Here they are upon you/Be upon your guard . . .").

Among the most diverting of the famous waulking songs composed in the time of Hercules Tailyeour was 'Lament For The Lost Harp Key', in which a mislaid tuning key becomes a symbol both ribald and bittersweet, as the harpist croons of misfortune in life and romance as well as the (hopefully fleeting) state of depression/dysfunction to which they have brought him. The lament's central image could also serve as a trope for poor political choices and corrupt civil or military leadership, and the lyrics were meant to provoke much-needed laughter, though its beautiful melody could also trigger tears: "Alas, my tale is distressing/ For me a pain and a loss/Since a weight came on my mind/And my equipment failed/Since I lost my harp key/I cannot find one like it anywhere/To be without it causes me much grief."

An ocean and several centuries distant, Hercules Tailyeour's inheritor had briefly departed Martha's Vineyard for the place he called "the New York island", there to pound out the title track of a new brace of waulking songs in which he admitted that, "Oh for sure one's always missing/And something is never quite right."

★   ★   ★

James Taylor had a family now, with Sarah ("Sally") an infant who inspired the new song, 'Daddy's Baby', in which James detailed his habit of concocting crib-side lullabies to quell her tears and win her affection.

Each day brought domestic urgencies and appointments quite

unaccustomed for the 25-year-old musician, who'd won stardom and the gal everybody longed for, yet carried a lot of inconvenient residual baggage from his former bachelor existence.

Being James Taylor was now a big business, with accountants, tour bookers and road crews and a friend turned manager in Peter Asher who had started out handling Taylor through an existing talent agency but was now fashioning a free-standing firm focused on him. The music world into which Jamie once escaped had lost all its secret passageways and hidden hatches. It had become a turreted pop alcazar with palace guards and courtiers.

"I'm not complaining, mind you," Taylor reflected wryly. "Let's face it: I mean, I could have been Pinky Lee, stranded doing daytime TV until I have a heart attack on the air" – as erroneously reported on September 20, 1955 when Lee fainted on-camera from a sinus condition while doing his live children's variety show at NBC-TV Studios in Burbank, California – "but I have this reputation of being this person who's always having a terrible time coping with everything. It's not the case, you know, when you examine the entire scheme. But I went from a position of simply darting in and out of the forest, striking and then heading back into the underbrush again, to where I was out there in the open trying to keep the castle!"

Just as Taylor found his kingdom-sized dance card increasingly filled, many of his cohorts were beckoned away by equally tight agendas. In between the time when Kootch and the Jo Mama band finished recording Carole King's *Music* and approached the follow-up *Rhymes & Reasons* (released October 4, 1972) there was another Jo Mama (1971's *J Is For Jump*) to expand an Atlantic catalogue begun with their eponymous '70 début. Then came The Section, an act Kortchmar had created with Russ Kunkel, Lee Sklar, and Craig Doerge, which cut two albums for Warner Bros., *The Section* (1972) and *Forward Motion* (1973) – after which Danny had his *own* Warner's album to do, *Kootch* (1973).

These activities left all parties little free time to play with Taylor in any sense of the word, so James had to find new musical companions. His next studio ensemble of session cats and technicians was largely friends and associates of Carly (who sang on five of *Walking Man*'s 10 tracks) and her own musical support system.

Chief among them were David Spinozza, who worked extensively on *Hotcakes* and became the producer of *Walking Man*, plus keyboardist Kenny Ascher, percussionist Ralph McDonald, drummer Rick Marotta, and a tasteful horn section highlighted by the Brecker Brothers. Also key to the new configuration were several top, jazz-tempered players: guitarist Hugh McCracken, bassist Andy Muson, and organ/piano whiz Don Grolnick.

Hoisting the flag for absent Jo Mama members was Ralph Schuckett on electric piano. Other blasts from the past who offered dashes of sentimentality – albeit with a topical thrust – during work on *Walking Man* were Paul McCartney and his wife Linda, who dropped in to do backing vocals on 'Rock 'N' Roll Is Music Now' and 'Let It All Fall Down'. The former track examined the history of American exploitation, recalling how a white man "sailing his ship up on the sea" had led directly to shackling "the black man to a tree". Taylor drew an analogy with the 20th century progression of prosperous R&B into its racist/larcenous apex in the white rock and gold mine of the late '59s and early '60s; once you checked the high-handed math and the human toll, Taylor implied, the practical result was the same.

'Let It All Fall Down' went straight for the jugular of Richard Nixon, whom Taylor had hoped to help rout from power since he and Carole King co-headlined a benefit concert in April 1972 with Barbra Streisand that raised a quarter of a million dollars for Democratic presidential hopeful Senator George McGovern. That Nixon would win by a landslide against McGovern, only to be brought low by Watergate and other high crimes and misdemeanours, was just another of the sudden twists of a twisted age.

"The country was feeling how petty and small-minded the whole thing seemed, and that the main job of power was to hold on to power through dirty tricks," said Taylor of writing 'Let It All Fall Down'. "I just remembered Nixon's foot-dragging on Vietnam, too, and being angry enough to want to write a song about it."

So Taylor penned one of his angriest pieces, marvelling at how Nixon persisted in telling lies, and how the country persisted in believing them. America was moving into a long night of general disbelief, cushioned by prosperity, that fed a decadence seeping into every nook and nano-cranny of the nation's psyche.

Hyper-materialism and technological mesmerism were the formidable distractions proffered to take citizens' minds off a democracy too demoralising to invite participation, and Americans were quite accepting as it reeled from the wraparound embrace of cocaine-coated disco parties to the dull glow of Atari's *Pong* video game. The Defence Department's Advanced Research Projects Agency computer web (Arpanet) was already allowing university-based researchers for the Defence Department to share resources, and by the start of 1974, most of the Arpanet's intra-computer traffic was in something called E-mail. You could buy an Altair 8800 build-it-yourself computer (no keyboard, monitor or software yet) and the Sony Betamax was on the horizon. Given the American penchant for ready self-absorption, the culture was embarking on a dance of dependence with such substitutes for original experience. *Walking Man* was a premonitory flight from the coming occlusion.

A twilight sojourn, Taylor's album was filled with a sense of separation from familiar things, but its mood was deep and dusky rather than dismal. Like a hike through an empty wood at dusk, it grew darker and quieter as the moon slipped behind snow clouds and huge flakes began to drop in fluttering folds. The scene *Walking Man* summoned was hardly forbidding, but its greatest appeal was to those who themselves had been there before. The music was dissatisfied with the status quo and hankering for a cloaked, cloistered form of natural quarantine: like the Vineyard in the depths of the off-season, or midnight on an autumnal Morgan Creek.

Discussing the stark black and white cover of the album, dominated by a tight close-up from photographer Richard Avedon of Taylor in a shapeless woollen sweater, James was well aware of the subtle surprise the image presented.

"*Walking Man* was a statement about my liking for the idea of walking onward," James elaborated. "For the Avedon cover shot, I just pulled out a watch I had been carrying for some time and used it as a prop. And part of the idea was autobiographical, marking my time in music."

In the cover image, it appeared at first as if Taylor was sauntering towards the camera, apparently interested only in what drew his centred stare – yet one's eye soon darted downward to the lower left, attracted by an initially overlooked object in James' cupped hand. Upon his palm sat a shiny pocket watch, its cover snapped open so the light could find its face and announce another message of the picture: time is swiftly passing.

The series of glances required for one to grasp the full range of details in the cover photo always culminated in a psychic shiver of recognition with its last subliminal point: winter was drawing nearer; Taylor's sweater wouldn't be sufficient to keep him warm.

"The 'walking man' was a combination of my father and the fall of the year and winter coming," Taylor explained. "October is my favourite month, but I used to have a terribly strong reaction to fall and the end of summer, and I still have it. So the album was about the coming of winter in many senses, and the way I feel about it.

"I panic a little bit when I feel it coming on. It's always reminded me a little bit of having to go back to school. By school, I mean boarding school. And maybe it's also the primal thing of realising that winter means you're going to have to put up with a tough time; the dark, difficult cold times that you have to be prepared for."

Taylor would also note that "*Walking Man* was the first record I made without Peter Asher" as producer, although Asher did provide some backing vocals. "David Spinozza, the New York guitarist and arranger, did the producing," James explained. "It was an East Coast album, without Kootch, Lee, and my LA community of friends. And it was the first time I worked with Don Grolnick. The tone of it, generally speaking, was low."

Yet there were some touches of humour. On the final track, 'Fading Away' (which Taylor privately called 'Faye Dunaway') he had a whimsical seduction line about there being "something out in the garden" he wanted to show his lover. Taylor also acknowledged the degree to which his own spirit seemed to be undergoing some waulking: "I'm a shrinking man, a sinking man."

And if 'Me And My Guitar' sounded egotistical at first, it was actually Taylor's most unsparing and endearing toteboard of his follies and inadequacies. He knew all about his instrument's changeless ability to keep him company but he regularly deduced it was also his most effective entree into the presence of others – whether it was a waiting audience, or friends who came by for tea.

As with Taylor's modern counterparts, the Scottish waulking songs of yore were unfailingly honest, and attempted to create an aura of community amid the hard tasks at hand. Waulking songs addressed private admissions and public issues, love and death and deeds of wars. Many such songs also borrowed pieces of popular ballads, much as James lifted a mordantly askew quotation of Carole King's 'You've Got A Friend' – "Nice to know I've got a friend/Puts his power right in my hand" – for his 'Lost Harp Key'-like 'Me And My Guitar'. To make the waulking songs last for the duration of mill hands' hours–long toil, choruses and lines were regularly repeated, deepening their meaning. But it was deemed ill luck to sing a waulking tune twice over the same bolt of cloth. In work and in life, one moved on.

Put me anywhere but here, the album seemed to implore, its author's main character sounding like a stunned cog in a wheel as he said he was "moving in silent desperation".

Walking Man proclaimed a need for distance and sanctuary, with virtually every song akin to 'Hello Old Friend' in its prominent mention of travel, the sea, crossing over water, the lure of foreign lands from Europe to China, and the pleasures of Nantucket and the Tide-water South. For added emphasis were a cover of Chuck Berry's 'The Promised Land', and 'Ain't No Song', an impeccably restrained aria to restive inadequacy, written by Spinozza and Joey Levine.

Taylor's *Walking Man* also contained songs that were real refine-ments or stylistic departures from work on his previous albums. The two most atmospheric such cuts on *Walking Man* were 'Daddy's Baby' and 'Migration', with their extensive use of the ethereal Vox Humana vocal filter/pitch transposer. They were also the most satisfying tracks, as Taylor seemed to give himself up to his strongest emotions and glim-mers of self-knowledge. Thinking out loud on 'Baby', with his newborn child in his arms, he held nothing back; and when he sang in 'Migration' about why music made his life work, he talked to it as if it were a kindly spectre, part angel and admonitory spirit guide whom he addressed as the "mystery muse". How well, he asked the shadowy seraph, had he done so far?

"I see music," he confessed in 1997, "as a clear connection to the physical laws that govern the universe. Harmony, the overtone series – our responses are so immediate that they drop us out of our dream.

You need to put your foot on the rock sometimes, and music is the way to do that.

" 'Migration' comes from a very spiritual place," Taylor explained. "I consider myself a spiritual person, with a lot of spiritual motivation, but I just missed the boat with religion, I guess. To talk about transition, and about the limits of consciousness, it's an old theme: the idea of people having an idea of what they're doing but it's mostly an illusion, and something else much larger and more profound is making us move. That was the song's suggestion."

Completed at the end of April 1974, *Walking Man* was preceded by a four-week spring promotional tour, that began in Moorehead, Minnesota and wound up at Nassau Coliseum on Long Island, New York, Taylor's band consisting of Spinozza and McCracken on guitars, Muson on bass, Marotta on drums, and Grolnick on keyboards.

Once *Walking Man* was issued in June, another three-week tour was organised for July to coincide with the release that month of the album's first single, 'Daddy's Baby' b/w 'Let It All Fall Down'. Joining the second road trip was guest star Linda Ronstadt, and the enhanced line-up was dubbed The Manhattan Dirt Riders. In August, another single was floated, 'Walking Man' b/w 'Daddy's Baby', but like it's predecessor, it made no chart appearance.

Walking Man was Taylor's most self-revelatory album thus far, because it faced up, artistically and humanistically, to all the things he could not find on his own, all the places his music would not be able to take him, all the ways he needed to stretch himself in order to grow as an artist and a person. James sang, in words weary but not unwelcoming, that he would need the help of others if the rest of his migration was going to be meaningful.

For listeners who preferred the romantic myth of a distressed but boyishly accessible troubadour, the severe weather readings on the adult-minded *Walking Man* may have proved too much cold truth in one place, since it would always remain Taylor's poorest selling album. A quarter-century later, regardless of the pensive beauty of its brand of waulking songs, *Walking Man* would still not be a gold record.

Like Robert Frost, who was born in sunny California but raised in the surly Merrimack Valley mill town of Lawrence, Massachusetts, Taylor had stopped by woods on a snowy evening; and the woods were lovely, dark and deep. But he could not stay in this safe and empty place. He had his own promises to keep, and miles to go before he'd sleep. At 26, James understood he would have to walk onwards or waulk alone.

19

Family Man

In the autumn of 1974, it had been exactly 11 years since Warner Bros. had formally acquired Frank Sinatra's Reprise Records on September 3, 1963 and begun to turn both of the labels into something beyond a Burbank wax museum. A decade previously, the company's roster was still an overextended cocktail party hosted by the Sinatra Rat Pack (Sammy, Dino, etc.) with a guest-list crammed full of tottering TV hosts, ageing baseball players and long-in-the-tooth screen idols — namely Art Linkletter, Don Drysdale, Alice Faye — plus an undefinable/unsaleable act called Arturo Romero & His Magic Violins. The commercial points of pride in '63 had been the platinum *My Son, The Celebrity*, chubby comic Allan Sherman's album sequel to the double-platinum *My Son, The Folk Singer*; and *Trini Lopez Live At PJ's*, thanks to Lopez's number 11 hit, 'If I Had A Hammer', itself a pass at Peter, Paul & Mary's earlier Warners' cover of Lee Hays and Pete Seeger's 1949 folk warhorse.

But under Chairman Mo Ostin and President Joe Smith's tutelage, the Warner-Reprise family was now a contemporary presence in every sense, from the valleys of its short-lived line of quadrophonic records (a fleeting fad predicated on four-channel sound via a quartet of speakers) to the relative peaks of its '73 album sales with Alice Cooper's platinum *Billion Dollar Babies*, Eric Weisberg's gold *Dueling Banjos*, Jethro Tull's

James, 29, on the cover of the *JT* album, 1977. (*Courtesy Columbia Records*)

The Fabulous Corsairs with Alex at the mike with James (*far right*) on guitar, 1964.
(*Taylor Family Archive, courtesy Trudy Taylor*)

James and classmate in study hall at
Milton Academy, early Sixties.
(*Taylor Family Archive, courtesy Trudy Taylor*)

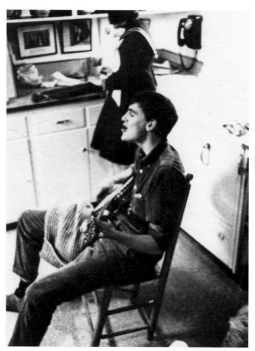

A "kitchen concert" with teenage James (*centre*) on
banjo, and sister Kate on dulcimer behind him.
(*Taylor Family Archive, courtesy Trudy Taylor*)

Manager-producer Peter Asher, James & Danny 'Kootch' Kortchmar, 1971. (*David Gahr*)

James in a Boston snowstorm, 1970. (*Taylor Family Archive, courtesy Trudy Taylor*)

Carole King, 1974. (*Michael Ochs Archives/Redferns*)

Paul Simon & Art Garfunkel in the mid-1960s.
(*Harry Goodwin*)

James Taylor, circa September 1971, at the time of the release of the single 'Long Ago And Far Away'.
(*Warner Bros. Records*)

THE SIMON SISTERS SING
THE LOBSTER QUADRILLE

and other songs for children
Columbia Children's Library of Recorded Books.

Lucy & Carly
The Simon Sisters sing for Children
Music by Lucy Simon

After Carly Simon became a superstar in late 1972-early '73 with 'You're So Vain' from her Elektra *No Secrets* album, the Simon Sisters late Sixties collection for Columbia Records' Children's Record Library series was reissued in 1973 with a vintage Simon Sisters portrait on the front cover. On the back of the reissue were another shot from the Simon Sisters' folkie days, and a childhood image of Carly (*left*) and Lucy (*right*).
(*Album art and photos: Courtesy Columbia Records*)

James Taylor appearing on *Top of the Pops* in London performing 'You've Got A Friend', August, 1971. (*LFI*)

Before… James, trying to get a laugh out of Carly, who's pregnant with Sally, 1973. (*David Gahr*)

After… The expectant parents, smiling through. (*David Gahr*)

gold *Passion Play* (on Chrysalis Records, but distributed in the US by Warners), and of course Sinatra's gold post-retirement album, *Ol' Blue Eyes Is Back*.

However, Warners was cold by December 1974, with Gordon Lightfoot's 'Sundown' being the only gold single of the year, and Maria Muldaur's self-titled solo album for Reprise earning a gold certification on May 13 by dint of her hit single of early spring '74, 'Midnight At The Oasis'. And since young star James Taylor had evidently cheered up – he was spotted on December 24 singing Christmas carols on the streets of Hollywood with Carly Simon, Joni Mitchell and Linda Ronstadt – Warner Bros. really needed him to pull his weight to help the company ledgers.

Basically, Warners wanted Taylor to rejoin *its* family, and come back out to LA to work with Lenny Waronker (son of Liberty Record founder Sy Waronker) who'd been appointed Vice President/Director of A&R in April 1974, and Warner-Reprise staff producer Russ Titelman. Thus beckoned, Taylor responded in kind. So James and Carly began making plans to move West with their toddler daughter Sally for several months. Daddy had fresh songwriting underway before the relocation, however, and his new output would express an artistic handshake between the two coasts.

The title track of what Taylor intended to call the *Gorilla* album was inspired by a visit James says he paid to the Central Park Zoo and its gorilla cage "after a fight with Carly". The songwriter stood awhile looking at "Congo the gorilla, who was there at that time, and I thought about the idea of the gorilla going home in my place." James was sceptical his spouse would note the difference.

A less facetious and more forlorn embodiment of the misunderstood creature lost in the wilds of urban life was offered in another song Taylor picked for the record, called 'Wandering'. A traditional lament popularised in the depths of the Depression, it accurately described the untrammelled vagrants and landless farmers who worked odd jobs for meals in the countryside, or hopped freight cars in flight from dead end poverty. While the melody came from an old Irish ballad, the lyrics were grafted from turn-of-the-century labour chants and word-of-mouth testimony to tell a tale of starvation in the midst of abundance.

The song acknowledged dangers in the life of the wastrel drifter, but took cold comfort in stoic acceptance, all the while implying that such an existence felt most natural: "I've been wanderin' early and late/ From New York City to the Golden Gate/And it don't look like/I'll ever stop my wanderin'."

Early in December 1974, James, Carly and little Sally, who was almost one year old, rented a house on Hazen Drive off Coldwater Canyon Drive, way up at the furthermost tip of Beverly Hills in the brambled slopes where the coyotes came out at night to prey on household pets. What was intended to be a two-month stay elongated into more than four, at a rent of $3,750 per month. (The premises' previous tenants had included Elizabeth Taylor and Mick and Bianca Jagger, a point the realtor had mentioned when setting the exorbitant figure Carly called "repulsive".)

Each morning Taylor kissed his wife goodbye, hugged Sally in her highchair as she was spoon-fed her pabulum, and drove down through the lush 1930's-era gentility of Bowmont, Cherokee, Coldwater, and Beverly Drives to Sunset Boulevard, where he'd head for either the Warner Bros. Recording Studio in North Hollywood or the Burbank Studio over the hill on the Warner lot.

After a few days of this somewhat rarefied but sensibly domesticated routine, Taylor began to feel like a contract player from the heyday of the Hollywood studio system.

"It was like making studio pictures in the '30s," he recalled. "Lee Herschberg, the engineer, and Lenny Waronker and Russ Titelman were all staff people at Warner Bros. Russ and Lenny had produced Ry Cooder and Randy Newman, and I was crazy about both of those artists, so I asked Lenny and Russ to take me on.

"I would go there every day and punch in, and do a day's work. It was a very matter-of-fact, established and workmanlike way of making albums. A producer basically takes responsibility for the entire project, but sometimes a producer credit can mean active musical participation, and sometimes it can mean being the organisational resource. Lenny and Russ were very involved musically with opinions and suggestions, as well as being liaisons with the company. They were aware of great people on the scene who were available and how to utilise them, like [guitarist/vocalist] Lowell George, [drummer] Jim Keltner, [bassist] Willie Weeks, percussionist Victor Feldman, Nick DeCaro, who wrote some nice string arrangements, and Valerie Carter, who sang on 'Angry Blues'."

Also integral to the vibe was Kootch, who suggested Taylor bring more R&B into his sets, and emboldened him to consider a song like Holland, Dozier and Holland's Motown smash for Marvin Gaye, 'How Sweet It Is To Be Loved By You', a number six hit for Gaye in 1964 on Motown's Tamla subsidiary. Taylor described his redo of the soul standard as "a Major 7th version of the Marvin Gaye" rendition, and he sang it with flair, Carly's siren-styled harmony vocal adding a sexy subtext, as if his love interest had invaded his very conscience. David Sanborn's sax leapt off the edge of Clarence McDonald's fountain of fat piano chords on the chorus, making his horn (and the song) appear to walk on air. Back on terra firma, the double drums from Russ Kunkel and Jim Keltner, Lee Sklar's bouncing bass and Russ's swinging tambourine all kept the bottom of 'How Sweet' solid but kinetic, as if it were a mêlée rumbling up from a street fair. This was music for the park on Sunday, and it found its way there via radio in May of 1975, when it was shipped as a single along with the album.

Unforced and extemporaneous in tone, *Gorilla* had many more such songs, like 'Music', 'You Make It Easy' and 'Mexico', which had stream of consciousness snippets of the sinful fantasies Southern California affords – each a daydream about the odd anonymity of stardom, the attractions of casual adultery, or the proverbial pleasures of nocturnal border towns. The narrator of the songs envisions places he's never been and indulgences he's never dared, but Tinsel Town makes them so effortless to reel through on a Moviola in his head.

Ideas can eddy in less agreeable directions, too, and many a West Coast sunset can veer one's reveries back on themselves in darkening vertigo. 'I Was A Fool To Care' was an excursion into romance that only depleted the bedevilled lover, and 'Angry Blues' was the sound of someone too impatient with himself to change his rationalising ways and push himself away from the table arrayed with all his bad habits. 'Love Songs' watched honest ardour as it makes its local rounds, being shut out here, greeted suspiciously there, the hapless emotion as epitomised by the questing clarinet of Jules Jacob; would it ever find the perfect hosts in such a cynical town?

Two songs near the close of *Gorilla* do what Taylors have done for two centuries: gaze out to the sea in search of solutions. 'Lighthouse' pictured a perfect voyage, the passenger outward bound; the lucky ship slicing the swells off the coast of Africa, headed for South America. But the lighthouse itself seemed stranded, high on a bluff, a sad sentinel with only a shipwreck on its rocks for company. The original Isaac Taylor might have felt this way after the death of his brother John, the only person who shared his memories of their Atlantic crossing; and his great grandson Isaac could have known such pained seclusion as he entered adolescence with no mother to soothe him and an incapacitated father to stoke his shame.

In former days such feelings were kept bottled up among the Taylors, but James' virtue as an artist was his instinct to share them with the world, telling others in distress that if they heard his songs on the radio they might like to sing along.

Gorilla's concluding statement was 'Sarah Maria', extolling his daughter's eyes' potential to challenge the moon and the stars as celestial means by which the sexton of one's heart could chart a course. For all the wandering yet undone, the singer longed to let his child lead the way for a while, putting his hand in hers as she tugged the album cover's stooped apeman in tropical suit and sandals out of the heart of darkness and into the noonday sun.

Los Angeles was in the middle of a political and cultural renaissance during the making of *Gorilla*, with three-term conservative mayor Sam Yorty defeated in 1973 by Thomas S. Bradley, a former policeman and city councilman and the first African-American to hold that office. Once obsessed with material acquisition, LA had lately turned its municipal energies to the arts, education, ecological balance and cultural uplift. A new Music Center completed in 1969 by Welton Becket and Associates was in a Late Modern style that mingled imperial Rome with medium-cool toga party, but its Mark Taper Forum, Ahmanson Theater and Dorothy Chandler Pavilion helped make the county of the '70s a mecca once more for commercial architecture.

On the down side, crime in the tourist-bound Hollywood district had increased 7.6 per cent since 1969. But that section of the city continued to reflect the steady expansion of the recording industry and supportive enterprises such as FM radio, helping to prompt the LA City Planning Commission to adopt a new master plan for Hollywood redevelopment that saw only mixed success at redeeming its gawker status as a "trip through a sewer in a glass bottom boat". But the City of Angels kept trying to redeem itself, so the time seemed right to celebrate the oceanside metropolis and its tentative tread towards regeneration, with the Pacific soul-pop of 'How Sweet It Is To Be Loved By You' riding the thermals to number five on the Hot 100 in the summer of '75.

Gorilla immediately put Taylor back on the gold standard, and when Kootch, Sklar, Kunkel and Clarence McDonald hit the road for a four-week spring tour that started in Indianapolis and ended with three sold-out evenings at Carnegie Hall, Kortchmar noted a lighter step from Stringbean as he strode the stage.

"Up to *Gorilla*," said Kootch, "we played mostly sitting down, but after that album was out we'd do a *show* – James would dance around and we'd open up the arrangements, and let us all stretch out and make the best known songs breathe more. Before that, when James would go onstage, it was like his skin was on fire, with his eyes on his toes and an 'Aw, shucks' terror about the sets. Now we had fun."

The momentum of Taylor's high spirits was such that another four-week tour was booked to begin on July 2, playing 12 cities with multiple dates in six of them, and when *that* went swimmingly, James headed back out alone in September for an eight-city solo stand. 'Mexico' was issued as a single in October, its guest vocals by stars David Crosby and Graham Nash helping to attract Top 40 AM stations and FM outlets too. It skidded to number 49, but radio kept it active in recurrent play.

Carly also got an album out in 1975, her recording begun eight weeks before Taylor's and taking twice as long. It was accomplished under Richard Perry's direction at a slew of Los Angeles and Burbank studios during the family's West Coast encampment. Carole King added vocals to 'Attitude Dancing' the number 21 single authored by Simon and Jacob Brackman, and James sang and played on 'Look Me In The Eyes', 'Slave' – the first two based on the approval she sought from her husband – as well as 'Playing Possum' and the record's second single, 'Waterfall'.

But *Playing Possum*, which sold respectably but didn't go gold, sparked much more attention for Norman Seeff's album jacket photography of Sally's mom in black boots and matching negligee than for its music. Simon said, "I felt very sexy when I wrote most of the songs" and then amended "sex" with "*sensual*". But "self-conscious" would have been accurate, too, with Simon anxious to return to her usual svelte form as her 15-month-old daughter drew her back out into public view, the pair spotted often around Beverly Hills in her leased Mercedes.

Carly was uniquely beautiful, pregnant or otherwise, and wrote beautiful songs, like 'Look Me In The Eyes', but she still didn't believe it herself, couldn't trust the conventional evidence.

As Taylor got happier, and Simon, who hadn't toured on her own since 1972, stayed at home, an unease crept up between them, with Carly's remark to others whenever James left their Hazen Drive lair becoming something of a spousal mantra: "He goes away forever every day."

★ ★ ★

After over a decade in the recording industry Taylor was hitting his stride as a professional and it suited him. He smiled more, had a brighter disposition, worked more efficiently, and wanted to preserve that new-found continuity. Thus James, wife and child found themselves out in Los Angeles on the cusp of 1976 so dad could go to work again.

This time they rented a certain mansion on Rockingham Avenue in Brentwood, the compound later to become infamous as the site of a murder for which football legend O. J. Simpson would be charged (and convicted, at least in the civil trial). Such odious events lay 18 years in the future, and for his part Taylor was currently basking in the new optimism at Warner Bros. that he'd helped fuel.

In 1976, Warner Bros. Records moved from its old quarters above the film studios' machine shop at 3701 Warner Boulevard to a sleek redwood "ski lodge" at 3300 Warner Boulevard. Designed by A. Quincy Jones, the graceful four-storey offices were filled with atriums, sunlight, modern art and plants – and soon festooned with the clever posters, placards and promotional toys reinforcing Warners Bros.' goofy but ingratiating pride in its "family".

The same team that spawned *Gorilla* was back in formation, Waronker, Titelman and Herschberg meeting with Taylor to show off the new Warner Boulevard digs, and telling him they were raring to get another gold record plaque to hang in the front lobby.

Kootch, Sklar and Kunkel, the three Musketeers of hand-tooled Los Angeles rock, were likewise excited. (Kootch had cleared his schedule after the advent of yet another band, Attitudes, which cut two albums for George Harrison's Dark Horse Records; *Attitudes*, 1976, and *Good News*, 1977, with fellow members Jim Keltner on drums, Paul Stallworth on bass and keyboardist David Foster.)

Even Crosby and Nash were again on hand to splash supplemental harmonies around Warner Bros. Recording Studios in North Holly-wood, and other guests (Stevie Wonder, Art Garfunkel, Bonnie Raitt) would soon take part in the festivities.

Taylor also had yet another iron-clad working title for the endeavour that would get contorted by pressing time. "I had wanted to call this one *Inside Pocket*, meaning a groove, a good place," said James, "but I sort of listened to Peter Asher on that one." It became *In The Pocket*.

The new song with the main chance of getting attention as the lead single was 'Shower The People', and it had a philosophy that would imbue the entire album, helping to make it Taylor's first masterpiece.

"I wrote 'Shower The People' in 1975," James explained. "Basically it's a positive, universal-love kind of anthem. And if there's a point to the song, aside from encouraging people to express whatever love they feel, it's about contributing positively to the world, making things better.

"And really the way to do that is immediately and locally. It's not just to talk about what needs to happen on a global level. If you know somebody and you can improve their experience by your contact with them – then *that*'s the thing to do. Identify the people you care about and make them feel better. That's how to make the world better. You don't need to reorganise the United Nations."

The track itself was almost churchy in its charms, Victor Feldman's orchestra bells and vibes angled in the mix to double exquisite harmony passages from Carly. When the single appeared on the Hot 100 in the July 4 issue of *Billboard* it became the virtual soundtrack of that summer, a canticle so lovely it brought public tears to many eyes. Oddly, the song rose only to number 22, yet its hold on the popular heartstrings endured into the next century.

And so did Taylor's strong attachment to its theme. "There's a very simple message to that song," he asserted much later. "It's basically saying to go ahead and come out with it – meaning love. Don't wait! Suffering is a human condition and it's always there, but I know that it's great for me when somebody can give me instruction on how to get through it in a song."

These same sentiments were shot through other material on the *In The Pocket* sessions, notably 'A Junkie's Lament', with its frank talk about the ravages of methadone, 'Daddy's All Gone', about the torments of time away from loved ones in the dreaded mode of an Ike Taylor, the almost hallucinatory ethos of 'Slow Burning Love', and cuddly caress of 'Everybody Has The Blues'. But advice on surviving woes was also a winning aspect of 'Family Man', a funky romp with horns from Michael Brecker and Steve Madaio that proclaimed Taylor's unwillingness to return to the bad old touring days of disappearing in an auto full of strangers on a blink's notice with no luggage. Hollering out the flippant hallmarks of *All In The Family*-hood, James was filled with affection rather than mischief: "Sears and Roebuck!" (who had balked at stocking Carly's visually risqué *Playing Possum* album) and "Howard Johnson! Colonel Sanders! Station wagon! Briggs and Stratton! Second Mortgage!" Simon, Raitt, Alex Taylor and Valerie Carter also sounded like they were having a ball on back-up singing duties for 'Family Man'. The *bonhomie* of the moment was a counterweight to some of the more sobering but no less consummate cuts on the disc.

'Captain Jim's Drunken Dream', on which Garfunkel harmonised with James, was the sour soliloquy of a seaman exiled from a Caribbean lifestyle he was no longer fit to lead; and Stevie Wonder's vocal pairing (plus harmonica) with his host on 'Don't Be Sad 'Cause Your Sun Is Down' was the hardest James had ever been on himself for the moodshifts that played havoc with his private life.

Bobby Womack's 'Woman's Gotta Have It' was Taylor's finest R&B reinterpretation, with a rock-steady vocal and a knowing edge to his advice about absentee lovers and the damage they can do. 'Nothing Like A Hundred Miles' had the faint heat of a fading sundown as Crosby and Nash helped James animate the inner voice of a rounder without anyone left to miss him.

But *In The Pocket* sparkled with more dashes of wise perspective. The greater distance James got on the degree to which his hobby had become an occupational hazard all its own, the more his sense of humour about such absurdities blossomed. 'Money Machine' was a hilarious lampoon of popular music's lavish sense of self-entitlement, and Taylor here was no virgin, playing off a verse of 'Fire And Rain' to assert, "I've seen fives and I've seen tens!"

With six Warner Bros. albums to his credit after the release of *In The Pocket*, which hit the charts on Independence Day just as 'Shower The People' had, Taylor was now a full-fledged member of the same corporate brood that brought the work of Frank Sinatra to market.

James was a fan of Sinatra's but he deflected most insinuations that the elder statesman had markedly influenced him, except to say, "I don't phrase anything like Sinatra at all except the way he ritards things," i.e. *ritardando*, gradually becoming slower, delaying.

Subtle traces of that technique appeared on *In The Pocket*'s 'Golden Moments', the pretty but decidedly dolorous ballad that was the album's coda after 'Family Man'. If you heard only the dominant phrases near the song's opening about how all the singer's golden moments would shine like the summer sun, one might guess the moody track to be contented in tone.

Closer examination found the song's character confessing he'd sold all his sorrows for gold and thrown all of the lucre away on "a good time and a song"; he was now with someone whose name he couldn't remember and in a place where no one could reach him or notice he's gone.

'Golden Moments', in its way, is a lot like Sinatra circa *In The Wee Small Hours* (Capitol 1955), or *September Of My Years* (Reprise, 1965), sounding reflective and in transparent denial – and making no bones about either outlook. If Sinatra ever had a private life it was only cursory in its secrets, because Frank put the hollowness and hunger he felt into the foreground of his art. Unlike other crooners and singing entertainers of his era, whether Bing Crosby, Nat "King" Cole, Perry Como or Tony Bennett, Sinatra wanted you to forget *nothing* about how he felt in the moment. Even if you knew about his domestic life, his kids, his sentimental attachments, his insensitive disengagements, he wanted you to understand what lay underneath even them: the emotions that craved public release.

From the very beginning, Taylor was as blunt as a pop troubadour could be about his drug life, his personal failings, his urges and impulses, ugliest fears and mistakes, sharpest opinions, and humblest ideals. All of these were in his songs, which were thick with psychic suffering, acute depression, hospital jargon, junkie code and allusions to needle use, sexual intrigue, political positions, little victories, personal awakenings.

And in the same manner that Sinatra shone a harsh, unyielding light on high life in the nightclub Hades he inhabited, with its seamy saloon slip-ups, bad dice and low companions, so Taylor encapsulated the pathetic pastimes of a smack freak in a couplet on *In The Pocket*'s 'A Junkie's Lament': "An empty hand in the afternoon/Shooting for the moon."

For all the swagger or soft inflection, both singers let patrons see and hear that their art wasn't just show business and diversion. They wanted a feeling to pass between artist and audience that might make one soar in spirit or flinch in recognition. If you liked just the sounds of the notes, fine, but the rest of the facts stayed in plain sight, every night, until you were ready for them.

After the gold certification trophy for *In The Pocket*, Taylor finished off his current Warners contract with a *James Taylor/Greatest Hits* set that included re-recordings (because the Apple masters were lost) at LA's Sound Factory in October '76 of 'Something In The Way She Moves' and 'Carolina In My Mind', both produced by Peter Asher. Added to the 12-track package along with 'Fire And Rain', 'Sweet Baby James', 'Country Road', 'You've Got A Friend', 'Don't Let Me Be Lonely Tonight', 'Walking Man', 'How Sweet It Is (To Be Loved By You)', 'Mexico' and 'Shower The People' was a live version of 'Steamroller', recorded at the Universal Amphitheater in LA in August 1975.

Greatest Hits was in the stores at the end of November and went platinum in a twinkling, with sales in the US alone exceeding 11 million units by the year 2001. Taylor was eager to renew his vows to the family in Burbank but, mysteriously, they failed to pick up James' option. Peter Asher reportedly said to Warners, "You need to renegotiate with us," but they said, "No, we don't."

"So we went back and forth for a while," according to Taylor, "and they actually just basically stopped talking to us, or stopped responding to us. That's not unusual for a record company to do that. Peter said, 'If you're not gonna take us seriously, and you haven't picked up this option, we're gonna start to talk with other record companies. By the time they took notice of it, Columbia had already made an offer and that basically started a kind of bidding war between us."

As Taylor later recalled, within three days of Columbia's offer, as tendered by executives Walter Yetnikoff and Al Teller, Warner Bros. woke up and belatedly started to negotiate, "but Columbia was offering *twice* what Warner Bros. was offering initially. Warner Bros. came back up. Columbia again doubled their offer." And then sweetened it some more.

"Despite the fact that Warner Bros. decided they didn't want to lose me and sent Mo and Lenny and [staff producer] Teddy Templeman to fly to the East Coast and try and twist my arm into not accepting this Columbia deal, I was committed to going with Columbia. So I signed with them and went over."

But none of this entirely explains Taylor's dissatisfaction with his Warner Bros. deal, and for that clarification, it's best to start at the beginning of that relationship and let James do the talking:

"Peter basically signed me to a company called Marylebone, which I co-owned with him, and then he signed Marylebone to Warner Bros. Then he sold Marylebone for stock in escrow at 44 dollars a share."

Marylebone Productions Ltd, was named for the fashionable West London vicinity in which Asher had a property. Once the ancient seat of a royal hunting residence, the village of Marylebone had evolved since the 17th century from the site of a famed outdoor garden featuring the orchestra of Thomas Arne (composer of 'Rule, Britannia!'), to the neighbourhood where Charles Dickens lived from 1839–51 and wrote *The Old Curiosity Shop*, *A Christmas Carol* and *David Copperfield*, and then the modern address of the London College of Dance and Drama.

"So Peter had made a deal with Warner Bros. Records for stock," Taylor related. "They put a huge amount of stock in escrow and we would basically draw the stuff down. In other words, at a fixed rate of 44 dollars a share, they put all this stuff in an escrow account, and every time we earned 44 dollars on the contract they'd give us a share. And it was one for him and one for me.

"It seemed like he [Peter] was getting a lot to me but he pointed out to me that the way he had structured things, I wouldn't be getting any more if I had been in a straight royalty situation so I agreed to it; I took his advice on it.

"What happened then was the stock went down to 7 dollars a share, so that every time we made 44 dollars I'd have 7, and this was on a stock royalty rate anyhow, so I really, basically wasn't making record royalties for any of my Warner Bros. days.

"It was a drag, so I kept talking with them about giving me a break on this thing, or reconsidering this thing. 'Cause I didn't have anything to do with it. So my contract was running and running, and I was making records just 'cause I wanted to make records. But it was also depressing to be at a company and making them a whole bunch of money and not making anything off these records!"

So Taylor was seeing money accrue from touring and publishing and mechanical rights but no direct money at all from record sales?

"No, no money at all from record sales."

Because you were getting the Warner Bros. stock at the going price in lieu of record royalties.

"Yeah! And I got rid of all my Warner Bros. stock. I could have held onto it, and Peter did. He held onto it until the price came back up again, and ended up doing really quite well. But I had sold out, on the advice of my financial people, of the stock I had gotten from them. So I basically took a bath on my Warner Bros. catalogue!

"I think the average royalty rate on the *Greatest Hits* – which has sold something like 14 million [worldwide] at this point – and all these other ones was basically 40 cents a record."

By the summer of 2001, *James Taylor/Greatest Hits* had sold some 11 million units domestically, which by Taylor's math would mean he'd earned approximately $4,400,000 – with the numbers increasing to about $5,600,000 when adjusted for the total global sales figure of 14 million. After the big tax bite was accounted for over the course of the 25 years the record was thus far in release, Taylor's own profits from one of the most commercially formidable hits collections ever issued would be startlingly modest.

"So I felt sour," said Taylor. "I really didn't want to continue making records for Warner Bros."

20

Secret O' Life

Many a tipsy tourist or disoriented off-islander veering accidentally onto one of the dozens of unmarked Martha's Vineyard roads that marble the north-west horn of the forest bordered by James Pond, Vineyard Sound and Lake Tashmoo would have been much surprised by the sudden sight at the end of a gravel-strewn clay capillary of the playful summer house of James Taylor, Carly Simon and their children, Sarah Maria and Benjamin Simon Taylor, the latter born on January 22, 1977.

A stately grey-shingled jumble of railed porches, tiny porticoes, solariums, buttressing outbuildings and playful windows painted in fluorescent lemon and coral pink, the mildly monastic structure was dominated by a 45-foot tower that seemed equal parts maritime window's walk and Cape Cod minaret.

Like the Isaac Taylor house perched above the wharf in New Bern, North Carolina, this self-commissioned retreat was a statement of purpose by its proud owner – a conscious stand against the stiff winds and stern winter weather of the North Atlantic island he adored – with many of the home's newer, more nonchalant touches owed to a tug of war with the tastes of his wife of five years.

Since their marriage, they'd spent most summers on the Vineyard, with the better portion of the winters accorded to Los Angeles, and work on the clapboard structure continued in any season when weather permitted. The original shack James lived in during his first year on the 65-acre parcel of land had become a guest house, and another one-room bungalow built by friends was absorbed into the main building as a music room.

There were low rock walls in final stages of production, a circular garden being planted, and an aged Ford tractor in use to mow the field displayed before the floor-to-ceiling windows in the dining room. Ceiling laths, joints and trusses were left exposed indoors, and small rooms and baths appeared off the main living areas with random logic. Sally's toy-filled room was downstairs, with dad's own christening cup in her private bath, and the master bedroom was upstairs – as was a handy crib for baby Ben, who was still being breast fed.

In James' and Carly's simple white boudoir was a queen-sized bed placed before tall white curtains, the mattress covered with a fine embroidered quilt of multi-coloured leaf circlets, with five square and circular throw pillows at its head, and a snow-white year-round down blanket laid across its foot. On the left side of the bed was an L-shaped corner bookcase of blonde wood on which sat a boxy white desk phone, a narrow filofax alphabetical card directory, some silver-framed family pictures, and a globular white lamp on a short stainless steel stem with black metal base. This niche of the chamber was one of Carly's beloved spots, where she often chatted on the phone in the evenings, her children dozing on the bed around her.

Her subdued, self-contained husband was often downstairs during the wee hours, a warm south-westerly land breeze pushing through the screens to stir his droopy chocolate brown moustache and shoulder length hair, as he pored over books about plants, geology, science, history and the sea, or played his acoustic guitar and scribbled ideas on a pad of paper. Parked outside on the pebble-dimpled driveway were a dusty Audi, which James usually drove, and the blue Mercedes Carly preferred.

Beside a stereo in a small downstairs den were copies of her two latest albums, *The Best Of Carly Simon*, which came out during the '75 Christmas season and went gold, and last summer's *Another Passenger,* cut in Los Angeles with a bevy of musicians and staff borrowed from the Warner Bros. stable (producer Ted Templeman, The Doobie

Brothers, Van Dyke Parks, Little Feat) in addition to James, sister Lucy Simon (currently a solo artist for RCA) and close friend Libby Titus, who recorded for Columbia.

Another Passenger sold modestly and spent only 13 weeks on the charts, its highest upsurge to number 29, despite the presence of still more guest stars (Linda Ronstadt, Jackson Browne) as backing singers. Its principal single, Carly's version of Doobie Michael McDonald's 'It Keeps You Runnin', peaked at number 46 on the Hot 100, while the Doobie's own edition of the track topped it at number 37.

Part of the problem was Carly's unshaken aversion to touring and performing, coupled with her resolve not to spend nights away from her children. When asked what her favourite track on *Another Passenger* might be, she told people it was 'Fair Weather Father', an airy cut, accented by celeste and viola, in which the lyric criticised a mate who allegedly doesn't like to hear the day's mishaps or the baby's tears, all the while insisting the mother of his kids be a trucker and a gardener and glamorous ingenue, too. But the song's main character forgives her man in the middle verse as he rises at night to console both her and their squalling babe.

This, then, was the capricious yet comfy house that James had built by the late 1970s, in contradistinction to the commanding, discriminating structure Isaac erected in the late 1790s. But James had also become a gentleman merchant, no less so than distant forebear Isaac, except that James' trade was mainly in products of his own unassuming creation.

James was a land owner too, quietly purchasing choice lots around the Vineyard, many of them terrain he left unspoiled, and he also held the deed to 365 acres on Nova Scotia, near the sea lanes his ancestors' ships had frequented when crossing to or from Scotland. James was now an experienced mariner, as well, with a scull he regularly rowed on the nearby ponds for exercise, and a small sailboat in which he gave friends afternoon rides on Menemsha Pond or across to the Elizabeth Islands. He and his brother Hugh and old friends from the South would also take larger craft for long-range voyages to the Bahamas.

But mainly James plied the local waters, which each summer occupied his imagination as with anyone who chooses to live on a small piece of glacial atoll surrounded entirely by ocean. Triangular Nantucket Sound, over thirty miles across from one corner to another, was formed by Cape Cod, the Vineyard and the island of Nantucket, and traversed daily by the ferries of the Martha's Vineyard Steamship Authority, or the Hyline, Island Queen, Schamonchi, and Patriot Party Boat lines as they shuttled automobiles and passengers between the Vineyard, the mainland (via Woods Hole, Falmouth, New Bedford, Hyannis) or Nantucket.

Most summers, the waters of Nantucket Sound were warm enough for swimming, calmer than on the Atlantic side, and gratifying for fishermen, who hooked ample striped bass and bluefish from either boats or the beach. Yet seamen knew these waters to be some of the most dangerous on the New England coast, with rapid changes possible in wind direction and velocity, and extreme caution required when navigating in thick weather. Menemsha Bight (a bight being a gulf of water between two promontories, as well as a loop of seaman's rope) was the first shelter boats found when entering the Cape Cod and Chilmark/Tisbury bounded channel of Vineyard Sound. It was a roily anchorage at best, but once past the jetties that protect Menemsha Basin, there were sufficient finger piers for overnight moorings.

Lake Tashmoo's inlet came next, and it was dredged to seven feet for easy entry on the rising tide, with the harbour anchorages at least ten feet deep. But the shoals in the channel needed a skilled hand at the helm. Vineyard Haven's harbour, still along to the north-east, was also well sheltered and filled with power boats and impressive yachts, but the tidal current at the opening between East Chop and West Chop (chop in this instance not denoting windswept sea but rather being 18th-century British slang for jaw) was often ripping past at a treacherous 4½ knots.

Once safely in the Vineyard Haven harbour at an anchorage or slip, larger boats were often surrounded by virtual schools of dinghies. They would be streaming in the direction of dockside gas and diesel fuel pumps at the town wharf, the A&P supermarket on Water Street, the post office, the ice machines at the Cumberland Farms outlet – or the dimly lit Black Dog Tavern (open for fishermen's breakfast at 6.30 a.m.) and its screened-in companion bakery, both of which sold the annual silhouette edition of the Black Dog T-shirt that was becoming *de rigueur* for civilian swabbies on the Eastern Seaboard, college-age backpackers, and (most alarmingly) status-conscious visitors from Boston, Manhattan and Washington, DC.

Unknown to tourists but essential to year-round islanders were Vineyard Haven's Maciel Marine, Ltd, where boat repair and local towing and salvage were conducted, and the Gannon and Benjamin Marine Railway yard, where wooden boats of all types and sizes were designed, built and mended.

The Vineyard's other two principal harbours were at Oak Bluffs, four miles eastward, where anchorage was prohibited by tight manoeuvring conditions but multiple side-by-side moorings could accommodate 300 boats; and Edgartown, where many ships came in under sail, sliding past the Middle Flats' shoal to starboard, and rural Chappaquiddick Island to port. The tide was usually strong where it crossed at the sharp bend inside the lighthouse. Those not intent on immediate services usually anchored in Katama Bay, where weekend captain Walter Chronkite could often be spotted at the wheel of his yawl, *The Wyntie*.

Settled in 1642 and incorporated in 1671, with the candle and whale-oil stores of its 18th century heyday since supplanted by demure restaurants and gift shops, Edgartown was named for the son of James II, King of Scotland from 1437 to 1460. (But in Montrose, Scotland, any gift shops near the quayside were currently overshadowed by huge vessels flying foreign flags, with 1977 being a boom year in shipping – much of it from Mid-Atlantic coastal ports in the American South.)

The once nearly extinct osprey could be seen circling the waterfront of Edgartown to feed on fish in June '77, and the same genus of white-headed hawks were spotted doing likewise on the opposite side of the ocean in Montrose Harbour. White-tailed deer were commonplace as they idly fed in the Menemsha Hills, whereas red and roe deer were the usual meanderers in the grasslands and woods around Montrose and Marykirk. Nonetheless, in the main, the faraway region from which Isaac Taylor had sailed to America bore a remarkable modern resemblance to Martha's Vineyard, with the mortarless rock walls dividing its farms or crofts, the clay cliffs and creamy sands of Montrose's Lunan Bay all but identical to the shoreline of Chilmark and Gay Head. Indeed, there were stretches of tree-shrouded country lanes within the

Balmanno and Kirktonhill estates that might easily be mistaken for portions of Middle or South Road between Chilmark and West Tisbury.

That the Taylors could have gravitated to an Atlantic seaboard outpost so similar to the Angus coast of Scotland – whether from seals swimming in its shallows, or mussel and reed beds nurturing the same migrant geese, or high bluffs being breeding stations for kindred sea birds – was a tantalising fact of which James and family were largely heedless, yet it loomed behind their actions and impulses.

★   ★   ★

Up-island on his own rough-hewn estate, James was composing material for *JT*, his first Columbia album, and he had collaborated with his wife on the only song they would write together for one of *his* records. Called 'Terra Nova', it spoke of the elemental attractions of their Vineyard hideaway, with its beckoning ring of sea; its resident fellow Taylors that he loved, missed and still struggled to understand; and his periodic sails from the island's harbours into the far horizon, which fostered one of the fondest feelings he'd ever known. And as a descant-like coda for 'Terra Nova', Carly added a two-stanza poem that she sang herself about Lamberts Cove, praising the boats on its glimmering tides, the morning hazes burned off by its calorifying sun, and the nagging private yearning that sometimes evaporated along with the mists.

But 'Another Grey Morning', one of her husband's newest compositions for his next record, told a different story – of the times when the Vineyard sun didn't show at all, and the father of the house was in a poor state of mind and body, and Mom couldn't get a solid bounce from him, though she pleaded for any emotion – positive or negative – that would dislodge the malaise. Then, according to the lyrics of 'Grey Morning', the baby would awake in tears, a foghorn would answer mournfully, and each of the household's inhabitants would retreat into their own silences, all of them hungry to know how much they really mattered to each other.

One answer came in 'Your Smiling Face', a pop sonnet written expressly for three-year-old Sally in all her flaxen-haired glory as she scurried across the meadows of the Lamberts Cove property in circus-striped play dresses and scuffed white sandals.

Another hint arrived in a song Taylor also wrote for the album that was a piano-paced plaint about the human connection, and human frailty. 'There We Are', deemed by James to have been delicately influenced by 'Falling In Love' from the 1938 Rogers & Hart musical, *The Boys From Syracuse*, fortified *JT*'s introspective vein. Set somewhere on a beach, where land, sea and sky cautiously converged, 'There We Are' told of a delicate locus in which two adults could linger like children, walking hand in hand, talking to each other in a way that finally made mutual sense. And James did something else he hadn't done before, stating in plain earshot of the rest of the planet that, "Though I never say I love you . . . Carly I do love you." Decades later, Simon would still tearfully confide to others, "If I ever hear it on the radio, I'm gone for the day."

The whole family would soon be gone from the Vineyard for a bit longer than that, since James' recording schedule was already booked: March 12–April 24, 1977 at The Sound Factory in Los Angeles. Mom, Dad, Sally and Ben were flying out well before that to stay at Lou Adler's Bel Air home, which the producer-owner of Ode Records had lent them for the duration.

The album Taylor was preparing would be a highly personalised successor to *In The Pocket*. Its title, *JT*, was his nickname among his musician friends, including Kootch, whose playing and ideas helped determine its polished contours. But the ease of its personal logistics was credited to Carly.

"I've always been very grateful to Carly for putting her own priorities aside and moving the family out to Los Angeles to allow me to make that record," said Taylor. "Carly was very accommodating; she took the kids out West, she did various work here and there in Los Angeles, but basically held down the home front and supported me while I did daily work on this album.

"This was a period of time when I was still doing drugs," he noted, "and I needed things to be on a pretty even keel in order not to go overboard."

Peter Asher was in charge of production, and discussed each of James' songs with him to ascertain its respective strengths and weaknesses. "Basically I would play Peter the songs," said James, "and we would tend to rehearse a number of them in order to keep studio costs down. Then we'd go somewhere and work through the tunes. But it was a good time. Val Garay engineered and mixed, Clarence McDonald played keyboards, Lee Sklar and Russ Kunkel played on it. Danny Dugmore did steel guitar, and Kootch played most of the guitars." He also brought valuable material and ideas to the party, providing one of *JT*'s best uptempo tracks, a humorous 1975 songwriting effort about an errant paramour called 'Honey Don't Leave L.A.'

Kootch also nudged Taylor to do Otis Blackwell's 'Handy Man', an R&B hit on MGM's Cub label in the winter of 1960 for Alabama-born singer Jimmy Jones, and then a number 22 cover for Michigan rocker Del Shannon in 1964 on Amy Records.

"The 'Handy Man' thing was a Jimmy Jones cover that Kootch suggested," Taylor affirmed, remembering the clever song of amorous persuasion from his Carolina boyhood. "It was 9 o'clock one night and we had already cut two things that day but Kootch said, 'Let's give this a try.' I came up with the arrangement immediately but Danny trimmed it a little bit because I was too chordy with it. Then Leah Kunkel" – wife of Russ and sister of The Mamas and The Papas' Cass Elliot – "came in a couple of days later and overdubbed that fabulous harmony part on it."

Suddenly *JT* had another single prospect that shot to the head of the class, being released on June 3, 1977, 21 days before *JT* was racked in shops. The song leapt to number four on the Hot 100, making it Taylor's highest charting since 'You've Got A Friend' six years earlier. 'Your Smiling Face' would get its own chance as a single in September after a 17-city summer tour (whose band included new back-up singers David Lasley and Arnold McCuller), the latter song becoming a Top 20 crowd rouser.

" 'Your Smiling Face' was a good, light-hearted pop love song," said Taylor after it had become a fixture in his live shows. "It has some falsetto stuff that I was unable to do for a long time. When you abuse your voice for a long period of time the falsetto tends to go, you lose it. I'm just now getting it back."

Ruminating on the buffed results of the rest of *JT*'s tracks, Taylor viewed 'Looking For Love On Broadway' as being "about the futility of doing just that. You see people wandering around the city as the sun goes down or as the evening wears on, and you just feel people carrying their hearts around that way, longing for a connection and for meaning. It drives us all, motivates everybody. It's that very repetitive and very common thing people will tease out, or appeal to – and have no idea whether they're selling us a movie, a box of soap, or an automobile. And I guess that's a song about longing a lot myself."

'If I Keep My Heart Out Of Sight' was allied with 'Broadway' as an interior monologue about chary reactions and careful reserve. "That's a song that I've always been proud of," said Taylor, "and the chord changes have always pleased me." Less appealing in theme but effective in its pungent thrust was 'I Was Only Telling A Lie', which Taylor termed "a nasty love song; it's abusive but doesn't celebrate that abuse – it exposes it.

"As for 'Bartender's Blues'," Taylor continued, "I think it's an okay but lightweight song – although George Jones later recorded it [as the title track of *Bartender's Blues*, Epic Records, 1978]. 'Traffic Jam', however, is fun. It was written on the spot and Russ Kunkel actually played cardboard boxes on it. It's definitely an LA creature, that song, with a little bit of insight into life on the freeways. But it took as long to write it as it takes to sing it."

He also enjoyed 'Honey Don't Leave L.A.', a concert showpiece for the band; punctuated on record and at shows by David Sanborn's pealing sax, it would get to number 61 in February 1978 as the late-breaking third and last single from *JT*.

Overall, Taylor felt *JT* was "a really good album that stands out as one of my best, with mostly really good material; I lucked out."

"And I think," he added, in reference to his new Columbia affiliation, "that you do get a certain amount of energy from changing horses." But his most fervent comments about the album ultimately settled upon the 3½-minute miniature near its close, 'Terra Nova'.

"I still get a little choked up when I hear 'Terra Nova'," Taylor explained. "I like what it says about loving my 'lovely' mom and my 'lonely' dad and my brothers and sister. It talks about being pulled away from the world that you're truly in, and also the constant need we have to return to that world."

JT's front and back cover photos, by David Alexander and Jim Shea, showed a studious looking Taylor, his haircut and aspect little changed from his time at Milton Academy; shaved off was the moustache and shed were the rumpled clothes of his bachelor days, replaced by crisp white shirts and v-neck sweaters.

But on the album's liner sleeve was a curious picture that looked wacky at first blush but grew increasingly clenched and emotionally confined in its body language as one contemplated it further. Taylor's description of his balled-up torso – a tense bundle of bowed head, spindly arms, yellow T-shirt, brown cord trousers and argyle socks – as documented by David Alexander for the sleeve image opposite the album lyrics was sufficient to give one pause about poor James' idea of a sight gag in 1977:

"For the inner sleeve, where I'm pressed into a space, I designed a plexiglass cube that was a section of a pyramid whose lines were exactly the points of perspective from the camera plate, so that as you looked at it you didn't see the inside or outside of it. It expanded with the per-spective, so everything was right on edge. When you forced yourself into it, you were actually in a cone or pyramid about three feet deep, so as you forced yourself into it you totally used up the space."

JT entered *Billboard*'s Top 200 Albums chart on July 9, 1977, and it would sell two million copies in the US alone – a domestic bonanza on a regular release rivalled only by *Sweet Baby James*. 'Handy Man' got Taylor a 1977 Grammy Award in the Best Pop Vocal Performance, Male, category, and the rest of the boldly deliberative record contained a lot of songs indispensable to the Taylor canon.

Prominent among them, though it never received sustained airplay, was 'Secret O' Life', a track intended to be touching but not without a sly Scottish twinkle in the eye o' its author/beholder, who titled the tune to resemble the quaint spelling of such Lifesaver candy flavours as 'Pep O Mint' and 'Wint O Green'.

"The Lifesaver is always the 'O' in the name," said Taylor with a laugh. "To write a song with that title seemed a bit presumptuous, so I wanted to tone it down a little bit and step back off it. I didn't want it to be as serious as it sounded. But I remember writing that song in a small pool of sunlight, a patch, while sitting on the stairs of my house built back in the woods on Martha's Vineyard. It was one of those nice after-noons, and that song was a quick one – the first verse and the chorus happened really quick.

"I guess I was lucky to be playing my guitar at the time the thing came out. It was in the early summer, late May–early June, and the sun was coming in, and the leaves were new on the trees, and I was playing this really nice guitar. I was feeling really good, feeling great, and it was a gift."

But Ike Taylor thought he discerned an underlying apprehension in the testimony on 'Secret O' Life' that its vivacious music was meant to alleviate. "In my contact with him we virtually never talk about what he's writing and how his music is going," Dr Taylor admitted regarding his son, "but when I hear his songs I can always tell *exactly* when he wrote it based on our conversations, and that song shows his feeling at the time he wrote it.

"I would judge 'Secret O' Life' to be written," Ike advised evenly, "when he was wondering where his career was leading."

21

Company Man

To be a good husband, a good father, a good brother, a good son and a good friend were goals to which James Taylor aspired in the 1970s, and all eyes were on him during late 1977 and early 1978 to see how he was faring.

The arrival of Ben was a defining moment for which his father, now 29, had not entirely been prepared, and it brought on a free-floating enfeeblement of anxious self-doubt that greeted James in sporadic waves. Primarily, James wanted to become one of the key things his own father had not been, which was a man of his word in terms of kindly promises and genial commitments, i.e. the casual vows on which average people depend the most. In this spirit, James had always resolved to look out for Kate, in ways spoken and unspoken, and he wanted to follow through on their enthusiastic talk of doing more recording together.

Since 1975, Kate had been living with songwriter/producer Charles Witham (born December 6, 1944), the son of a Raytheon executive from Ipswich on Massachusetts' North Shore. Charles' mother had grown up in Newburyport and her family knew Mae Woodard, Trudy Taylor's sister, and other members of the Woodard clan.

Charles, who came of age in suburban Newton and started vacationing on the Vineyard in 1964, was introduced to Kate by James in 1971 and they immediately fell in love and began living together (they would not formally wed until December 22, 1988). After several years of intermittent touring based on the momentum of her '71 solo record, "I came back to the Vineyard," Kate recounted, "and I was establishing a home, 'cause I really didn't have one and I was really in need of making one, and that became my focus." On November 5, 1975, Kate gave birth to her first child, Elizabeth Menemsha Witham.

"Then, in late '76, James came to visit," Kate recalled, "and he said, 'I want to talk with you about making another record.'"

Kate had avoided returning to music in any full-time professional sense, afraid it would mean disruptions in her home life of the sort she'd seen as a child when her father served in the Navy at the South Pole. But she missed recording, and James decided to draw his shy sister out gradually, rekindling her studio juices with just a single. After several postponements, James took Kate into Atlantic Recording Studios in Manhattan in August of '77 to remake 'It's In His Kiss (The Shoop Shoop Song)', a hit on Vee-Jay Records in 1964 for Greenwood, Mississippi R&B singer Betty Everett.

"James brought that song up, and it was the first thing we went in and did for my next album," said Kate, her brother governing the arrangement as well as the production, believing it'd be perfect for his bashful sibling's surprisingly sassy soul-growl. "And when we were finishing it," she recalled, "we were in the studio late at night doing the last bit of harmony. All of a sudden in walks Mick Jagger! My jaw dropped, and I could not go on."

Petrified to record in such exalted company, Kate came out of the vocal booth to say hello and Jagger saw she was very flustered. He moved to go, but elected to settle her nerves first with a brief reminiscence.

"Six years earlier, when I was in LA doing my first album," as Kate later recounted, "I'd had a bicycle and I'd left it at Peter Asher's house, and Mick came by one day and asked Peter's secretary if he could borrow it. So on the way back out the door, the last thing Mick said to me was, 'Thanks for the use of the bike!'"

The tension of resuming a recording career thus dispelled, Kate jumped into cutting her single's B-side 'Jason & Ida', a song she'd written with Duane Giesemann as a love token to two children of Vineyard friends: "Two beautiful pure spirits."

James and Carly added vocal harmonies, and 'It's In His Kiss (The Shoop Shoop Song)' b/w 'Jason & Ida' was released by Columbia at the end of the month, surfacing on the Hot 100 on September 3rd and hitting number 49 over the course of seven weeks.

The ice broken, Kate completed *Kate Taylor*, her second album, with plenty of family aid. She recorded James' new 'Happy Birthday Sweet Darling', written for his road manager Eric Barrett (legendary former roadie for Jimi Hendrix), and another new song James authored with former Flying Machinist Zach Wiesner, an affecting ode to personal courage called 'Slow And Steady'.

As work progressed on *Kate Taylor*, James was contacted by Paul Simon, who lived down the block from his and Carly's apartment at 135 Central Park West in Manhattan. Paul asked James to sing with Simon & Garfunkel on a cover of Sam Cooke's '(What A) Wonderful World', a song Cooke co-wrote with Lou Adler and Herb Alpert for Keen Records back in 1960. Taylor was touched by the invitation from his respected folk-pop contemporaries, since Garfunkel had earlier sung on 'A Junkie's Lament', and all three of their paths had overlapped for years throughout their early British scuffling and its ricocheting impact on the American charts.

The trio convened in Paul's apartment, came up with a pleasingly subtle vocal mesh, and cut Cooke's syrupy classic with producer Phil Ramone in New York, the song hitting number 17 in early 1978 and appearing on Garfunkel's gold *Watermark* solo album. (In another year, Paul Simon would be plucked away from Columbia by Warner Bros. in a move many industry observers interpreted as a score-settling tit-for-tat by Taylor's former label after losing *their* premier singer-songwriter.)

Meanwhile, work on *Kate Taylor* was winding up. Also cut for her long-awaited solo sequel were husband Charles' 'Tiah Cove', Livingston Taylor's 'Rodeo', Ethan Signer and Clay Jackson's 'Smuggler's Song', plus Ike Turner's 'A Fool For Love', and a gender-minded rewrite of 'Stubborn Kind Of Fellow', Marvin Gaye's 1962 soul teaser, now titled 'Stubborn Kind Of Woman'. James and Lew Hahn co-produced *Kate Taylor*, and both Alex and Hugh Taylor sang beside Kate and James throughout, with Don Grolnick, the Brecker Brothers, guitarist Cornell Dupree, flautist David Amram, bassist Will Lee, guitar-singer

John Hall of the group Orleans, Atlantic arranger Arif Mardin and sister-in-law Carly all on board.

But the highpoint of Kate's exceptional 11-song set, released on May 4, 1978, was 'Harriet Tubman', a searing latter-day spiritual by bassist/composer Walter Robinson, who'd been a frequent presence on Livingston Taylor's albums. Introduced by tolling piano figures from Richard Tee, with a gospel chorus led by Jessy Dixon, the stirring piece told the saga of African-American abolitionist Araminta "Harriet" Tubman, a former slave who made some 19 trips to the South after her own escape in 1849 to bring chattelised blacks to freedom in the North by means of an "Underground Railroad" network of safehouses and hiding places – some of which ran through Boston, the Merrimack Valley and the New Hampshire/Maine border to Quebec.

Tubman was a leading "conductor" along these clandestine routes, organised between the Carolinas and northern New England, and Louisiana and Ontario, with offshoots established between Texas and Mexico, and Florida and Cuba/Andros Island. Robinson's engrossing song of these African-American thralls' desperate flight as led by the brave female guide and her "first mate" trail scout was spectacular in its force of mood, and boded well for a full musical production Robinson hoped one day to mount.

Once *Kate Taylor* was done, James divided his time in early 1978 between assisting on Carly Simon's *Boys In The Trees* album, which was produced by Mardin and released in April, and refining his compositions for *Working*, a musical adapted and directed by Stephen Schwartz from a book by journalist Studs Terkel, which would open for a brief Broadway bid on May 14, 1978.

Boys In The Trees was without question the most fully realised album Simon would issue in the years before 2000, unerring in its evocation of a young woman coming of age physically, emotionally and experientially. The delicate but steadfast force of Arif Mardin's instrumental settings was electrifying, each pluck, *ping*! and spacious orchestral placement of vocal parts enforcing the sense of penetrating a still pool of impossible depth.

Simon concentrated on the use of her head voice, rather than the higher pitches that often flattened her tone, and the effect was of an unhurried flow of emotional clarity and allusive power. From opening track 'You Belong To Me', which she co-wrote with Michael McDonald by long-distance collaboration, to the title cut, which trenchantly conveyed the barefoot excitement of a summer evening's adolescent sensations, the pervasive rightness of feel was well-nigh flawless. Simon's saturnine 'Back Down To Earth', her restrained rendering of Boudleaux Bryant's 'Devoted To You', and the gently jocular calypso of Carly's own 'De Bat (Fly In Me Face)' each convinced with calm facility, and 'Haunting', her unadorned art song closing side one, would have stopped any show on Broadway that season.

As with side two's expectant mating dance of 'Tranquillo (Melt My Heart)', written by Simon with Taylor and Mardin; the translucent desire of 'You're The One' and 'In A Small Moment'; the assertive accord of 'One Man Woman' (penned for her by James) and the frankly sentimental 'For Old Time's Sake' by Simon and Jacob Brackman, there were no false notes in the almost-too-brief two minutes and 28 seconds of the sad madrigal that was 'Haunting'.

"Basically," Simon observed, "you don't have to see somebody for a long, long time for them to still be inside of you. There's no way of killing it off; it's a kind of obsession. And some people do have that effect on me. I have a good memory, especially for emotions, and I don't get over strong feelings."

That Taylor played, sang on, or had a role in writing many of the tracks on *Boys In The Trees* was significant, but it was Mardin's grasp of Simon's truest gifts as a pop elegist that made the crucial difference. And for the 'Haunting' track, Simon's pride of performance disappeared almost entirely behind the substance of the song.

Boys In The Trees had a great deal to say about love and its remains, like the endurance of its inner tremors, despite the mereness of tangible lasting evidence. With modesty and care, Simon made listeners embrace and surpass the music to think only of the arresting might of its meaning – for oneself and others.

★ ★ ★

'Millworker' achieved this quality, also, in the musical *Working*, its declarative account of a ruined life so unyieldingly honest it ennobled the singer even as it rang with the truth of real defeat. But James Taylor only wrote the song for *Working*, 'Millworker' being one of three pieces (besides 'Brother Trucker', and the music to Graciela Daniele and Matt Landers' 'Un Mejor Dia Vendra') provided at the request of Stephen Schwartz to help to transfer the gist of Terkel's oral history of ordinary working people into a revue-like stage presentation. Taylor's tuneful (and inconspicuously Celtic) 'Millworker' oratory was performed in the show by Robin Lamont and it was a sublime, if under-esteemed, slice of stage magic, Lamont summoning the exact measure of last-ditch dignity the material demanded.

The theme itself was ostensibly that of a misbegotten mill girl from the cotton looms of Lowell, Massachusetts in the mid-1800s. The harsh but not wholly negative lives of these 19th century child labourers were immortalised first-hand in Harriet H. Robinson's memoir of her own 1835–48 employment (she was ten when hired) at a mechanised loom in the factory town (formerly Chelmsford) renamed for Bostonian industrialist Francis Cabot Lowell. Constructing his first prototype in nearby Waltham based on ideas appropriated during a British trip, Lowell conceived a bale-to-spindle waterpower plant that revolutionised American textile manufacture, and became a tourist magnet for British guests to the Boston area.

The Lowell Factory Girls were neither tawdry nor downtrodden; rather they started out as an object lesson in the civilised method of enticing and housing a stable young work force in the largest manufacturing centre of its kind in the United States. The mode of hiring was in keeping with local Yankee customs of contracting matrimony-destined girls of decent backgrounds to act as "niece"/helpmates for well-off families, payment going towards the young woman's trousseau.

Employment in the Lowell mills was not indenturing or compulsory but a matter of felicitous opportunity. Summer hours were six days a week, 12 hours a day, with breaks readily secured for shopping or personal errands, and winter saw a dawn to sundown regimen, i.e. standard labour shifts of the era as in upland agriculture. But mill work was not as back-breaking. Employers did not discourage modular months of off-and-on enlistment, given the large pool of traditionally female textile workers in Massachusetts, whom Robinson commended for their world-widening interest in cash wages of $3 to $3.50 a week, as opposed to the thankless – and salaryless – drudgery found on backwoods family farms. (Facets of these realities were embodied by the mill girls in the stage company of Rogers & Hammerstein's *Carousel*, whose original 1945 cast starred John Raitt, future father of singer Bonnie.)

The Lowell mills' cordial climate of personal advancement changed, however, when hard economic times descended after 1836 and compelled wage cuts, as well as occasioning stingy schemes like required church attendance (at $6 per annum – three weeks yearly pay – for pew seating) and the withdrawal of subsidies on room and board.

Strikes led to general investigations of child factory labour, whose standards in New England were often far below Lowell's superior level, and the Female Labor Reform Association was formed to agitate for union representation. By 1860, "the fair unveiled Nuns of Industry, Sisters of Thrift", as celebrated in an 1848 Lowell magazine piece by John Greenleaf Whittier, Trudy Woodard Taylor's distant relative, were gone from their respectable boarding houses. Their New England legacy of temporary employ among non-proletarian strivers passed in later generations to women akin to the college-age Kate Taylor, who had worked as a waitress alongside hundreds of other girls in the region's resort restaurants.

As far as James Taylor's own accumulating toil between late '77 and the onset of '78, he composed 'Millworker' in a locale in the Lamberts Cove house that was "about six feet away from the place where I wrote 'Secret O' Life'. One warm night I was in bed with Carly, and I woke up about 1.00 a.m. and I walked downstairs to the desk where there was a pen and one of the sketch pads that Carly buys so many of for the kids. I turned on a little desk lamp and I wrote the second verse real quick. I don't know if I had been dreaming it before I woke up but it was a real channelling experience.

"It started out as a truck driver song, strangely enough," he said, "with the first verse talking about 'me and my machine, for the rest of my life'. It doesn't actually refer to a specific character in that Terkel book, but it was inspired by those interviews of people talking about their work and their life. My mother and her family were from Newburyport, and right up in Lowell is where the big textile mills were, on the Merrimack River, which was the heart of the Industrial Revolution in this country, and later they were down in New Bedford, near the Vineyard."

In Taylor's imagining, his millworker would not be one of the country-mouse offspring of a secure independent tiller or outland artisan but rather a naive lower class sewing girl who took a grimy, dangerous factory post believing she would get the pretty bonnets and lending library cards the Lowell Girls sported. Instead she met a drunken co-worker, who died and left her with three children to feed. Driven to such jobs and personal alliances due to poverty, and then trapped when one's kinfolk or marriage partners expired in a local wave of disease, such girls could subsequently be shunned even for domestic "help" above the level of common black and Irish servants (the Irish then ranked lower than the blacks).

For mental respite, Taylor had the song's lonely labourer reflect on her father's seminal kindnesses, as well as her granddad's accounts of sailors in trading vessels who were lost at sea, further situating the song's main points within the mists of stories he himself half-recalled from his Carolina childhood. James was also excited to have created a uniquely poised and righteous character whose perspective was a female one.

"There haven't been many, certainly, from me," he acknowledged, "and I ran upstairs to Carly and read it to her and she said" – groggily – "'*Uh, yuh, ril gud.*' It's tough to wake Carly up for a response because if you succeed it'll be three hours before she can get back to sleep again. I don't know who I'm giving this advice to, but to all you people out there: *Don't wake Carly up in the middle of the night!*"

Another thing disturbing Simon's sleep patterns during the late 1970s was her husband's socialising with new found companions from the cast of the late-night NBC television programme, *Saturday Night* (later renamed *Saturday Night Live*), which began its programming life on October 11, 1975.

The programme's founding executive producer, Lorne Michaels, had created the Not Ready For Prime Time Players overnight by hiring most of the often Michael O'Donoghue-directed regulars (Gilda Radner, Bill Murray, Chevy Chase, etc.) on *The National Lampoon Radio Hour*, and spin-off *National Lampoon's Lemmings* and *The National Lampoon Show* Off-Broadway stage productions. There was one fellow Michaels was reluctant to take on, though, and that was *The Lampoon Show*'s director and star, former Second City improv phenom John Belushi. But O'Donoghue and the other writers pushed for Belushi (who was himself a talented writer) and after an audition in which he portrayed a samurai pool shark, he was in.

Born in Chicago's Norwegian American Hospital on January 24, 1949, the son of Albanian immigrant Adam Belushi and his Akron, Ohio-bred wife Agnes, John had been a husky, outgoing ham since his adolescent days in Wheaton, Illinois. He was co-captain of the Wheaton High football team, and drummer/leader of at least two rock bands (The Vibrations, The Ravens).

Belushi moved to New York in 1973 with high school sweetheart Judy Jacklin and they first visited Martha's Vineyard together in June 1974. After they were married in Aspen, Colorado on New Year's Eve, 1976, they continued to frequent the Vineyard.

Kootch introduced Taylor to Belushi at a summer '76 party at Peter Asher's LA house; later that year, James was a musical guest on *Saturday Night Live*. Between skits on Legionnaires' Disease, host Lily Tomlin's Ernestine The Telephone Operator schtick, and Gilda Radner's Emily Litella spiel about "crustaceans" hijacking an airplane, Taylor sang 'Shower The People', Jr. Walker & 'The All Stars' '(I'm A) Road Runner', and 'Sweet Baby James'.

Subsequent summer rendezvous on the Vineyard with the Taylors as the Belushis rented houses in Gay Head and Chilmark cemented the ties between James and John, and they often went fishing together or body surfing off Lucy Vincent Beach. The bond was based on humour, mutual affection for left-wing politics and music, especially R&B, blues and soul; love of the outdoors, especially the sea; an affinity for clambakes, beer drinking, Fourth of July fireworks, and fish sandwiches at Sandy's roadside stand in Vineyard Haven, and the shared experience of growing up with difficult-to-please dads.

Others gathered into the Vineyard circle of summering buddies included *Saturday Night Live* cast member Dan Aykroyd, playwright/songwriter Timothy Mayer, journalist and TV/film writer Mitch Glazer, and local businessman/shop owner Larry Bilzerian. Also a big fan of Belushi's was Alex Taylor, who admired John's taste in music and his welcoming comradeship.

Children also tended to like Belushi, and a prank John always played when visiting the Lamberts Cove house was to pause in the doorway as the pint-sized Ben pulled his trouser legs. "Has anybody seen BEN?"

John would call out, in mock exasperation, looking every place but down at the tot. "I was supposed to meet him *here* to take him for ice cream, but I can't find him anywhere! Please tell him I looked *everywhere* for him!"

"I'm right here!" Ben would squeal. "Can't you see?!" Until Belushi would pivot towards the door and then spin back, scooping Ben into his big arms and then driving them both in his jeep to the Aquinnah snack bar below the Gay Head lighthouse.

Carly, however, didn't connect with Belushi's offhand amity and absence of ceremony. His spontaneity made her seem stilted, and the fact that her mother Andrea doted on Belushi just muddled matters more. Often ill at ease with her own spouse, Carly could not find her social balance when John was added to the equation for late dinners at the Ocean Club in Vineyard Haven, or early suppers she cooked at Lamberts Cove. Most of all, Belushi did drugs (mostly pot at the time), and drank with regularity, two things she could not abide.

Nothing untoward occurred on the island when Taylor and Belushi and company congregated, just a lot of laughter, grilled tube steaks, and high-spirited wit. But James was moving gingerly through doubts and fluctuating dependencies that kept Carly on edge under the best of circumstances. Belushi represented another unwanted human yardstick to measure the widening distance between Mom and Dad at Lamberts Cove.

And then there was the pressing need for Taylor to funnel more hit product to Columbia Records as per his lucrative new agreement; whose evolving terms would ultimately entail a dozen records, in addition to contingencies negotiated for a litany of side projects like *Working*, whose Columbia Masterworks original cast album finally reached stores on June 20, 1978.

The year came to a conditional close for James and Carly with the September issue of 'Devoted To You', their duet from *Boys In The Trees*, the song vaulting to number 36.

Elsewhere on the American home front, the deadline for the (doomed) ratification of the Equal Rights Amendment was extended to 1982. The Wampanoag Indians, who had saved America's original Plymouth Plantation settlers from starving, lost their lawsuit to recover 13,700 acres of tribal lands seized in 1870.

Things were no more fair or logical in global matters. The US announced it would resume full diplomatic relations with the human rights-riven People's Republic of China on January 1, 1979. While in Guyana, 911 members of Jim Jones' People's Temple, including more than 200 children, were found dead of mass suicide. And high above the earth, four probes from the Pioneer Venus 2 satellite began sending data about the atmosphere (carbon dioxide) and surface conditions (rocky, volcanic terrain) and weather (dense clouds of sulphuric acid) of the ethereal planet named for the Roman goddess of vegetable gardens and feminine chastity.

★ ★ ★

On January 4, 1979, recording commenced at the Sound Factory in Los Angeles for Taylor's second Columbia album. Kootch, Kunkel, Grolnick, Sklar, Schuckett, Sanborn, Spinozza, Nash, Lasley, McCuller, guitarist Waddy Wachtel, Asher, Garay, and the rest of the staunch caravan turned out, including Carly and her brother-in-law Alex. Not in attendance was Abigale Haness, whom Kootch was divorcing. And there were no Beatles or Carole King, but James cut splendid versions of Lennon and McCartney's 'Day Tripper' and Goffin and King's 'Up On The Roof', to keep the faith.

The latest album in progress was to be tagged *Flag*, an appellation intended to denote a "personal statement", as James put it. "It represents you; you put it out there; you express; let's run it up the flagpole."

Although the triangular colour patterns on the cover of *Flag* inadvertently proved to be the nautical signal for "man overboard", the jacket's blue/aqua backside had no particular symbolism in the international code of naval signals at sea. If one split the difference, the implied title was something closer to *Waving, Not Drowning*.

A series of often-scathing character studies, *Flag* kicked off with the sardonic 'Company Man', which looked hard at the star-making appliances and mammoth record sales explosions of the late 1970s, a period in which an act was either "multi-platinum" for each piece of product (6 times over in the case of Peter Frampton's 1976 *Frampton Comes Alive*, and 16 times as much for Fleetwood Mac's 1977 *Rumours*) or made to feel invisible in corporate circles.

" 'Company Man' couldn't have made the record company very

happy," Taylor said, since it indicted an industry at the height of a gran-diosely greedy cycle. "But it was just a comment, like 'Hey Mister, That's Me Up On The Jukebox' was on the fact that it takes a young man to play *only* for money – which will only turn you old."

The song that followed in *Flag*'s track sequence was 'Johnny Comes Back', which Taylor called, "A dark tune; it's basically about someone who's keeping someone interested in them because he's got them strung out. It talks about 'Where she'd get that tear in her eye/ Whoever said she could leave me.' That sort of stuff. But I've always liked 'Johnny' and occasionally we'll reheat it and take it out for concerts."

Another tale of knotted flirtation occurred later on *Flag* with 'I Will Not Lie For You'.

"The lyric seems kind of prissy and snotty and petty," Taylor allowed, "but it took seven minutes to write the whole thing: *boom*. Me and Russell Kunkel had built a small cabin, a guest cottage in the woods near my Vineyard house, and I had been working out there one day to make a record. That night, I knew that if I left the guitar in the cottage it might freeze there, and I went to get it and I just picked it up and the song came right out of the guitar!

"I went back in my house, played it for Carly. She said, 'Nice song.' I said, '*Yeah.*' She said, 'Are there any more out there?' I said, 'I dunno; you leave a guitar out there and you might catch another one!'"

But Taylor was not without misgivings about the irascible side of his songmanship: "Although I did not write 'You've Got A Friend', I sometimes expect someone to come up to me after I've sung it and say, 'You call yourself a *friend*?' Often, I feel really presumptuous about the things I write. Yet I write them in an overwhelmed state, and it's not like ordinary feelings I have most of the time."

The same reasoning applied for amiable gambols on *Flag* like 'Chanson Francaise' and 'Is That The Way You Look?' And Taylor said the run he and the band took at 'Day Tripper' was "just one of those things where we had time at the end of a day and somebody starts playing a groove, and before you know it, it's a track." As for the cover of his own 'Rainy Day Man', he said, "I always thought it was a great song, and thought it had come a long way since I first did it. Bonnie [Raitt] had covered that song [on her 1974 *Streetlights* album]; and since

George Jones has re-recorded all *his* songs every time he'd change a record label, I thought that, 'If George can do it, I can too.'"

The resurrection of 'Up On The Roof' in an arrangement slightly redolent of his duet on it with Carole King at Carnegie Hall in 1971 was even more purposeful. "'You've Got A Friend' and 'Up On The Roof' are two greats of her's, written on her own or with Gerry Goffin," mused Taylor, "but there are countless others. She has just been a source for me of well-constructed, solid songs and elegant lyrical architecture – and an inspiration in terms of how good she was at coming up with commissioned work. In a way, *Flag* was an attempt at and celebration of that kind of craft."

And it would pay off when the album was released on April 26, 1979, *Flag* going gold on the strength of 'Up On The Roof', which hit number 28 on the Hot 100. Taylor appeared on *Saturday Night Live* to perform 'Roof', 'Johnny Comes Back' and 'Millworker', also squeezing in a small acting role in a sketch opposite Belushi, Aykroyd and host Michael Palin as a deckhand sailing with the "manly men" aboard the good ship The Raging Queen.

As with *Flag*'s revamped 'Millworker' and the citizens' band radio-celebrating 'Brother Trucker' (on which James and Alex did a joint vocal), one of the best and bleakest dramatic monologues on the album is its closing song, which also began as an assignment for another circumstance. "'Sleep Come Free Me' was intended to be for *Brubaker*" – the 1980 Robert Redford prison movie – "but ultimately they weren't interested," Taylor explained. "The song was an attempt at trying to get into the frame of mind of someone who wishes their time would go away." A brilliant, anguished oath by an isolation-scarred 28-year-old inmate who'd seen 10 years inside his dungeon, it jerks with jagged spasms from Kootch's electric guitar, and shuts down at the end with the clank of a steel door being yanked shut courtesy of Deputy Sheriff Larry Tourquet.

The only slightly less grim 'B.S.U.R' (i.e. 'Be As You Are') took the artful premise of turning letters and numbers into sentences as popularised by the books (like CDB! and CDC?) of author-illustrator William Steig. As kids, Taylor and his sister Kate enjoyed those Steig texts and played those games, and the adult James used a similar technique to convey a marital contretemps.

"I wanted to write the whole song out in letters," said Taylor of stanzas that gauged the nuptial union in question to be a bleeding movie, guessing game and masquerade, " 'cause I thought it would look nice on a lyric sheet. So I wrote 'BSUR' and Carly was fine about the song, *sang* on it, but other people were appalled that I could put our relationship on the line that way. She's written a song called 'Fair Weather Father' that seems to paint me pretty ugly, but I sang back-up on it, and I don't take it seriously."

A songwriter, like a novelist, can't help but draw from his life to some extent, especially if he seeks to be accurate about what he knows. But did the people close to Taylor object to the personal quality of certain song narratives?

"What it comes down to," Taylor emphasised, "is this: you choose what is obviously, at best, a near-miss at a moment that is heavily subject to mood, time and musical style. If they think it's a true representation of what goes down between you and them then they're simply off the mark.

"I feel as though an intimate relationship between people is a separate thing; it's an oasis. And it doesn't operate in terms of right or wrong. Although when intimate couples argue, they so often make the point of who's done what right and who's done what wrong. In other words, they speak in terms of transgressions, in terms of codes of behaviour. And they keep *immaculate* score.

"It's no good to keep score. That just doesn't help, because it's denying the value of the intimacy of the situation. That's debasing it, putting it on a more general basis. Why do that?

"Of course, there are things that people should and shouldn't do," he conceded, "and that's why you get angry at people. But an intimate relationship transcends that. To put business on the street – maybe messing with someone – I think that's a risk you take in a relationship anyway.

"I think if you mess up, some of it is forgivable. And then there's a situation where the relationship is decaying, and there's no chance for them to get back together and make it right after it's finished."

22

That Lonesome Road

A dog licked his face, and then he finally saw the light. It was the spring of 1979, and James was sprawled, semi-conscious, on his back. He had passed out, sometime before sunup, upon the lawn in front of his little white cottage outside the village of Plymouth, Montserrat, a Leeward Island that had been discovered (1493) by Columbus, colonied (1632) by the English, self governed since 1960, and nearly blown apart the evening before.

At least that's what the steady pounding in his noggin was alleging to Taylor. He had been spending late afternoons or early evenings hanging out with Jimmy Buffett, whose *Euphoria II* sailboat was anchored in the harbour off Old Road Bluff while Buffett made his *Volcano* album at George Martin's AIR Studios.

The record was purportedly named for Galway's Soufriere, the smouldering magma cauldron on Montserrat that would erupt more than a decade later and eradicate this overgrown cay of a Caribbean paradise. Those troubles were in the future, however. Taylor's current woes were linked to how he had been spending his *late* evenings, and what islanders called the "real" origin of Buffett's album title: a drink called the Volcano.

Dreamed up along the snaky footpaths between a Plymouth tavern called the Agouti and the Village Place, a low-ceilinged groggery above

the hillside hamlet of Salem, the Volcano was the thirst chaser of preference whenever the two taverns' cold Carib Beer ran low or the dawn
got too near for comfort. The fundamental recipe for a Volcano,
according to Village Place bartender Danny Allen: (any) four kinds of
rum, grenadine, pineapple juice, orange juice, and Montserrat lime
juice. Taylor, brothers Alex and Hugh, and Buffett had been downing
these libations with a will in the last few days, and the stray alarm clock
of sorts that was the hound dog poised over Jamie's squinting features
was telling him it was getting much later than he'd guessed.

"Yeah, well, I don't have too much moderation in my drinking,"
Taylor admitted to this writer a few months after the incident. "If I get
intoxicated, sometimes I lose control. And I've sometimes made mistakes when I was too high that I deeply regret. I can get real sad thinking about things I've said to people and ways I've made people I love
feel because I was so out of it. But those things are in the past."

Taylor was on a downward spiral of depression and disenchantment
– with himself, with his life. Friends steered him to an Alcoholics
Anonymous group ("High-bottom Upper West Side drunks," as he
described them) that met in a hall off Central Park West near his home.

James had been somewhat productive on the Montserrat safari,
singing with Buffett for *Volcano*'s 'Treat Her Like A Lady' and adding
guitar and vocals to 'Sending The Old Man Home'. Hugh and Alex
Taylor sang behind their brother in the harmony backdrop for the
tracks 'Lady I Can't Explain' and 'Survive', under the intemperate
pseudonym The Embarassing Stains. But mostly the Eastern Caribbean
interlude had been about wanderlust and drinking. Alcohol was already
a dangerous proposition for Alex, whose 1974 Dunhill album, *Third
For Music*, drew little notice; Alex's career had been stalled by alcohol,
and treatment hadn't kept him on the wagon. Now James was in the
danger zone.

His *Flag* album entered the *Billboard* charts on May 12, 1979 achiev-
ing platinum sales like Carly's *Boys In The Trees* (the best-selling non-
anthology album of her career). Taylor felt more assured about
addressing, both in his music and in his confidences, the extent to
which he was on the verge of unravelling. Others in his professional
circles slipped over the edge on which he teetered: actress Laurie Bird,
his co-star in *Two-Lane Blacktop*, committed suicide on June 16, 1979,

in the East Side penthouse she shared with beau Art Garfunkel, leaving Art and others shattered.

Many of the songs on *Flag* had graver underpinnings than Taylor had previously admitted to. 'Sleep Come Free Me' had actually been precipitated, "a couple of weeks before that," by a frightening blackout he'd undergone after a public drinking bout at a friend's affair that he hadn't been able to curtail. He got locked for no good reason into an obstinate acoustic guitar rendition of fellow Massachusetts folkie Taj Mahal's 'She Caught The Katy And Left Me A Mule To Ride' (Mahal adapted it from the original by Yank Rachel, Sleepy John Estes' mandolin player, for Mahal's 1968 Columbia album, *The Natch'l Blues*) and Taylor refused all requests to cease and desist.

"I got *so* drunk that I blacked out a whole rampage of awful behaviour," said Taylor of the obsessive binge. "I don't know where I got the energy for it. I can remember that I played 'She Caught The Katy', which I love, at a party for something like eight hours straight, and when someone finally threatened, or offered, to beat me on the head lest I keep [i.e. out of fear he might continue] playing the song, I actually bit a big hole in the guitar. And this guitar belonged to a good friend of mine, so it was a *bad* thing to have done.

"I had also recently watched a TV programme on angel dust, where some poor bastard killed a man and couldn't remember afterwards. So I began to think of how some person could wake up with no memory of what he had to pay for with his time in prison. When I came to, I heard for days about my behaviour – some people just gave me dirty looks – so I wrote that into the song."

Ashamed, yet able to retreat into work, Taylor made a great effort to keep himself in check and productive, but he kept drinking. In this respect, he was again at odds with his worse fear: becoming like his father.

"The work is always the last thing that goes," as Trudy Taylor had admonished about the alcoholic lifestyle, "because it holds their lives together."

Ike Taylor had remarried in 1979 to lawyer Suzanne Sheets and though living in Boston he was still on the part-time staff at the UNC Medical School at Chapel Hill in the Department of Social Administrative Medicine, and had recently been flying down to attend meetings on–campus for the first time since 1971. Ike was also an associate director of administration at the Boston University Medical Center and was about to add an administrative post at B.U.'s Hubert H. Humphrey Cancer Research Center. Dividing his days between North Carolina, Boston's Beacon Hill, he sometimes saw his grown children, but not his first wife. "He would never want to see me," Trudy later said, "although I wanted that, and I tried." Ike was planning to start a new family with Suzanne. And *he* was still drinking heavily.

Son James' raft of activities was even more extensive. Swept up in the tailwind of a hit album, Taylor's itinerary – excerpted from the road ledger prepared by Peter Asher's office – between July 1979 and September 5, 1980, when sessions for a new album were to start in Los Angeles, had been prodigious:

JULY 3, 1979: Six-week summer tour begins in Memphis, 25 shows in 17 cities (including five nights at LA's Greek Theater), concluding Aug. 17 at Berkeley's Greek Theater. Two nights at Ohio's Blossom Music Center taped for *Showtime* cable television. Band: Kootch, Kunkel, Sklar, Grolnick, Wachtel, Sanborn, Lasley, McCuller.

SEPTEMBER 19–23, 1979: Participates in *No Nukes* 'Concerts For A Non-Nuclear Future' at Madison Square Garden by MUSE (Musicians United For Safe Energy); shows filmed, recorded.

DECEMBER, 1979: *No Nukes* all-star 2-LP album released (Asylum/WEA), certified RIAA gold. James heard on six tracks – with Doobie Brothers and John Hall ('Power'), with Carly Simon and Graham Nash ('The Times They Are A-Changin'), with Carly ('Mockingbird'), with the Doobies ('Takin' It To The Streets'), and on his own ('Captain Jim's Drunken Dream', 'Honey Don't Leave L.A.').

MAY 15, 1980: *Saturday Night Live*, 100th Show. James sings 'Cathy's Clown', 'Sunny Skies', 'Take Me To The Mardi-Gras' with Paul Simon, David Sanborn.

JULY 18, 1980: *No Nukes* feature-length movie opens in New York City; includes live album performances plus 'Stand And Fight' by James (co-written with Jacob Brackman).

AUGUST 3, 1980: Four-week tour begins in Memphis; 23 shows

in 18 cities (including attendance record-breaking four nights at Pine Knob, Mich.) concluding Aug. 30 at Merriweather Post Pavilion, Columbia, MD., with special guest Kim Carnes. Band: Sklar, Grolnick, Wachtel, Lasley, McCuller, Dan Dugmore on pedal steel, Greg "Fingers" Taylor on harmonica (no relation) and drummer Rick Marotta. Tour represents *live* rehearsal-performances for upcoming album.

SEPTEMBER 5, 1980: Album sessions begin at Record One Studio in LA

For Trudy Taylor's part, she still resided at her beachfront Chilmark house but travelled annually to Ireland and China, was heavily involved in social and environmental causes, wrote prose and occasional magazine and newspaper articles, worked on a book about Chinese peasant and vernacular architecture, and spent as much time with all her children and grandchildren as possible, even taking them along on her overseas jaunts. Her home was an orderly but exuberant repository of all her offspring had done, the dining room, kitchen and hallway of its elegant quasi-Japanese floor-plan brimming with neatly arranged files, rows of recordings, scrapbooks of photos and scrupulously hung artwork and gimcracks from the eldest boy to the eager new grandson.

Livingston, who returned to the record business with three well-received albums (*Three-Way Mirror*, Epic Records, 1978; the retrospective *Echoes*, Capricorn, 1979; *Man's Best Friend*, Epic, 1980) had prospered on the concert circuit and wed long-time love Maggie Shea on May 1, 1976.

Hugh, who had a number of boating and real estate interests on the Vineyard, married Jeanne Ayer Smith on April 15, 1974 and they now had two kids: Alexandra Taylor (born May 6, 1975) and Isaac Cole Taylor (born October 25, 1977).

Kate and Charlie were raising Elizabeth and her stepsister Aquinnah May Witham, and Kate released a superb R&B/country soul album on Columbia in 1979; produced by Barry Beckett at Muscle Shoals Sounds Studios in Alabama, with Hugh, Alex and Liv pitching in on vocals, it was called *It's In There . . . And It's Got To Come Out*. On March 24, 1981, Kate would give birth to another daughter, Aretha Theodosia Angelique Witham.

Alex was doing well recording commercials and jingles. He'd also begun touring in 1980 with Skin Tight, a group from Fort Worth, Texas that moved to the Vineyard to work with Kate and him.

Carly was busy with Ben and Sally, her recording shoehorned into slots around their schedules. *Spy*, a 1979 album inspired in part by Anais Nin's erotic memoir, *Spy In The House Of Love*, was produced by Arif Mardin, and its lead-off single was 'Vengeance'. While a somewhat harder-edged offering than usual, it still sounded too familiar to excite. It sputtered out at number 48 and the album inched up to number 45 before expiring.

Simon's 1980 *Come Upstairs* record (her first of three for Warner Bros.) was one of the weakest she would ever release and betrayed the insecurity of a neglected homebody, but it jumped to number 36 thanks to 'Jesse', a gold single that shot to number 11 and sounded like someone's crush note to a re-encountered old flame. On tour in October to promote 'Jesse', she began haemorrhaging onstage in a pre-mature menstruation diagnosed as triggered by extreme stress. Backstage she collapsed, sobbing uncontrollably.

"My sister Lucy was there with me," said Simon, "and said, 'There's no reason why you ever have to put yourself through this again. There are other ways of getting yourself out in front of the public.' I started seeing a psychiatrist again, and I decided that at this time in my life, when things are so difficult for me in other ways, I shouldn't aggravate my nervous condition anymore." She cancelled the last six shows of the tour, and was sued by promoters.

James took time out from his own touring to be with a recuperating Carly and help out on a project spearheaded by Lucy Simon: *In Harmony – A Sesame Street Record*, an album on which various artists (Linda Ronstadt and Wendy Waldman, George Benson and Pauline Wilson, Billy Joel, Doobie Brothers, Bette Midler, Al Jarreau, Dr. John and Libby Titus) joined with the Simon and Taylor families to write and/or record expressly for children.

One of the most acclaimed (and imitated) such endeavours of the post-World War II baby boomers' own nest-building heyday, *In Harmony* won a well-deserved 1980 Grammy for Best Children's Recording and spawned an equally good sequel (*In Harmony 2*).

The title track of *In Harmony* was credited to "Kate Taylor and the

Simon-Taylor Family", Livingston did 'Pajamas', the Doobie Brothers covered Lucy and Carly's vintage 'Winken, Blinken And Nod', Lucy sang 'I Have A Song' and Carly, tellingly, provided a bittersweet piece called 'Be With Me'. James and the now six-year-old Sally cut the most endearing track of all, 'Jelly Man Kelly', which was her reconceptualisation of Kootch's 'Machine Gun Kelly'.

"Sally is listed as co-writer of that song," Taylor noted proudly. "She and I used to sing it in the car."

"Ben has an unrecorded song," Taylor added, "that he made up with Tim Mayer called 'Stupid Chicken': 'Stupid chicken/In the kitchen/ With Baba Rum Raisin/Making stupid chicken stew for you!' It's a nice song, and Tim was riffing off someone coming on strong about Baba Ram Dass and the surrender trip of idolising someone – and Ben picked it right up."

Even in the midst of gross overwork, James was grappling to regain the light touch with which his music often shone by involving his children in the act of song-making. When he played these days around family and immediate friends, he did the silly, informal things in his repertoire that the general public rarely heard. One such tune was 'I Guess I'll Always, Always, Always', which had no additional lyrics beyond the repetition into near-infinity of "always". Sung slowly and with thoughtful inflection and handsome chords, 'I Guess I'll Always, Always, Always' only revealed its true non-structure after about 50 or 60 seconds – and it always got a good laugh.

Another silly song – "I occasionally play it at picnics" – which James was finally urged to cut after he unveiled it in several concerts was 'Mona', about a pet pig.

"I was thinking about killing my pig because I'd had it for a long time and it was old," said Taylor, "and I then had a new baby, Ben. My brother Alex noted that the pig sometimes got out and was rambunctious. In fact, I saw it kill another little pig once. So Alex said, rightly, 'That pig might kill one of your kids. You gotta be careful.' I'm afraid it's true, so I had been considering bumping her off, and I wrote a song about it."

Besides wanting to keep his children safe and happy, Taylor wanted them to see where many of his other songs came from, and where his ancestors originated. In 1980, he took Carly and the kids to London, travelling by ocean liner. He showed them his old basement flat in Beaufort Gardens and the gas heater with the insatiable appetite for two-shilling pieces. Then they all took the West Highland Railway far north to the so-called Coastal Strip at Fort William, Scotland, a beautiful and fertile part of Inverness-shire, situated on the herring-filled Loch Linnhe at the foot of Ben Nevis, Britain's highest mountain.

"My father used to tell me that his ancestors came from a place called Marykirk, which was near Montrose," a place far south-east of Fort William, he told Carly and the kids. "I think they were some sort of seafaring merchantmen – they had their own boat to sail to North Carolina."

After driving around awhile, gazing at the rolling hills and some of the prettiest landscape Taylor had ever seen, James and family caught the train back down from whence they came.

"James is really a country boy, likes being on the loose and disorganised," Carly commented at the time, "and it's one of our incompatibilities. When he comes back from the road, there's always a feeling of anticlimax, of relief followed by 'Jesus, *now* what?' It seems that sons cannot help following in their father's footsteps, whether they like the path or not."

Back in America, waiting for Taylor, were all the song paths necessary to complete an album he'd decided to call *Dad Loves His Work*.

"I was riding back East on a plane one time," James reflected, "and had a conversation with a guy next to me. Both of us were talking about how our work took us away from our families. And I had an evocative memory as we spoke of my own father continually being pulled away from us by his work. When you have to leave your family to do your job, you can say, 'Daddy has got to go out and make some money so we can live' and if you're responding to guilt, you can say, 'It's for you, I do it for you.' But I realised that, if possible, the best thing to do – and I've done this with my kids – is to say, 'I love doing this, I'm going to do this because I love it. Dad loves his work.' Because if it's true it's more honest than saying, 'It's a sacrifice that I do for you.' And it's also more celebratory."

"James' work is extremely good for him," Carly said in response to her husband's outlook. "It holds him together. And he's usually most healthy physically and mentally when he's on tour. But while he feels justified by his *Dad Loves His Work* philosophy, it's still difficult for his children, especially Ben."

"On *Dad Loves His Work*, I think Jamie wants his children to know that although he's away a lot and seems very burdened by his life, he loves his work, and they shouldn't worry about him," mused Ike Taylor at the time. "As for me and him, I don't contribute to his life now, except when he needs me or when somebody's ill."

During 1980, three-year-old Ben was found to have a serious ailment – a dysplastic (abnormally developed) kidney that ultimately resulted in the removal of one of his (toxic) kidneys, and James went to his own dad for counsel.

"When Ben got sick – he was sickly all his life – James called for advice," said Ike. "I called friends at Columbia Presbyterian, which led to an accurate diagnosis of Ben's kidney problem. I got a great deal of satisfaction out of being able to help. This dad certainly loves *his* work; I've been very happy with my career. I can't get all the work I used to manage, but I'm having a good time. Sadly, my absence from home was almost constant.

"James and I talk from time to time," Ike added, "about his life and mine. My impression is that James is fairly well-satisfied himself with what he's accomplished. I read in the newspapers about troubles in his family. What do you say? James is in his thirties and it's a fact of life that our expectations tend to be moderated as the years go by."

But not always. The music that emerged on *Dad Loves His Work* was not about denial, defeatism or diminished expectations. Rather it saw James taking an unsparing look at everything he and Carly and his own father and even his own ancestors had done to themselves, each other and even those surrounding them.

Beginning with 'Hard Times', he addressed the difficulties of holding an "angry man" and a "hungry woman" together.

Next, on 'Her Town Too', Taylor and songwriter friend J.D. Souther examined a long-standing relationship that had reached an insurmountable impasse. "J.D. Souther and I wrote and sang that song about a couple who were long-term friends and had an acrimonious break-up," said James. "It was a tender, well-meaning song about how difficult it was to be friends to both of them at that time. For no good reason people thought that 'Her Town Too' had something to do with

Carly and me but in fact it was entirely about the ex-wife of a mutual friend."

In terms of the album's song sequence, up next was " 'Hour That The Morning Comes', a song that sounded angrily self-critical. 'Hour That The Morning Comes' is about a number of people at a party," Taylor detailed. "The first one is Carly, who doesn't get drunk and has a good time without hurting herself. The second guy with his head *kacked* – that's a junkie's term – in his lap, is just someone who's feeling miserable. The next person, the fool with the lampshade on, is somebody else I know, and the 'secret agent man' is a dealer, or somebody with an angle he had to play at the party."

A sense of redemptive possibility arose on *Dad Loves His Work* with 'I Will Follow', which could be taken as a declaration to save a relationship, or a determination to keep searching until the right one came along. " 'I Will Follow', like a lot of the songs that I write, had a spiritual feel to it," Taylor said. "That song is about surrender, and I suppose I would have to say it's my favourite on the album, but 'Believe It Or Not' " – the subsequent cut, about winning an elusive heart – "is good too."

As for the inciteful 'Stand And Fight', it was commissioned for the 1980 film, *Times Square,* a tale of teens hanging out in New York's notorious urban agora, with a script by Jacob Brackman as produced by Robert Stigwood. "Jake wrote a lot of the *Times Square* script to coincide with the songs we'd written," said James, "but for some reason Stiggie said, '*Nooo*.' It was a very frustrating experience for Jake. He didn't expect to be stonewalled by Stigwood. I felt bad about 'Stand And Fight' being pulled.

"I played the song for Waddy Wachtel and Kootch, Russ Kunkel and Don Grolnick at the soundcheck for the *No Nukes* concerts and they dug it and picked it up in no time at all."

"I was amazed to find, during the first time I went to Italy to play [in September 1985]," Taylor added, "that the Italian Communist Party had used that song as their theme. In fact, when I played Pisa, the promotion of that concert was somehow connected with the local Communist Party machinery! Of course, communism in Italy is very different from elsewhere, but clearly it was a very kinetic song for them."

The most downbeat track on *Dad Loves His Work* was 'Only For

Me', its heart-sore mood accentuated by beautifully forlorn pedal steel from Dan Dugmore. In the lyric, a young man speaks of discovering an older man he knows in a bar, the older chap in an acute state of intoxication but still lucid enough to explain the pain that put him there. Asking the young man to sit at his table, the drunk begins to tell a story of a father who couldn't face the responsibility of his own family and dared to run away, leaving everyone behind – including the son who worshipped him.

Hearing the story told with all the humility and sorrow it merits, the young man suddenly makes another discovery: he has the power to forgive the unforgivable. And as he does so, he feels a rapturous light erupt between the old man and himself unlike anything he's ever known. Of all the songs Taylor would write, whether about shooting smack and other self-degradations, or the most uplifting daily aspects of love and charity, 'Only For Me' was the sole tune he said he found too difficult to discuss. Indeed, it would be another 16 years before he could bear to do so.

Regarding the infectious 'Summer's Here', Taylor wanted fans to know, "That was the character talking. I don't *hate* any time of the year, but I like fall the best."

The chantey that was 'Sugar Trade' was social commentary of an uncommonly intense type as Taylor traced the chain of responsibility that can make a seaman or ship owner feel justified in being a small part of a great enterprise – even if that business has an inhuman side to it. Constructed like a shipboard work song of the sort so prevalent in the great days of sail, 'Sugar Trade' was also a chilling parable, reminding all hands that it takes a lot of courage to go to sea; and yet if someday one finds oneself being swallowed up by its fury, it's best to be certain the mission was worthy of one's demise, and not as feckless as a farewell note in a bottle "with nothing to say".

"We were down in the basement of J.P.'s at East 75th Street, me and Buffett," Taylor recalled of the song's inception, referring to the notorious Upper East Side musicians' and actors' watering hole owned by Miami-born sailor/restaurateur Jimmy Poulis. "Oh man, in the basement of that joint, getting into trouble! Then I took the lyric up to Mayer in the Vineyard and he added the 'crown and the cross' stuff." Taylor explained that the verses which started out as a kind of bar-room yarn/lark became a deadly serious examination of the slave trade and the manner in which it still mars modern culture – as well as a disquieting exercise for all three songwriters. Taylor, for one, said he had no idea how deep his revulsion for the subject ran until he'd probed it.

'London Town' was a re-enactment of the trip Taylor made with Simon and their children in 1980, as well as other solo trips in the time since his Apple years. "I was amazed to be walking those streets, 10 years down the line," he said. The topic turned wrenching for Taylor on December 8, 1980, when John Lennon, a neighbour of his on the Upper West Side, was senselessly murdered outside the Dakota apartment building by a demented young gunman. The shots fired just before 11 p.m. were audible throughout the area, most people first assuming they were a car backfiring, but then feeling oddly uneasy.

Thinking back during the weekend of Lennon's death on the immediate acceptance James found at Apple, Taylor remembered Lennon with fond regard and fierce respect. "The atmosphere at Apple was casual and hectic," said James, "and getting things done there was as informal as strolling down the block to the deli for a sandwich. There was no heavy vibe; it was 'Sure, let's go!' Peter played my tape for Paul and John, and I was on the label.

"I had a couple of conversations with John during that early time in the studio and I remember him as being very busy and devoted to his craft. I watched him work on the two or three versions of 'Revolution' and he was really going after it. His energy was very intense and he believed very passionately about most of what he wrote. It was obvious that the song was a response to a lot of people making demands on him concerning his radical point of view, and you realised that by our adulation of the group, we were all making it more and more difficult for them to continue. But they must have had a positive will beyond what I could contemplate, and John especially was writing a lot and doing *very* adventurous things."

The last song on *Dad Loves His Work* was 'That Lonesome Road', and Taylor must have known it was a foreboding slice of the "self-definition" he'd reluctantly accepted his songs as destined to become. Six months after *Dad Loves His Work* entered the *Billboard* album chart on March 21, 1981 – the gold record rising to number 10 and its 'Her Town Too' single getting to number 11 on the Hot 100 –

Carly announced her separation and pending divorce from her husband.

Talking in fall '81 at the Lamberts Cove house, which Taylor gave her as part of their settlement because it would be the least disruptive for the children, Simon said, "There are good reasons for the decision. Our needs are different; it seemed impossible to stay together."

Years later, she would write an unpublished short story examining how the constant renovation of the house and grounds became a hectic decoy distracting them from the drama indoors; Carly called for a cobblestone driveway and a pond, and James lobbied for separate dwellings for the dog, tractor and pig, plus a windmill. But when the penultimate bridge arched over the courtyard which they'd both petitioned the carpenters for was completed, so was their union – commemorated since by the "white elephant" of a shrine Carly and their children still inhabited.

Yet during her '81 speculations amid the harvest equinox, Simon remarked only that, "James needs a lot more space around him – aloneness, remoteness, more privacy. I need more closeness, more communication. He's more abstract in our relationship. I'm more concrete. He's more of a . . . poet, and I'm more of a . . . reporter."

Smiling wanly, her full lips turned thin with a ripple of emotion that seemed uncertain of its course. "Basically," she said, "he just wasn't willing to dress up like Louis XIV before we went to bed every night. I really *demand* that of a partner." She burst into grateful laughter.

As the day wore on, and the autumn light angled itself more sharply and then fell sombre, Simon followed suit. Her next album was to be called *Torch*, she said, and it had a torch song on it by a favourite of James', Hoagy Carmichael. The piece was 'I Get Along Without You Very Well'. She recited some of its lyrics, most of which meant the polar opposite of their assured disavowals. But as Sally was heard crying from the other end of the house, and Ben called out for attention, she expressed herself not in terms of Hoagy Carmichael but rather in a paraphrase from 'Haunting'.

"Sometimes, if you're in a complete relationship, feelings have a chance to die out," she said. "But if a relationship has ended prematurely for some reason, or it can't be fulfilled for another reason, the haunting goes on, the obsession, the dreams about the person" – she stopped, sighing heavily – "and the feeling that he is forever locked inside."

23

Home By Another Way

James was on the road in the Far East in the autumn of 1981, touring Japan and Australia. And during each of the next four years, he would venture out on both a winter and a warm-weather tour for blocks of four to six weeks each (i.e. approximately ten weeks annually).

He bought an apartment off West End Avenue to be near the children during the New York school year. On the Vineyard he built a small, one-floor, U-shaped bungalow overlooking Menemsha Pond, with rooms for himself and the kids, plus a kitchen, modest deck and flanking screened-in porches for summer sleeping and dining.

A "fisherman's shack", he called it, and put in electric heat for the winter, although a wood-burning stove in the living room saw the most use. Later, he built a small boathouse down by the water for his kayak and sculls – although Ben liked to play and camp out within it as he got older.

There were other plans along the way that never saw fruition, some small, like an unrecorded "jive" song written in 1980 with Jacob Brackman called 'Take Me Back, California'; some medium-sized, like a double live album of his early '80s shows alternately titled *Fish Scales* and *Bicycle Built For A King*, with photographs for the proposed cover art of James cycling bare-chested in a sports coat on Lucy Vincent Beach.

Alex Taylor continued to tussle with his drinking problems as he and wife Brent raised baby James (now 14) and their 16-year-old adopted son, Edward. The titles of songs on Alex's 1981 *Dancing With The Devil* blues album for Ichiban Records were a random reflection of the pressing issues in his world: 'House Of Cards', 'Can't Break The Habit', 'Birds Of A Feather', 'Change In Me', 'No Life At All', and of course the title track.

Then there was Taylor's Lighthouse Lager, which was to be brewed by James on the Vineyard (along with a Lighthouse Ale) in a joint venture with Hugh Taylor. "We've done research over the last couple of years and learned as much as possible, going up to places like Sonoma, California to check out one of the smallest breweries in the world," Hugh Taylor explained in October of 1981. "Preliminary plans for this summer include designing the building and figuring out a brewing schedule. Our yearly output would be 10,000 barrels for island consumption – what Budweiser does in 10 minutes.

"The beer will be bottled in fully returnable bottles and we'll pick up our empties – although we know we'll lose bottles off-island to souvenir collectors," he continued, "and it will be packaged in a four-pack that will be priced like a six-pack, ideally in a six-sided bottle so they cling together like a honeycomb. All the beer will be pasteurised – a fresh beer delivered *cold* every 14 days to all local Vineyard outlets. Our logo will be a beam of light coming from a lighthouse like the one at Gay Head, with 'Taylor' printed across it.

"James and I were on the phone last night at 11 p.m.," Hugh enthused, "talking beer from Martha's Vineyard to LA, where James had a stopover before going to Honolulu for a show. He's really psyched, and I told him I hope he's working on some good drinking songs. For now, we're gonna call the parent company J&H Brewing but that could change depending on how many siblings are involved. We're still learning all we can, but we should be brewing by late spring of next year."

Since Hugh was involved with a charter boat and ferry business in Menemsha and his real estate interests, and James went away after Christmas for a six-week winter tour starting in Cleveland on February 1, 1982, conversations, more research and a timetable for the brewery were still being co-ordinated by Hugh via regular phone calls to James.

Questions of whether the enterprise, which had a credible business plan, would have even got underway or remained just an engaging notion were entirely swept aside, however, by something friends of James and Hugh learned on the afternoon of March 5, 1982.

Judy Belushi heard the door of her Manhattan townhouse open, the lock obviously released by a friend who knew the push-button combination, but whoever it was had suddenly begun bounding up the stairs, taking several at a time.

"Judy!" he yelled, and she recognised the voice of Dan Aykroyd, who burst into the room with his hand covering his head as if wounded. "I . . . I don't know how to tell you this," he gasped, gagging on his own words. "I don't know what to say . . . I."

"Danny, what is it?" she screamed, seeing he was about to cry. "Has John been hurt?"

"No, honey," he answered softly, shaking his head. "He's dead."

All his life, John Belushi had been the vibrant overachiever and social linebacker who ran interference for others. As an adolescent coming of age in a household his own mother described as "very European in outlook", John was the one who petitioned his conservative restaurateur dad for permission, among other things, for his sister and two brothers to speak freely at the dinner table.

As John reflected in 1978, "I used to tell my father, 'This is America, Dad, you're not in Albania anymore. You made it out and escaped to a free country. Let's enjoy that freedom, let's at least loosen up at home.'"

A big brother to dozens of fellow performers and entertainment industry figures, whether actors, musicians or those who worked behind the scenes, getting them jobs, gigs and parts, loaning them money, sharing his contacts, paying sincere attention to their hopes and even paying their rent, John had forged an image of invincibility. And while he could be a hard partier of the first rank, he had never faltered in his forward career motion.

As Judy Belushi would recall, "He was the star of the country's top money-making movie, *Animal House*, on its way to becoming the top money-making comedy of all time. He was a cast member of *Saturday Night Live*, the number-one late-night television show, and he had released his first music album with his band, The Blues Brothers. On

January 24, 1979, John's thirtieth birthday, the album became number one on the charts. No other performer has ever held all three top positions simultaneously."

And no one lost so much so quickly in the next 14 months. Perhaps because no one around John entirely comprehended the degree of the clinical depression under which Belushi would be barely functioning in the last brief span of his life, because it came on so insidiously, and he concealed his affliction so relentlessly.

Belushi was initially deeply dispirited by the $40 million flop that was *1941*, an unfunny comedy directed by Stephen Spielberg about the Japanese attacking Los Angeles during World War II. It also hurt the careers of many of Belushi's co-stars, including Treat Williams and Nancy Allen, but Belushi felt it was his fault for not carrying the picture.

When pal Michael O'Donoghue tried to cheer him up by bursting the "big deal" bubble around the debacle with a droll button he'd made a batch of that read: JOHN BELUSHI 1949–1941, the burly actor laughed but half believed it.

Belushi rebounded with the huge success in 1980 of *The Blues Brothers* film, but once the glow of that comedy and its hit soundtrack subsided, he distrusted the 'blockbuster or bust' mentality of the period. Yet John was having difficulty finding less broad vehicles that could help establish him as a comic actor of genuine range.

Continental Divide, a 1981 romantic comedy opposite Blair Brown got excellent reviews but tepid box office response, and *Neighbors*, a surreal 1981 picture that reunited him with partner Aykroyd, also fared poorly with ticket buyers. The chief benefit of the latter project had been personal, since it got actress/friend Kathryn Walker back to work after the devastating death from a fall in Hawaii in 1980 of fiancé Doug Kenney, an actor/writer for *Animal House* with whom John had been close since their seminal *National Lampoon Radio Show* collaborations. A further side-effect of restoring Walker's spirits was the affection that bloomed between her and James Taylor when Tim Mayer, a chum of Kathryn's from her years at Harvard, introduced them to each other at a brunch Mayer hosted on the Vineyard in July, 1981.

In the last months of 1981, Belushi had been hustling to get other film projects green-lighted under a deal he had with Paramount

Pictures, most importantly *Noble Rot*, a comedy he was co-writing with Don "Father Guido Sarducci" Novello about life in the vineyards of a winery.

When that script was put on hold, Belushi's expansive degree of dejection contracted into despair. He tried to smother it with drink and harder drugs. He begged his old friends like Taylor to come out and carouse with him, but nobody played that hard anymore; it was the early '80s and they'd outgrown '70s sybaritism as their marriages and children demanded more of their free time and mad money.

Belushi died of a needle-injected dose of heroin and cocaine, a circumstance that shocked his closest friends into disbelief.

"Nobody who loved him wanted to go out and play any more," as friend Mitch Glazer later put it, "and the people John *did* find to play with didn't love him."

John Belushi, 33, was buried on March 9, 1982 after funeral services at the First Congregational Church of West Tisbury on State Road. Kathryn Walker and James Taylor had been with Judy Belushi on an almost constant basis in the last four days since Belushi's death on the 5th, helping her to make the arrangements.

In keeping with the customs of the Albanian Orthodox Church, there was an open casket throughout the proceedings, and at the appointed moment for mourners to file past, Taylor joined the line and approached. When he reached the coffin, he stood close enough that his belt buckle touched the bier. He took what Judy Belushi later described as "a long, very intense, sad look at John", who had been just ten months younger than him. Later at the cemetery gravesite, under a cold grey sky, Taylor lifted his guitar and sang 'That Lonesome Road'.

★   ★   ★

"John's death was a wake-up call for me," said Taylor. "There were a number of wake-up calls; I didn't exactly turn on a dime immediately, it took another 10 months or so before I got serious about leaving my mess."

Another rude awakening was the demise of Taylor's *Two-Lane Black-top* co-star, Beach Boy Dennis Wilson, who drowned while intoxicated in the waters of Marina del Rey on December 28, 1983. "The last time I saw Dennis," Taylor reflected, "I was out visiting Peter Asher in Los Angeles [in 1983]. I had had a traffic accident and I was talking to a cop. And Dennis came over, looking absolutely wild, in some altered state, in rough shape. He came over to tell the cop not to give me a hard time . . . And a month later he was dead."

As for Belushi, his "was a lesson that spoke really loud to me," said James. "Nothing John was doing would have indicated that he should have died before me or anybody else."

Taylor fulfilled his concert commitments over roughly the next year and a half (among them five weeks of dates with early fan Karla Bonoff). He then cleared his schedule – from mid-September of '83 (the year his divorce from Carly was signed) for the next four months. With Sally due to turn ten and Ben soon to be six, James decided he must put substance abuse out of his life forever.

By January, after his children's birthdays, he was due to fly to Montserrat to start cutting another album, his fourth for Columbia and first in three years. He wanted to make a record clean, and call it *That's Why I'm Here*.

"The basis of the 'That's Why I'm Here' song, for which I named the album, was threefold," said Taylor. "The first verse was about hooking back up with an old musician friend of mine who I had fallen out with.

"The second verse was about John Belushi's death. The words 'brown bread' are Cockney rhyming slang for 'dead', and that verse is about 'There but for the grace of God go I.' The last verse was about career pressures and personal responsibilities and putting both in balance.

"When I started that album in Montserrat," Taylor continues, "I had given up methadone in January. I was booked into AIR Studios, but obviously I should have taken care of myself and cancelled it. I was completely bombed out, shattered. I had bottomed out from my addiction and I had gone in for a cure that should have taken four months and I did it in 19 days. And when I got down to Montserrat I was in no shape to do anything."

Yet, somehow, with understanding from all concerned, including recording/mixing overseer Frank Filipetti and the musicians, who included Bill Payne of Little Feat, keyboardist Clifford Carter, drummer

Rick Shlosser, guitarists Jeff Pevar and Dan Dugmore and a big-voiced addition to the McCuller/Lasley vocal choir named Rosemary Butler, Taylor got two strong tracks in the can: a courtly version of the Buddy Holly jewel, 'Everyday' (originally the B-side of Holly's 1957 hit, 'Peggy Sue') and the up-tempo love plea, 'Turn Away'.

Buoyed in body and mind in the aftermath by Walker, Taylor kept to his resolve and stayed clean through a 4-week spring tour of the Midwest and Southwest and then a 6-week summer trek with Randy Newman. But the event that altered him musically in the same manner Belushi's loss had changed him emotionally was the Rock In Rio Festival of January 14–15, 1985.

"I treasure the spark of insight and vitality I got from the Latin music I was exposed to in Brazil," Taylor said. "I appeared at the Rock In Rio Festival there just as democracy was flowering again in the country. During my trip to Rio de Janeiro I was headed back up emotionally and physically. What happened down there to me, the wonderful reception from the crowds and fellow musicians, sustained me in a major way. When I got back in the studio afterward" – at Right Track Recording in New York – "it was like a year later."

Of the material he polished at Right Track with the aid of Don Grolnick and Bill Payne, he confessed a special satisfaction with 'Only One' – "a nice sort of anthem, a sweet love song written as a kind of Valentine for Kathryn, because that was around the time I met her" – which featured Don Henley and Joni Mitchell on backing vocals. Taylor also considered 'Song For You Far Away' to be "a strong song too – that was written for [the 1982 movie] *E.T.* But somewhere between [Stephen] Spielberg and John Williams, who had other music in mind, it didn't get used.'

'Going Around One More Time' was a cover of Liv's 1978 track from his *Three-Way Mirror* album; 'My Romance' was the Richard Rodgers and Lorenz Hart song from the 1935 Broadway show *Jumbo*, and 'Limousine Driver' was a spoof on rock celebrity by James. 'Mona' landed on record with a classy harmony vocal from Graham Nash, and 'The Man Who Shot Liberty Valance' was Taylor's take on Gene Pitney's (unused) 1962 hit theme song from the John Ford western.

Radio seized on 'Everyday' as the single from *That's Why I'm Here*, taking it to number 61 and embedding it in Adult Contemporary play-lists for the next 15-plus years. But the track that meant the most to Taylor was 'Only A Dream In Rio' whose prismatic arrangement, heightened by its prelude in 6/4 time, evinced the elegant earthiness of Brazilian pop long before such worthy follow-ups as the David Byrne-compiled *Beleza Tropical: Brazil Classics 1* of 1989, or Paul Simon's 1990 *The Rhythm Of The Saints*.

Accompanied by percussionist Arto Moreira, 'Only A Dream In Rio' told an entrancing tale of renewal.

"I had checked into a hotel room on the beach at Ipanema, and Gilberto Gil, the beloved Brazilian artist, had lent me a guitar that was sitting in my room when I got there. I picked up that guitar, and the song was right inside it."

★ ★ ★

The wedding invitation, etched in red script, asked guests to celebrate the marriage of Kathryn Walker and James Taylor with "Wedding Cake And Waltzing" at Synon Hall in the Cathedral of Saint John the Divine in New York on Saturday December 14, 1985. During toasts at a small, wedding-party dinner after the main ceremony and before the waltzing, Kootch stood and got the biggest laugh of the night when he raised his glass and said, "I knew James Taylor before he was sensitive."

By the mid-'80s, that image of the pre-eminent sensitive singer-songwriter was a mixed blessing for Taylor, setting him apart from the shifting cynicism of the time but reminding many that the general public had yet to go beyond the pop hits and into the compositional and thematic depth of his body of work. Though the hardcore bought enough copies to push *That's Why I'm Here* into platinum status, most music fans were unaware he'd made his best record since *JT*. He was 36 now and beginning a new life with a woman outside the realm of rock'n'roll.

A distinguished actress as well as Harvard Phi Beta Kappa and Fulbright scholar in music and drama, Walker, born January 9, 1943, had long been close both to fellow Harvard graduates Doug Kenney (who advanced from mid-'60s campus roles as an editor of the Harvard *Lampoon* and president of the Spee Club, a university social club, to a role as one of the founding editors – along with Henry Beard and Rob Hoffman – of *The National Lampoon*), and to Timothy Mayer, whose intense involvement in theatre during his years (1962–66) at Harvard led to a life-long theatre career that included productions at the prestigious Goodspeed Opera House in East Haddam, Connecticut as well as Broadway credits such as co-authorship of the book for the 1982 Broadway musical hit, *My One And Only*.

Mayer, Kenney and Walker were part of a circle of mid-'60s Harvard chums (Lindsay Crouse, John Lithgow, Paul Schmidt, Honor Moore, Stockard Channing, Tommy Lee Jones, George W.S. Trow) who vaulted out of its ivory towers to embody a more accessible cultural vanguard. Walker had entered Harvard for a masters in Celtic studies after graduating in 1964 from Wells College in Aurora, New York. In 1970 after studying at the London Academy of Music and Dramatic Arts under her Fulbright Fellowship, she moved to Manhattan, and won an Emmy in 1975 for her lead role in 13-part *The Adams Chronicles*. She played Abigail Adams, wife of President John Adams and mother of future chief executive John Quincy Adams, during the clan's 1750–90 era. Walker also starred in *Special Bulletin* (1983) and *The Murder Of Mary Phagan* (1990) – both Emmy winners; several acclaimed PBS American Playhouse programmmes (John Cheever's *O Youth And Beauty*, Reynolds Price's *Private Contentment*, and John Updike's *All The Way Home*), and network dramas such as *FDR: The Last Years* with Robards, *Family Reunion* with Bette Davis, and *Mrs. Delafield Wants To Marry* with Katharine Hepburn. ("I played the daughter of Hepburn's character," said Walker, "which was a fascinating role to have opposite Hepburn.")

Walker co-starred on Broadway with Christopher Plummer in Neil Simon's *The Good Doctor*, with Jason Robards in Eugene O'Neill's *A Touch Of The Poet*, with Richard Burton and Elizabeth Taylor in *Private Lives*, with Ian McKellen in *Wild Honey*. Besides *Neighbors*, her films included *Blade* (1973), *Slap Shot* (1977), *Too Far To Go* (1978), *Rich Kids* (1979), *D.A.R.Y.L.* (1985) and *Dangerous Game* (1993).

A witty, attractive and outgoing brunette who loved good talk and conviviality, she brought fresh air and intellectual stimulation of high and hale varieties into Taylor's everyday affairs, from literature, fine art, cinema, dance, and photography, to the theatre. And while they bought homes together in Washington, Connecticut and Santa Fe, New Mexico, she was equally happy to spend nights grilling swordfish and playing Trivial Pursuit with her and Taylor's friends at his Chilmark shack.

On the Vineyard or in New York, Carly had been wary of mixing various circles of James friends, but Kathryn was oblivious to such concerns, encouraging everybody to get to know each other on their own terms whether it was her former Harvard actor pals, or Jimmy and Jane Buffett, North Carolina poet/novelist/playright Reynolds Price, screenwriter Mitch Glazer and actress spouse Wendy Malick, Michael O'Donoghue and musician wife Cheryl Hardwick, film and record producer Laila Nabulsi; the Belushis; Aykroyd and wife Donna Dixon; or local neighbours in either place, regardless of their background or pedigree – as long as they brought something intelligent and entertaining to the mix.

Walker had a knack for devising worthwhile occasions for everyone to congregate, donate their talents and gain pleasure from each other's abilities, as when she and Harvard professor William Alfred co-founded the Athens Street Company in 1989 to perform poetry, music and original theatre. One acclaimed result was *Among Animals* in 1992, an evening of music, dramatic readings and light verse whose stage company included Alfred, Channing, Hardwick, O'Donoghue, Price, Moore and Schmidt, as well as actors Bill Murray, Christopher Walken, Brooke Shields, humorist Fran Lebowitz, Walker's husband James – and their dog Flea, who ran out to James at an unscripted juncture.

Débuted at Sanders Theater in Cambridge, Massachusetts to benefit Cleveland Amory's Fund for Animals (on whose board Walker served), *Among Animals* was also presented at Wellesley College, and in Manhattan (and later adapted for a BBC film) – each time with parties afterwards that renewed or kindled more friendships.

Walker did not equate fun with substance abuse or self-indulgence or excess. Never judgemental, she just had no time for outlets with a self-destructive tilt.

"James and I met at a horrible point in both our lives," she said, "when I was shattered with grief after the death of Doug Kenney, and James was in the fight of his life with drugs and alcohol. We both wanted and *had* to be our real selves."

She assisted greatly in helping Taylor gain the grit and volition to go to Alcoholics Anonymous – as James himself volunteered afterwards to friends – and stood by him with forbearance during each level of his detoxing and withdrawal, along with the bed-sweats, seizures, outcries and violent recurrent nightmares that accompanied them.

"It was a terrible time," she says, "but to make it seem as if I was a dutiful nurse mopping his brow wouldn't be right. It was much harder and more intense than that, a very wrenching and even ugly thing neither of us wanted to go through but had to."

James called her "Kitty", she called him "Bim", and the lines in the song 'That's Why I'm Here' about waking him up in the middle of the night to "tell me everything's alright", are his tribute to her for aggressively engaging rather than disavowing his drug and alcohol problems, and for never looking down on him for the monkeys dug into his back with dagger-deep claws. Since even her earliest encounters with him were unattached to his performer's persona, Walker never tried to segregate Taylor's bleeding warts from the rest of who he was and wasn't.

"James and I met at a point in both our lives when we were open to a fresh start, to the *need* for a new beginning," said Walker, "but we came together through close mutual friends in a way that allowed him to be his actual self and also be original around me, and vice versa. He also had enormous energy and great gifts of interest and appreciation. We also just fell madly in love with each other, and that love made us both feel we could actually go on with our lives at that point."

Walker also encouraged Taylor's interests in political and social issues, the role of music in theatre, and in naturalism, zoology and animal rights – which got him outdoors for pursuits that transcended either touring or the athletics he needed to get his mind off his addictions.

In the May 1987 issue of *National Geographic*, Taylor read a story entitled "At Home With The Arctic Wolf", by L. David Mech, the cover of the magazine and the piece itself graced with the astoundingly intimate wildlife photos of Jim Brandenburg. The text spoke of the "vocal repertoire" of the environmentally threatened grey wolf and the white Arctic wolf, which had made their stands in the northern woods of Minnesota, Canada and Alaska's Arctic tundra, noting how a pack discovered by the intrepid *Geographic* team would lift their early morning howls in unison "in a wilderness concerto".

The piece touched something fundamental in Taylor, who appreciated the allure of isolated creatures that sang out of primordial instinct, answering the Arctic sun as it warmed their lairs or warned them of dangers – like humans.

"I contacted Jim Brandenburg, who's a friend," Taylor recalled, "and got some portrait photos of timber wolves in Northern Minnesota, picking one for the cover of *Never Die Young*," his next album, which he recorded at the Power Station in New York after sensibly booked blocks of 1986–87 touring that took him to Australia, Hawaii, Scandinavia, France, England, both parts of divided Ireland, Belgium, Italy and to Brazil (twice).

"For me," Taylor explained, "the photo I chose was evocative of nature, but I had also gotten tired of seeing my picture on the front of my album covers. Most of all, I loved the fact that the wolf was singing."

The notion of a timber wolf in mid-aria as the image heralding the stark beauty of *Never Die Young* in 1988 also struck chords in Taylor's core audience of fans, who embraced its songs about the importance of personal integrity, the pleasures of small town life, and the nobility of all living things, and made the transporting release a platinum record. But as per usual, Taylor's appealing work contained surprising under-textures of the sort found throughout nature, whether human or otherwise.

Much of the musicality of these textures was made possible by drummer Carlos Vega, known for his supple jazz and Latin percussion on recordings by Lee Ritenour, George Benson, Milt Jackson, Luis Miguel and Julio Iglesias, in addition to adroit pop, rock, R&B and country sessions with Neil Diamond, Linda Ronstadt, Bonnie Raitt, Randy Newman, Teddy Pendergrass, Patti Labelle, Vince Gill and Randy Travis. Though the man himself was taciturn, Vega's style was conversational in tone and articulate in touch, and he would aid Taylor's studio and concert sound immeasurably over the next ten years.

Produced by Don Grolnick, the record had some of Taylor's most open-souled ballads, including 'First Of May', in which he said were cached some of the "relatively few" lyrics of his "that border on being rude" as they "talk about 'A rite of Spring/A horizontal thing/The sweetest sort of dance/Hidden in among the plants.'"

An equally lustrous and light-tempered track like 'Baby Boom Baby' gradually revealed itself not as a pledge of love but rather a plea from an unrequited suitor who wondered, "How can I miss what I never knew?" as he fumbled to renew an acquaintance that still haunts his heart.

Just as clever in its emotional ambush was 'Home By Another Way', co-written with Timothy Mayer, in which the saga of Jesus' nativity and subsequent flight with his parents from the evil King Herod turned from Bible anecdote into practical advice on the urgency of leading an original life – especially considering "how the gods play the odds".

Taylor also loved the intricate title track. "Some think of it as being about young people who have died and gone to 'another land beneath another sky' and that's not true," said James. "It's actually about one person looking at an idealised, mythical couple, and while there's envy there, the person is rooting for them and saying, 'Hold them up!' and praying they'll make it. The emotional foundation of the story is the person telling it, saying, 'I don't have a chance of making it out of what-have-you – a dying steel town, a *barrio*, an addicted existence, a war zone – but I hope to hell *they* make it, and survive,' and that they 'Never give up/Never slow down/Never grow old/Never die young.' "

Timothy Mayer, 44, died of cancer on April 9, 1988, and James was at the burial site on April 12 in Cotuit, Massachusetts, holding his guitar tightly as he sang 'Home By Another Way'. At a subsequent reception at the Mayer family's house, Walker seemed doubly sad after her new husband mentioned an upcoming tour. Later, standing on the porch outside, she looked forlorn as she told friends, "James is going away again."

On November 21, 1989, Liv Taylor turned 39, gave up alcohol, took up aviation, bought a plane, and soon fulfilled a boyhood dream of flying.

Sally, 15, and Ben, 12, were growing up fast, and James began to do something Ike never did: take his kids everywhere he went, whenever they could go. They accompanied him on tours, which Sally prized, because she got to sing back-up, and Ben really dug, because he'd taken up the guitar at 10, and Dad could teach him chords. James was an exercise buff, so they all got into mountain biking, white-water rafting, sailing, hiking. Each year they'd plan for the big six-week special vacation dad and the two offspring took annually, which included European jaunts, and explorations of Asia, the Caribbean, and various corners of North America. And since James had divorced their mom (who married writer Jim Hart on December 23, 1987) and tackled his bad habits while his children were very young, a clean slate was still possible.

"He and my mother separated almost before I can remember," said Ben, "so I don't have memories of him being around the house. Apart from a brief initial phase, I don't ever remember being upset."

But there was one problem with their ultra-available dad. "There is a little bit of rivalry between Sally and me," said Ben. "The quality of time I spend with any father is diluted when there is another child around to get some of the attention. For selfish reasons, I try to keep time with my father and time with my sister separate. I hate to admit it but we've always been rivals for his attention."

This immersion in adolescent wiles put James in mind again of his own coming of age trials; after concerts in Australia and US – and guesting on brother Hugh's 1990 *It's Up To You* album on the Village Green label – James and producer Grolnick cut 1991's *New Moon Shine*.

"The phrase 'new moon shine' refers to moon shine whiskey in the song 'Copperline'," explains Taylor, who co-authored the graceful ballad in 1991 with novelist Reynolds Price (*Kate Vaiden, Blue Calhoon, Roxanne Slade*). "It also refers to a different kind of moon shine – meaning a different kind of intoxicant – and then it also refers to the idea of a certain kind of light coming from a new moon, so it has the contradiction of darkness and something radiating out of it. It's a play of words on the necessity of redemption.

"I really liked the title," Taylor added, "which was suggested by Reynolds and Kathryn, who sat around and talked about it for a while; it came out of a discussion."

But what triggered all this talk in the first place were Taylor's own meditations on his childhood in Chapel Hill, notably the time idly passed as a little kid along the cold, sparkling, and snake-infested length of Morgan Creek. " 'Copperline' is a photo album snapshot that harkens back to my childhood," he conceded with a laugh. "None of it is real accurate – but none of it is inaccurate, either."

Still, the best stuff is too good to make up.

James in Los Angeles, February 1988, on the eve of the release of 'Never Die Young'.
(*Timothy White Collection*)

Vineyard Haven, Martha's Vineyard, in the 1940s. (*Timothy White Collection*)

Trudy Taylor, motor boating across Menemsha Pond in the late Eighties.
(*Taylor Family Archive, courtesy Trudy Taylor*)

Alex Taylor, King Snake Records
publicity shot, 1989.

Hugh Taylor, 2000, showing a
marked resemblance to 18th
century ancestor Isaac Taylor.
(*Taylor Family Archive,
courtesy Trudy Taylor*)

The modern Taylor family seal,
designed by Kate Taylor.
(*Taylor Family Archive*)

Livingston Taylor, 1999. (*John Goodman*)

Kate Taylor, on the cover of her 1999 single
'Auld Lang Syne'. (*Front Door Records*)

James Taylor in Boston, June 1987. (*Timothy White Collection*)

James Taylor under sail in the Atlantic in the 1980s. (*Taylor Family Archive, courtesy Trudy Taylor*)

Sally Taylor, 2000, on the road, in the mountains. (*Blue Elbow Records*)

Ike Taylor, in the summer of 1996.
(*Taylor Family Archive, courtesy Trudy Taylor*)

Actress Kathryn Walker, early 1980s.
(*Timothy White Collection*)

Kathryn Walker and fiancé James, playing Trivial
Pursuit, Chilmark, Mass, summer 1984.
(*Timothy White Collection*)

Trudy Taylor, 1996, from the cover of her limited edition book of prose, *My Delights*.
(*Taylor Family Archive, courtesy Trudy Taylor*)

Kirtonhill pasture, 1998. (*Timothy White*)

Ruins of gatehouse entry to Kirtonhill.
(*Timothy White*)

Surviving wing of Kirtonhill manor, 1998.
(*Timothy White*)

Balmanno estate as it appears today.
(*Timothy White*)

Guests congratulate newlyweds James and Caroline "Kim" Taylor after their
Boston marriage ceremony, February 2001. (*Corinne Schippert*)

'Raised Up Family', 1999, left to right, Caroline 'Kim' Smedvig, Ben Taylor, Trudy Taylor & Sally Taylor,
together in New York City. (*Jessica Kusmin/Taylor Family Archive*)

James Taylor, summer 1997, steering his sail boat across Menemsha Pond.
(*Kelly Lynch/Timothy White Collection*)

"And a lot of the songs on *New Moon Shine* have that quality," Taylor agreed of the album that entered the *Billboard* 200 album chart on October 19, 1991 and quickly went platinum. "For example, 'Like Everyone She Knows' is observing a sense of emotional empathy for a young person who's new in the city. I've known what that's like. The song has a little of my early days coming into New York City in the mid-'60s by way of Boston and Chapel Hill, and also a bit of the time when I went to London to make my way before getting signed by The Beatles to Apple Records."

This keen sense of empathy and its larger scheme was probed in the anti-war story of 'Native Son'.

"It's written about a friend I grew up with named Mark Burnett, who went to Vietnam as a medic and shot himself after he got home," said Taylor. "The song was about the impossibility of coming home and reintegrating himself after what he'd seen in that war."

And then there's 'Shed A Little Light', a tabernacle-like choral tribute to Dr Martin Luther King – "It was declarative and out in the open, boldfaced," noted Taylor, and inevitably sets up a sharp contrast between such heroes from Taylor's liberal/activist Southern upbringing and later leaders like Ronald Reagan, who get a different sort of review on 'Slap Leather'.

"'Slap Leather' was about Reagan, whose first thing after he left office was to go to Japan to speak to a convention of Japanese businessmen for $2 million," Taylor explained in 1998. "He had a payment value for being President of the United States; that was very unseemly to me. Another matter in the song was how narrow our view of the Gulf War was. We're counting the rockets, acting like it was just a media event, like a 'Big Mac falafel'. But the Iraqi people, who're not an evil enemy and are more like prisoners – they were doing most of the dying."

'Down In The Hole' had its own ghastly details in its imaginings of "a person who suffers from severe depression" that's so oppressive he believes he's snared in a subterranean world. But Taylor himself sounded as if he had the strength to think back on such intervals, recreating them rather than being a diarist stuck in the moment, his vocals vigorous and nuanced with storytelling flair.

"My vocals have been changing in recent years," he said at the time, "and I'm a little bit more aware of how I'm yelling and screaming onstage. I don't think people identify me with my hollering side, but actually there are quite a few songs in my set that require a lot of stress on the old instrument, and I've been thinking about backing off on some of those.

"I've had vocal coaching in the last few years from a woman in New York named Ann Countryman and more recently from another woman in New York named Marge Rivingston," Taylor noted. "Basically the way I got into voice study was that in travelling with Arnold [McCuller] and Rosemary [Butler], I've seen how serious they are about their instruments and how they train them. They eventually brought it home to me that if I was going to be doing six shows a week in a row routinely for a three-hour set, my voice *wasn't* going to hold up. I'd fall to pieces tonally and be suffering and sacrificing to compensate."

The result of such coaching was that Taylor's vocals became more sophisticated.

"I think that's true," he said. "I'm more aware of how in-tune every vocal is, and I work more carefully on performance aspects – but you can go too far with that too. If you allow a singer who's at all compulsive in the studio to run away with himself, you end up removing all the soul and personality to where it gets streamlined. Singing is not meant to sound 'finished'. It's meant to live. In mid-air. A good producer will tell you when to stop listening to yourself."

New Moon Shine had a great producer in Don Grolnick, and by his strategic use of horns, and of vocals where organ or other keyboards might normally be – and vice versa – he made the aural textures of the record breathe. Clifford Carter's synthesizers and programming were also used well but with keen restraint.

"There are a lot of significant things happening in my music and myself since I cleaned up and tried to take responsibility for my life," said Taylor in 1991. "Perhaps I accept myself and my circumstances a little bit. I know I'm trying to. I'm not being so evasive or demurring so much anymore. Kathryn has been a big part of this new sense of freedom and well-being.

"One of the things that I do notice with this album," he ventured, "is that it's a little less painful to sit with material and work with it, and *then* watch it go out into the world. I now have the patience to send it out there in its fully imagined state."

"Sometimes I think of those early sessions as removing a massive bandage," he said in reference to the *James Taylor* and *Sweet Baby James* albums. "The more quickly I pulled it off, the less painful I presumed the violent action was. I'd give it a nice, quick *rriippp!* and pray the wounds underneath were healed. Sometimes they were. But sometimes they weren't – *yeow!*

"Professionally," added Taylor, "people have been telling me in recent years that my music is fresher, more complete-sounding and in a good place," said Taylor. "But at the start of this decade I also had a dark reaction to my music – that I'd perhaps stayed too long in one place, being a horse in a familiar harness. The only answer to such a 'crisis' was that I avoided taking it too seriously."

And being a singer-songwriter seemed at last a creditable profession.

"Tin Pan Alley is a good, solid, respectable and yet humble category for someone to refer to yourself as," he agreed with a grin. "Songwriting is an honourable profession. Look at Gershwin and Irving Berlin. And singing for your supper is no crime.

"Look at people like Hoagy Carmichael, Cole Porter, Moss Hart. I met Yip Harburg once; he was a friend of Kootch's parents. He wrote my favourite line in a song."

What song was that?

"The lion's song about courage in *The Wizard Of Oz* – 'What makes the hottentot so hot?/What put the 'ape' in apricot?/What have they got that I ain't got?/Courage!' I'd like to have said that!" He burst out laughing.

"But making progress in your life is simply a matter of not getting caught in a little *tiny* trap," Taylor ruled, turning sombre. "If you stay relatively conscious and sober eventually you do learn and integrate things. I'm used to thinking of life in terms of addiction. One of the things that's at the heart of addiction is that the thing you're compulsive about becomes everything. The object is the obsession. Literature is everything. Sex is everything. Jesus is everything. Cocaine is everything. Music is everything.

"None of that is so, of course. Life is not an object. And only *everything* is everything – and each thing contributes, for better or worse."

297

And on *New Moon Shine*, Taylor and Grolnick and their fellow musicians, particularly the painterly drummer Carlos Vega, made listeners believe that the sky opened and the earth shook within the spirit of a young boy living on Copperline, and they served up a credible sense of someone leading a psychic underground existence 'Down In The Hole'.

But the album was also significant for its guest collaboration with Danny Kortchmar, who played a cutting acoustic guitar and shared the production credits with Grolnick on the coltish tale of love's convolutions, '(I've Got To) Stop Thinkin' 'Bout That', which Kootch would later recall as, "The first tune that James and I ever actually sat down together to write."

Kootch also co-produced the track that is quite possibly the finest narrative piece Taylor has ever composed, 'The Frozen Man'. " 'The Frozen Man' was written based on an idea I had after reading another article in *National Geographic*," said James. "The article was about a sailor found buried in the permafrost, a British expeditioner who died while trying to find a northern passage above the Arctic Circle."

The lyric is constructed as a first-person account of a human archaeological find from the subject's own startled standpoint, the miraculously revived sailor remembering a tempest "reaching up to swallow me whole", the icy shock of being tossed overboard stopping his heart in mid-beat. After being encased in polar ice for a century, the Frozen Man is awakened in a hospital by an inquiring nurse. Bewildered, he tells his angelic attendant how he lost his brothers and other hands at sea, and then pines for all he's been cursed to have outlived.

Provided with a peg leg and a new eye, the Frozen Man is a notorious freak of nature who frightens children and becomes a tabloid sensation. He is permitted to visit the graves in Liverpool, England, of his wife and daughter, as well as his own vacant tomb, and these experiences leave him desolate. The song is the sad tale of a displaced life – but also an allegory for fame, success, and the right choices made for the wrong reasons.

One can gain the whole world and forfeit one's soul – as the New Testament has always warned. But 'The Frozen Man' makes it appear as if civilisation is evolving towards a stage where it may be able to suspend free will, thrusting the whole world upon someone in order to steal his or her private essence.

The Frozen Man is a guest at the party by decree – denied the dignity of a refused invitation, let alone a natural exit. He is the Walking Man robbed of all sense of purpose, duty and direction. He personifies the theme of 'Long Ago And Far Away', wherein things don't turn out as one planned – but taken to its cruellest extreme.

Marking time with its gentle knell of ringing acoustic guitar chords, terse shakers and doleful bass drum, the Frozen Man is humanity brought to its knees, bereft of comfort or closure, compelled to come back and bear interminable witness to everything it could not control or change or undo, as if in an uncaring/dismissive dress rehearsal for the Last Judgement. Not even Scrooge was handled so forcibly or roughly by the Ghosts of the Past and Future.

'The Frozen Man' eclipsed even 'Fire And Rain' (which had a reciprocal melody line) in its tender, piteous consideration of human powerlessness, and Kortchmar and Grolnick's production was impeccable in its lovely austerity. At the point Taylor wrote 'The Frozen Man', he said he "wasn't aware of that story" from his own ancestry of Isaac Taylor's brother John being washed overboard and then rescued during his forebears' 1790 voyage from Montrose to New Bern. Yet the song captured perfectly the mood of high jeopardy and immense loneliness the sea represents for all those travelling under sail in threatening tides.

'The Frozen Man' also carried the sobering air of life's second chances, as well as the terrible clarity such lucky breaks can lend to beneficiaries.

New Moon Shine ended with the vista of a vast, uneasy ocean in Taylor's reading of a Scottish lament, an *iorram* or rowing song (with roots in the traditional 'Waly, Waly Up The Banks'), called 'The Water Is Wide'.

"I knew that song from the folkie days," said Taylor. "There may have been a version from Jean Redpath around the house, and people used to perform it in coffee houses. In this case, Mark O'Connor plays the lovely fiddle part. I think the melody's sad but hopeful power is its own explanation of why certain songs last."

Yet it could explain why mutually supportive relationships like the one portrayed in the song do not always last. In the years following *New Moon Shine*, as Taylor's children took up more of his time, and the touring preserved on the 1993 *James Taylor (Live)* two-disc collection became a bi-yearly inevitability, and her own theatre and film work continued, Taylor and Kathryn Walker began to grow apart. The aim had been to build a flexible life together, honouring the past but repairing the present to make it work better for both of them in the future. As precedents have indicated, it wasn't that simple.

After Taylor and Carly Simon had broken up, Simon said of his problems that she "thought drug addition was like a virus, that he would get rid of it. It would run its course and go away . . . I was totally naive." And of his deeper demons, like the winter he dreaded on the calendar and feared in himself, she said, "I didn't know James felt that way about winter, but winter always seemed to remind him of the rejections he felt as a child."

In the winter of 1994, Simon was thinking back on her own sense of rejection as her mother died in February of lung cancer. Carly remembered how Andrea Simon withheld approbation almost as much as her father had – and often to more cutting effect. In 1989, weeks after Carly had received the Academy Award for 'Let The River Run', the theme song from the film *Working Girl*, her mother had toasted Carly at a dinner party with the withering salute, "You're not the best singer, you're not the best composer, but you got the Oscar."

Old emotional patterns found new counterparts in the mirror; by December 1994, Carly still had not moved into a common residence with her husband of seven years, Jim Hart, but said that Hart "stays over all the time" at her homes.

In contemplating her first husband just before their marriage broke up, Simon had also noted that Taylor "has a fear, a great dread, of imminent catastrophe, and he wants to have his own self-contained oasis on the Vineyard, where we can farm our own land, draw water from our own well, and so on." Time would reveal that Simon sought a similar sort of mental remove for herself, but while she was still with James, she believed she'd be included in his ideal refuge: "He often talks about how we'll live in safety when 'the catastrophe' comes."

As fate would have it, Kathryn Walker was the person who was there when the catastrophe inside Taylor came out. She saw all the battered underplanking and shifted ballast, the loose rudder and broken masts; she watched the torn sails flapping and heard the wind howl in the rigging, and beheld every part of JT that had been damaged or temporarily lost at sea during the middle passage between the decline of Jamie and the long deferred appearance of grown-up James Vernon Taylor. The shared decade of pain and redemption and psychic quartermastering that ensued was exhausting.

But so was the aftermath, because in order to stay clean and detached from his addictions, Taylor needed to stay active in every sense, burning off the nervous, nettlesome anxiety that drugs and drink had previously subdued. The healthful daily activity was fine, but the constant creative motion he also needed – the insatiable urge to travel and tour and fill time with work that could take him out of his crowded head – was far too demanding for Kathryn after the ordeal that preceded it. It was time for both of them to let go.

Four years after their divorce in 1996, Walker expressed her private thoughts about first meeting Taylor a year after the death in August 1980 of Doug Kenney, and then about the 15 years of their lives – ten of them as man and wife – that they spent together:

"Although we were around the same circles, James and I didn't really meet until the year after Doug's accident. I was in awful shape and my doctor had put me on some useless anti-depressant. My friend Tim Mayer put James, who was famously knowledgeable about pharmaceuticals at the time, on the phone to advise me about the drug I was taking. In the course of the conversation I told him that his was the only music I could stand to listen to in the months after Doug's death. Something in his voice, I said, and no false notes.

"'False notes?' he said, as if I'd said 'dead rat'. We laughed and I started to like him. He has something in his voice that's very clean and from the source. It's like a clear lens; the light comes through by itself. No matter what he sings it's there. Whatever his other talents, that's his gift. It *is* a gift. It actually seems to make people feel better. That's probably why he got so many letters from people in mental institutions. I don't know many singers who have that. I know a couple of actors I've worked with who do. Jason Robards has it and so does Christopher Walken. The light shines through. It's beyond just being talented.

"James was also handsome, smart and very funny, something I missed, missing Doug. He looked like a godsend to me. And was.

"Complications followed, as they do. Fifteen years is a pretty long

301

time. And maybe celebrity isn't really the gift of the gods. But talent is. Even now when I hear his voice singing somewhere out in the world it surprises me and I think, 'Oh, very nice, James'."

That's Why I'm Here, Never Die Young and *New Moon Shine*, the music that Taylor made during his years with Walker, was an attempt to let listeners know that it was possible to look forwards and backwards at the same time if one lives long enough to enjoy the privilege. It was about an 11-year-old's love for a 1959 Sam Cooke hit like 'Everybody Likes To Cha Cha Cha', or a celebration of a colourful friendship one could learn from on 'T-Bone' (but originally titled 'Santa Fe'), and an irrepressible desire to burst out with the rapture of feeling loved and happy and clean as a whistle on 'Sun On The Moon', 'Sweet Potato Pie' and 'Valentine's Day'. And also the ability to pity the story of a 'Runaway Boy' once so familiar and now so alien as to almost be a stranger.

Most of all, this music was about the love that makes one need to hold on, and finally allows one to let go. As intoned on the closing track 'The Water Is Wide', an obscure Scottish balladeer may have said it best:

> The water is wide, I can't cross over
> And neither have I wings to fly
> Build me a boat that can carry two
> And both shall row, my love and I.
>
> Oh love is handsome and love is fine
> The sweetest flower when first it's new
> But love grows old and waxes cold
> And fades away, like summer dew.

24

Native Son

James was going away again. On the road in Scandinavia in February 1998 on the eve of the Grammy Awards ceremonies at Radio City Music Hall in New York, he fretted over the notion of flying home just in case he won anything. But he was generally advised by confidants, business associates and representatives at his record company that such lofty honours were unlikely for his current, critically acclaimed *Hourglass* album and he had best continue his European tour.

Taylor was in Norway, away from his local base at the Grand Hotel at 31 Karl Johann's Gate in Oslo for a skiing trip in the town of Geilo, when he learned by phone at 5 a.m. that *Hourglass* had won Grammys for 1997 in the Pop Album Of The Year and Best Engineered Album (Nonclassical) categories. Both trophies were accepted in New York by Frank Filipetti, recipient of *Hourglass*'s engineering honour.

Several weeks earlier, Trudy Taylor had secretly been informed that Taylor would also be the recipient later in 1998 of The Century Award, *Billboard*'s highest honour for distinguished creative achievement. That December, Taylor himself was on hand in Las Vegas at the Century Award presentation during the annual *Billboard* Awards on Fox Television. After he received his trophy from singer Shawn Colvin, who sang on *Hourglass*, Taylor thanked his mother and family, ex-manager Peter Asher (who had amicably resigned and exited the management firm he'd founded to join Sony Music Entertainment as a Senior Vice President) and new manager Gary Borman whose Borman Entertainment Company also represented country star Faith Hill. Then James singled out "my old pal Kootch, Danny Kortchmar, who got me started in this business, and who promised that he'll let me know when it's time to leave."

"James is the archetypal singer-songwriter," Kortchmar had privately observed many months before. "He's *the* mould, as a solo artist backed by a consistent touring band, writing confessional songs before almost anybody – songs that remained personal even as they became universal. Dylan achieved the universal aspect, but not the personal vulnerability.

"Working and touring with James for decades, I used to want him to rock out more – until I realised that what he wanted to do was actually calm people in a unique, quirky way," confided Kortchmar, who was back doing select sessions and shows with Taylor after contributing to and co-producing Don Henley's solo albums (*I Can't Stand Still*, 1982; *Building The Perfect Beast*, 1984; *The End Of The Innocence*, 1989), and producing Neil Young (*Landing On Water*, 1986) and Billy Joel (*River Of Dreams*, 1993).

"James, he's a guitar virtuoso who subverted folk forms with a lot of major 7ths and higher inversion chords," added Kootch, "and he mixed influences like Stephen Foster, Pete Seeger, Aaron Copland, Lightnin' Hopkins and The Beatles so they disappeared into the James Taylor stew. His songs sound like blues, like Christmas carols, and like a church choir too, yet it all essentially comes only from him."

"He's just good, James, you just like *watching* him," mused Paul McCartney in March 2001. "And his guitar playing, too, is incredible. He's got the whole act together, he's lovely."

"I see family allusions in much of his work, and a core confidence in the rightness of exposing his inner self," said Ike Taylor of his son in 1981. "'Fire And Rain', for instance, was a great expression of his sensitivity but also of his will. And my greatest belief is in his creative will."

"My son ministers through his music," said Trudy Taylor. "He picks up the themes of what's good in the past, and he gives them a unified clarity in the present." Such observations by Taylor's mother were also a fitting description of the Grammy-winning *Hourglass*.

Hourglass had been built up informally but deliberately in sight of the sea, in a bungalow on Menemsha Pond near Taylor's own house on Martha's Vineyard. It contained affecting material that highlighted all James' various strengths, from love tokens ('Another Day', whose melody dates back to 1985 sessions on Montserrat), paeans to seaboard adventure ('Yellow And Rose', about the British Crown's forcible early settlement of Australia by means of deported convicts; and a cover of Livingston's 'Boatman' from Liv's 1996 *Bicycle* album), plus topical narratives, including 'Gaia', which James called, "Your basic tree huggers' anthem" based on planetologist John Lovelock's theory that the earth is a living organism he dubbed Gaia, for the Greek earth goddess; and 'Line 'Em Up', a commentary on disgraced President Richard Nixon and rituals of power.

"If that song's about anything," said James of 'Line 'Em Up', he felt it was "about how things repeat themselves. Nixon didn't do us any favours; he was one of the main things that deflated the possibilities of the '60s. There's this guy who's really in a position of leadership for the entire world, and he's obsessed with the pettiest kind of vengeance on his supposed enemies. But the political system selects for that kind of pettiness. So I'm referring to Nixon, but I'm actually talking about his footsteps. I focused on the speech Nixon gave on the White House lawn when he resigned" – on August 9, 1974 amid the Watergate scandal, with Vice President Gerald Ford (who later pardoned Nixon) sworn in as 38th US president the same day.

"And then," James recalled of Nixon, "he had to put one foot in front of the other to get to the helicopter to leave, and the way he did it was by lining up his people and saying goodbye to each one. He's using the line of people to supposedly say this tearful goodbye, but what he's actually doing is trying desperately to get to the helicopter and get his ass out of there?" Taylor laughs. "I'm not sympathetic to Nixon, because he debased the office. But on some level I am, in the same way you have to feel sympathy for every sentient soul on the planet."

Regrettably, Nixon proved to be yet another inadequate father figure.

"Yes," said Taylor, nodding, "and we all react each time like a family. These days, family structure is breaking down. And the more unlikely it is that you will actually make it out from your family and into the world in any kind of survivable form, the more useful it is for others to see and understand the bridge anyone's had to build to do it successfully. These ways of leaving the family and establishing yourself are an ongoing prospect, especially if your job as a creative person is to illustrate that process, that transition, that escape. And you also offer other ways of coping and of celebrating."

To this end, *Hourglass* contained other examples of Taylor's various fortes, whether power ballads ('Little More Time With You'), jazz waltzes ('Up From Your Life'), witty romps (hidden track 'Hangnail'), revived standards ('Walking My Baby Back Home', a big hit on the Brunswick label in 1931 for Nick "The Singing Troubadour" Lucas), and secular hymns: 'Up From Your Life' and 'Up Er Mei', the latter about a 1993 hiking trip he took with his children to the Er Mei Mountain in China's Sichuan province.

And then there was 'Enough To Be On Your Way'. This song from *Hourglass* encompassed Taylor's reactions to the deaths in the 1990s of Ike Taylor who was utterly worn out in body and spirit, and brother Alex (who died due to an alcohol-related heart attack in 1993 on March 12, James' birthday).

"I miss Ike terribly," said Trudy Taylor. "My feelings for him never changed. I would never have considered divorcing him if it hadn't been for his drinking. The disease took control of him and ultimately made it impossible to reach him.

"But I never stopped loving him," added his first wife, who never considered remarrying. "He was the love of my life." Of their first son, she said, "Losing Alex was so difficult. Alex was so protective of us family; he took care of us until alcoholism took care of him."

Alex had been in Sanford, Florida, recording a sequel for the independent King Snake Records label to his critically lauded 1989 album *Voodoo In Me*. Guesting on the previous record had been brother James, singer Gregg Allman, and blues guitarist Donald Kinsey's band, The Kinsey Report, and the best material from *Voodoo* included original songs 'Time On The Inside' and 'Vanessa'. Alex aimed to surpass himself on the new effort – to take the blues fire he'd felt on such projects as his brief 1986 alliance with Boston harpist James Montgomery in their R&B group (The East Coast Funkbusters) to a new peak, while putting his latter days as a jingle artist for Levis and Kentucky Fried

Chicken behind him forever. Alex had also cut a country track, 'You're My Woman', with producer Rik Tinory that he'd asked Garth Brooks to appear on.

But work came to an abrupt halt on Friday March 10 after Alex lapsed into unconsciousness at the recording studio, his condition brought on by acute alcohol intake. Alex was rushed to a local hospital while comatose, and succumbed on Sunday March 12, never having regained consciousness.

The final public performance by Alex Taylor, who was often co-billed in New England in the 1980s with Boston-based blues artists like Montgomery, had been a gig at the Cambridge, Massachusetts House of Blues on New Year's Eve. Two years later, on November 20, 1995, Alex's son, 28-year-old baby James, was married to 26-year-old Natasha Bee.

Also lost during the 1990s was Ike's second wife, the former Suzanne Sheets, who succumbed to cancer; and James' best friend, keyboardist-arranger Don Grolnick, a lymphoma victim, as well as drummer Carlos Vega, found dead at 41 in his home in Los Angeles on April 7, 1998 from a self-inflicted gunshot wound. No one had seen it coming, least of all James, who had just returned with Vega after completing his European concert schedule and was due to reunite with him following a few weeks vacation to start the US leg of the *Hourglass* tour in New York.

Overcome with horror and grief, Taylor took the news very hard, especially after Grolnick's illness and untimely death at New York's Mount Sinai Hospital in 1996 at the age of 48, at which time James had said of Don, "He was my cherished friend and the most remarkable musician I have known. It's going to take a while to figure out what to do without him."

After this latest tragic loss, Taylor could not bear to comment beyond a brief written statement he prepared himself, confessing how much he missed the soft-spoken and retiring Vega "as a friend and artist", and noting, "It has been a great privilege and delight working with Carlos and wonderful to have collaborated with so talented a player." At Taylor's request, Vega was replaced for the May 29 show at the Beacon Theater (due to be taped for a live television special and DVD) and some subsequent dates by mutual friend Steve Jordan, the well-known songwriter/drummer and producer (Keith Richards, Aretha Franklin, Robert Cray, Fabulous Thunderbirds) who had also appeared on the *New Moon Shine* album. Jordan called Vega "a stabilizing force in any group that he played in, which is the reason this thing is so shocking to everyone, because the circumstances of his departure were so incongruous with his life, at least the way we saw it."

Vega was survived by his wife, Teri, and daughters Marissa and Alexis.

"The idea of 'Enough To Be' is of somebody who can't get home, who can't find home, and it's *late* for them to find home, late in their lives," said James. "A lot of the initial focus came from Alex's dying, and the mention in the lyric of smoke and a storm refers to an actual event after his cremation, when the ashes that went up a smokestack in Florida seemed to turn into an amazing storm that followed us home from that ceremony, tearing up the East Coast from Carolina to Massachusetts.

"As for the 'family' I refer to in the second verse of 'Enough', it's the family of mankind, all of us a bit fucked up and searching for home."

James' brother Livingston knows the feeling, and tries to transcend it by filling a thermos with coffee, and taking off in his single-engine Cessna plane. "I've always had flying dreams," he said one afternoon at home in Weston in 1999, "ever since I saw a TV commercial as a kid for a short-lived cereal called Sugar Jets. And I've always had this weird sense of how to float above and look down at myself. I've only panicked one time in my plane, when my dashboard lights went out one night in the mid-1990s. I had to get out a flashlight to read the instruments and the vertical speed indicator told me I was flying straight up.

"The panic rose up my body to my ears, and it was just about to go over my eyes when I told myself, 'Stop this panic! DON'T DO THIS!' And I calmed down, righted the plane, and landed. Since then I've been in other sticky situations, like getting caught in ice clouds and freezing up, and another time in the '90s my engine went dead from a broken valve and I had to glide into an emergency landing in Groton, Connecticut, but I've never let myself panic again. One of my great pleasures is being alone in my plane at 10–12,000 feet, smoking a cigar, sailing along."

Livingston would find himself alone more than usual by spring 2001, as completion of a new home on the Vineyard coincided with a separation from Maggie, his wife of 25 years.

Carly Simon had to rediscover the pleasures of music-making after a bout with stage-one cancer, being diagnosed with a breast tumour in 1997. In October, she underwent a mastectomy and then chemotherapy treatments. While recovering, she lived briefly during 1998 in a four-storey townhouse at 37 West Cedar Street on Beacon Hill in Boston – until neighbours complained of hearing her rehearsing through the walls. Despite having invested a year's worth of renovations in the property, including a roof deck, she put it back on the market after two weeks. Having already given up her long-time apartment on the Upper West Side – which her children had already exited in favour of their own post-adolescent lodgings – she decided to turn the Lamberts Cove house into her primary residence and moved all her things from Boston and New York there.

Finally based, to her surprise, on the Vineyard, Simon began recording there, and released her first album in nearly five years (the last being 1997's *Film Noir* set of movie standards) in May 2000. The latest album was composed largely during a year's worth of 8-track sessions in her daughter Sally's old bedroom in the Lamberts Cove house; produced with David Field, Frank Filipetti and Teese Gohl, the record was entitled *The Bedroom Tapes*. Initially inspired by jukebox exposure to a version of George and Ira Gershwin's 'Embraceable You', the project was called *When Manhattan Was A Maiden* until that title song was dropped. Simon settled on eleven new pieces including 'Big Dumb Guy' and 'I'm Really The Kind' (both with backing vocals by Ben Taylor), 'Scar' (about her mastectomy) and 'In Honor Of You (George)', a tribute to George Gershwin, who died of a brain tumour in 1937.

Outside projects for 2001 included a co-starring sanction of Janet Jackson's use of "You're So Vain" on Janet's *All For You* album in a revamped edition entitled "Son Of A Gun (I Betcha Think This Song Is About You)," the latter version widely interpreted as revenge music targeting Jackson's estranged husband Rene Elizondo.

While reconciled to life on the Vineyard, Simon could not help lamenting that she saw even less than usual of her low-profile spouse of 13 years, Jim Hart, who often worked for long periods in New York.

During the '90s, Hugh and Jeanne Taylor renovated a house they'd built in 1971 on the Gay Head Cliffs, turning it into the seven-room Outermost Inn with the best restaurant on the island, and guests could sail with them daily on their catamaran, *Arabella*. On summer evenings, son Isaac Cole Taylor could sometimes be heard singing to himself around his parents' inn before he headed down-island to the Agricultural Hall for another gig. (It's an unspoken tradition among many year-round Vineyarders to beep one's car horn when passing the cemetery where John Belushi is buried, to salute his spirit.)

Livingston's own salute to the late Ike Taylor, 'My Father's Eyes', the song about his dad's "irreparable heartbreak" that Liv played at Ike's 1996 memorial service, would appear on *Snapshot*, Liv's end-of-the-century solo anthology on his own Whistling Dog Records.

Accompanying Liv's brother James to their father's memorial service that warm November morning in Boston's Back Bay had been Caroline "Kim" Smedvig, the petite and comely director of public relations and marketing for the Boston Symphony Orchestra. On Christmas Eve, 1999, Taylor got on his knee in the couple's home in Chesnut Hill, Massachusetts, just outside Boston, and proposed marriage to the 44-year-old Smedvig, presenting her with an antique Tiffany diamond ring. "It was a very traditional, old-fashioned proposal," said Smedvig. "I guess he really is a romantic."

As the *Boston Globe* noted three weeks later: "The marriage will be Smedvig's second and Taylor's third." The couple had met in the early '90s when Taylor made his orchestral concert début with Boston Pops conductor John Williams, and began dating in 1995. They had planned to be wed in Tanglewood, the summer home of the Boston Symphony.

But as the engagement stretched on through 2000, the marriage site was shifted to Boston, with Tanglewood relegated instead as the planned site of a mid-summer 2001 reception for family and friends. Keeping pace in the interregnum was the much anticipated arrival (on April 5, 2001) of twin boys, named Henry ("the name," noted James, "of my mother's father, a fisherman") David, and Rufus Logan, by means of in-vitro fertilisation and a third-party surrogate mom/"gestation carrier" who agreed to bring the older couple's biological offspring to term. "We have been looking forward to this for ages," said Kim when word of the arrangements became known.

The nuptials, which were likewise kept quiet until the eve of the event, proved to be a small ceremony held on Sunday, February 18, 2001 in the Lindsey Chapel of Boston's Emmanuel Episcopal Church, with fifty family and friends in attendance, most of them with immediate ties to the couple. The bride, 46, wore a strapless ivory Vera Wang dress and the groom, due to turn 53 in a few weeks, was attired in a grey-teal suit designed by Yohji Yamamato and dark bow tie. Sir Andre Previn and cellist Yo-Yo Ma performed at the rite, and Boston Pops conductor laureate Williams gave Smedvig away.

On that same date back in February 1956, father Ike Taylor had written a short letter to James from his Navy clinic in Antarctica, telling his son, "This may be the last I'll be able to write and mail to you for many months" because the mail boat was leaving. "This letter should reach you just about on your birthday," said Ike, "and I want to wish you a very happy one.

"I sleep right in the hospital so when someone is sick I am right where I can help him," noted Ike of his remote sub-zero outpost, adding, "I am having a very good time and like this place very much."

Also in the newspapers on Taylor and Smedvig's wedding day were reports that a team of US scientists at the South Pole were gathering data from portable weather instruments installed on iceberg B-15A. The floating mass, 100 miles across and 30 miles wide, had broken off earlier from the Ross Ice Shelf and was currently 90 miles from Ike's old base at McMurdo Station. "It's a prenatal study of icebergs," explained a spokesman for the iceberg scientists. "We want to catch the birthing . . . We want to find out: is the slow march of a crack across the ice shelf from tidal movement or some climate mechanism?"

In terms of the Taylor family and Ike's legacy of separation and isolation, similar questions remained as-yet unanswered. But the more things changed across the landscape that begat the Taylors, the more the past imposed its shadows. In Montrose, Scotland on February 19, an educational lecture was given in the town about Antarctica and the challenges of offering medical care at the South Pole. At the same moment, officials for the Port of Montrose were boasting on its website that new quayside storage facilities and the flexibility of berths and stevedoring on both sides of the harbour had allowed the port to establish substantial new trade: "The secret of the port's success lies in its approach to customers. Attentive individual service, competitive pricing, fast efficient loading and unloading ensure that users return to Montrose time and again."

But not all of February 2001's entries and exits from the land of the Scots were proceeding efficiently. In what seemed like a stanza left out of 'The Frozen Man', the Scottish press recounted a sad human interest tale of a native son inadequately interred. It seems a small group of family and friends had gathered on a frigid hillside in a one-time royal burgh far below Edinburgh for the funeral of a former textile worker, only to witness a grave mistake: "Undertakers heightened the misery of the mourning family by bringing the wrong body to the cemetery."

★   ★   ★

"The more successful or thwarted you are as an isolated individual," mused James to the author, "the more you need reconnection." Such thoughts may also explain why James went to great lengths at the end of the decade to appear between tour dates as a surprise guest at a concert thrown by the quarter-century old *People* magazine in The Theater at Madison Square Garden to honour Carole King. At the finale, Taylor suddenly joined Babyface Edmonds to help sing 'You've Got A Friend' to the 57-year-old King.

King had responded in kind on June 15, 2000, when Taylor was inducted into the Songwriters' Hall of Fame, telling those gathered in the New York Sheraton hotel ballroom a moving anecdote: "In 1969, I was a singer in James Taylor's band, and James would do a solo section, where he would play acoustic guitar solo. And while the other musicians were off doing drugs and having sex, I would stand in the wings and listen to every note and every word, because these songs were so amazing, they were so warm and personal and they were so beautifully crafted. They completely inspired me to sit down and actually write a few for myself. I had been writing with Gerry Goffin and Toni Stern prior to that – still did, still do – but I was able to reach inside myself and write songs in a more personal way because he inspired me to do that."

Danny Kortchmar next stepped to the mike to tell an impish tale about the day in the early '60s that Taylor elected to "rat me out!" to his parents after egging him to "boost" a trinket from a Martha's

Vineyard antique store. Once the guffaws in the ballroom died down, Kootch got serious: "I want to quote from [Henry David] Thoreau: 'To affect the quality of the day – that is the highest of the arts.' And that's what James does, he affects the quality of the day, and he reminds you of your own humanity." A visibly touched Taylor came to the podium to embrace King and Kortchmar.

Taylor was an instrument of additional fond gestures during the 1990s as when he popped up at old friend Mitch Glazer's second marriage, to actress Kelly Lynch in December 1992 in Los Angeles, to sing Chuck Berry's wedding-minded 1964 hit, 'You Never Can Tell'; and then closing the decade by recording both a stirring piece in honour of his son, titled 'Benjamin', as well as a tender version of Stephen Foster's 'Hard Times Come Again No More' for the Yo-Yo Ma/Edgar Meyer/ Mark O'Connor album *Appalachian Journey*, released by Sony Classical in March 2000.

More music emerged from Taylor, notably the (1998) song 'Belfast To Boston', which his mother would later fly to Ireland to see him perform, proud of her son as he sang, "Send no more vengeance across the sea/Just the blessing of forgiveness/For my new countrymen and me." Taylor also duetted with Mark Knopfler on the title track of Knopfler's much praised 2000 Warner Bros. album, *Sailing To Philadelphia*. In the song, inspired by Thomas Pynchon's novel *Mason & Dixon*, Taylor portrayed astronomer/surveyor Charles Dixon, partner of Jeremiah Mason, who took a wooden ship with his friend from England to America in the mid-1700s to create what proved to be the cartographic boundary between the "slave" and "free" states in the Civil War, the Mason-Dixon Line.

James Taylor – Greatest Hits Volume 2, a Columbia Records-era companion to one of the most successful (if not personally remunerative) recordings in history hit stores on November 7, 2000. And despite the loss of an irreplaceable notebook of lyrics and musical notes that was stolen from his and Kim's Trump International Hotel room in Manhattan in May 2000, he persevered through 2000 and early 2001 in the writing of yet another album, whose working title was *As If*.

Among the new songs under consideration for the album were (all names tentative) 'Caroline I See You', 'Fourth of July', 'Come With

Me On My Way', and 'Raised Up Family', the last a statement about the developmental importance of pulling away from family ("God bless the child who can live on his own!") to forge one's own independent path in life.

A small backlog of other tracks included 'Belfast To Boston', and a rendition of Woody Guthrie's 'Pretty Boy Floyd', the sad tale in song of poor Georgia farmboy Charles Arthur Floyd, a Depression-era robber whose fame as 'Public Enemy No. 1' climaxed with FBI agents gunning down the 30-year-old criminal in East Liverpool, Ohio in 1934.

James also found time in January 2001 to reprise his personal and professional 1985 turning point at Rock In Rio by performing at its third concert incarnation in Brazil. His set before 180,000 people was highlighted by 'Only A Dream In Rio'. And he sang with Sting on 'Fill Her Up', their joint country-rock romp from Sting's Grammy-winning 1999 *Brand New Day* album.

But one of the most indelible things James Taylor did for himself, his family and his friends at the turn of the millennium was *Hourglass*. "The *Hourglass* record, my first all-new work in five years, was postponed by the dying of Alex," Taylor explained. "And then it was interrupted by the loss of my father, his second wife, and then the family duties that came with that – including looking after the three young children they left parent-less. And I also lost my manager, Peter Asher, who got out of management entirely and became an executive at Sony Music!" He shrugged haplessly. "These things brought me full circle in my sense of everything I've inherited from my past.

"As I've said, I used to deeply dread the end of summer and the coming of winter," he continued, "the 'Walking Man' song and album in '74 being a combination of symbolism about my father and the coming of Old Man Winter. But after a while you want to be a little bit fonder of your burdens, because they're what make life interesting, and they're basically what your work is in this life."

This was the same mindset that moved Kate Taylor in 1997 to return to the Arlington School at McLean Hospital to deliver an alumnus speech to its graduating class. "I told them that they were gonna be okay," she recalled later with a chuckle. But Kate said something more to those students:

Not always being sure where our paths are leading can often result in a sense of wonder and gratitude as the mysteries unfold. What a wonderful thing it is to find yourself at a place in time where the freedom of choice is available to pursue your long held dreams, and at a pace that suits your inner rhythms. There are so many paths that you can choose to set out upon in pursuing your personal quest. The scenery will certainly vary according to your particular choice. You needn't worry about getting to where you're going to because, to paraphrase a line from songwriter Erica Wheeler, "You are the destination of your beautiful road."

When she was 16, Kate Taylor devised her own family symbol, a crescent moon and single wavelet of sea enclosed in a circle. When Kate first went to England with James to audition for Peter Asher in the summer of '69, she had the symbol tattooed on the top of her foot, and James also got a tattoo of the symbol. As other Taylors got the same tattoo, it became the contemporary equivalent of the family crest of the Taylors of Kirktonhill. The day Sally Taylor turned 18 she got the same sign tattooed in the centre of her upper back.

"To me," said Sally, who began touring at the end of the 1990s to sell her own *Tomboy Bride* and *Apt. #6S* albums (the latter named for her parents now-forsaken Upper West Side apartment), "the sign represents who I am at the core of my being: beauty, integrity, eternity, stability, and truth." And Kate herself included the symbol in the artwork for the first single (a version, accompanied by James, of Robert Burns' 'Auld Lang Syne') from her fourth album-in-progress, tentatively entitled *Beautiful Road*.

While in the final stages of co-producing *Beautiful Road*, Kate's husband Charlie died suddenly on September 12, 2001 in Boston after a long illness. Another standout track on *Beautiful Road* was a song of Charlie's that Kate sang with James called "I Will Fly."

Kate remarked a few days after Charlie's death that "For anyone who is grieving, 'I Will Fly' will bring immeasurable comfort. Charlie was very earthbound, but it is obvious that his spiritual vision was crystal clear. His words fill you up, shining a light on the depth of meaning that they held for him." His widow cited the final verse of the song: "I will fly on wings of peace/To that place above the clouds/The bluest sky, the golden sunlight/The truest love, the sweetest sound."

25

Enough To Be On Your Way

James Taylor had been seated for much of a rainy, millennium's-edge afternoon in the back dining room of the Minetta Tavern Restaurant, the ancient left-wing/show biz hangout at the corner of Minetta Lane and MacDougal Street in New York's Greenwich Village.

This place, of course, was where he and Kootch often ate Italian entrees and swapped song ideas for their evening sets with The Flying Machine before walking one block over to their nightly Night Owl regimen.

Taylor hadn't been back to this historic watering hole (which straddles the Minetta Stream upon which the Village was originally settled) since the mid-'60s. The ghosts in its precincts − some friendly, some fierce − precipitated much of the expansive reflections upon which he and his lunch guest had been feasting.

"The situation in New York could easily have killed me several times," ruled Taylor, referring to time spent in these narrow Village streets as a teenager addicted to drugs. "I had been falling into dry holes," he continued, as he poked at his pasta, the smooth, angular planes of his narrow face growing taut. "There were some real misfires."

From a distance or in photographs, the balding Taylor often seems spindly and worry-worn, but up close his personal aura was of timeless sinew and a boyishly patrician serenity. Attired in a dark brown turtle-neck jersey, caramel corduroy slacks and rubber-soled leather brogans, the thin but big-boned frame was crisply muscled. And the almost-shy gaze atop the gracile torso was startlingly clear-eyed, his calm but formidable intelligence coiled with a similar, understated dignity.

Whenever the table talk veered off into the wildlife or topography of New England or the Tidewater South, Taylor's aptitude matched that of the most astute naturalists, and as politics arose, he pressed the once-audacious leftist outlook of his pro-Civil Rights, staunchly activist Southern upbringing with a statesmanlike poise. Taylor came of age in a stratified, post-colonial world that crashed to earth of its own insup-portable weight. It was a dangerously shifting realm in which even the momentary loss of one's wits might mean the loss of one's life – and he understood that.

But as he gradually learned from his boyhood onwards, his own family comprised an equally hazardous and unsteady sphere, riddled with ingrained suffering, sudden peril and intrinsic trapdoors, the drink and depression and addictive impulses of his ancestral kin reinforcing a fear of, and shame towards, the closeness that could save them.

"I was arguing with a friend of mine recently," he said softly, "and she was saying that she thought our emotional responses to music were as learned as our emotional responses to language, but I don't – and I still disagree with her.

"I think that one of the main motivations for writing music is to get out, to get off, and ultimately to get relief from separation. That's why music has lived forever in church in the South, and elsewhere, and it probably comes from that religious setting, from that need for connection.

"I have that need," he continued, "and that's why a lot of songs that I write can turn out to be this kind of religious music without having any obvious religion in them. I believe that the emotional response we have to music is so immediate it suggests an underlying or overlying reality and a huge emotional content for us, regardless of what the lyric is.

"The thing about songs, for me, is that I write songs that *I* want to hear. I write them because I need to hear them and I haven't heard them yet." A distant smile, and his eyes shone with emotion. "Because I believe, most of all, that just by being music, it's religious."

Long silence. The colour slowly returned to Taylor's face, and he and his guest began to discuss the fatherly significance and family symbolism of Ike's rescue mission of 30 years before, when Ike – for surely the only time ever – dropped everything in his own life, and hurried to Greenwich Village and the heroin-stricken James.

Ike then drove himself and his son through a sundown and a sunrise until they were back once again down along the ominously titled fall line – that noisy, treacherous and beautiful point at which waterfalls occur as the hard, rocky shelf of the Carolina Piedmont Plateau gives way to the softer stone of the Atlantic Coastal plain.

Greater Raleigh, North Carolina, beside the Neuse River on the doorstep of drowsy Chapel Hill, was and is in a fall line vicinity. An experienced sailor will tell you that the fall line is the head of navigation, the utmost inland point navigable from the sea. And that's probably why this spot on the map had always felt particularly right to somebody who was the direct descendant of the seminal Isaac Taylor. It was the farthest a man could stray from the sea and still feel certain of finding his way back home.

"To focus on that cavalry charge of my father's, now that he's gone, is a great thing for me," Taylor said at lunch, because James finally realised, three decades later, that his dad was not just retrieving his son but trying to take him to the safest place he knew. So James decided, in an allegorical stroke, to share the moment with his own son.

"The initial idea for 'Jump Up Behind Me' on *Hourglass* came from my father coming and saving me," James recounted. "The idea of the lyric was of someone swinging a person up onto a horse behind him, and taking the person home. I had this very strong image of being on the side of the road, collapsed, and my father finding me.

"And then I also made it about finding my true love, and wanting to take her back across the water."

To Scotland?

"Yeah," he nodded, "or to the Orkneys, or some mythical place that you leave when you're young but return to when you're old."

Taylor had recently been discussing 'Jump Up Behind Me' with son Ben, who'd commenced his own recording career in 1994 with a single rendition on the Giant label of 'I Will', a song from The Beatles' '68 *White Album*. The son had clearly acquired his father's taste in British pop, but also a questioning bent regarding lyrical tail-spinning.

As James recounted: "My son Ben says, 'Okay, so you've found this ideal woman, your true love. You've followed this road 'til you reach the sea; you're gonna catch the tide; you're gonna set your horse free. Fine. Then what?'"

"I tell him, 'Ben, it's mystical, magical, it's gonna be okay,'" said Taylor with a grin, aware his son must soon write songs that pass muster for his own Sony Music deal. "'Besides, Ben,'" I told him, "'it's basically a *fantasy* song!'"

(On January 25, 1998 Ben had accompanied his touring father to Glasgow, Scotland, for a traditional Robert Burns Night supper – roughly the equivalent of America's Thanksgiving – during which a piper played and a reading was done of Burns' 1786 poem/tribute to the national dish of boiled sheep stomach stuffed with a pudding of minced liver, oatmeal, suet, onions and spices, *To A Haggis*. Ben also began performing songs of fantasy and reality at his dad's shows, singing back-up on 'Shower The People', duetting on a cover of Little Feat's 'Dixie Chicken', and singing his own 'Broken Tonight'.)

As the waiter came to offer some coffee, Taylor decided he'd like to drink his cup in the front section of the restaurant, near a window looking out on the Cafe Wha? where, he fondly recalled, Jimi Hendrix performed in the era of The Flying Machine. Taylor angled his elongated carriage into the cramped booth nearest the street, and began sipping his decaff.

"As I've said, for most of my life, my father basically was inaccessible, not available to me," James mulled. He stopped, seeming to hesitate with another recollection. And then, softly, eyes downcast, he said, "There was another song like 'Jump Up' that I recorded in 1980. It was a song called 'Only For Me', which was on the *Dad Loves His Work* album.

"'Only For Me', although I think it's a flawed song, did something for me. It's a completely fictitious thing, but a personal recapitulation of father and son energy was at the centre of it emotionally. In the song I had encountered my father in an alcoholic decline in a bar, having not seen him for all of my life – that's basically what the song is about."

In halting bursts, Taylor talked/recited the lyrics, which recalled his father, then nearly 60 years old: "Out of sight of the light in the window/His mind in his whiskey/And his body in a folding chair/Far beyond repair."

As his son entered his line of "vision", Ike made "his decision" and he stood to his feet to greet him, although sitting back again proved "a long way down".

James sized up his parent, knowing he'd been there, too, and said he was there to look after him. "Young man," Ike answered, "you're looking pretty green/Like a stranger to this kind of place." Ike insisted his son sit beside him, peer into his face, and hear a story he'd never told: "There was a father and a son/But that was long ago/And when the time came to run/I just couldn't say no/So I left them behind."

The lyrics finished with the statement that these are moments we've all seen before, when, "in times of great sorrow" our "human compassion will flow from a well that has long run dry." And then James sang, "It happened to me . . . only for you, from one who was lost and found."

"He finally came across, even slightly apologetic for his own failings," concluded Taylor, wrestling with his reserve as his eyes gleamed. "On that night when he came to take me home, and then with that song, after so much time, my dad and I finally made a lasting connection."

Taylor in many ways resembled another wandering Scot with a lyricist's ominous life-view. Poet Robert Burns' relations with his own father were strained to the last, the parent confessing before his death in 1784 that there was one member of the family for whose future he feared. "Oh father, is it me you mean?" asked his abject son, approaching the deathbed. Learning, as his father repeated his qualms, that it *was* him he meant, Burns turned away to the window in tears, with that final public token of his parent's caring as the only understanding they ever shared.

Burns and Taylor also had a dark mutual fascination with the coming of winter. Burns called it "the best season for devotion", and he penned a verse entitled *Winter, A Dirge*, to preserve his outlook:

> The sweeping blast, the sky o'ercast,
> The joyless winter-day,
> Let others fear, to me more dear
> Than all the pride of May.

The Tempest's howl, it soothes my soul,
My griefs it seems to join,
The leafless trees my fancy please,
Their fate resembles mine.

During the centuries when the Taylors began to build boats and take leave of the Angus coast, Scotland was astorm over issues of religion and creed, chief among them the conservative notions of predestination versus a liberal doctrine of free will. Between such conflicts stood the Freemason's Lodge to which the Taylors of Montrose were pledged, where trust held sway in a divine architect who ordains a fellowship of faith that fits a grand design.

Then as now, there were many who felt the origins of humanity's free choice lay in Heaven, where each soul volunteered to assume a specific life and legacy in order to define, as well as deserve, eternity. Thus, mortal destiny is the work each soul elects to complete. Our reward is either a joyful return home – or exclusion from Paradise by the angelic equivalent of the tyler (the Lowland Scottish pronunciation of the Norman-French *Tailleur*, i.e. one who cuts), a customary sentry who stands outside Masonic lodge meetings with a drawn sword.

James Taylor rose from his chair in the front lounge of the Minetta Tavern Restaurant and prepared to greet the world again. For half a millennium, the biggest goal of all the Taylors has been to change the course of their own family history by striving to confront and surmount its greatest failings. In finally accomplishing this, James is the forerunner of a new chapter, a new tradition, a new way of symbolising *in hoc signo vinces*.

"I think I'm getting better at being a friend, and a parent, and a sibling, and a child," he said as he gulped the last swallow of his coffee. "I don't know how good I am as a companion, but a woman named Kim has helped me there, and I'm starting to feel good about that, too."

As the rainy day man stepped out of the restaurant, the sun broke through, and Taylor suggested a stroll through the area's residential back streets.

"The other song on *Hourglass* that means a lot to me is 'Another Day'," said James as he stepped off the sidewalk onto the asphalt and turned west past the Cafe Wha?, retracing the path of the old Minetta Stream as it had meandered to the Hudson and thence out to sea. "It took me over 13 years to finish 'Another Day'," he explained, "which is about withdrawal and making it to morning, when the sun comes out and you believe in the fact of yet another day. I really started writing it in 1983, and at that time I was thinking a bit about John Lennon and that Beatles song from *The White Album*, 'I'm So Tired'.

"I always thought that song was about John Lennon experiencing withdrawal from some substance or other, having a terrible night of kicking – or at least that's how I identified with it. And that's what my song's about: that bad night, *and* the way you feel about the next day.

"But right now," he concluded with a smile, "I feel like I can walk down Minetta Lane as a different man."

Ten minutes later he hailed a taxi, riding uptown to make an appointment, phone Kim, and then head out to the airport to make a tour date. By then, the sun was almost down. James was going away again.

APPENDICES

Notes on Sources

The immediate roots of this book are in a conversation James Taylor and I had in the kitchen of James Cagney's former farmhouse on Martha's Vineyard in August, 1997, when Taylor agreed to allow me to trace the personal and creative history of his family, dating back to the Taylor's origins on the Angus coast of Scotland. But the deeper underpinnings of the project lay in an earlier, 20-year journalistic relationship.

The author first met Taylor in the summer of 1977 in J.P.'s, a music industry hang-out on Manhattan's Upper East Side. At the time I was the Managing Editor of *Crawdaddy* and he had just released his initial album in his long-term contract with Columbia Records, *JT*. Over the course of our initial half-hour talk, which concerned a mutual interest in the geography, colonial history and sea-faring lore of the Atlantic coast, we established a cordial personal and professional acquaintance that endures to this day.

Besides writing numerous in-depth articles on Taylor for *Rolling Stone*, *Musician*, *Billboard* and other publications, and conducting various television and radio interviews with him, including a live nationwide interview-and-performance special for the Westwood One Radio Network in 1988, Taylor and I have had running conversations over the decades about history and its deeper intimate and intercultural impact.

Whether talking on airplanes, in studios, in restaurants, in his home at the time, or my own, in Massachusetts, California, New York, North Carolina, so many of these discussions ultimately centred upon the inescapable legacy of the past, and its nagging message that we must each learn from former days in order to move forward into fresh terrain and original lives.

I am deeply grateful to James, his late father Ike, his mother Trudy, and all his siblings – Alex, Livingston, Kate, Hugh, and James and Carly Simon's own offspring, Ben and Sally – for talking with me over the last quarter-century about their works and their lives. And I'm particularly grateful to James and Trudy for extending an extraordinary degree of trust and cooperation over the last five years of writing and research for this book project.

While allowing this writer to continually check facts and re-verify the soundness of perspectives and assumptions regarding their family saga as published not just in the 20th century but in the four centuries that preceded it, the Taylor family had no editorial control over this book, and no such accreditation or authorisation was either requested or extended.

For my part, I was particularly concerned that the original Isaac Taylor of the 1700s and his modern inheritor, James' dad, be rendered with accuracy and concrete understanding. In order to help ensure this was possible, the Taylors guided me to the historical and private papers of both Isaac Taylors as preserved, respectively, in Wilson Library at the University of North Carolina at Chapel Hill, North Carolina, and at the Dartmouth College Library in Hanover, New Hampshire.

Trudy also allowed me to pore over her files of family correspondence and mementos spanning the history of her own clan, the Woodards of Maine and Massachusetts, as well as the lifelong records of her and Ike Taylor's lives and those of their children. I looked through several hundred years of Woodard and Taylor genealogical data, photo archives, personal diaries, private correspondence and even the letters exchanged between Ike Taylor and his wife and children as their family unfolded and faced emotional hardships, such as when Ike served in Antarctica from 1955 to 1957 with the United States Navy's Operation Deepfreeze.

These documents number in the many thousands of pages, and those quoted in this text are further informed by innumerable others not specifically cited but nonetheless supportive in the outlooks described. Unless otherwise noted in the book, all quotations in the text are taken directly from 25 years of interviews with the author. This also includes the Simon family, including Andrea, Joanna, Lucy, Carly and Peter, all of whom I've interviewed besides visiting their house in Riverdale while it was still the central rallying point for them. I also viewed Carly at work in the studio for her *Boys In The Trees* and *Torch* albums.

Besides visiting or being present at the historical points described in most of the houses, summer bungalows and pivotal households detailed in the modern portion of this story, this writer travelled to Montrose and Marykirk, Scotland to see the surviving buildings and grounds of the Taylor's Kirktonhill and Balmanno estates, as well as Tailor's Close on the west side of the High Street of Montrose – the original location of the Taylor's firm when the family served as tailors to the monarchs of Scotland as well as crown-sanctioned seafaring traders from the region.

If members of the Taylor ancestry are quoted in distant eras in the course of the text, their statements are taken directly from letters, diaries, ledgers, documents and other personal papers that exist in the historical record and were examined for this purpose. The author is particularly grateful to Sheila Simpson, Fiona C. Scharlau and John Doherty of the Angus Archives at the Montrose Library, especially Mrs. Scharlau, who took me on a personal tour of the Taylor family's 17th- and 18th-century environs in Montrose, and to Mrs. Simpson, who personally drove me all over Marykirk and the Kirktonhill and Balmanno estates, from its medieval church and graveyard, where ancient Taylors were baptised, wed or interred, to its great houses – including the surviving portion of the main mansion in which Mrs. Simpson's own family now resides.

In order to supplement prior on-site research in Kingston, Jamaica on its maritime history and role in trade between Britain and the American South, as well as travels to Monserrat and other Caribbean islands related to this story, I repeatedly journeyed to North Carolina – especially to the Raleigh-Durham and Chapel Hill region and to coastal New Bern. There were visits to the Taylor's former residences in the Carrboro and Chapel Hill areas, as well as all their historical properties in New Bern, and the former Glenburnie plantation on the Neuse River outside New Bern, now known as Glenburnie Park.

Greatly helpful in this research and exploration were noted New Bern author/historian Peter B. Sandbeck; Victor T. Jones, Jr., in the Local History and Genealogy section of the New Bern-Craven County Public Library; Joanne Gwaltney at the New Bern Historical Society; Richard A. Shrader at the Academic Libraries/Wilson Library at the University of North Carolina at Chapel Hill; Amy Westbrook at the Chapel Hill/Orange County Visitors Bureau, James Lehrer at the Carrboro Branch of the Orange County Public Library in Chapel Hill, and Bill Jones at the Public Information Office of the North Carolina Department of Transportation. For research in Western North Carolina, I am indebted to the Forest Supervisor, Asheville, North Carolina; the Burnsville, North Carolina Chamber of Commerce; and the staffs of the historical societies of Morganton, North Carolina and Burke County, North Carolina.

I am also thankful to the Stockbridge Chamber of Commerce, the Greater Merrimack Valley Convention and Visitors Bureau, the Berkshires Visitors Bureau; the Shipley School, Bryn Mawr, Pennsylvania; the Newburyport Chamber of Commerce; the Austen-Riggs Hospital, and Milton Academy for information and enlightenment.

At the invitation of the Taylor family, I attended the reception in 1998 at the Governor's Mansion in Raleigh, North Carolina as well as the induction ceremony at the Sheraton Imperial Hotel in Research Triangle Park, North

Carolina, when James was among the recipients of the North Carolina Award. I would like to thank Betty Ray McCain, Secretary of the North Carolina Department of Cultural Services, and Deputy Secretary Elizabeth F. Buford for their help and assistance on this occasion, as well as James himself (and his then-fiancée Kim Smedvig), Hugh and Jeanne Taylor, and Trudy Taylor for their evening-long insights and reminiscences regarding life in North Carolina during the 1950s and 1960s. Trudy Taylor was also kind enough to give me an informal tour of the governor's mansion while recalling the local turmoil of the civil rights struggles in North Carolina during the years of the Taylors' residence in the Carrboro and Chapel Hill areas.

All first-hand descriptions of James Taylor's songwriting come directly from him; and whenever possible, the narrative is informed by direct observation. For example, when details are provided on how Taylor tacked his skiff on Menemsha Pond in the past or present, it's because Taylor took the author out onto those waters in his boat to demonstrate and recall such incidents. If a guitar technique is explained, it's because Taylor picked up his guitar and showed the author his methods; the same is true for accounts in the past and present of his own actions and activities, with Taylor often on-site with the author as he pointed out or recounted the particulars. Over the years, the author has also been present in either the studio or less formal settings for compositional aspects of the creation of many of Taylor's albums, including *Flag, Dad Loves His Work, That's Why I'm Here, Never Die Young, New Moon Shine,* and *Hourglass.* Taylor has also played me tapes of raw demos from his Warner Bros. years, sent me early editions of assorted tracks during his tenure at Columbia, and shared demos and rough mixes of work-in-progress ranging from an unrecorded demo of a tribute song to Bob Marley, and tapes of his unissued *Bicycle Built For A King* live set, to an unreleased version of 'Belfast To Boston'.

I would also like to thank Livingston and Maggie Taylor for opening their home and their memories to my family and I in the autumn of 1999 during final research on this book, with Liv also sharing his own interest in family lore and its historical underpinnings in both New England and North Carolina. I am also greatly thankful to Kate Taylor and her husband Charles H. Witham for sharing their memories and personal documents with me, including rare and unreleased recordings and such private materials as the actual text of Kate's 1997 address to the graduating class of Arlington School at McLean Hospital in Massachusetts.

Danny "Kootch" Kortchmar provided an invaluable wealth of insights and reminiscences to me over the entire course of this project, as well as numerous suggestions on how to sharpen, expand and otherwise improve on early drafts of the manuscript. I cannot thank him enough for his thoughtful interest and assistance.

Besides watching dozens of James Taylor concerts from the balcony, the orchestra, the wings or backstage since the late 1960s, the author has met, talked with and/or directly observed the creative processes of many of the pivotal musical and career-related figures around James Taylor, including Carole King, Jimmy Buffett, Don Henley, Randy Newman, Peter Asher, Lenny Waronker, Russ Titelman, Arif Mardin, George Massenburg, Frank Filipetti, Jill Dell'Abate, Joe Smith, Mo Ostin, Jerry Wexler, Michael "Mickey" Kapp of Kapp Records, Taj Mahal, Buffy Sainte-Marie, and key players in James' bands such as Rick Marotta, Russ Kunkel, Waddy Wachtel, Don Grolnick, Steve Jordan, Bob Mann, Dan Dugmore, Bill Payne, Clifford Carter, Lee Sklar, Rosemary Butler, Arnold McCuller, David Lasley, Valerie Carter, Kate Markowitz, and the late Carlos Vega. And I thank them all for their cordial goodwill and/or assistance over the years, including their performances on my radio specials with James, which were co-produced with Andy Denemark.

For memories of Taylor's Apple Records period, I am enormously grateful for insights over the years from Peter Asher and from interviews I conducted in the 1980s, 1990s and 2000s with Paul McCartney and George Harrison. I also thank Joni Mitchell and Paul Simon for years of in-depth interviews illuminating the modern impact of the singer/songwriter as well as the specifics of their own work, creative roots, and associations with James.

I am especially grateful to Kathryn Walker for years of help, encouragement and trust, and to the late Timothy Mayer, a close friend, collaborator and inspiration for James, as well as mutual friend the late Michael O'Donoghue.

Also deserving of much thanks for help over the years are the late John Belushi and his widow, Judy Jacklin Belushi, as well as the rest of the Belushi family.

I'd like to thank the editors of my many James Taylor articles and profiles during the last three decades, including Jann Wenner, Barbara Downey Landau, Harriet Fier, Terry McDonell, Bill Flanagan, Vic Garbarini, and Howard Lander, the president and publisher of *Billboard* and one of my wisest editorial counsels.

Gratitude also to Gary Borman, Taylor's manager at Borman Entertainment; and to James' long-time personal assistant, Cathy Kerr, who now manages Randy Newman. Both Gary and Cathy have always gone out of their way to be helpful and supportive of this and other James-related projects and I am greatly appreciative. More thanks to William Whitworth, Editor Emeritus of the *Atlantic Monthly*, who read the entire manuscript and offered excellent suggestions, and to Bruce Fishelman Esq. and George Stanbury Esq. for help and advice and to legendary photographer David Gahr, who made a gift of his historic photos of James, Kootch, Peter Asher and Carly included in these pages. And to Nikki Lloyd for her photo research, to Kate Canfield and Scotsman Jeff Nisbet for image scanning and restoration, as well as to Chloë Alexander for her cover design, and to Norman Seeff for his timeless portrait.

Sincere thanks to Jim Stein, as well as Tracy Brown, and most particularly to my Omnibus Press editor of over two decades, Chris Charlesworth, who fervently believed in this project from the start. Thanks also to my friend and fellow author, Johnny Rogan, whose editorial advice was invaluable.

I am also indebted to Owen Laster of the William Morris Agency for uncommon faith and assistance.

The two people most helpful in encouraging me in this text are my best friend, Mitch Glazer, who's also my best editor, and my loving wife, Judy, without whom I could never have written this or any book. I also thank my sons, Alexander and Christopher, for their own special understanding and inspiration.

MAPS

Angus Council Cultural Services, Angus Archives, Montrose Library. MONTROSE CIRCA 1600–1700.

Angus District Libraries & Museums Service, 1989. THE MONTROSE TOWN TRAIL/THE ROYAL BURGH OF MONTROSE, 2nd edition, 1989.

Arrow Map, Inc. MASSACHUSETTS/EASTERN MASSACHUSETTS ROAD MAP, Bridgewater, MA. 1997.

Automobile Club of Southern California, and California State Automobile Association. STREET MAP OF CENTRAL AND WESTERN AREA, METROPOLITAN LOS ANGELES.

Baedeker, Mairs Geographischer Verlag. SCOTLAND, COUNTRY MAP, 1995.

Craven County Convention and Visitors Bureau. HISTORIC HOMES AND SITES.

Forest Service, Toecane Ranger District, Burnsville, North Carolina. SOUTH TOE RIVER TRAIL MAP, May 1990.

JCS Publications. MONTROSE & BRECHIN, Ordnance Survey Maps with the permission of the controller of Her Majesty's Stationery Office, 1998.

MARYKIRK, SCOTLAND, 1883; surveyed in 1862–3–4.

National Geographic Society, Cartographic Division, Washington, DC, September 1957. ANTARCTICA.

National Geographic Society, Cartographic Division, Washington, DC, July 1994. BOSTON TO WASHINGTON, CIRCA 1830.

North Carolina Department of Transportation. NORTH CAROLINA 1997–98 STATE TRANSPORTATION MAP.

Paul, Jan, and Tom Simmons and Cindy Ann Tyminski. WELCOME TO THE ISLAND OF MARTHA'S VINEYARD, Martha's Vineyard Printing Company, 1997.

Pulkownik, Bryon. UNIVERSALMAP: HANDY MAP OF RALEIGH, NORTH CAROLINA, STREETMAP, Seeger Map Company, 1996.

Rand McNally. RALEIGH/DURHAM: WAKE, DURHAM & ORANGE COUNTIES – "THE TRIANGLE" – STREETFINDER, 2000.

Walkables. WALKABLE STOCKBRIDGE, Lenox, MA., 1997.

Wood, John, ed. PLAN OF THE TOWN OF MONTROSE, 1822.

BOOKS

Adams, David G., Gordon Jackson and S.G.E. Lythe, eds. THE PORT OF MONTROSE: A HISTORY OF ITS HARBOUR, TRADE AND SHIPPING. Tayport, Fife, Scotland: Hutton Press, Ltd., 1993.

Albion, Robert G., William A. Baker, and Benjamin W. Labaree. Marion V. Brewinton, Picture Editor. NEW ENGLAND AND THE SEA. Mystic, Connecticut: Mystic Seaport Museum, Inc., 1994.

Atkinson, Norman Keir. THE EARLY HISTORY OF MONTROSE. Montrose: Angus Council Cultural Services, 1997.

Barnett, Colin W. THE IMPACT OF HISTORICAL PRESERVATION ON NEW BERN, NORTH CAROLINA: FROM TRYON PALACE TO THE COOR-COOK HOUSE. Winston-Salem, North Carolina: Bandit Books, Inc., 1993.

Barrett, John G. THE CIVIL WAR IN NORTH CAROLINA. Chapel Hill: The University of North Carolina Press, 1963.

Belushi, Judith Jackin. SAMURAI WIDOW. New York: Carroll & Graf Publishers, Inc. 1990.

Biddelcombe, George. THE ART OF RIGGING. New York: Dover Publications, Inc., 1990.

Bishir, Catherine W., and Michael T. Southern. A GUIDE TO THE HISTORIC ARCHITECTURE OF EASTERN NORTH CAROLINA. Chapel Hill: The University of North Carolina Press, 1996.

———— And Jennifer F. Martin. A GUIDE TO THE HISTORIC ARCHITECTURE OF WESTERN NORTH CAROLINA. Chapel Hill: The University of North Carolina, 1999.

Bonn, Thomas L. UNDER COVER: AN ILLUSTRATED HISTORY OF AMERICAN MASS MARKET PAPERBACKS. New York: Penguin Books, 1982.

Bordman, Gerald. AMERICAN MUSICAL THEATER: A CHRONICLE. New York: Oxford University Press, 1992. AMERICAN THEATER: A CHRONICLE OF COMEDY & DRAMA, 1914–1930. New York: Oxford University Press, 1995.

Branch, Taylor. PARTING THE WATERS: AMERICA IN THE KING YEARS, 1954–63. New York: Simon & Schuster, 1988.

————. PILLAR OF FIRE: AMERICA IN THE KING YEARS, 1963–65. New York: Simon & Schuster, 1998.

Brander, Michael. THE SCOTTISH HIGHLANDERS AND THEIR REGIMENTS. New York: Barnes & Noble Books, 1971.

Bullock, Steven C. REVOLUTIONARY BROTHERHOOD: FREEMASONRY AND THE TRANSFORMATION OF THE AMERICAN SOCIAL ORDER, 1730–1840. Chapel Hill: The University of North Carolina Press, 1996.

Cannon, John, and Ralph Griffiths. THE OXFORD ILLUSTRATED HISTORY OF THE BRITISH MONARCHY. Oxford: Oxford University Press, 1997.

Cash, W. J. THE MIND OF THE SOUTH. New York: Vintage Books Edition, 1991.

Cawthorne, Nigel. THE SEX LIVES OF THE KINGS AND QUEENS OF ENGLAND. London: Prion/Multimedia Books Ltd., 1994.

Chafe, William H. CIVILITIES AND CIVIL RIGHTS: GREENSBORO, NORTH CAROLINA AND THE BLACK STRUGGLE FOR FREEDOM. New York: Oxford University Press, 1981.

Cherry, Conrad. GOD'S NEW ISRAEL: RELIGIOUS INTERPRETATIONS OF AMERICAN DESTINY. Chapel Hill: The University of North Carolina Press, 1998.

Claiborne, Jack, and William Price, eds. DISCOVERING NORTH CAROLINA: A TAT HEEL READER. Chapel Hill: The University of North Carolina Press, 1991.

Doerflinger, William Main. SONGS OF THE SAILOR AND LUMBERMAN. Glenwood, Illinois: Meyerbooks, 1990.

Dufek, Rear Admiral George J. OPERATION DEEPFREEZE. New York: Harcourt, Brace and Company, 1957.

Duncan, Roger F., and Paul W. Fenn, W. Wallace Fenn, and John P. Ware. THE CRUISING GUIDE TO THE NEW ENGLAND COAST. New York: W.W. Norton & Company, 1997.

Emerson, Ken. DOO-DAH! STEPHEN FOSTER AND THE RISE OF AMERICAN POPULAR CULTURE. New York: DaCapo Press, 1998.

Emrich, Duncan. FOLKLORE ON THE AMERICAN LAND. Boston: Little, Brown & Company, 1972.

Epstein, Dena A. SINFUL TUNES AND SPIRITUALS: BLACK FOLK MUSIC TO THE CIVIL WAR. Urbana and Chicago, Illinois: University of Illinois Press, 1981.

Escott, Paul D. MANY EXCELLENT PEOPLE: POWER AND PRIVILEGE IN NORTH CAROLINA, 1850–1900. Chapel Hill: The University of North Carolina Press, 1985.

Finson, Jon W. THE VOICES THAT ARE GONE: THEMES IN 19TH CENTURY AMERICAN POPULAR SONG. New York: Oxford University Press, 1994.

Franklin, John Hope. DEMOCRACY BETRAYED: THE WILMINGTON RACE RIOT OF 1898 AND ITS LEGACY. Chapel Hill: The University of North Carolina Press, 1998.

———. THE FREE NEGRO IN NORTH CAROLINA, 1790–1860. Chapel Hill: The University of North Carolina Press, 1995.

Furnas, J.C. THE AMERICANS: A SOCIAL HISTORY OF THE UNITED STATES, 1587–1914. New York: G.P. Putnam's Sons, 1969.

Gillett, Charlie. THE SOUND OF THE CITY: THE RISE OF ROCK AND ROLL. New York: Da Capo Press, 1996.

Green III, John B. A NEW BERN ALBUM: OLD PHOTOGRAPHS OF NEW BERN, NORTH CAROLINA AND THE SURROUNDING COUNTRYSIDE. New Bern, North Carolina: The Tryon Palace Commission, 1985.

Haigh, Christopher, ed. THE CAMBRIDGE HISTORICAL ENCYCLOPAEDIA OF GREAT BRITAN AND IRELAND. Cambridge: Cambridge University Press, 1995.

Hamm, Charles. YESTERDAYS: POPULAR SONG IN AMERICA. New York: W.W. Norton, 1983.

Harrison, George. I, ME, MINE. New York: Simon & Schuster, 1980.

Hibbert, Christopher, and Ben Weinreb, eds. THE LONDON ENCYCLOPAEDIA. New York: St. Martin's Press, 1983.

Hobsbawm, Eric, and Terence Ranger. THE INVENTION OF TRADITION. Cambridge: Cambridge University Press, 1996.

Holzman, Jac, and Gavan Daws. FOLLOW THE MUSIC: THE LIFE AND HIGH TIMES OF ELEKTRA RECORDS IN THE GREAT YEARS OF AMERICAN POPULAR CULTURE. Santa Monica, California: FirstMedia Books, 1998.

Humphries, Patrick. THE BOY IN THE BUBBLE: A BIOGRAPHY OF PAUL SIMON. London: New English Library/Hodder and Stoughton, 1988.

Jackson, Kenneth T., ed. THE ENCYCLOPEDIA OF NEW YORK CITY, New Haven/New York: Yale University Press/The New York Historical Society, 1995.

Johnson, Randy. HIKING NORTH CAROLINA. Helena, Montana: Falcon Publishing, Inc., 1996.

Keay, John, and Julia Keay. COLLINS ENCYCLOPAEDIA OF SCOTLAND. London: HarperCollins Publishers, 1994.

Kemp, Peter, ed. THE OXFORD COMPANION TO SHIPS AND THE SEA. New York: Oxford University Press, 1988.

Kennedy, David M. FREEDOM FROM FEAR: THE AMERICAN PEOPLE IN DEPRESSION AND WAR, 1929–1945. New York: Oxford University Press, 1999.

King, Dean, with John B. Hattendorf. Maps by William Clipson and Adam Merton Cooper. HARBORS AND HIGH SEAS: AN ATLAS AND GEOGRAPHICAL GUIDE TO THE AUBREY-MATURIN NOVELS OF PATRICK O'BRIAN. Henry Holt and Company, Inc., 1996.

Kinsley, James, ed. BURNS: COMPLETE POEMS & SONGS. Oxford, England: Oxford University Press, 1969.

Kishlansky, Mark. A MONARCHY TRANSFORMED, BRITAIN 1603–1714. London: Allen Lane/The Penguin Press, 1996.

Klein, Joe. WOODY GUTHRIE: A LIFE. New York: Delta Books, 1999.

Larkin, Jack. THE RESHAPING OF EVERYDAY LIFE, 1790–1840. New York: HarperPerennial, 1988.

Levenson, Thomas. ICE TIME: CLIMATE, SCIENCE AND LIFE ON EARTH. New York: Harper & Row, 1989.

Lewisohn, Mark. THE COMPLETE BEATLES CHRONICLE. New York, Harmony Books, 1992.

———. THE BEATLES RECORDING SESSIONS: THE OFFICIAL ABBEY ROAD STUDIO SESSION NOTES, 1962–1970. New York: Harmony Books, 1988.

Leyburn, James G. THE SCOTCH IRISH: A SOCIAL HISTORY. Chapel Hill:
The University of North Carolina Press, 1962.

Linscott, Eloise Hubbard, collector/ed. FOLK SONGS OF OLD NEW
ENGLAND. New York: Dover Publications, 1993.

Lomax, John A., and Alan Lomax. AMERICAN BALLADS AND FOLK SONGS.
New York: Dover Publications, 1934.

Mackie, J.D. A HISTORY OF SCOTLAND. London: Penguin Books, 1991.

Malone, Bill C. COUNTRY MUSIC U.S.A. Revised Edition. Austin, Texas:
University of Texas Press, 1985.

————. SINGING COWBOYS AND MUSICAL MOUNTAINEERS:
SOUTHERN CULTURE AND THE ROOTS OF COUNTRY MUSIC.
Athens, Georgia: The University of Georgia Press, 1993.

Mancuso, Chuck. POPULAR MUSIC AND THE UNDERGROUND:
FOUNDATIONS OF JAZZ, BLUES, COUNTRY & ROCK 1900–1950,
Dubuque, Iowa: Kendall/Hunt Publishing Company, 1996.

McNeil, W.K. SOUTHERN MOUNTAIN FOLKSONGS. Little Rock, Arkansas:
August House Publishers, Inc., 1993.

McIntyre, Ian. DIRT & DIETY: A LIFE OF ROBERT BURNS. London:
Flamingo/HarperCollins Publishers, 1996.

Merwe, Van Der. ORIGINS OF THE POPULAR STYLE: ANTECEDENTS OF
TWENTIETH-CENTURY POPULAR MUSIC. Oxford, England: Clarendon
Press, 1992.

Meyer, Duane. THE HIGHLAND SCOTS OF NORTH CAROLINA,
1732–1776. Chapel Hill: The University of North Carolina Press, 1961.

Miles, Barry. PAUL McCARTNEY: MANY YEARS FROM NOW. New York:
Henry Holt & Company, 1997.

Morrison, Dorothy, and Alex I. Mouat. MONTROSE OLD CHURCH – A
HISTORY. Montrose: Montrose Review Press, 1991.

Mrozowski, Stephen A., Grace H. Ziesling, and Mary C. Beaudry. LIVING ON
THE BOOT: HISTORICAL ARCHAELOGY AT THE BOOTT MILLS
BOARDING HOUSES, LOWELL, MASSACHUSETTS. Amherst,
Massachusetts: University of Massachusetts Press, 1996.

New Bern Historical Society. GHOST STORIES OF OLD NEW BERN. New
Bern, North Carolina: New Bern Historical Society Foundation, 1991.

O'Brian, Patrick. H.M.S. SURPRISE. London: William Collins Sons & Co. Ltd.,
1973.

————. THE WINE-DARK SEA. New York: W.W. Norton, 1994.

Paasch, Captain H. PAASCH'S ILLUSTRATED MARINE DICTIONARY. New
York: Conway Maritime Press, 1997.

Perone, James E. PAUL SIMON: A BIO-BIBLIOGRAPHY. Westport, Connecticut: Greenwood Press, 2000.

———. CAROLE KING: A BIO-BIBLIOGRAPHY. Westport, Connecticut: Greenwood Press, 1999.

Peterson, Richard A. CREATING COUNTRY MUSIC: FABRICATING AUTHENTICITY. Chicago: The University of Chicago Press, 1997.

Phifer, Edward. W. BURKE: THE HISTORY OF A NORTH CAROLINA COUNTY. Morganton, North Carolina: Burke County Historical Society, 1982.

Pitzer, Sara. NORTH CAROLINA: OFF THE BEATEN TRACK. Old Saybrook, Connecticut: The Globe Pequot Press, 1999.

Powell, William S. NORTH CAROLINA THROUGH FOUR CENTURIES. Chapel Hill: The University of North Carolina Press, 1989.

Pugh, Ronnie. ERNEST TUBB: THE TEXAS TROUBADOUR. Durham, North Carolina: Duke University Press, 1996.

Purser, John. SCOTLAND'S MUSIC. Edinburgh: Mainstream Publishing Company, Ltd., 1992.

Robinson, Harriet H. LOOM & SPINDLE, OR LIFE AMONG THE EARLY MILL GIRLS. Kailua, Hawaii: Press Pacifica, 1976.

Rodgers, Carrie. MY HUSBAND JIMMIE RODGERS. Nashville, Tennessee: Country Music Foundation Press, 1995.

Rogers, John G. ORIGINS OF SEA TERMS. Mystic, Connecticut: Mystic Seaport Museum, Inc., 1985.

Salgado, Gamini. THE ELIZABETHAN UNDERWORLD. New York: St Martin's Press, 1992.

Sandbeck, Peter B. THE HISTORIC ARCHITECTURE OF NEW BERN AND CRAVEN COUNTY, NORTH CAROLINA. New Bern, North Carolina: The Tryon Palace Commission, 1988.

Sandburg, Carl. AMERICAN SONGBAG. New York: Harcourt Brace Jovanovich, Publishers, 1990.

Sanjek, Russell, and David Sanjek. AMERICAN POPULAR MUSIC BUSINESS IN THE 20TH CENTURY. New York: Oxford University Press, 1991.

Schlereth, Thomas J. VICTORIAN AMERICA: TRANSFORMATIONS IN EVERYDAY LIFE, 1876–1915. New York: HarperPerennial, 1991.

Schlesinger, Sr., Arthur M., and Dixon Ryan Fox. Revised and Abridged by Mark C. Carnes. A HISTORY OF AMERICAN LIFE. New York: Scribner, 1996.

Schreuders, Piet. PAPERBACKS, U.S.A.: A GRAPHIC HISTORY, 1939–1959. San Diego, California: Blue Dolphin Enterprises, Inc., 1981.

Scott, John Anthony. THE BALLAD OF AMERICA: THE HISTORY OF THE

UNITED STATES IN STORY AND SONG. Carbondale and Edwardsville, Illinois: Southern Illinois University Press, 1983.

Seeger, Pete, and Bob Reiser. CARRY IT ON: THE STORY OF AMERICA'S WORKING PEOPLE IN SONG AND PICTURE. Bethlehem, Pennsylvania: A Sing Out Publication, 1991.

Seeger, Pete, and edited by Jo Metcalf Schwartz. THE INCOMPLEAT FOLKSINGER. Lincoln, Nebraska: University of Nebraska Press, 1992.

Sheppard, Muriel Early. Photographs by Bayard Wooten. CABINS IN THE LAUREL. Chapel Hill: The University of North Carolina Press, 1991.

Shields, David S. CIVIL TONGUES, POLITE LETTERS IN BRITISH AMERICA. Chapel Hill: The University of Chapel Hill Press, 1997.

Smout, T.C. A HISTORY OF THE SCOTTISH PEOPLE. London: Fontana Press/HarperCollins Publishers, 1985.

Snider, William D. LIGHT ON THE HILL: A HISTORY OF THE UNIVERSITY OF NORTH CAROLINA AT CHAPEL HILL. Chapel Hill: The University of North Carolina Press, 1992.

Thomas, Hugh. THE SLAVE TRADE: THE STORY OF THE ATLANTIC SLAVE TRADE, 1440–1870. New York: Simon & Schuster, 1997.

Tick, Judith. RUTH CRAWFORD SEEGER: A COMPOSER'S SEARCH FOR AMERICAN MUSIC. New York: Oxford University Press, 1997.

Tomes, John. BLUE GUIDE: SCOTLAND. London: A & C Black Publishers Limited, 1996.

Tullos, Allen. HABITS OF INDUSTRY: WHITE CULTURE AND THE TRANSFORMATION OF THE CAROLINA PIEDMONT. Chapel Hill: The University of North Carolina Press, 1989.

Turnage, Sheila. NORTH CAROLINA. Oakland, California: Compass American Guides, 1998.

Ulrich, Laurel Thatcher. GOOD WIVES: IMAGE AND REALITY IN THE LIVES OF WOMEN IN NORTHERN NEW ENGLAND, 1650–1750. New York: Vintage Books/Random House, 1991.

Valentine, Tom. OLD MONTROSE. Ochiltree, Ayrshire, Scotland: Stenlake Publishing, 1997.

Vickers, James. IMAGES OF AMERICA: CHAPEL HILL. Dover, Nee Hampshire: Arcadia Publishing, 1996.

———. And Thomas Scism and Dixon Qualls. CHAPEL HILL: AN ILLUSTRATED HISTORY. Chapel Hill: Barclay Publishers, 1985.

Von Schmidt, Eric, and Jim Rooney. BABY LET ME FOLLOW YOU DOWN: THE ILLUSTRATED STORY OF THE CAMBRIDGE FOLK YEARS. Amherst, Massachusetts: University of Massachusetts Press, 1994.

Warner, Anne. TRADITIONAL AMERICAN FOLK SONGS, FROM THE ANNE & FRANK WARNER COLLECTION. Syracuse, New York: Syracuse University Press, 1984.

Watson, Harry L. AN INDEPENDENT PEOPLE: THE WAY WE LIVED IN NORTH CAROLINA, 1770–1820. Chapel Hill: The University of North Carolina Press, 1983.

Weisman, JoAnne B., ed. THE LOWELL MILL GIRLS: LIFE IN THE FACTORY. Carlisle, Massachusetts: Discovery Enterprises, Ltd., 1991.

Whitburn, Joel. TOP POP ALBUMS: 1955–1996. Menomonee Falls, Wisconsin: Record Research, Inc., 1996.

———. TOP POP SINGLES, 1955–1999. Menomonee Falls, Wis.: Record Research, Inc. 2000.

———. POP MEMORIES, 1890–1954: THE HISTORY OF AMERICAN POPULAR MUSIC. Menomonee Falls, Wis.: Record Research, Inc. 1986.

———. TOP COUNTRY SINGLES, 1944–1997. Menomonee Falls, Wis.: Record Research, Inc., 1998.

———. TOP COUNTRY ALBUMS, 1964–1997. Menomonee Falls, Wis.: Record Research, Inc., 1997.

———. TOP R&B SINGLES, 1942–1999. Menomonee Falls, Wis.: Record Research, Inc., 2000.

———. TOP R&B ALBUMS, 1965–1988. Menomonee Falls, Wis.: Record Research, Inc., 1999.

———. POP HITS, 1940–1954. Menomonee Falls, Wis.: Record Research, Inc., 1994.

———. BUBBLING UNDER SINGLES & ALBUMS. Menomonee Falls, Wis.: Record Research, Inc., 1998.

White, Timothy. ROCK LIVES: PROFILES AND INTERVIEWS. Revised & Updated Edition. New York/London: Henry Holt & Company/Owl Books/Omnibus Press, 1991.

———. MUSIC TO MY EARS: THE BILLBOARD ESSAYS. Revised & Updated Edition. New York: Henry Holt & Company/Owl Books, 1997.

———. THE NEAREST FARAWAY PLACE: BRIAN WILSON, THE BEACH BOYS, AND THE SOUTHERN CALIFORNIA EXPERIENCE. New York/London: Henry Holt & Company/Owl Books/Pan-Macmillan, 1994, 1996.

Wolf, Stephanie Grauma, ed. VARIOUS AS THEIR LAND: THE EVERYDAY LIVES OF EIGHTEENTH-CENTURY AMERICANS. New York: HarperPerennial, 1993.

Wolfe, Charles, and Kip Lornell. THE LIFE & LEGEND OF LEADBELLY. New York: HarperPerennial, 1992.

SELECTED ARTICLES, PAMPHLETS AND DOCUMENTS

The author read through decades of back issues of BILLBOARD, ROLLING STONE, MUSICIAN, FOLK ROOTS/fROOTS, SING OUT!, BROADSIDE, DOWN BEAT and other publications for material on James Taylor and folk music.

Also probed were several centuries of North Carolina's newspapers, including the Morganton NEWS-HERALD, the GREENSBORO DAILY NEWS, THE CHAPEL HILL WEEKLY, the JOURNAL AND SENTINEL of Winston-Salem, North Carolina, the ASHEVILLE CITIZEN-TIMES, the DURHAM MORNING HERALD, THE CHARLOTTE NEWS, THE CHARLOTTE OBSERVER, THE BULLETIN of the University of North Carolina School of Medicine, THE ALUMNI REVIEW of the University of North Carolina at Chapel Hill, the NORTH CAROLINA GAZETTE of New Bern, North Carolina from the 1790s onward, and the JOURNAL OF THE NEW BERN HISTORICAL SOCIETY. Also used in research were over 50 years of THE BOSTON GLOBE and VINEYARD GAZETTE.

The Wilson Library at the University of North Carolina at Chapel Hill allowed the author to study the private papers of the first Isaac Taylor in America, including the legal documents and ship manifests sent between New Bern, North Carolina and Kingston, Jamaica pertaining to the seizure and later auction of Taylor's ship, the *Rainbow*. Also studied by the author were the Inventory of the Estate of Isaac Taylor, and the Will of Isaac Taylor.

Documents listed below include materials obtained from Montrose, Scotland Customs Records at the Dundee City Archives, Scotland; the National Library of Scotland, and the National Maritime Museum, London, England.

Anderson, Mrs. John Huske. "North Carolina Women of the Confederacy". Fayetteville, North Carolina: North Carolina Division of the United Daughters of the Confederacy, 1926.

Angus Archives, Angus Council, Montrose Library, Montrose, Scotland. Taylors of Kirktonhill, descendant tree, Robert Taylor/register report/custom report.

———. Family tree of James Taylor and Christian Card/Ciard.

———. Old Parish Register for Kincardineshire.

———. Extracts from Montrose Town Council minutes, 1617–1639.

———. Extracts from Montrose Town Council minutes, 1703–1710.

———. Extracts from Montrose Town Council minutes, 1710–1733.

———. Extracts from Montrose Town Council minutes, 1733–1757.

———. Extracts from Montrose Town Council minutes, 1758–1771.

————. Extracts from Montrose Town Council minutes, 1771–1794.

BOSTON GLOBE. "Simon Has Hart But No Roommate." December 24, 1994.

Boyer, David S. "Year of Discovery Opens In Antarctica." NATIONAL GEOGRAPHIC, September 1957.

Brenner, Marie. "I Never Sang For My Mother." VANITY FAIR, August 1995.

Cornyn, Stan, and Ellen Pellissero. "What A Long, Strange Trip It's Been." Unpublished Warner Bros. corporate history, 1981.

Fong-Torres, Ben. "A Session With 'Fired Up' Carly Simon: 'Oh My Gosh, Here's This Body Again!'' ROLLING STONE, May 23, 1975.

Frazier, Paul W., and Calvin L. Larsen. "Across The Frozen Desert To Byrd Station." NATIONAL GEOGRAPHIC, September 1957.

Friedman, Roger. "Carly Comes Around Again." FAME, January, 1989.

Jervise, Andrew. "Marykirk," EPITAPHS AND INSCRIPTIONS, Vol.1 pp. 132–5, 353, 1875.

Knight, Frank & Rutley, Auctioneers. "Brief Summary of the Particulars of Kirktonhill Estate." pp. 1–28, 1924, for auction to be held Wednesday, January 14, 1925, 2 p.m.

Low, James G. HIGHWAYS & BYWAYS, Chapter XIII, "Tailors To The King."

Low, Rev. A.C. "Parish of Marykirk." New Statistical Account of Kincardineshire, pp. 297–309, 1843.

McClure, Rev. J.C. "Marykirk In The Olden Time: A Lecture Delivered to the Parishioners," November 22, 1901. Montrose, Scotland: Printed at the STANDARD Office, 1902.

Mech, L. David. Photographs by Jim Brandenburg. "At Home With The Arctic Wolf." NATIONAL GEOGRAPHIC, May 1987.

Morse, Steve. "James Taylor Wraps Up An Important Year." BOSTON GLOBE, November 12, 2000.

Naglin, Nancy. "One Love Stand: Laboring In The Vineyard With Carly Simon." CRAWDADDY, September, 1976.

Place, Jeff, and Guy Logson. Annotations for WOODY GUTHRIE, THE ASCH RECORDINGS, Vols. 1–4, Smithsonian Folkways Records, 1997, 1998, 1999.

School of Medicine and Medical Alumni Association Bulletin, The University of North Carolina. Volume XVI, No. 2. Spring–Summer 1969.

Sinclair, Sir John. Statistical Record of Scotland, Vol. 18, pp. 608–643, "Parish of Marykirk," 1796.

Smith, Giles. "The Man Whose Drug Intake Worried John Belushi!" Q Magazine.

Statistical Account of Scotland, 1791–1799. "Parish of Marykirk." Vol. XIV: Kincardineshire and South and West Aberdeenshire. E.P. Publishing Ltd, 1982.

Taylor, Trudy. Taylor family tree, May 5, 1997.

Taylor, Isaac. "The Isaac Taylor Papers (M-3049)." Manuscript Department, Southern Historical Collection, Wilson Library, The University of North Carolina at Chapel Hill.

Taylor, Isaac. "Isaac Taylor Papers." Stefansson Collection, Dartmouth Library.

———— Annex D, Part Seven. Medical Report, U.S. Naval Air Facility, McMurdo Sound, Antarctica. December 20, 1955–January 22, 1957.

Verna, Paul, "Drummer Carlos Vega, 41, Dies." BILLBOARD, April 25, 1998.

White, Timothy. "James Taylor: The Century Award – A Portrait of the Artist." BILLBOARD, December 5, 1998.

————. "The Handyman's Tale." MOJO, September, 1997.

————. "Old Wounds, New Bandages: James Taylor On The Mend." MUSICIAN, 1988.

————. "James Taylor, American Troubadour." 'Music To My Ears,' BILLBOARD, July 17, 1993.

————. "George Harrison Reconsidered: After All Those Years of Mania and Moptops, Dark Suits and Deep Blues, Here Comes The Fun." MUSICIAN, November, 1987.

————. "Paul McCartney: Farewell To The First Solo Era." MUSICIAN, February 1988.

————. "Unpublished Joni Mitchell interview." March 17, 1988.

————. "James Taylor Grins And Bears It." ROLLING STONE, June 11, 1981.

————. "Father & Lovers: Carly Simon Learns To Say Goodbye." ROLLING STONE, December 10, 1981.

————. "After Innocence: Ex-Eagle Don Henley and Comrade Danny Kortchmar Aim For The Heart Of The Mattter." L.A. STYLE, February, 1990.

————. "Meet Joe Smith: An Anecdotal History of Rock 'n' Roll." L.A. STYLE, November, 1987.

————. "No Secrets: Carly Simon . . . Rock's Savvy Siren." ELLE, January 1986.

————. "Jerry Wexler: The Godfather of Rhythm & Blues", *Rolling Stone*, November 27, 1980.

Williamson, Nigel. "Relative Values." SUNDAY TIMES MAGAZINE, March 15, 1998.

Woodard, David. "Last Will." York County, Maine. 1865.

Woodard, Trudy. "Diary and Daily Reminder." 1940.

————. "Diary." 1941.

Discography

THE RECORDINGS OF JAMES TAYLOR AND FAMILY

What follows is a select discography of the principal recordings of James Taylor, his brothers, sister, and offspring. This information is intended to serve as a companion to the text and an informal guide/overview, rather than a compendium-style recording history.

James Taylor has sung back-up, offered musical accompaniment and otherwise been a credited and uncredited guest on hundreds of recordings by colleagues and cohorts. (An example of the latter was James' animated appearance on the February 24, 1994 "Deep Space Homer" episode of Fox-TV's *The Simpsons*, during which he sang a customised version of 'Fire And Rain'.) Taylor's siblings and grown children have made a comparable range of contributions to the recordings of others. Thus, this reference section encompasses primarily the central canon rather than the complete scope of such work. It is intended to instruct the enthusiast, while offering a handy guide for the archivist.

JAMES TAYLOR TRACKS
Early demo sessions

TRACKS ON US SINGLES

THE FABULOUS CORSAIRS
Demo tracks cut by The Fabulous Corsairs at two-track studio in Raleigh, North Carolina owned by Jimmy Katz; A-side written by Alex Taylor.

You're Gonna Have To Change Your Ways/Cha Cha Blues   1964

THE FLYING MACHINE
Rough/incomplete tracks cut at Jubilee Records' Select Sound Studios, Manhattan circa 1967 included 'Night Owl', 'Knocking 'Round The Zoo', 'Rainy Day Man',

'Brighten Your Night With My Day', 'Kootch's Song' (instrumental), 'Something's Wrong' (instrumental track). Additional instrumental was added to several cuts in 1996.

Jay Gee/Jubilee

Night Owl/Brighten Your Night With My Day	1967

Euphoria

Brighten Your Night With My Day/Knocking 'Round The Zoo	1971

TRACKS ON US ALBUMS

Euphoria

JAMES TAYLOR AND THE ORIGINAL FLYING MACHINE	2	1971

Rainy Day Man
Knocking 'Round The Zoo
Something's Wrong (back track w/vocals)
Night Owl
Brighten Your Night With My Day
Kootch's Song
Knocking 'Round The Zoo (lead by D. Kortchmar)

Gadfly	219	1996

Night Owl (New Version)
Knocking 'Round The Zoo (New Version)
Rainy Day Man
Brighten Your Night With My Day (Intro)
Brighten Your Night With My Day
Kootch's Song
Something's Wrong (Instrumental Version)
Night Owl (Original Version)
Knocking 'Round The Zoo (Original Version Intro)
Knocking 'Round The Zoo (Original Version)

JAMES TAYLOR US/UK ALBUMS

Apple

JAMES TAYLOR, produced by Peter Asher	97577 2	1968

Don't Talk Now
Something's Wrong
Knocking 'Round The Zoo
Sunshine Sunshine
Taking It In

Something In The Way She Moves
Carolina In My Mind
Brighten Your Night With My Day
Night Owl
Rainy Day Man
Circle Round The Sun
The Blues Is Just A Bad Dream

Warner Bros.

SWEET BABY JAMES, produced by Peter Asher   1843   1970
    Sweet Baby James
    Lo And Behold
    Sunny Skies
    Steamroller
    Country Road
    Oh Susannah
    Fire And Rain
    Blossom
    Anywhere Like Heaven
    Oh Baby, Don't You Loose Your Lip On Me
    Suite For 20G

MUD SLIDE SLIM AND THE BLUE HORIZON,   2561   1971
       produced by Peter Asher
    Love Has Brought Me Around
    You've Got A Friend
    Places In My Past
    Riding On A Railroad
    Soldiers
    Mud Slide Slim
    Hey Mister, That's Me Up On The Jukebox
    You Can Close Your Eyes
    Machine Gun Kelly
    Long Ago And Far Away
    Let Me Ride
    Highway Song
    Isn't It Nice To Be Home Again

ONE MAN DOG, produced by Peter Asher   2660   1972
    One Man Parade
    Nobody But You
    Chili Dog
    Fool For You
    Instrumental I

New Tune
Back On The Street Again
Don't Let Me Be Lonely Tonight
Woh, Don't You Know
One Morning In May
Instrumental II
Someone
Hymn
Fanfare
Little David
Mescalito
Dance
Jig

WALKING MAN, produced by David Spinozza   2794   1974
Walking Man
Rock 'N' Roll Is Music Now
Let It All Fall Down
Me And My Guitar
Daddy's Baby
Ain't No Song
Hello, Old Friend
Migration
The Promised Land
Fading Away

GORILLA,   2866   1975
     produced by Lenny Waronker and Russ Titelman
Mexico
Music
How Sweet It Is (To Be Loved By You)
Wandering
Gorilla
You Make It Easy
I Was A Fool To Care
Lighthouse
Angry Blues
Love Songs
Sarah Maria

IN THE POCKET,   2912   1976
     produced by Lenny Waronker and Russ Titelman
Shower The People
A Junkie's Lament
Money Machine

Slow Burning Love
Everybody Has The Blues
Daddy's All Gone
Woman's Gotta Have It
Captain Jim's Drunken Dream
Don't Be Sad 'Cause Your Sun Is Down
Nothing Like A Hundred Miles
Family Man
Golden Moments

GREATEST HITS   2979   1976
Something In The Way She Moves (re-recording)
Fire And Rain
Carolina In My Mind (re-recording)
Country Road
You've Got A Friend
Shower The People
Mexico
Don't Let Me Be Lonely Tonight
Sweet Baby James
How Sweet It Is (To Be Loved By You)
Walking Man
Steamroller Blues (live)

Columbia

JT, produced by Peter Asher   34811   1977
Your Smiling Face
There We Are
Honey Don't Leave L.A.
Another Grey Morning
Bartender's Blues
Secret O' Life
Handy Man
I Was Only Telling A Lie
Looking For Love On Broadway
Terra Nova
Traffic Jam
If I Keep My Heart Out Of Sight

FLAG, produced by Peter Asher   36058   1979
Company Man
Johnnie Comes Back
Day Tripper
I Will Not Lie For You

Brother Trucker
Is That The Way You Look?
B.S.U.R.
Rainy Day Man (re-recorded)
Millworker
Up On The Roof
Chanson Francaise
Sleep Come Free Me

DAD LOVES HIS WORK, produced by Peter Asher   37009   1981
Hard Times
Her Town Too
Hour That The Morning Comes
I Will Follow
Believe It Or Not
Stand And Fight
Only For Me
Summer's Here
Sugar Trade
London Town
That Lonesome Road

THAT'S WHY I'M HERE,   40052   1985
     produced by James Taylor and Frank Filipetti
That's Why I'm Here
Song For You Far Away
Only A Dream In Rio
Turn Away
Going Around One More Time
My Romance
Everyday
Limousine Driver
Only One
Mona
The Man Who Shot Liberty Valance
That's Why I'm Here (Reprise)

NEVER DIE YOUNG, produced by Don Grolnick   40851   1988
Never Die Young
T-Bone
Baby Boom Baby
Runaway Boy
Valentine's Day
Sun On The Moon
Sweet Potato Pie

Home By Another Way
Letter In The Mail
First Of May

NEW MOON SHINE, produced by Don Grolnick   46038   1991
Copperline
Down In The Hole
(I've Got To) Stop Thinkin' 'Bout That
Shed A Little Light
The Frozen Man
Slap Leather
Like Everyone She Knows
One More Go Round
Everybody Loves To Cha Cha Cha
Native Son
Oh Brother
The Water Is Wide

JAMES TAYLOR (LIVE) 2-CD set   47056   1993
All newly arranged concert versions of material.
Sweet Baby James
Traffic Jam
Handy Man
Your Smiling Face
Secret O' Life
Shed A Little Light
Everybody Has The Blues
Steamroller Blues
Mexico
Millworker
Country Road
Fire And Rain
Shower The People
How Sweet It Is (To Be Loved By You)
New Hymn
Walking Man
Riding On A Railroad
Something In The Way She Moves
Sun On The Moon
Up On The Roof
Don't Let Me Be Lonely Tonight
She Thinks I Still Care
Copperline
Slap Leather

Only One
You Make It Easy
Carolina In My Mind
You've Got A Friend
That Lonesome Road

(BEST LIVE)–CD Extra   68096   1993
A two-CD set, plus a separate enhanced CD.
  Sweet Baby James
  Steamroller Blues
  Country Road
  Fire And Rain
  Don't Let Me Be Lonely Tonight
  Walking Man
  Mexico
  How Sweet It Is (To Be Loved By You)
  Handy Man
  Your Smiling Face
  Shower The People
  Shed A Little Light

(BEST LIVE)   1994
A single–album version.
  Country Road
  Don't Let Me Be Lonely Tonight
  Fire And Rain
  Handy Man
  How Sweet It Is (To Be Loved By You)
  Mexico
  Shed A Little Light
  Shower The People
  Steamroller Blues
  Sweet Baby James
  Walking Man
  Your Smiling Face

HOURGLASS,   67912   1997
    produced by Frank Filipetti and James Taylor
  Line 'Em Up
  Enough To Be On Your Way
  Little More Time With You
  Gaia
  Ananas
  Jump Up Behind Me
  Another Day

Up Er Mei
Up From Your Life
Yellow And Rose
Boatman
Walking My Baby Back Home

GREATEST HITS VOLUME 2   85223   2000
Secret O' Life
Handy Man
Your Smiling Face
Up On The Roof
Her Town Too
That's Why I'm Here
Only A Dream In Rio
Everyday
Song For Your Far Away
Never Die Young
(I've Got To) Stop Thinkin' 'Bout That
Copperline
Shed A Little Light
Another Day
Little More Time With You
Enough To Be On Your Way

'PULL OVER' SAMPLER   2001
Limited edition 3-song CD, a bonus with merchandise purchases at dates on Taylor's
2001 Pull Over Tour, has new song 'Caroline I See You', plus 'Song For You Far
Away', and live '(I've Got To) Stop Thinkin' 'Bout That' from '98 Beacon Theater
concert (on Columbia DVD 50171).

AS IF   Due in 2002
Tentatively-named studio sequel to HOURGLASS, assembled by Taylor with
producer Russ Titelman. As of July 2001 it consisted of session tapes of the following
possible material (exact titles subject to change): 'Fourth of July', 'Belfast To Boston',
'September Grass', 'Carry Me On My Way', 'Whenever You're Ready', 'Raised Up
Family', 'Cakewalk', 'Mean Old Man', 'Caroline I See You', 'Traveling Star', 'Are
You There?', and an exquisite rendition of 'Have Yourself A Merry Little Xmas'.
Many songs, such as 'Caroline I See You' and 'Fourth of July', are inspired by James'
courtship of Caroline "Kim" Smedvig Taylor, while 'Raised Up Family' alludes to
the ancestral passage of the Taylors from Scotland to America. Even in their
unfinished stages, the arrangements and vocal performances on the tracks under
consideration, particularly 'Fourth of July', 'Belfast To Boston' and 'September
Grass', are among the most stunning of Taylor's entire recording career.

Discography

JAMES TAYLOR SINGLES & EPs ON US/UK LABELS, A SELECTION

Apple

Carolina In My Mind/Taking It In (US, cancelled)	1969
Carolina In My Mind/Something's Wrong	1969
Carolina In My Mind/Something's Wrong (re-release)	1970
Carolina In My Mind/Something's Wrong (UK Edition)	1970

WALL'S ICE CREAM (UK EP)   CT 1   1969
Storm In A Teacup (by The Iveys), Something's Wrong (by James Taylor), Little
Yellow Pills (by Jackie Lomax), Pebble And The Man (Happiness Runs) (by Mary
Hopkins).

Warner Bros.

Sweet Baby James/Suite For 20G	1970
Fire And Rain/Anywhere Like Heaven	1970
Country Road/Sunny Skies	1971
You've Got A Friend/You Can Close Your Eyes	1971
Long Ago And Far Away/Let Me Ride	1971
Don't Let Me Be Lonely Tonight/Woh, Don't You Know	1972
One Man Parade/Hymn	1973
One Man Parade/Nobody But You	1973
Hymn/Fanfare	1973
Daddy's Baby/Let It All Fall Down	1974
Walking Man/Daddy's Baby	1974
How Sweet It Is (To Be Loved By You)/Sarah Maria	1975
Mexico/Gorilla	1975
Shower The People/I Can Dream Of You	1976
You Make It Easy/Woman's Got To Have It	1976

Elektra

Mockingbird (J. Taylor & C. Simon)/Grownup (C. Simon)	1974

Columbia

Handy Man/Bartender's Blues	1977
Your Smiling Face/If I Keep My Heart Out Of Sight	1977
Honey Don't Leave L. A./Another Grey Morning	1978
Up On The Roof/Chanson Francaise	1979
Her Town Too/Believe It Or Not	1981
Hard Times/Summer's Here	1981
Everyday/Limousine Driver	1985
Only One/Mona	1986
Never Die Young/Valentine's Day	1988
Your Smiling Face	1993
Little More Time With You	1997
Have Yourself A Merry Little Christmas	2001

JAMES TAYLOR ON OTHER ARTISTS TRACKS/ALBUMS, A SELECT CHRONOLOGY

Listed below are rare and unusual appearances on releases by artists other than such familiar Taylor collaborators as Carole King, Joni Mitchell, Carly Simon, Taylor's siblings and children, etc.

John Stewart

WILLARD   (Capitol ST-540)   1970
  Taylor lends guitar and/or vocals on 'Big Joe', 'Clack Clack', 'All American Girl', 'Oldest Living Son'.

Neil Young

HARVEST   (Reprise 2277-2)   1972
  Taylor adds vocals to 'Heart Of Gold', 'Old Man' (on which he also plays banjo).

HARVEST MOON   (Reprise 945057-2)   1992
  Backing vocals by Taylor on 'Frank Hank To Hendrix', 'War of Man', 'One of These Days'.

Tom Rush

LADIES LOVE OUTLAWS   (Columbia KC 33054)   1974
  Taylor sings harmony on 'Jenny Lynn'.

Crosby and Nash

WIND ON THE WATER   (MCA 31251)   1975
  Taylor sings on title track, plays guitar on 'Carry Me'.

Garland Jeffreys

GHOST WRITER   (A&M SP-4629)   1977
  Taylor sings on 'Cool Down Boy'.

Rosie

LAST DANCE   (RCA APL1-2415)   1977
  Taylor adds vocals to 'Out of Pawn'.

The Section

FORK IT OVER   (Capitol ST-11656)   1977
  The lead vocal on 'Bad Shoes' is Taylor.

Libby Titus

LIBBY TITUS   (Columbia PC 34152)   1997
  Taylor joins Carly Simon on vocal backing for 'Darkness 'Til Dawn'.

Discography

John Hall

JOHN HALL   (Asylum 6E-117)   1978
  Taylor joins Carly Simon in vocal harmonies on 'The Fault' and 'Voyagers'.

POWER   (Columbia 35790)   1979
  Taylor and Carly Simon sing with Hall on the title track.

George Jones

BARTENDER'S BLUES   (Epic PE-35414)   1978
  Vocal backing on Jones rendition of the title track is by author Taylor.

Don McLean

CHAIN LIGHTNING   (Millenium BXL1-7756)   1978
  Vocal backing on 'Since I Don't Have You' is by Taylor.

Art Garfunkel

WATERMARK   (Columbia 34975)   1978
  Taylor joins Garfunkel and Paul Simon on '(What A) Wonderful World'.

UP 'TIL NOW   (Columbia 47113)   1994
  Taylor plays and/or sings on 'Crying In The Rain', 'It's All In The Game'.

ACROSS AMERICA: THE VERY BEST OF ART GARFUNKEL
                  (Virgin/Hybrid 42655 26)   1997
  Joint live version with Taylor of 'Crying In The Rain'.

Karla Bonoff

RESTLESS NIGHTS   (Columbia CK 35799)   1979
  More than a decade after first catching Taylor at the Troubadour in LA, Bonoff's
  hero sings backup on her version of 'The Water Is Wide'.

Various Artists

THE BITTER END YEARS   (Roxbury RLX 300)   1974
  Taylor does live version of 'Riding On A Railroad'.

NO NUKES: THE M.U.S.E. CONCERTS FOR A NON-NUCLEAR
FUTURE   (Asylum 801)   1979
  Taylor performs 'Honey Don't Leave L.A.' and 'Captain Jim's Drunken Dream',
  duets with Carly Simon on 'Mockingbird' and with Simon and Graham Nash on
  'The Times They Are A-Changin', lends vocals to Hall's 'Power', Doobie
  Brothers' 'Takin' It To The Streets'.

IN HARMONY   (Warner Bros. 3481-2)   1980
  Taylor sings on 'Jelly Man Kelly' and title track.

IN HARMONY II   (Warner Bros. 3481-2)   1981
  Taylor sings 'Sunny Skies'.

STAY AWAKE   (A&M 3918)   1988
  'Second Star To The Right' is done by Taylor with vocal support from the
  Roches.

FOR OUR CHILDREN – TO BENEFIT PEDIATRIC AIDS RESEARCH
      (Walt Disney 60616-2)   1991
  'Getting To Know You' done by Taylor.

A LEAGUE OF THEIR OWN – MUSIC FROM THE MOTION PICTURE
      (Columbia CK 52919)   1992
  Taylor sings 'It's Only A Paper Moon' and 'I Didn't Know What Time It Was'.

SWEET AIRS THAT GIVE DELIGHT: FORTY SEASONS OF
MUSIC FROM THE STRATFORD FESTIVAL (Attic ACD 1378) 1993
  Performing with orchestra and choral support and/or combo in Shakespearean
  setting is Taylor on 'You Spotted Snakes', 'Sigh No More Ladies', 'Come Unto
  These Yellow Sands', 'Where The Bee Sucks', 'When Daisies Pied', 'Life On
  The Inside'.

CARNIVAL!   (RCA Victor 44769-2)   1997
  Taylor sings 'I Bought Me A Cat' live with the San Diego Symphony.

SNL 25: SATURDAY NIGHT LIVE, THE MUSICAL PERFORMANCES
VOL. 1   (DreamWorks 50205-2)   1999
  Contains 'Secret O' Life' by Taylor.

SING AMERICA   (Warner Bros. 9 47245-2)   1999
  Includes Taylor's 'Oh Susannah'.

Jimmy Buffett

VOLCANO   (MCA MCAD-1657)   1979
  Taylor sings on 'Lady I Can't Explain' and 'Sending The Old Man Home' and
  vocalises with brothers Alex and Hugh (billed as The Embarassing Stains) on
  'Treat Her Like A Lady' and 'Survive'.

HOT WATER   (MCAD-42093)   1988
  Taylor sings on 'Prince Of Tides', 'Pre-You', 'Great Heart', and joins Buffett and
  Timothy B. Schmit on 'L'Air de la Louisiane'.

BANANA WIND   (MCA/Margaritaville 11451)   1996
  Taylor shares vocals on 'False Echoes'.
    David Sanborn

HIDEAWAY   (Warner Bros. 3379-2)   1980
  Taylor sings on 'Carly's Song'.

Bill LaBounty

BILL LABOUNTY   (Warner Bros. BSK 3632)   1982
  Backing vocals by Taylor on 'Didn't Want To Say Goodbye',
  and 'Never Gonna Look Back'.

Discography

David Lasley

MISSIN' TWENTY GRAND   (EMI ST-17066)   1982
    Taylor sings on 'Got To Find Love', and Lasley covers the Taylor song 'Looking
    For Love On Broadway'.

Linda Ronstadt

GET CLOSER   (Asylum 960185-2)   1984
    Taylor shares vocals on 'I Think It's Gonna Work Out Fine'.

FOR SENTIMENTAL REASONS   (Asylum 960474-2)   1986
    'Straighten Up And Fly Right' features Taylor on support vocals.

Ricky Skaggs

LOVE'S GONNA GET YA   (Epic EK 40309)   1985
    Taylor shares vocals on 'New Star Shining'.

Graham Nash

INNOCENT EYES   (Atlantic 81633)   1986
    'Sad Eyes' features support vocals by Taylor.

Steve Winwood

BACK IN THE HIGH LIFE   (Island 830 148)   1986
    Harmony vocal by Taylor on the title track.

David Crosby

OH YES I CAN   (A&M 5232)   1988
    Taylor sings on title track.

Mark O'Connor

ON THE MARK   (Warner Bros. 9 25970-2)   1989
    'Old Blue' features Taylor's vocals and guitar.

LIBERTY   (Sony Classical 63216)   1997
    Taylor sings and plays on 'Johnny Has Gone For A Soldier'.

Mark Cohn

MARK COHN   (Atlantic 782178-2)   1991
    'Perfect Love' features Taylor on support vocals.

Manhattan Transfer

TONIN'   (Atlantic 82661-2)   1994
    Taylor sings 'Dream Lover'.

Milton Nascimento

ANGELUS   (Warner Bros. 945499-2)   1994
     Features joint rendition by Taylor and Nascimento on extended new
     arrangement of 'Only A Dream In Rio'.

John Sheldon & Blue Streak

BONEYARD   (Signature Sounds 1227)   1994
     Taylor contributes vocals to 'The Little Things' and served as executive producer
     of album.

Randy Newman

FAUST   (Reprise 9 45672-2)   1995
     Vocals by Taylor are featured on 'Glory Train', 'How Great Our Lord', 'Best
     Little Girl', 'Northern Boy' and 'Relax, Enjoy Yourself'.

Valerie Carter

THE WAY IT IS   (Countdown 77737-2)   1996
     Taylor sings on 'I Say Amen'.

Elio e le Storie Tese

EAT THE PHIKIS   (Aspirine/BMG-Italy 36094-2)   1996
     Taylor sings on 'First Me, Second Me (The Peak Of The Mountains)'.

Patricia Kaas

DAN MA CHAIR   (Columbia-France 483834-2)   1997
     Shares vocals and plays guitar on 'Don't Let Me Be Lonely Tonight'.

Spalding Gray

IT'S A SLIPPERY SLOPE   (Mercury 314-558288-2)   1998
     Taylor produced this monologue album by Gray on Martha's Vineyard.

Jonathan Elias

THE PRAYER CYCLE   (Sony Classical 60569)   1999
     Taylor joins The English Chamber Orchestra and guitarist John Williams to sing
     'Grace'.

Various Artists/Music For Our Mother Ocean

MOM III   (UNI/Surf Dog)   1999
     Includes 'Gaia'.

Various Artists

SATURDAY NIGHT LIVE – THE MUSIC PERFORMANCES, VOL. 1
1999
     Includes live 'Secret O' Life'.

Discography

Various Artists

SONY MUSIC 100 YEARS: SOUNDTRACK FOR A CENTURY 1999
    Pop Music: The Modern Era, 1976–1999 section includes 'Your Smilin' Face'.

Sting

BRAND NEW DAY   (A&M 694904432)   1999
    Featured as guest vocalist on 'Fill Her Up' is Taylor.

Elton John

AIDA   (Rocket 314-524628-2)   1999
    Songs by John and Tim Rice in new pop interpretation of the opera, with Taylor
    as guest vocalist/guitarist on 'How I Know You'.

Yo-Yo Ma, Edgar Meyer, Mark O'Connor

APPALACHIAN JOURNEY   (Sony Classical 66788)   2000
    In this sequel to Ma, Meyer and O'Connor's 1996 APPALACHIA WALTZ
    collaboration, Taylor sings 'Hard Times Come Again No More' and performs the
    guitar instrumental 'Benjamin'.

APPALACHIAN JOURNEY 4-TRACK SAMPLER   SK66762   2000
    Includes 'Hard Times Come Again No More'.

Various Artists

VHI Storytellers   (UM/Interscope)   2000
    Includes live version of 'Mexico'.

Maceo Parker

DIAL: M-A-C-E-O   (What Are Records? 045BYM)   2000
    Guest appearance by Taylor on 'My Baby Loves You'.

Mark Knopfler

SAILING TO PHIILADELPHIA   (WEA/Warner Bros. 044605)   2000
    Taylor sings on the title track.

Shawn Colvin

WHOLE NEW YOU   (Columbia)   2001
    Taylor is guest vocalist on 'Bonefields'.

Michael Brecker

NEARNESS OF YOU: THE BALLAD BOOK
                          (Uni/Verve 05B83E)   2001
    Taylor appears on two tracks of this jazz album, which includes a cover version of
    'Don't Let Me Be Lonely Tonight', which earned James a pop vocal Grammy.

LIVINGSTON TAYLOR TRACKS

Livingston actually embarked on a formal solo career slightly in advance of brother James. Liv was a regular on the Boston-Cambridge folk circuit starting in 1968, where he earned an early supporter in local journalist Jon Landau. Twenty-year-old Livingston was one of the first artists signed to Phil Walden's Capricorn Records label in 1970, and recorded steadily for major labels until 1980, when he took an eight-year hiatus from the practice. It was during those years, however, that he toured most heavily, became a frequent presence on local and national television, and forged a highly organised fan network on a successful independent par with such latterday alternative folk artists/entrepreneurs as Ani DiFranco.

Livingston created a company (Taylor Music, P.O. Box 620114, Newton Lower Falls, MA. 02462-0114) to service his increasingly international audience, built up a comprehensive database for touring and merchandising, and developed a range of products for devotees, including instructional guitar videos and audiotapes (LIVINGSTON TAYLOR'S EXCELLENT GUITAR LESSON; HIT GUITAR STYLES), his own record label (Whistling Dog Records), T-shirts and souvenirs. He also authored several acclaimed children's books with wife Maggie (PAJAMAS; CAN I BE GOOD?), and published a non-fiction guide to the artist's life (STAGE PERFORMANCE, Pocket Books, 2000) that reflected his distinctly droll concert style. These and other enterprises were further unified in the 1990s via an award-winning website (www.livtaylor.com). When not touring internationally or flying his own plane, Liv also could be found teaching at the Berklee College of Music in Boston.

LIVINGSTON TAYLOR US ALBUMS

Capricorn

LIVINGSTON TAYLOR, produced by Jon Landau   (SD 33-334)   1970
    Sit On Back
    Doctor Man
    Six Days On The Road
    Packet Of Good Times
    Hush A Bye
    Carolina Day
    I Can't Get Back Home
    In My Reply

Lost In The Love Of You
Good Friends
Thank You Song

LIV, produced by Jon Landau   (SD 863)   1971
Get Out Of Bed
May I Stay Around
Open Your Eyes
Gentleman
Easy Prey
Be That Way
Truck Driving Man
Mom, Dad
On Broadway
Caroline
I Just Can't Be Lonesome No More

OVER THE RAINBOW, produced by Ed Freeman   1973
Loving Be My New Horizon
Blind
Falling In Love With You
Let Me Go Down
Rodeo
If I Needed Someone
Pretty Woman
Somewhere Over The Rainbow
Oh Hallelujah
I Can Dream Of You
Lady Tomorrow

ECHOES, produced by Ed Freeman, Jon Landau (CPN-0220)   1979
Get Out Of Bed
On Broadway
Carolina Day
Lady Tomorrow
Caroline
Lost In The Love Of You
Loving Be My New Horizon
Can't Get Back Home
Gentle Man [*sic*]
Over The Rainbow
If I Needed Someone
Hush A Bye

Epic

THREE-WAY MIRROR, produced by Nick DeCaro (ESCA5447) 1978
Going Round One More Time
L.A. Serenade
Gonna Have A Good Time
Train Off The Track
I Will Be In Love With You
No Thank You Skycap
I'll Come Running
Living Without You
Southern Kids
How Much Your Sweet Love Means To Me

MAN'S BEST FRIEND, (ESCA7585) 1980
    produced by Jeff Baxter, John Boylan
Ready, Steady, Go
Dance With Me
First Time Love
Sunshine Girl
You Don't Have To Choose
Dancing In The Street
Out Of This World
Face Like Dog
Pajamas
Marie

Critique/ATCO

LIFE IS GOOD, (7 90941-2) 1988
    produced by Artie Traum, Scott Petito
Life Is Good
One Of The Things I Do So Well
City Lights
If I Were You
It's Love
Make It Love
Loving Arms
Louie
Glad I Know You Well
Falling In Love With You
Mary Ann
Rockin' Robin

Chesky

GOOD FRIENDS,   (JD97)   1993
      produced by David Chesky & Joel Diamond
  Out Of This World
  Jacques Cousteau
  Heart And Soul
  Carolina Day
  If I Only Had A Brain
  Grandma's Hands
  Blind
  Good Friends
  Pajamas
  Get Out Of Bed
  Save Your Heart For Me
  Fifth And Vine
  Bluer Than Blue
  In My Reply
  Somewhere Over The Rainbow
  Thank You Song

INK, produced by Joel Goodman and David Chesky   1997
  Isn't She Lovely
  First Time Love
  Hallelujah I Love Her So
  Fly Away
  Our Turn To Dance
  I Must Be Doing Something Right
  The Biggest Part Of Me
  Get Here
  Baker Street
  The More I See You
  The End Of The Innocence
  Never Can Say Goodbye

Vanguard

OUR TURN TO DANCE,   (VCD-79469)   1993
      produced by Artie Traum & Scott Petito
  Our Turn To Dance
  It's My Job
  I Must Be Doing Something Right
  No Easy Way To Break Somebody's Heart
  Make The Change
  My Father's Eyes

Silvered Wings
You Got The Right Guy
Someday You May Notice Me
Vacation
The Way You Look Tonight

Whistling Dog

UNSOLICITED MATERIAL   1994
A live album, originally sold at shows.
Intro/Life Is Good
Writing A Book
Jacques Cousteau
Olympic Guitar
Elusive Butterfly
Save Your Heart For Me
I Hate Country Music
I Must Be Doing Something Right
Railroad Bill
Pajamas
Jason (Waltzing With Bears)
Heart And Soul
No Easy Way To Break Somebody's Heart
On And On
The Dollar Bill Song
Carolina Day
City Lights
Earl's Breakdown
Eight More Miles To Louisville
Songs That Should Never Be Played On The Banjo
Goodnight
Over In The Soviet Union
Over The Rainbow

SNAPSHOT   1999
Recorded live in December 1998 at The Iron Horse, Northampton, Massachusetts.
I Believe
O Loretta
I'm Not As Herbal As I Ought To Be
The Dollar Bill Song
Bicycle
Olympic Guitar
You Can Take Me Home
Doggie Jail
Railroad Bill

Walking My Baby Back Home
The Way You Look Tonight
Our Turn To Dance
No Easy Way To Break Somebody's Heart
Piano Noodle
Loving Arms (with Joanne Cassidy)
Through The Fire (with Joanne Cassidy)
Songs That Should Never Be Played On The Banjo
My Father's Eyes
Glad I Know You Well

Coconut Bay

BICYCLE, produced by Scott Petito   1996
 I Believe
 I Belong
 Boatman
 Olympic Guitar
 Bicycle
 Don't Let Me Lose This Dream
 Oh Loretta
 Nobody Can Make Me Cry
 Looking To Love
 Dixie Chicken
 Last Letter

Razor & Tie

CAROLINA DAY: THE LIVINGSTON TAYLOR COLLECTION,
              (21612) 1998
 produced by Michael Ragogna and Stephen Stewart
 Get Out Of Bed
 Can't Get Back Home
 Carolina Day
 Good Friends
 Lost In The Love Of You
 Packet Of Good Times
 Caroline
 On Broadway
 I Just Can't Be Lonesome No More
 Loving Be My New Horizon
 Lady Tomorrow
 Somewhere Over The Rainbow
 Going Round One More Time
 I'll Come Running

I Will Be In Love With You
First Time Love
Pajamas
Hush A Bye

LIVINGSTON TAYLOR SINGLES ON US LABEL – A SAMPLING

Capricorn

Carolina Day/Sit On Back	1971
Get Out Of Bed/Get Out Of Bed (mono)	1972

Epic

I Will Be In Love With You/How Much Your Sweet Love Means To Me	1978
I'll Come Running/No Thank You Skycap	1979
First Time Love/Pajamas	1980

ALEX TAYLOR TRACKS

Founder of the R&B-inclined Fabulous Corsairs, the first band in which brother James played, Alex Taylor was a born blues/R&B belter who was signed to Capricorn Records in 1970. Over the course of three decades, he performed and recorded with such artists as James Montgomery, Jimmy Buffett, Cowboy, Gregg Allman, and the Kinsey Report, and built a strong reputation in the South, Mid-west and North-east. Of the five complete albums cut during his lifetime, the 1972 *DinnerTime* album was critically acclaimed as one of the best Southern blues releases of the era and is an enduring classic. Alex was completing a second album for King Snake Records at the time of his death on March 12, 1993.

ALEX TAYLOR US ALBUMS

Capricorn

WITH FRIENDS & NEIGHBORS	(860)	1971

    All In Line
    Baby Ruth
    C Song
    Highway Song
    It's All Over Now
    Night Owl
    Southbound
    Southern Kids
    Take Out Some Insurance

DINNERTIME, produced by Johnny Sandlin   (CP-0101)   1972
Album was re-released in 1999 as Capricorn 314 538 763-2.
- Change Your Sexy Ways
- Let's Burn Down The Cornfield
- Comin' Back To You
- Four Days Gone
- Payday
- Who's Been Talkin'
- Who Will The Next Fool Be
- From A Buick Six

Dunhill

THIRD FOR MUSIC   (50151)   1974
- A blues–rock collection by the singer.

Ichiban

DANCING WITH THE DEVIL,   1981
    produced by Bob "Rattlesnake" Greenlee
- House Of Cards
- Can't Break The Habit
- Let The Big Dog Eat
- Birds Of A Feather
- Change In Me
- Dancing With The Devil
- No Life At All
- Practice What You Preach
- Black Sheep
- Bait My Hook

King Snake

VOODOO IN ME   (CS15)   1989
- Spirited blues set by Alex, with liner notes by Dan Aykroyd, and guests including brother James, Gregg Allman, and the Kinsey Report. Tracks included Alex's own 'Vanessa' and 'Time On The Inside'.

KATE TAYLOR TRACKS

After forming her first band, Sister Kate's Soul Stew and Submarine Sandwich Shop in the late 1960s while attending the Arlington School at McLean Hospital, Kate was signed to Atlantic/Cotillion Records in 1970.

KATE TAYLOR ALBUMS ON US/JAPAN LABELS

Atlantic/Cotillion

SISTER KATE, produced by Peter Asher   (9045) 1971
(Digitally remastered and re-released on CD in 1998 on East/West-Japan as
AMCY-2588.)

 Home Again
 Ballad Of A Well-Known Gun
 Be That Way
 Handbags And Gladrags
 You Can Close Your Eyes
 Look At Granny Run, Run
 Where You Lead
 White Lightning
 Country Comfort
 Lo And Behold/Jesus Is Just Alright
 Do I Still Figure In Your Life?
 Sweet Honesty

Columbia

KATE TAYLOR, produced by James Taylor & Lew Hahn (35089) 1978
(Digitally remastered and re-released by Sony Music Entertainment-Japan as SRCS
6459.)

 A Fool In Love
 Smuggler's Song
 Harriet Tubman
 Stubborn Kind Of Woman
 Happy Birthday, Sweet Darling
 It's In His Kiss (The Shoop Shoop Song)
 Slow And Steady
 It's Growing
 Tiah's Cove
 Rodeo
 Jason & Ida

IT'S IN THERE . . . AND IT'S GOT TO COME OUT, (360349) 1979
  produced by Barry Beckett
 I Got The Will
 Kite Woman
 Ain't No Way To Forget You
 Loving You Was Easier (Than Anything I'll Ever Do Again)
 Ain't Too Proud To Beg
 Same Old Song
 You Can't Hurry Love

I'm A Hog For You Baby
Champagne And Wine
Ain't No Love In The Heart Of The City

Front Door

BEAUTIFUL ROAD,   (Due in 2002)
    produced by Charlie Witham and Scott Petito
Flying In The Face Of Mr. Blue
Beautiful Road
The Golden Key
Rain On The Water
Blue Tin Suitcase
He's Waiting
Shanty Song
Shores Of Paradise
I Will Fly
Auld Lang Syne

KATE TAYLOR SINGLES/TRACKS ON US LABELS, A SAMPLING

Columbia

It's In His Kiss (The Shoop Shoop Song)/Jason & Ida   1977

Sony/Word

STRONG HAND OF LOVE: A TRIBUTE TO MARK HEARD   1994
    A various-artists collection on which Kate contributes the track, 'Satellite Sky'.

Philo

CHRISTINE LAVIN PRESENTS: FOLLOW THAT ROAD
                                    PH1165/66   1994
    Two-CD set of highlights from Lavin's second annual Martha's Vineyard
    Singer/Songwriter Retreat. Includes Kate's 'Flying In The Face Of Mr Blue'.

Front Door

Auld Lang Syne (The Days Of Long Ago)   1999
    A special CD single in jewel case with booklet of lyrics and photos, produced by
    Charlie Witham and Tony Garnier, w/arrangement and guitar/vocal
    accompaniment by James Taylor.

HUGH TAYLOR TRACKS

While Hugh's professional focus has been on his guest inn/restaurant, real estate interests and other enterprises, he's found time over the years to serve as a fire chief on Martha's Vineyard – and to sing with his siblings. Hugh has often performed with his brothers and sister as The Taylor Family, and has sung on albums by James, Kate, Livingston and Alex Taylor, in addition to recordings by Carly Simon, Jimmy Buffett, Bill Wharton, David Sanborn, Michael Brecker, and others.

HUGH TAYLOR US ALBUMS

Village Green

IT'S UP TO YOU   (PCCY-00157)   1990
   A collection on which Hugh is supported vocally by all his siblings, particularly James. Tracks include the title song, 'World Of Difference', 'Brick By Brick', 'What Kind Of Fool (Do You Think I Am)' and 'Ol' 55'.

SALLY TAYLOR TRACKS

Sally maintains a regular tour schedule with her five-piece band, its concert dates obtainable from her website, www.sallytaylor.com

SALLY TAYLOR US ALBUMS

Blue Elbow

TOMBOY BRIDE   (79020-4 4-90092-2)   1998
   The Complaint
   Strangest of Strangers
   The Goodbye
   Happy Now
   Song 4 Jeremy
   Sign Of Rain
   When We're Together
   Tomboy Bride
   In My Mind
   Red Room
   Alone
   Unsung Dance

APT. #6S   69984-2   2000
   All This Time
   Split Decisions (background vocals by Ben Taylor)
   March Like Soldiers
   4 Kim (background vocals by Ben Taylor)
   Fall 4 Me
   Give Me The Strength
   Convince Me (background vocals by Ben Taylor)
   40 Years (background vocals by Ben Taylor)
   Nisa
   Without Me
   Immortal
   How Can I?

SHOTGUN   2001
Cuts on "demo" of her third album include: 'Victim', 'Girl In The Picture', 'Wait',
'Disaster', 'Dvoren', 'Justin Tyme', 'Driving Me Crazy', 'Memorial Day', 'Missing
Part', 'Hard To Swallow', 'C Thru', 'Amazing', 'October', 'Disaster' (2nd Version).
Fans were asked to vote on best 3–6 cuts for final, re-recorded CD.

SALLY TAYLOR US SINGLES/TRACKS

BMG/Arista

LETTERS NEVER SENT, Carly Simon   1994
Sally Taylor supplies backing vocals on her mother's album.

Atlantic

MUSIC FROM THE MOTION PICTURE ANYWHERE BUT HERE
                                       (83234-2)   1999
Soundtrack features selections from various artists, among them 'Amity',
co-authored and sung by Carly Simon and Sally Taylor.

BEN TAYLOR TRACKS

Ben's ongoing recording and touring activities (which include the concert
début of such songs as 'Broken Tonight' and 'Just In Time To Fall Down')
can be accessed via www.bentaylor.com.

BEN TAYLOR US ALBUMS

Sony/Work/Epic

GREEN DRAGON, NAME A FOX (AKA GREEN DRAGON NAME
OF FOX) 2001
> Tentative title(s) on test pressings of proposed 13-track début, which included 'Broken Tonight' and 'Jamie Loves The Ocean'.

Ben Taylor (self-funded/recorded)

FAMOUS AMONG THE BARNS 2002 (tentative)
> Independent project by Ben with his band. Includes backing vocals by Carly Simon, and by James Taylor. James' harmony backing on such tracks as 'Island' was done at Q Division Studios in Somerville, Ma. on Sunday, November 18, 2001. "That's a good band you've got behind you, Ben, and it's a good strong feeling in the song," said James following his overdubs on 'Island'. After the session, Ben commented, "Having my poppa sing on my record with me, this is the best day of my life."
>
> Tracks from the overall BARNS sessions include: Just Like Everyone Else, Day After Day, No More Running Away, Island, Let It Grow, Rain, I Am The Sun, Safe Enough To Wake Up, Mushroom Dance.

BEN TAYLOR US SINGLES/TRACKS

BMG/Arista

LETTERS NEVER SENT, Carly Simon 1994
> Ben Taylor supplies acoustic guitar and assorted vocals on his mother's album about family regrets and unfinished business. The project's best cut is Ben's collaboration with Carly on 'Time Works On All The Wild Young Men'.

Giant/Warner Bros.

BYE BYE, LOVE, Original Soundtrack (4/2-24609) 1995
> I Will (rendition of Beatles song, co-produced by James Taylor and Frank Filipetti)

I Will/CD-Cassette single 1995

Arista

FILM NOIR, Carly Simon 1997
> My Romance (Ben duets with Carly)

THE BEDROOM TAPES, Carly Simon 14627-2 2000
> Big Dumb Guy (Ben sings back-up)
> I'm Really The Kind (Ben sings back-up)

Ralph Lauren

My Romance   2000
  Re-recorded version of song by Carly Simon and Ben Taylor in 1999 Christmas
  TV commercial for Ralph Lauren fragrance.

Delias

FREE YOUR MIND   2000
  Sampler CD from mail order firm features tracks from various artists, including
  Ben Taylor's 'It May Take Some Time'.

Yvonnetipping.com

'Playing A Game'   2000
A track Ben co-wrote and recorded with Scottish singer–songwriter Yvonne
Tipping, a native of Bellshill, a surburb of Glasgow.

Index

Index

Index

Index